Irreconcilable Grievances

The Events That Shaped the Declaration of Independence

Patrick J. Charles

HERITAGE BOOKS
2008

HERITAGE BOOKS
AN IMPRINT OF HERITAGE BOOKS, INC.

Books, CDs, and more—Worldwide

For our listing of thousands of titles see our website at
www.HeritageBooks.com

Published 2008 by
HERITAGE BOOKS, INC.
Publishing Division
100 Railroad Ave. #104
Westminster, Maryland 21157

Copyright © 2008 Patrick J. Charles

Cover Design: Josh Yeston

All rights reserved. No part of this book may be reproduced or transmitted in any form or by any means, electronic or mechanical, including photocopying, recording or by any information storage and retrieval system without written permission from the author, except for the inclusion of brief quotations in a review.

International Standard Book Number: 978-0-7884-4566-8

In loving memory of Carl and Helen Charles

"Labour to keep alive in your breast that little celestial fire called conscience."
—George Washington's Rules of Civility 110

Table of Contents

1. Interpreting the Declaration of Independence   1

Part One: Diplomatic Failure and the Rights of Englishmen
2. Failed Peace   25
3. A Legal Independence   53

Part Two: To Turn Slaves Against Their Masters
4. Dunmore's Proclamation and Domestic Insurrections   85
5. Alternate Contributions   113

Part Three: Fire From the Sea
6. The Most Horrid Devastations Upon the Country   135
7. Portsmouth and the Tragedy of Norfolk   173

Part Four: The Inclusion of Indian Auxiliaries
8. The "Savage" Threat From the Frontier   213
9. Choosing Sides   247

Part Five: Foreign Alliances
10. The Hessian Contribution   273
11. The Need for Foreign Assistance   299

Index   327

Introduction

In today's political climate, many actions are driven through fear—fear of being attacked, fear of the loss of property, or the fear of losing the American way of life. The political climate of late eighteenth century America was not much different. Similar fears were the precursors to America's Declaration of Independence. While some of these fears were warranted, others were propagated by the false and inaccurate dissemination of information.

The story of the American Revolution has been told countless times. How the writings of John Locke, events of the Boston Tea Party, Boston Massacre, Stamp Act protests, Quartering Act, Boston Port Act, and Coercive Acts influenced the founding fathers to break away from Great Britain. Unfortunately, this does not portray a full depiction of factors attributed to the push for autonomy. From the first shots fired at Lexington and Concord through the spring of 1776, the majority of American colonists wanted to maintain their allegiance to the British Empire. It was only after certain events occurred within the first year of hostilities that the revolutionaries thought of declaring their independence.

The aim of *Irreconcilable Grievances* is to discuss the pertinent events from July 1775 to July 1776 that influenced a large majority of the revolutionaries to call for independence. Much like any political stance today, people held their opinion based upon personal experiences as well as deductive reasoning. While the evolution of political thought was essential in gaining the support of intellectual classes, the evolution of events themselves is what transcended to the average individual. Certain events within the first year affected individuals differently. If we were to interview each one of the signers of the Declaration of Independence and query as to what most compelled them to split with Great Britain, what would each answer? When one thinks of this question, they realize a large variance of answers would arise.

Acknowledgments

I would like to take the time to thank Gary Klinga who edited most of this manuscript. I would also like to thank the following individuals for also taking the time to look over and edit portions of the manuscript; LeAnn Starlin, Woody Holton, Joel Guilmartin, Mark Lender, Terry Golway and Michael McDonnell. Without their advice and corrections I don't know if this manuscript would have ever been completed.

The following institutions, libraries, and staff were instrumental in completing the manuscript—Library of Congress, National Archives, Indiana University's libraries, University of Michigan, Hiram College, and the Cleveland State University's Law Library. Invaluable information, help, support, and sources were provided by Caroline Cox, Philander Chase, Thomas Humphrey, Thomas Long, Muriel Atkin, Nemata Blyden, and Adele Alexander.

Lastly, this book would not have been possible without the continuing push, love, and support from friends and family—the Charles family, Burkhart family, Gusich family, Metcalf family, Morgan family, with special thanks to Jordan Gusich, Adam Morgan, Thomas Burns, all the brothers of Pi Kappa Alpha Delta Alpha (especially Josh Yeston for designing the cover), Lindsay Brown, Derek Newberry, Paul Vallee, my former and current brothers in arms in the Marines, Sherry Hong, all my friends at Cleveland State-Cleveland Marshall School of Law, Amy Stack, Drew Hertel, Adrian Clayton, Eric Varner, Tomar Thomas, Catelin Hevia, Grant Yochim, Laura Delucia, Emily Burkhart, the staff at Brigade, Mark Schamel, Carrie Love, and all the friends and family who I apologize for failing to mention.

Chapter One

Interpreting the Declaration of Independence

I fear We cannot proceed systematically, and that We Shall be obliged to declare ourselves independent States.
John Adams to Patrick Henry, June 3, 1774

Leo Cherne once wrote, "The average serviceman doesn't talk like Thomas Jefferson."[1] Although Cherne was describing those who had served in World War II, in his book *The Rest of Your Life*, the statement also aptly and poetically describes the veterans of the American Revolution. Men like Jefferson, John Adams, George Washington, and John Hancock did not typify the average colonial serviceman. These prominent leaders were, by comparison, well-spoken and educated men from the aristocratic class, and in no way represented the 22,000 plus men and women, mostly farmers and townspeople, who arrived at Cambridge following the Battle of Lexington and Concord or filled the ranks for the remainder of the conflict. In fact, it was the ordinary middle and lower class citizens who ensured the success of the Revolution. But first they had to be persuaded to fight for the cause. What primarily gained their loyalty to the cause of independence was not the romantic rhetoric of the eighteenth century, but a series of physical events, events that would shape the colonists' perception of the political issues between the colonies and Great Britain.

The story of the American Revolution has been told countless times. It has been widely held that the writings of John Locke and the pivotal events like the Boston Tea Party, Boston Massacre, Stamp Act protests, Quartering Act, Boston Port Act, and

---

[1] Leo Cherne, *The Rest of Your Life*, (Garden City, NY: Doubleday, Doran and Company, Inc., 1944), 14.

Irreconcilable Grievances

Coercive Acts all influenced the founding fathers to break away from Great Britain. It is true that these philosophical and physical forces were, in fact, listed as reasons precipitating the split with England in Thomas Paine's *Common Sense* and the Declaration of Independence, but such pronouncement were done primarily to provide a complete list of grievances to the British government. This list not only made the argument concise and circular but was politically essential when declarations were issued. Often overlooked is the fact that the Declaration of Independence was modeled after the document that was one of the main bases of the British Constitution--the Declaration of Rights of 1689.

Prior to the Declaration of Independence, Virginia issued their own Declaration of Rights, in which the sole intent was to "maintain peace and order in this colony and secure substantial and equal liberty to people."[2] The author, George Mason, detailed a list of rights that was penned to counter the British usurpations imposed upon the colony of Virginia, and in many instances, the entire thirteen colonies. Nearly all the grievances on Mason's Declaration of Rights would make the final draft of the Declaration of Independence. When comparing the two documents to the earlier petitions by the founding fathers, it becomes obvious the list grew longer and more detailed due to the series of events that occurred from the summer of 1775 to the spring of 1776.

An abundance of evidence exists to support the fact that the colonists were perpetually working towards reconciliation with the mother country. Only a minute segment of the population supported a push for independence prior to the spring of 1776. The vote for independence might not have even occurred had it not been for the timing of Richard Henry Lee's resolution in June 1776. Lee formally proposed "That these United Colonies are, and of right ought to be, Free and Independent States, that they are absolved from all allegiance to the British Crown, and that all

---

[2] Brent Tarter and Robert L. Scribner, *Revolutionary Virginia: The Road to Independence*, Vol.7 Part 1, (University of Virginia Press, 1983), Proceedings of May 15, 1776, Fifth Virginia Convention, 143.

Interpreting the Declaration of Independence

political connection between them and the State of Great Britain is, and ought to be, totally resolved."[3]

Just a month prior, in the preamble of the May 15 resolve for repression of British authority, Congress felt it was "absolutely irreconcilable to reason and good conscience, for the people of these Colonies now to take the oaths and affirmations necessary for the support of any government under the crown of Great Britain; and it necessary that the exercise of every kind of authority under the said Crown should be totally suppressed."[4] These words created a divide among the colonial representatives. Although there was little objection to the adoption of the actual resolve, which "recommended to the respective Assemblies and Conventions of the United Colonies…to adopt such Government as shall…best conduce to the happiness and safety of their Constituents in particular, and America in general," the preamble was barely adopted.

After two to three days of heated debate, the vote was 6 in favor, 4 against, with 2 abstaining and Georgia not voting. Although the Congressional resolve recommended that new governments be erected with the preamble directly charging the King, the delegates that voted in favor did not perceive the resolve as a push for independence. Congressional delegate James Duane of New York disagreed, and felt the preamble would be violating the instructions from the New York Convention directing him to work towards reconciliation.[5] Maryland's delegates left the Congress and only returned once they had affirmed their colony's convention which "prevented them from approving anything that might lead to independence."[6]

---

[3] Ibid, Proceedings of May 18, 1776, Fifth Virginia Convention, n. 1; *Journal of the Continental Congress*, Vol. 5, 425.

[4] Tarter & Scribner, *Revolutionary Virginia: The Road to Independence*, Vol. 7 Part 1, Proceedings of May 15, 1776, Continental Congress, "To Adopt Such Forms of Government," 140.

[5] Ibid, note 4.

[6] Pauline Maier, *American Scripture: Making of the Declaration of Independence*, (New York, NY: Alfred A. Knopf Press, 1997), 38.

Irreconcilable Grievances

John Adams urged, in a definitive manner, the assembly to push for independence, but he knew it would be best to prevent Massachusetts from moving too quickly to break ties; such a move might imperil her by separating her from the other colonies. He wrote, "The Union is our defence, and that must be most tenderly cherished."[7] His dreams were realized once news arrived from Virginia that the convention sitting there had "Resolved unanimously that the delegates appointed to represent this colony in General Congress be instructed to propose to that respectable body to declare the United Colonies free and independent."[8] The resolution caught Adams by surprise. He wrote to Patrick Henry:

> It has ever appeared to me that natural Course and order of Things was this; for every Colony to institute a Government; for all the Colonies to confederate, and define the Limits of the Continental Constitution; then to declare the Colonies a sovereign State, or a Number of confederated Sovereign States, and last of all, to form Treaties with foreign Powers. But I fear We cannot proceed systematically, and that We Shall be obliged to declare ourselves independent States, before We confederate, and indeed before all the Colonies have established their Governments. It is now pretty clear that all these Measures will follow one another in a rapid Succession, and it may not perhaps be of much Importance which is done first.[9]

The difference between the adoption of the May 15 resolve for repression of authority and Richard Henry Lee's vote for independence was the manner in which the delegates decided to come to a vote. Multiple state conventions and assemblies were in

---

[7] David Hawke, *A Transaction of Free Men: The Birth and Course of the Declaration of Independence*, (New York, NY: Charles Scribner's Sons, 1964), 121.
[8] Tarter & Scribner, *Revolutionary Virginia*, Fifth Virginia Convention, Proceedings of the Ninth Day of Session, May 15, 1776, 143.
[9] Robert J. Taylor, *Papers of John Adams*, Vol. 4, (Cambridge, MA: The Belknap Press, 1979), To Patrick Henry, June 3, 1776, 234-235.

Interpreting the Declaration of Independence

favor of independence, but Congress normally thought it in "vain to wait weeks or months for perfect unanimity since it was impossible that all men should ever become of one sentiment on any question."[10] Lee's resolve was different because its supporters were willing to give the colonies time to deliberate independence.

The vote for independence was moved to the first week of July. In the meantime, Congress thought it prudent to assemble a committee to prepare a Declaration of Independence that consisted of Thomas Jefferson, John Adams, Benjamin Franklin, Roger Sherman, and Roger R. Livingston. Thomas Jefferson would draft the document and many Congressional delegates worked hard to mobilize support for the initiative. Historian Pauline Maier points out it was not as important as to who mobilized what, as was "timing of the effort to mobilize popular support."[11] Timing was everything, from Virginia's decision to declare independence, to Richard Henry Lee's proposal in Congress, to the tabling of the vote for independence, and lastly, to the decision to have a Declaration of Independence ready and waiting even though enacting it had not been approved.

Not all the complaints listed on the Declaration for Independence triggered the sway of popular opinion, from the restitution of grievances, towards freedom from British oppression. From the first shots fired at Lexington and Concord through the spring of 1776, the majority of American colonists still wanted to maintain their allegiance to the British Empire. It was only after certain pivotal events occurred within the first year of hostilities that the revolutionaries thought of declaring their independence.

Even the most ardent patriots wished to see a settlement occur. Thomas Jefferson hoped Parliament was "thoroughly and minutely acquainted with every circumstance relative to America as it exists in truth" and was "persuaded this would go far towards disposing them towards reconciliation."[12] John Adams was initially for

---

[10] Maier, *American Scripture*, 43.
[11] Ibid, 69.
[12] Julian P. Boyd, *The Papers of Thomas Jefferson*, Vol. 1, (Princeton,

reconciliation but preferred any attempts to do so should be through a position of strength; he secretly hoped for the failure of the Olive Branch Petition in order for this to occur. He wrote to James Warren:

> You will see a Strange Oscillation between Love and Hatred, between War and Peace. Preparations for War, and Negociations for Peace. We must have a Petition to the King, and a delicate Proposal for Negociation &c. This Negociation I dread like Death. But it must be proposed. We cant avoid it. Discord and total Disunion would be the certain Effect of a resolute Refusal to petition and negociate. My Hopes are that Ministry will be afraid of Negociation as well as We, and therefore refuse it. If they agree to it, We shall have occasion for all our Wit, Vigilence and Virtue to avoid being deceived, wheedled, threatened or bribed out of our Freedom.[13]

Adams continued by writing, "We ought immediately to resolve all Ministerial Tyrannies, and Custom houses, set up Governments of our own, like that of Connecticut in all the Colonies, confederate together like an indissoluble Band, for mutual defence and open our Ports to all Nations immediately." One may assert this statement serves as evidence of Adams' desire to break away from England. To make such an assertion would, however, be misleading. Adams cites Connecticut's government because although it was under the authority of the king; it had the control to elect its own governor. Thus, what Adams insinuated was that he rejected some of the precedents within the Massachusetts charter, wishing to become more of a self-governing colony but not independent. In regards to Adams preference to "open our Ports to all Nations," he felt it would be a pertinent move that would push Parliament to open the door "as

---

NJ: Princeton University Press, 1950), To John Randolph, August 25, 1775, 241.
[13] Taylor, *Papers of John Adams*, Vol. 3, To James Warren, July 6, 1775, 60-63.

Interpreting the Declaration of Independence

wide as possible for Peace and Reconciliation."[14]

Henry Laurens swore on his "fortune & Life" that "not a Man in this province, wishes for independence upon Great Britain or but wishes to return to, & remain in that State of dependence & Subordination."[15] He felt the colonies would never submit to England's demands since "a conquest on the part of Administration in the present contest will prove an effectual defeat of the true interest in America." Laurens was referring to economics. He knew the task at hand for England was nearly unattainable since the continent was so large. As long as the colonial union was preserved, and regardless of the outcome of the conflict, "a vast national debt will place her."[16] Unless Parliament adhered to their demands, Britain would experience great economic suffering as a result. Much like Adams, Laurens preferred to be in a position of strength and would only work out reconciliation if it were upon "Constitutional terms."[17]

Through December 1775, only a small fraction of the revolutionaries felt independence should be declared, and these individuals were dubbed extremely radical. The fact is that every one of the grievances the colonies addressed to Britain was capable of being mediated. It was only once certain events transpired, while armed conflict was occurring, that most revolutionaries lost any trust they had remaining with the British government. If the events prior to Lexington and Concord were significant enough to cause America to seek its independence, then one must reasonably query, "Why did they wait until July 1776?"

Many of the grievances listed on the Declaration of Independence had already been listed and sent to England either in the Declaration of the Causes and Necessity for Taking up Arms and the Resolution of Congress on Lord North's Conciliatory

---

[14] Ibid, To James Warren, July 24, 1775, 89.

[15] David R. Chesnutt, *The Papers of Henry Laurens*, Vol. 10, (Columbia, SC: University of South Carolina Press, 1985), To John Laurens, April 22, 1775, 105.

[16] Ibid, To James Air, May 18, 1775, 130.

[17] Ibid, To John Laurens, June 23, 1775.

Irreconcilable Grievances

Proposal. These grievances were not the primary reasons for the push for separation; otherwise independence would have been pursued much earlier. It is not to say that these occurrences were insignificant in their own right towards the break with England, but they certainly were not effective enough to sway colonists who were neutral or loyal (and even many revolutionaries, since the army was perpetually struggling to gain recruits) to take up arms.

The Declaration of the Causes and Necessity for Taking up Arms was just one of several addresses issued by Congress in the summer of 1775 whose purpose was to justify to the colonists and the world the necessity for armed resistance. It attributed the arming of the colonists to being "prohibited from the Fisheries in the Seas near their Coasts," a "perpetual Auction of Taxations where Colony should bid against Colony, all of them uninformed what Ransom would reddem their Lives; and thus extort from us, at the point of the Bayonet," and the sending of "large Reinforcements of Ships and Troops" instead of replying to their petitions.[18] Most importantly, these military reinforcements, led by Thomas Gage, ventured to Concord in order to retake stolen munitions. Munitions that were previously at the British garrison Fort William & Mary in Newcastle, New Hampshire prior to being raided by John Sullivan.[19] The fort was only defended by a

---

[18] The Declaration for the Causes and Necessity for Taking up Arms also makes reference to General Guy Carleton's "instigating the People of that Province and the Indians to fall upon us; and we have but too much reason to apprehend, that Schemes have been formed to excited domestic Enemies against us." Taylor, *The Papers of Thomas Jefferson*, Vol. 1, 217. This means Jefferson was listing the inclusion of Indians as auxiliaries and the encouragement of slave revolts in June 1775. At this time there was no evidence to support either claim. Both were purely propagated on fear and rebel hearsay. It would not be until the fall of 1775 that evidence of either began to surface. These charges did not make the Olive Branch Petition or the Congressional response to Lord North's Conciliatory Proposal probably because there was no evidentiary basis for them. Both claims would make the Declaration of Independence and were a strong contributing factor towards independence.

[19] James H. Stark, *The Loyalists of Massachusetts and the Other Side of*

Interpreting the Declaration of Independence

corporal's guard, and since the fort contained large quantities of ammunition, arms and supplies, it was deemed an easy target.

Gage's attempt to retake the munitions was a significant contributing factor that influenced the revolutionaries to take up arms. This action reinforced the fear they had been stating all along: the British government was trying to subject them to a state of servitude. This fear of slavery was reinforced once Gage, "further emulating his ministerial Masters," declared the colonists:

> [T]o be Rebels and Traitors...justice cannot be administered by the common law of the land...from whence results a necessity for using and exercising the law martial; I have therefore thought fit, by the authority vested in me, by the royal charter to this province, to publish, and I do herby publish proclaim and order the use and exercise of the law martial.[20]

In the Declaration of the Causes and Necessity for Taking up Arms it stated this along with the butchering of "our Countrymen," and the burning of Charlestown as other trepidations for the colonies' physical defense. In closing, the document stated "our cause is just...our union is perfect," and "if necessary, foreign Assistance is undoubtedly attainable." What Congress wanted to make clear was they were negotiating from a

---

the American Revolution, (Boston, MA: W.B. Clarke Co., 1910), 51.

[20] Alden T. Vaughn, *Chronicles of the American Revolution*, (New York, NY: Grosset & Dunlap, 1965), Proclamation of Governor Thomas Gage, June, 12, 1775, 179-181. On the same day, Gage also wrote to the Ministry requesting the employment of Indians as auxiliaries since "the Rebels have shewn us the Example, and brought all they could down upon us here." Moreover, on that same day, Gage wrote, "things are now to come to that Crisis, that we must avail ourselves of every resource even to raise the Negroes, on our cause." Carter, *The Correspondence of General Thomas Gage with the Secretaries of State, and with the War Office and the Treasury*, Vol. 1, Thomas Gage to Lord Barrington, June 12, 1775, 684. Some event or mindset must have influenced Gage on this day. By this point, he most assuredly saw the war no longer as an argument over Parliamentary policy. He now viewed the conflict as a war for independence.

position of strength but also wanted to assure "that we mean not to dissolve that Union which has so long and so happily subsisted between us, and which we sincerely wish to see restored."[21] The purpose of their taking up arms was "in defence of the Freedom that is our Birthright, and which we ever enjoyed till the late Violation of it."

The Olive Branch Petition was adopted two days after the Declaration for the Causes and Necessity for Taking up Arms. It was a second Congressional petition to the King, and like the Declaration of Causes, it provided the ideology behind the revolutionaries' forming of armed resistance. It did not charge the King at fault for their denial "to share in the blessings of peace and the emoluments of victory and conquest." The petition charged the Majesty's ministers with "the delusive pretences, fruitless errors, and unavailing severities that have from time to time been dealt out by them in their attempt to execute this impolitic plan." It was the ministers that compelled them to "arm in our own defence", since they had engaged them "in a controversy so peculiarly abhorrent to the affections of your still faithful colonists."[22] Also, much like the Declaration for Causes, the petition reaffirmed the colonies' intention to remain loyal to the crown. It stated:

> We not only most ardently desire the former harmony between her and these colonies may be restored but that a concord may be established between them upon so firm a basis, as to perpetuate its blessings uninterrupted by any future dissentions to succeeding generations in both countries...We beg leave further to assure your Majesty that...our breasts retain too tender a regard for the kingdom from which we derive our origin to request such a reconciliation as might in any manner be inconsistent with her dignity or her welfare.

---

[21] Boyd, *The Papers of Thomas Jefferson*, Vol. 1, Declaration for the Causes and Necessity for Taking up Arms, Final Draft, 213-218.

[22] Ibid, Second Petition from Congress to the King, July 8, 1775, 219-222.

Interpreting the Declaration of Independence

The Resolution of Congress Regarding Lord North's Conciliatory Proposal gives the most detailed list of the issues between the revolutionaries and the British government during the early goings of the conflict. Passed in Philadelphia on July 31, 1775, the resolve was a reply to Lord North's attempt to prevent any further discontent between the colonies and the mother country. Unfortunately, the proposal was dated February 20 and had arrived too late to have its intended diplomatic effect. By the time it had reached Congress, the British Army was already garrisoned within the Boston peninsula and the revolutionaries had seen the capabilities of their rag-tag army at the Battle of Bunker Hill. The possibility of a resolution being worked out quickly would now be difficult since many of the influential members of Congress saw themselves as negotiating from a position of strength.

Lord North's proposal offered to eliminate the tea tax so long as the colonies promised to pay the salaries of civil authorities regularly. There was a disagreement among the colonists whether this was a fair. Some thought the British government had not conceded enough, while others felt they had conceded too much. In the end, the rebels translated Lord North's resolution more as a ploy to let their guard down and secondly, as a means to reinstate the Declaratory Act in which Parliament could bind the colonies in "all cases whatsoever." The proposals were not, therefore perceived by the rebels as an attempt at peace. The revolutionaries' retort was the "proposition seems to have been held up to the world to deceive it into a belief that there was nothing in dispute between us but the mode of levying taxes."

In short, Lord North's proposal did not discuss the real issue at hand, which was that the colonies should be "entitled to the sole and exclusive privilege of giving and granting their own money." Congress thought the colonies deserved the right to determine their appropriation of taxes so it will not be "wasted among the venal and corrupt for the purpose of undermining the civil rights of the givers, nor yet be diverted to the support of standing armies,

Irreconcilable Grievances

inconsistent with their freedom and subversive of their quiet."[23] The issue of standing armies was just one of the grievances listed by Congress. The record also included:

> We are of opinion the proposition is altogether unsatisfactory because it imports only a suspension of the mode, not a reunification of the pretended right to tax us: Because too it does not propose to repeal the several Acts of Parliament passed for the purposes of restraining the trade and altering the form of government of one of our Colonies; extending the boundaries and changing the government of Quebec; enlarging the jurisdiction of the Courts of Admiralty and Vice Admiralty; taking from us the rights of trial by a Jury of the vicinage in cases affecting both life and property; transporting us into other countries to be tried for criminal offences; exempting by mock trial the murders of Colonists from punishment; and quartering soldiers on us in times of profound peace. Nor do they renounce the power of suspending our own Legislatures, and the legislating for us themselves in all cases whatsoever. On the contrary, to shew they mean no discontinuance of injury, they pas acts, at the very time of holding out this proposition, for restraining the commerce and fisheries of the Provinces of New England, and for interdicting the trade of other Colonies with all foreign nations and with each other.[24]

When one compares this list of grievances and the prior petitions with the list in the Declaration of Independence, a strong resemblance can be appreciated. The majority of the complaints which appear on the Declaration had been stated a year earlier. The following, which appears on the Declaration of Independence, had already been addressed in some form or fashion a year prior to it being resolved:

---

[23] Boyd, *The Papers of Thomas Jefferson*, Vol. 1, Resolutions of Congress on Lord North's Conciliatory Proposal, The Resolutions as Adopted By Congress, July 31, 1775, 230-33.
[24] Ibid.

Interpreting the Declaration of Independence

He has refuted his Assent to Laws, the most wholesome and necessary for the public good.

He has forbidden his Governors to pass Laws of immediate and pressing importance, unless suspended in their operation till his Assent should be obtained; and when so suspended, he has utterly neglected to attend to them.

He has refused to pass other Laws for the accommodation of large districts of people, unless those people would relinquish the right of Representation in the Legislature, a right inestimable to them and formidable to tyrants only.

He has called together legislative bodies at places unusual, uncomfortable, and distant from the depository of their Public Records, for the sole purpose of fatiguing them into compliance with his measures.

He has dissolved Representative Houses repeatedly, for opposing with manly firmness his invasions on the rights of the people.

He has refused for a long time, after such dissolutions, to cause others to be elected, whereby the Legislative Powers, incapable of Annihilation, have returned to the People at large for their exercise; the State remaining in the mean time exposed to all the dangers of invasion from without, and convulsions within.

He has endeavoured to prevent the population of these States; for that purpose obstructing the Laws for Naturalization of Foreigners; refusing to pass others to encourage their migrations hither, and raising the conditions of new Appropriations of Lands.

He has obstructed the Administration of Justice by refusing his Assent to Laws for establishing Judiciary Powers.

Irreconcilable Grievances

He has made Judges dependent on his Will alone for the tenure of their offices, and the amount and payment of their salaries.

He has erected a multitude of New Offices, and sent hither swarms of Officers to harass our people and eat out their substance.

He has kept among us, in times of peace, Standing Armies without the Consent of our legislatures.

He has affected to render the Military independent of and superior to the Civil Power.

He has combined with others to subject us to a jurisdiction foreign to our constitution, and unacknowledged by our laws; giving his Assent to their Acts of pretended Legislation.

For quartering large bodies of armed troops among us.

For protecting them, by a mock Trial from punishment for any Murders which they should commit on the Inhabitants of these States.

For cutting off our Trade with all parts of the world.

For imposing Taxes on us without our Consent.

For depriving us in many cases, of the benefit of Trial by Jury.

For transporting us beyond Seas to be tried for pretended offences.

For abolishing the free System of English Laws in a neighbouring Province, establishing therein an Arbitrary government, and enlarging its Boundaries so as to render it at once an example and fit instrument for introducing the same absolute rule into these Colonies.

Interpreting the Declaration of Independence

For taking away our Charters, abolishing our most valuable Laws and altering fundamentally the Forms of our Governments.

For suspending our own Legislatures, and declaring themselves invested with power to legislate for us in all cases whatsoever.

How the radicals of thirteen divided colonies united to break the shackles of British oppression is an amazing story, but what is equally intriguing is how each of the colonies was affected differently within the first year of the war. Each colony's particular geographical location, cultural influences, and exposure to the conflict played a pertinent collective role in deciding what influenced their desire for autonomy. Much like any political stance today, people held their opinion based upon their personal experiences, as well as deductive reasoning. Certain events within the first year affected individuals differently. Lord Dunmore's proclamation to free the slaves did not significantly affect New Hampshire as much as it affected Virginia and South Carolina. The same can be said of the British Navy's ability to prohibit commerce within New England's waters. The southern colonies were not considerably affected economically by such measures. The best way to underscore this point is to bring up the following hypothetical situation. Were we to interview each one of the signers of the Declaration of Independence and query as to what most impelled them to split with Great Britain, what would each answer? Predictably, when the question is asked, one cannot help but realize that a large variance of answers would arise.

What also must be remembered is that the American Revolution was North America's first English civil war in which arms were taken up. A small revolution occurred within certain localities following the Glorious Revolution in England in 1689, but in its particular case, violence was minimal and the transition in government was less problematic. Those who would support independence during the American Revolution made up no more than forty percent of the population. There was an equal amount of individuals that wanted governmental reform, a redress to the

Irreconcilable Grievances

grievances since the Treaty of Paris in 1763, but they did not want to break their ties with Britain. These individuals either split from the revolutionary movement when petitioning turned to armed conflict or once independence was seriously sought.

The story of the Tories is not well known by most Americans, and for good reasons. Prior to the Declaration of Independence, the revolutionary interim governments established effective reforms that persecuted any who did not agree with their political objectives. By the time independence was declared, it was almost too late for the Tories to effectively unite for their cause. The threats of loss of property, mauling, and even death were perpetuated against the loyalists throughout the war, thus preventing them from taking arms.[25] The point is that there was a large variance of public and political opinion existing within the colonies throughout the war. Each event during the first year of the war affected each person differently.

The news of the Hessian mercenaries being employed can serve as an example. It had multiple effects upon the colonists. For the revolutionaries it had a dual effect. For some it gave them a strong reason to distrust any form of reconciliation with Great Britain, pushing them to rally to the cause. For others, it brought trepidation, since Hessian soldiers were known for their fierceness. For the loyalists, it also would have possessed a dual effect. For some, it gave conviction that the British government was taking the rebellion earnestly and sending the proper reinforcements to quell it, while for others it meant the rebellion had gotten out of hand.

Those who would initially write the story of the Revolution primarily viewed American independence as an inevitable occurrence or a struggle between good and evil.[26] George

---

[25] Force, *American Archives,* Fourth Series, Vol. 5, Continental Congress, March 14, 1776, 1638; Lorenzo Sabine, *Biographical Sketches of Loyalists of the American Revolution*, Vol. 1 (Boston, MA: Little Brown & Company, 1864), 281, 309.

[26] Bernard Bailyn, *The Ordeal of Thomas Hutchinson,* (Cambridge, MA: Harvard University Press, 1974), viii.

Interpreting the Declaration of Independence

Bancroft saw the rebellion against King George III as part of a pageant of freedom. He believed Americans possessed a God-given love of liberty and that their history proved it.[27] John Adams viewed the Revolution as a stage in the maturing of American society. He alleged that, since the landing of Europeans on the continent, independence had been "in the minds and hearts of the people from the beginning."[28] Many have asserted this American ethnocentric notion, which points out that the colonists initially came to America to resist European oppression. Therefore, it was only a matter of time before the colonists overthrew imperial rule. This assertion is not entirely inaccurate since many oppressed groups came to America to find a new start but to assert that their hidden motive from the beginning of colonization, was to start their own country is inaccurate. Sir Herbert Butterfield emphasizes the earliest historical writings that follow a controversial event are still deemed a significant part of the event itself. Even though the incident might have ended, the result is still in doubt, emotions are still deeply engaged and, thus, attempts to clarify what happened tend to be heroic.[29] Historical omissions of this type are common following any revolution, and examples can be found throughout the world.

Even today, some historians still portray the War for American Independence in this light. Throughout the twentieth century, fresh examinations of the war were introduced, such as Philip Greven's assertion the parent-son relations had changed significantly for the generation that fought the revolution. Greven argues that by Andover, Massachusetts' fourth generation, "Thomas Paine's call for independence...from the mother-country and father-king might have been just what Paine claimed it to be--

---

[27] Kenneth S. Lynn, *A Divided People*, (Westport, CT: Greenwood Press, 1977), 89.
[28] Wallace Brown, *The Good Americans: Loyalists in the American Revolution*, (New York, NY: William Morrow and Company, 1969), 19.
[29] Herbert Butterfield, *Whig Interpretation of History*, (New York, NY: Norton, 1965).

Irreconcilable Grievances

common sense."[30] This theory was elaborated on by Edwin Burrows and Michael Wallace, claiming Americans initially "accepted British control and authority because the objective disparity between British power and colonial power created in them a deep personal sense of comparative weakness and inferiority." It was only once demographic and economic growth occurred that the colonies "transformed the collective image of the colonies from one of weakness and inferiority to one of strength and capability."[31]

Although this theory seems to fit within the story of the American Revolution, it omits the facts that the colonies had petitioned the crown in multiple past instances since their colonization, the events of the Glorious Revolution in America and, regardless of being under the authority of the crown, the colonies had been self-governing since 1689. It was only once King George had taken an active role in managing the colonies that the friction, known as the American Revolution, was sparked between the colonial governments and Britain.

Historians will continue to seek out new interpretations of the American Revolution, but finding unanimity in such theses for the entire colonies is nearly impossible. Each colony was created by individuals with different cultural backgrounds and for various intentions; each colony was unique in its own right. Thus, the cultivation of individuals in these areas occurred differently. Sure, there were some similarities, but it has been consistently shown that the northern, middle, and southern colonies held different ideals and beliefs. Scholarship has also shown, in colonial times, there was also a distinctive societal difference between coastal

---

[30] Philip J. Greven, *Four Generations: Population, Land, and Family in Colonial Andover, Massachusetts,* (Ithaca, NY, 1970), 281.

[31] Edwin G. Burrows and Michael Wallace, "The American Revolution: The Ideology and Psychology of National Liberation," *Perspectives in American History 6*, (1972). This source was found in Robert Weir's "Rebelliousness: Personality Development and the American Revolution in the Southern Colonies," *The Southern Experience in the American Revolution*, (Chapel Hill, NC: The University of North Carolina Press, 1978), 28.

Interpreting the Declaration of Independence

regions and western settlements. Therefore, the revolution must also be examined by region, colony, and localities, rather than only trying to find common psychological and philosophical trends throughout. There were events that revolutionaries from all localities viewed as detrimental to their constitutional rights, but each individual was primarily motivated towards seeking independence differently, depending on their education, political beliefs, psyche, religion, race, economic status, age, culture, ethnicity, and socialization.

There is no doubt the evolution of political thought was a large contributing factor that influenced most of the leaders of American Revolution to distance themselves from Britain. The majority of colonists were not formally educated, though. This means other factors would have played a more dominant element in gaining their support. For these individuals, physical events spoke volumes. By continuing to examine the Declaration of Independence in comparison to the resolutions a year prior, we see a compilation of grievances that were physical events which most colonists could easily comprehend as barbarous atrocities, events that needed no political or psychological explanation accompanying it. The offenses by the Crown spoke for themselves. They include:

He has abdicated Government here, by declaring us out of his Protection and waging War against us.

He has plundered our seas, ravaged our coasts, burnt our towns, and destroyed the lives of our people.[32]

He is at this time transporting large Armies of foreign Mercenaries to compleat the works of death, desolation, and tyranny, already begun with circumstances of Cruelty & Perfidy scarcely parallelled in the most barbarous ages, and totally

---

[32] The *Declaration for the Causes and Necessity for Taking up Arms* did cite the burning of Charlestown as a reason for taking up arms. This occurred well after the Battles of Lexington and Concord had already taken place, thus was not really a factor in what that said petition was arguing.

Irreconcilable Grievances

unworthy the Head of a civilized nation.

He has constrained our fellow Citizens taken Captive on the high Seas to bear Arms against their Country, to become the executioners of their friends and Brethren, or to fall themselves by their Hands.

He has excited domestic insurrections amongst us, and has endeavoured to bring on the inhabitants of our frontiers, the merciless Indian Savages whose known rule of warfare, is an undistinguished destruction of all ages, sexes and conditions.[33]

Lastly, there was a grievance that was not listed in the final draft of the Declaration of Independence. It affected the Southern colonies greater than the Middle or New England colonies, and drove more Southern revolutionaries to independence than any other measure the British employed. It will be discussed in great detail in the subsequent chapter, and was primarily left out due to its hypocritical nature. It stated:

> He has waged cruel war against human nature itself, violating its most sacred rights of life and liberty in the persons of a distant people who never offended him, captivating and carrying them into slavery in another hemisphere, or to incur miserable death in their transportation hither. this piratical warfare, the opprobrium of infidel powers, is the warfare of the Christian king of Great Britain. [determined to keep open a market where MEN should be bought and sold,] he has prostituted his negative for suppressing every legislative attempt to prohibit or to restrain this execrable commerce [determining to keep open a market where MEN should be bought and sold]: and that this assemblage of horrors might want no fact of distinguished die, he is now exciting those very people to rise in arms among us, and to purchase that

---

[33] This grievance was also listed in *Declaration for the Causes and Necessity for Taking up Arms*. There was no evidentiary support for this claim and certainly not before either Lexington & Concord or John Sullivan's raid on Fort William & Mary in December 1774.

liberty of which he had deprived them, by murdering the people upon whom he also obtruded them: thus paying off former crimes committed against the liberties of one people, with crimes which he urges them to commit against the lives of another.

Physical events such as the recruitment of Indians, employment of slaves, effects on the military front, Hessian mercenaries, King George's address to the colonies, the burning and harassment of coastal towns, and deceitful attempts of reconciliation that were seen as a means to distract and enslave the colonists. These events thus revived the seventeenth century ideology that the people have a natural right to purge themselves from unjust rulers. This form of political thought was affirmed twice in England's Civil Wars a century before. In both cases, especially the latter one in 1689, it affirmed Englishmen's constitutional and natural rights. American revolutionaries were fully aware the sacrifices their forefathers faced in order to secure these rights, and the revolutionaries undoubtedly felt it their duty to honor their ancestors and themselves by fighting for what was deemed just.

Part One:

Diplomatic Failure
And The
Rights
Of
Englishmen

Chapter Two

A Failed Peace

Is it possible to come to a reconciliation with people that have treated us with so much barbarity?
                    John Winthrop to John Adams, April 5, 1776

If there was one adversity that could alter the American Revolution from a struggle over a restitution of grievances to a war for independence, it would be the breakdown of useful diplomatic avenues for the rebels to pursue. Thomas Cushing predicted, in February 1775, that if the colonies' diplomatic "hopes should be called off by the intemperate and violent conduct of the mother country after the conciliatory offers that have been made by the continental congress...and administration should determine to carry into execution the late acts of parliament by military force, the people of America, I am persuaded, will make the last appeal."[1] It began with the reception of King George's speech in Parliament on October 26, 1775. It was during this speech that the king asserted the American rebellion was being "manifestly carried on for the purpose of establishing an independent empire." The speech (coupled with the Prohibitory Act), is what Thomas Jefferson was referring to when he penned in the Declaration of Independence, "He has abdicated Government here, by declaring us out of his Protection and waging War against us." Thomas Lynch commented to George Washington, "Do not the Speeches of the King and his Minister hold a very different Language from those of last year!"[2]

---

[1] Richard Henry Lee, *Arthur Lee, LL.D.*, (Boston, MA: Wells and Lilly, 1829), 275.
[2] Abbot & Twohig, *The Papers of George Washington*, Revolutionary Series, Vol. 3, Thomas Lynch to George Washington, 109.

Irreconcilable Grievances

News of the King's speech did not reach the Continental Congress until January 8, 1776, but it was not the first and only time the King had made such a statement. On August 23, he issued a proclamation stating the colonists had "proceeded to open and avowed rebellion," encouraged by persons in England whose "traitorous conspiracies" would be duly punished. The comment led radicals such as James Warren to believe that Congress should "no longer" hold "any doubts, and hesitancy, about taking...Effectual strokes."[3] Nearly a year earlier, on November 18, 1774, the King had written to Lord North that the "New England Governments are in a state of rebellion," and "blows must decide whether they are to be subject to this country or independent."[4] The reception of the King's speech was met with astonishment, especially by those moderate and conservative revolutionaries who hoped reconciliation was imminent. For radical revolutionaries, such as Samuel and John Adams, the news reaffirmed their belief that nothing short of a push for autonomy should be the goal of the colonies. Samuel Adams wrote to James Sullivan, "I have seen the Speech which is falsly & shamefully called most gracious. It breathes the most malevolent Spirit, wantonly proposes Measures calculated to distress Mankind, and determines my Opinion of the Author of it as a Man of wicked Heart."[5] Adams hoped the colonies shall now "act the part which the great Law of Nature points out," thinking it was "high time that we should assume that Character" of independence.[6]

Richard Henry Lee thought the "despotic intentions of the British" were only "further demonstrated by the King's speech"

---

[3] Robert J. Taylor, *The Papers of John Adams*, Vol. 3, James Warren to John Adams, November 14, 1775, 304.

[4] W. Bodham Donne, *The Correspondence of King George the Third with Lord North 1768-1783*, Vol. 1, (New York, NY: De Capo Press, 1971), Letter 263, November 18, 1774, 214-215.

[5] Harry Alonzo Cushing, *The Writings of Samuel Adams*, Vol. 3, (New York, NY: Octagon Books, 1968), Samuel Adams to James Sullivan, January 12, 1776, 257-58.

[6] Ibid.

and the "express declaration...of both houses of Parliament."[7] He felt these political actions served as evidence that the British intended to "subdue at every event, and to enslave America after having destroyed its best Members."[8] Nathanael Greene believed the "Tyrant's last Speech closes all hopes of an Accomodation," leaving the colonists "no Alternative but Freedom or Slavery," the latter being "too horrible to think on, the former too dessirable to lose."[9] He shared similar sentiments with Jacob Greene when he penned, "George the Third's last speech has shut the door of hope for reconciliation." Although the King was making "great preparations...to prosecute the war," Greene had "no reason to doubt the success of the Colonies" in upcoming battles.[10] Greene also thought the King's speech called for "the necessity of making a declaration of independence," the first revolutionary to coin the phrase.[11] Washington disclosed his feelings on the subject of King George's speech to Joseph Reed, stating:

> With respect to myself, I have never entertained an Idea of an Accomodation since I heard of the Measures which were adopted in consequence of the Bunkers Hill fight. The Kings Speech has confirmd the Sentiments I entertained upon the News of that Affair...and, if every Man was of my Mind the Ministers of G.B. should know, in a few Words, upon what Issue the cause should be put. I would not be deceived by artful declarations, or specious pretences...nor would I be amused by unmeaning propositions, but in open, undisguised, and Manly terms proclaim our Wrongs & our Resolutions to be redressed. I would tell them, that we had born much...that

---

[7] James Curtis Ballagh, *The Letters of Richard Henry Lee*, Vol. 1, (New York, NY: De Capo Press, 1970), To Patrick Henry, April 20, 1776, 176-7.

[8] Ibid, 177.

[9] Richard K. Showman, *The Papers of Nathanael Greene*, Vol. 1, (Chapel Hill, NC: The University of North Carolina Press, 1976), To Christopher Greene, December 20, 1775, 168.

[10] Ibid, To Jacob Greene, December 20, 1775, 167.

[11] Ibid.

Irreconcilable Grievances

we had long, & ardently sought for reconciliation upon honorable terms...that it had been denied us...that all our attempts after Peace had provd abortive and had been grossly misrepresented...that we had done every thing that could be expected from the best of Subjects...that the Spirit of Freedom beat too high in us, to Submit to Slavery; & that, if nothing else would satisfie a Tyrant & his diabolical Ministry, we were determined to shake of[f] all Connexions with a State So unjust, & unnatural. This I would tell them, not under Covert, but in Words as clear as the Sun in its Meridian brightness.[12]

General Washington felt so adamant that he even shared these private sentiments with John Hancock, with whom he was usually very cautious in addressing his personal feelings on matters. He similarly wrote, "he had never entertained an Idea of Accomodation" since he heard "of the Meausres which were adopted in consequence of" the Battle of Bunkers Hill." To Washington, the King's speech simply "confirmd" these "Sentiments."[13]

King George's speech was particularly shocking to many Congressional delegates since it was believed they had taken the measures necessary to work out an amends with the Mother Country when they dispersed the Olive Branch Petition, ratified on July 8, 1775. Samuel Chase was part of the minority who held a conversing opinion, stating it was "Just as I expected," and was "not disappointed" when the King dismissed it.[14] To get an idea of the mindset of revolutionary leadership, it must be remembered that the events of Lexington and Concord, as well as the Battle of Bunker Hill, had already echoed throughout the colonies. The

---

[12] Abbot & Twohig, *The Papers of George Washington*, Revolutionary Series, Vol. 3, To Lieutenant Colonel Joseph Reed, February 10, 1775, 288.

[13] Ibid.

[14] Taylor, *The Papers of John Adams*, Vol. 3, Samuel Chase to John Adams, January 12, 1776, 401.

A Failed Peace

rebels thought they were definitively bargaining from a position of strength. Their militia and minutemen armies had held off, arguably, the most professional soldiers in the world with but few casualties. This success even propelled the radical James Warren to envision the Olive Branch Petition to possibly serve as a "Mantle to Cover the Nakedness of the Ministry" in order to "Screen them from the Shame of being forced to a retreat by the Virtue of Americans."[15]

The revolutionaries had pressured the British government to overturn almost every form of unpopular legislation by staying the course. Their own ancestors had stood firm to secure the rights and liberties believed to be owed to them through the English Constitution. Therefore, it seemed entirely reasonable to the majority that their petition would not fall upon deaf ears. Their belief was deemed with even greater favor, since they were now petitioning King George, whom many felt was not at fault for the unpopular taxes and legislation. Certainly he would listen to good reason and uphold the rights of Englishmen?

By contrast, Samuel Chase was among those Congressional representatives who suspected the Olive Branch Petition would be an unsuccessful endeavor. Some even hoped the petition would fail sequentially to force autonomy. Joseph Ward wrote that when they are "done playing with petitions and making kites for George, I expect we shall exert our united vigor in a direct line to 'Liberty Peace and Safety,' and soon reach the summit of human happiness and glory."[16] Ward expected the summit to arrive when "Wisdom and Fortitude…will guide our political helm until we arrive at the haven of perfect Freedom."[17] John Adams shared Chase and Ward's skepticism. Although he might have signed the Olive Branch Petition, Adams most assuredly "thought the gesture futile, even inimical to the colonies' best interests."[18]

---

[15] Ibid, *The Papers of John Adams*, Vol. 2, James Warren to John Adams, September 11, 1775, 131-33.

[16] Ibid, Joseph Ward to John Adams, October 23, 1775, 237.

[17] Ibid.

[18] Ibid, 9.

Irreconcilable Grievances

Notwithstanding the conflicting viewpoints, the Olive Branch Petition did not stand a chance in influencing King George's opinion on the rebellion. He seemed to have already made up this mind even before its arrival and urged for strong decisive action by his military commanders, Vice Admiral Samuel Graves and Thomas Gage. Unfortunately, there was little for the King to be enthusiastic about regarding the success of his commanders. Gage thought it was "beyond" his "Capacity to Judge what ought to be done," but was firmly against yielding. He warned Lord Barrington if they strayed from the course, Parliament would "have not a spark of Authority remaining over this Country."[19] Although Congress was pressing for a reconciliation to be worked out, Gage was pessimistic. He was convinced the rebels had a hidden agenda, as was made plain in the reports in the local publications. False and incomplete reports convinced Gage that the rebels "mean absolute Independence…which are meant to delude and deceive the Multitude."[20] By August, Gage had become completely convinced of the rebels' designs, conveying it to Lord Dartmouth:

> The Designs of the Leaders of the Rebellion are plain, and every Day confirms the truth of what was asserted years ago by many intelligent People, that a Plan was laid in this Province and adjusted with some of the same Stamp in others for a total Independence; whilst they amused People in England, called the Friends of America, as well as many in this Country with feigned Professions of Affection and Attachment of the Parent State, and pretended to be aggrieved and discontented only on Account of Taxation; That they have designedly irritated Government by ever Insult, whilst they artfully poisoned the Minds of the People, and ripened them for Insurrection. They would still deceive

---

[19] Clarence Edwin Carter, *The Correspondence of General Thomas Gage with the Secretaries of State, and with the War Office and the Treasury*, Vol. 1, Thomas Gage to Lord Barrington, March 28, 1775, (Archon Books, 1969), 671.

[20] Ibid, Vol. 2, Thomas Gage to Lord Dartmouth, July 24, 1775, 410.

A Failed Peace

and lull the Mother Country into the Belief that nothing is meant against the Nation, and that their Quarrel is only with the Ministers; but it is hoped the Nation will see thro' the Fallacy and Deceit. It matters not who holds the Helm of the State, the Stroke is leveled at the British Nation, on whose Ruins they hope to build their much Vaunted American Empire, and to rise like a Phoenix out of the Ashes of the Mother Country.[21]

News of inaction and failure from his commanders had not swayed the King but rather infuriated him. He felt he had conceded much, revoking one unpopular tax after another, while reports of insurgencies and rebellion continued. Only through an overwhelming show of force could the colonists be put into line. However, the King's initial plan to quell Massachusetts was largely unsuccessful due to inadequate troop estimates and logistical support, and largely because he and his advisors did not realize the degree to which the rebellion extended. It was thought to have been, for the most part, limited to Massachusetts, giving the British Navy an opportunity to requisition supplies from the neighboring colonies.[22] Such a seizure, however, was never realized. Furthermore, Britain's assumption had dire consequences, for their army would be trapped in Boston, starving, undermanned, and lacking adequate munitions, all essential keys to encountering another army. King George felt he had learned from his mistakes; now that he knew the colonists' true designs, he could act accordingly by sending sufficient troops and supplies to force the colonists into submission.

With reports of the dismal situation of the British army in Boston reaching England when the King delivered his speech to Parliament, debate heated up in both the House of Lords and House of Commons on whether to "put a speedy end to these

---

[21] Ibid, Thomas Gage to Lord Dartmouth, August 20, 1775, 412.
[22] Carter, *The Correspondence of Thomas Gage with the Secretaries of State and with the War Office of the Treasury 1763-1775*, Vol. 1, 181.

disorders by the most decisive exertions."[23] Upon the completion of the King's October 26 speech, business resumed in the House of Lords. Lord Camden immediately stood and proposed an adoption to "such measures for the healing of the present unhappy disputes between the mother country and the Colonies."[24] Camden's petition for reconciliation was ignored. As it happened, his appeal for adoption was out of Parliamentary order, for it "had always been the rule in that House, not to enter upon any business till the Speech from the Throne had been taken into consideration," thus it received no attention on the floor.[25]

Viscount Townshend was the first to address the House regarding the speech. He urged the members to "support his Majesty with our lives and fortunes," since the rebellion manifests for the "purpose of establishing and maintaining an independent empire."[26] Viscount Dudley concurred with Townshend, believing "that none but men of the worst dispositions, and most pernicious designs, would encourage the claims of America, and that, as they had been wrong almost in everything else, he was glad to find that they have been mistaken in their predictions relative to the distresses which the dispute with America would bring upon this nation."[27]

The speech was not well received by all. The Marquis of Rockingham, for one, "condemned the speech," and contended the measures "were big with the most portentous and ruinous consequences."[28] The Earl of Coventry did not see war as an option. He thought Britain should "either…relinquish all connection with the Colonies" or "adopt conciliatory measures." The idea of "conquering" the colonies was, in his opinion, too "wild and extravagant." Even in the event of victory, the colonies "would be worth nothing," since success would call "for such a

---

[23] Force, *American Archives*, Fourth Series, Vol. 6, 2.
[24] Ibid, 3.
[25] Ibid.
[26] Ibid, 4.
[27] Ibid.
[28] Ibid, 5.

standing military force to keep them in subjection, as we could never be able to support."²⁹ The Duke of Grafton "could not vote for" the King's proposal, but would certainly "give the Address...a negative." He had previously supported the Administration's efforts to subdue Massachusetts but asserted he had "been misled and deceived."³⁰ Doctor John Hinchcliffe, Bishop of Peterborough, held similar sentiments. He had voted for the initial sending of troops because it was believed "the Americans would not fight." Now, that it was obvious they "can and will fight," a reconciliation needed to be explored. The rebels might have lost the battles, but "considering the stand they made, and the intrepidity of the troops they had to contend with, they were not disgraced by their defeat." Lastly, Hinchcliffe did not see the purpose of a "ruinous and expensive war" if "there is scarce a man in this country who thinks now that America...will not submit to taxation."³¹ Lord Lyttleton "totally disapproved of the Address," feeling the Ministry was only assuming the Americans were seeking independence while they have "not declared to be in rebellion."³²

The Olive Branch Petition was also brought up in the debate over the King's speech. The Earl of Shelburne queried, "How comes it, that the Colonies are charged with planning independency, in the face of their explicit declaration to the contrary, contained in that Petition?"³³ To him, it was not logical to resolve their dispute by force when it was "contrary to fact, contrary to evidence" that the Americans were seeking independence. Shelburne argued it must then be the Lord's intention, "by...perpetually sounding independence in the ears of the Americans to lead them to it," or by compelling them into it, "which must be our ruin?"³⁴

---

²⁹ Ibid.
³⁰ Ibid, 6.
³¹ Ibid, 8-9.
³² Ibid, 8.
³³ Ibid, 12.
³⁴ Ibid.

Irreconcilable Grievances

By the end of the debate in the House of Lords, the minority's cries for reconciliation proved unconvincing. The majority was too impressed with the "tenderness with which his Majesty has proceeded" to not offer their support.[35] They felt the King was not only diplomatic in conveying his speech, but he even stated his goal was to restore the colonies "to the free exercise of its trade and commerce, and to the same protection and security, as if they "had never revolted."[36] The Earl of Sandwich stated "the only true cause" why the disorders in America had increased was because of support of individuals within this House who spoke of reconciliation. It was their "open and avowed support and countenance…to the rebels, by men who, under a pretended regard for their country, encouraged, from the worst motives, an unnatural rebellion," to its current state.[37]

To the majority, the argument was simple. Reconciliation, as was proposed by the Duke of Grafton, "was in fact giving up the whole contest, and at once relinquishing our rights of sovereignty, and every possible benefit we are entitled to claim in the way of trade and commerce."[38] Now, that Parliament felt they were properly informed of the actual state of rebellion, it was believed proper action could be carried out. The Earl of Dartmouth pointed out "it was never supposed, if America united, that to reduce them would be the work of one summer." The force initially sent there was only for the "safety and protection of the Province of Massachusetts Bay," not for the entire continent.[39] By sending a sufficient force, it was believed the issue would eventually be resolved by fear or force.

Debates in the House of Commons were no different, and nor was the end result. Major John Dyke Acland knew that "reducing America to just obedience" was "not without its difficulties" but

---

[35] Force, *American Archives*, Fourth Series, Vol. 6, 3.
[36] Ibid, 2.
[37] Ibid, 6-7.
[38] Ibid.
[39] Ibid, 10.

A Failed Peace

felt they "must be overcome, not yielded to."[40] He made the point to the members of the House that "it cannot now be contended that America is not in a state of war," since "they now hold a higher tone," and presumed an "invincibility of strength."[41] Sir Adam Ferguson agreed with the minority that the Continental Congress had not actually declared themselves independent but "certainly had done so in general terms."[42] Alexander Wedderburn was more vocal in his support for action. "Relinquish America, and you also relinquish the West Indies," he shouted. His argument was that Britain must bargain from a position of strength, stating "Establish, first, your superiority and then talk of negotiation." Wedderburn queried, "Did Rome, when Hannibal marched triumphantly up to her walls, sue for peace?" Henry Dundas made sure the assembly considered how reconciliation would be perceived by the other European powers. He believed all of Europe "would say we had felt our inability to enforce our rights, and therefore were glad to accommodate on any terms."[43] Much had been spent on the French and Indian War, which had determined England was the dominant force on the continent. The French and Spanish might foresee reconciliation as a sign of weakness, thus the use of force was necessary in order to preserve the western British Empire from encroachment by other European powers.

Edmund Burke led the minority in pushing for a compromise, speaking for nearly two hours. He forecast how the British would be viewed in history as tyrants for pursuing a civil war with its colonies. Burke thought the Americans had gone too far and were not justifiable in what they had done; but they no longer wanted to make "England appear like a porcupine, armed at all points with Acts of Parliament."[44] Charles James Fox, too, thought the colonists "were not justifiable in what they had done" but were

---

[40] Ibid, 18.
[41] Ibid.
[42] Ibid, 23.
[43] Ibid, 49.
[44] Ibid, 44.

"more justifiable for resisting" than if they "submitted to the tyrannical acts of British Parliament." Fox appealed to the hearts of his colleagues by asking, if it would not be the choice of every Englishman to "aim at freedom" rather than "submit to slavery?"[45] John Wilkes thought the war "fatal and ruinous to our country," since it "absolutely annihilates the only great source of our wealth," namely, commercial trade.[46]

The motion to accept the King's proposal easily passed, 278 for, and only 108 against. A committee, led by Major Acland, was assembled to address the king regarding the decision. The address closed by stating:

> And we hope and trust that we shall, by the blessing of God, put such strength and force into your Majesty's hands, as may soon defeat and suppress this rebellion, and enable your Majesty to accomplish your gracious wish of re-establishing order, tranquility, and happiness, through all the parts of your united empire.[47]

Although the Olive Branch Petition arrived in England on September 1, 1775, the contents were not officially deliberated upon in Parliament until November 7, nearly two weeks after the King's speech to Parliament. Before a debate on the petition could occur, it was requested that John Penn, Governor of Pennsylvania, and messenger of the petition, be called upon to authenticate it. On November 10 he was examined and, prior to being probed, was given a list of questions to be asked. Penn was asked if there were any questions "he wished to decline answering," but he assured Parliament there were none "so solicitous to avoid."[48] The Earl of Dartmouth was the first to question Penn. Penn was queried as to whether the war was in "defence of their liberty" or "for the purpose of establishing an Independent Empire?"[49] Penn

---

[45] Force, *American Archives*, Fourth Series, Vol. 6, 44.
[46] Ibid, 22.
[47] Ibid, 47.
[48] Ibid, 124.
[49] Ibid, 125.

A Failed Peace

confirmed what the petition stated, that the war was carried on in "defence of their liberties, as they think," and thought "they do not carry on the war for Independence."[50] Dartmouth also inquired about the ability of the colonies to wage a war against the British. How many men were fit to bear arms, how many would fight, and could they produce gunpowder and cannon? Penn supposed sixty thousand men from Pennsylvania "would willing come forth" to bear arms, and he affirmed that the colonists' ability to produce gunpowder and cannon sufficient to carry on a war.

Regarding Parliament's reception of the colonists' petitions, Penn answered that the colonists were "dissatisfied" and "had conceived great hopes" in the success of the Olive Branch. Furthermore, he stated, if conciliatory measures were not speedily pursued, it would not be long before an alliance with foreign powers was imminent. The Earl of Sandwich was the next member to question Penn, inquiring into the legitimacy of the Continental Congress in representing the desires of all the colonists. Penn assured the Earl that "no one opposed" Congress, as "it seemed to be the general wish of the people."[51] The Earl of Denbigh was the third and last member of the House of Lords to question the governor. Denbigh made the record clear on Parliament's legal right to tax the colonies. He mentioned the Pennsylvania charter's clause concerning Parliament's right to taxation, and he asked if the colony was willing to be taxed? Penn knew the clause but did "not believe Pennsylvania would be satisfied to be taxed" by Parliament or by their own elected government.[52]

Penn's testimony would not change Parliament's position, but his responses affirmed both sides' position on the war. The Duke of Richmond felt Penn confirmed his greatest fears, that "they had resources within themselves for the subsistence of their armies." The Duke was uncertain whether the Americans "had or had not the courage to make use of arms," but he knew they "were at least

---

[50] Ibid.
[51] Ibid, 128.
[52] Ibid.

expert in the mode of using them."[53] The Earl of Shelburne believed Parliament's right to tax the colonies "was so fundamentally wrong," it was not worth a war even though it was "derogating from the dignity of Parliament to treat with an assembly not legalized as a Congress."[54] Their right to taxation had been commercial, but expedients to obtain an acknowledgement of that right proved ineffective, and thus Shelburne felt "the more we consider it, the more we must be convinced...we have no right to tax America."[55]

Shelburne and some others might have been willing to dispense with some Parliamentary power, but the majority did not wish to give up their right to tax. Lyttelton attacked Shelburne's motion, asking the assembly whether they would relinquish their dominion "over those worst of Rebels, and tamely submit to transfer the seat of empire from Great Britain to America?" The Earl of Sandwich replied by stating he certainly would not "surrender the right of Parliament to its rebellious subjects."[56] Furthermore, the Earl added that, although the "Lords in Opposition" were "very sincere" and "genuine" in their attempts to work out reconciliation, he believed the dispensing with any Parliamentary power was to "render the rights of this country into the hands of the Colonies."[57]

The Olive Branch Petition was not accepted by the King or either House of Parliament, and even though it was rejected, it propelled the minority to continue to find new outlets for a compromise. On November 7, Temple Luttrell proposed that every member should "exert his utmost endeavor to restore peace and commercial prosperity to the mother country and her colonies." He wanted Parliament to be open to receiving "proposals for reconciliation from any General Convention, Congress, or other collective body...suspending all inquiry into

---

[53] Force, *American Archives*, Fourth Series, Vol. 6, 128.
[54] Ibid, 130.
[55] Ibid, 131.
[56] Ibid, 135-6.
[57] Ibid, 136.

A Failed Peace

the legal or illegal forms under which such Colony or Colonies may be disposed to treat."[58] Surprisingly, the motion passed, even though such an action would be technically admitting Congress to be a legal legislative body, which it was not.

On a separate occasion, Edmund Burke appealed to the House of Commons by forwarding a petition from the English towns of Westbury, Warminster, and Trowbridge concerning the economic impact of the war. The King's order prohibiting all commerce with the American colonies had caused a severe decline in trade, while raising unemployment in the commercial towns affected. The townspeople hoped that the King would "adopt such lenient measures as may restore this great kingdom and her Colonies that affectionate intercourse with each other."[59] Burke supported the bill by stating there were three plans Parliament could adopt. They could have a "simple war, in order to a perfect conquest," adopt "a mixture of war and treaty," or resolve a "peace grounded on concession."[60] Burke stated why he felt a "simple war" or "mixture of war and treaty" was not within the best interests of the Ministry. He believed only by compromising with the colonists' desires for liberty, could Parliament work out a long lasting peace; otherwise, hostilities would continue to develop until autonomy became the colonies' final goal. The bill passed in the negative, 210 against, and 105 in favor.

What Parliament would pass in terms of a conciliatory bill was Lord North's Prohibitory Act. On December 22, 1775, the act prohibited the American colonies from "all manner of trade and commerce" and declared that any ships found trading "shall be forfeited to his Majesty, as if the same were the ships and effects of open enemies." Such ships were unable to be "claimed or sued for in the Courts of Admiralty."[61] The act repealed the Boston Port Act and two other acts restraining colonial trade. Lastly, it

---

[58] Ibid, 139-41.

[59] Ibid, 171.

[60] Ibid, 172.

[61] Chesnutt, *The Papers of Henry Laurens*, Vol. 10, John Laurens to Henry Laurens, November 24, 1775, 513.

authorized the King to "appoint Commissioners to grant Pardons & receive the Submissions of any Province, County, Town or District."[62] George Hay supported the act, since it was the "best way to terminate a war in which we have been involuntarily involved with."[63] British Attorney General Thurlow "approved of it" because it maintained the right of taxation but "left an opening to America of a permission to raise her share of the supply towards the common defence by granting it in her own Assemblies."[64]

The Prohibitory Act was not received well by the rebels. It technically placed them out of the protection of the Crown, declared them to be the enemies of England, ordered them to be treated as such and allotted the confiscation of their property. Various rumors about the act's peace commissioners developed. The rebels' greatest fear was the commissioners were not going to negotiate with Congress but with each province separately. While the bill was still under debate in Parliament, John Laurens wrote to his brother Henry that the Prohibitory Bill was "calculated only to destroy that Unanimity which renders America so formidable." He felt the Ministry's designs were to engage "each particular Province in separate and uncertain Treaties" in order to tempt "weak Individuals to desert the cause."[65] Their fears were well founded, since the act only allotted the commissioners to treat with provinces, counties, towns, and districts. No provision in the act allowed the commissioners to work out reconciliation with Congress.

News of the Prohibitory Act arrived in the colonies in late February and was not read before Congress until February 27. It was so offensive to Joseph Reed that it, coupled with "a thousand other Proofs of a bitter & irreconcilable Spirit," made him query why a "strange Reluctance in the Minds of many to cut the Knot"

---

[62] Abbot & Twohig, *The Papers of George Washington*, Revolutionary Series, Vol. 3, 379 n 19.

[63] Force, *American Archives*, Fourth Series, Vol. 6, 188.

[64] Ibid, 190.

[65] Chesnutt, *The Papers of Henry Laurens*, Vol. 10, John Laurens to Henry Laurens, November 24, 1775, 510-11.

A Failed Peace

with Great Britain still existed.[66] William Henry Drayton had "never heard of so atrocious a procedure," and felt it "had no parallel in the registers of tyranny."[67] The conservative Robert Morris thought the act, coupled with the burning of colonial towns, "prepared Men's minds for an Independency that were shock'd at the idea a few weeks ago."[68] George Washington would write, "was there ever any thing more absurd, than to repeal the very Acts that have introduced all this confusion and bloodshed & at the same time enact a Law to restrain all Intercourse with the Colonies for opposing them."[69] John Adams was also "amazed" how such an act could be possibly "endured in any one Spot in America."[70] He wrote to James Warren that the act tied with King George's speech "convinced the doubting and confirmed the timorous and wavering" on the issue of independence. Benjamin Kent, moreover, believed this and the recent "hundred" series of events will propel the colonies to be "wholly divorced from that Accursed Kingdom."[71]

The Prohibitory Act's sole intent was to both force and negotiate a peace but, in fact, propelled the opposite. A month prior to the act's arrival, some moderate and conservative rebels were optimistic about a potential peace agreement being negotiated with Lord Drummond (Thomas Lundin). Drummond did not claim or possess any official authorization from the British government to conduct negotiations. His plans for peace were

---

[66] Abbot & Twohig, *The Papers of George Washington*, Revolutionary Series, Vol. 3, Joseph Reed to George Washington, March 3, 1776, 406.

[67] Force, *American Archives*, Fourth Series, Vol. 5, 1028.

[68] Paul H. Smith, *Letters of Delegates to Congress, 1774-1789*, Vol. 3 (Washington, DC: Library of Congress, 1976-79), 244, 431, 258. Found in Maier, *American Scripture*, 28.

[69] Abbot & Twohig, *The Papers of George Washington*, Revolutionary Series, Vol. 3, George Washington to Joseph Reed, February 26-March 9 1776, 375.

[70] Taylor, *The Papers of John Adams*, Vol. 4, John Adams to William Heath, April 15, 1776, 120.

[71] Ibid, Benjamin Kent to John Adams, April 24, 1776, 145-46.

Irreconcilable Grievances

propagated on conversations with American moderates from New York in the fall of 1774 and with Lord Dartmouth and Lord North in England between December 1774 and September 1775.[72] During the first two weeks of January, Drummond discussed his plan for reconciliation with several members of Congress, including Thomas Lynch. Lynch was optimistic, writing to Washington that the "King and his Minister" were allegedly only offering their "vigorous support" of their rights and "the terms of 1763," while Drummond is willing to "give much more."[73] Drummond's terms seemed too good to be true, so Lynch "doubted" this information but was assured the "Ministry wanted nothing but a Shew of Revenue to hold up Parliament."[74]

Some rebels were greatly concerned with how the Ministry's actions contradicted one another. John Hancock wrote that the British "are determined to exert themselves and to send a considerable force against us...though at the same time they pretend to say that they will offer terms of accommodation."[75] The King's speech to Parliament in October was quickly circulated widely throughout the colonies. It confirmed more troops were in route, including the possibility of foreign assistance. The situation seemed suspicious to many rebels, but moderates like Hancock thought Congress must be ready "For should an accommodation take place the terms will be severe or favorable in our proportion to our ability to resist."[76] Washington wholeheartedly agreed with Hancock's comments, stating they "ou[gh]t to be on a respectable footing to receive their Armaments in the Spring."[77] Although the General agreed, he confessed he did not know how his army "shall be provided with the Means" to resist, since he lacked the essentials, men, arms, and

---

[72] Abbot & Twohig, *The Papers of George Washington*, Vol. 3, 111 n 3.

[73] Ibid, Thomas Lynch to George Washington, January 16, 1776, 109-111.

[74] Ibid.

[75] Ibid, John Hancock to George Washington, January 29, 1776, 210-11.

[76] Ibid.

[77] Ibid, George Washington to John Hancock, February 9, 1776, 278.

A Failed Peace

ammunition.[78] Lynch held similar sentiments and preferred to negotiate from a position of strength. Drummond had proposed the suspension of arms through the winter, but Lynch "turned a very deaf ear."[79] Although Drummond proposed "very generous terms," Lynch thought it best to "wait a little."[80] He was waiting for positive news regarding the campaign against Quebec in order to increase the strength of the American bargaining position.

The news of Quebec was not what Lynch had hoped for. The American defeat at Quebec set back potential negotiations, since the loss stirred feelings of hostility towards the British. It was the first moral defeat the Continental Army faced. They had lost the Battle of Bunker Hill in June but at little cost compared to the British. The loss at Quebec severely weakened the American negotiating position. Though the loss stalled negotiations, Lynch did try to revive the talks. Meanwhile, Drummond's attempt at peace failed for other reasons. The diplomatic failure would primarily rest on General Washington's refusal to cooperate. It started when Washington was supposed to forward a letter from Lord Drummond to Brigadier General James Robertson, the British barrack master general at Boston. Instead of doing what was requested of him, he sent the letter to Congress, an action that humiliated the delegates who had been in discussions with Drummond.[81] Washington wrote his sentiments on the proposal to Hancock, stating:

> As I never heard of his Lordship being vested with power to treat with Congress upon the Subject of our Greivances, nor of his having laid any propositions before them for an Accomodation, I confess it surprized me much, and led me to form various conjectures of his motives, and Intended application to General Howe & Admiral Shouldham for a passport for the safe Conduct of such Deputies as Congress

---

[78] Ibid.

[79] Ibid, Thomas Lynch to George Washington, January 16, 1776, 110.

[80] Ibid, n 3.

[81] Ibid, Thomas Lynch to George Washington, February 5, 1776, 252-253 n 2.

might appoint for Negotiating Terms of Reconciliation between Great Britain and us. Whatever his Intentions are, however benevolent his designs may be, I confess that his Letter embarrassed me much, and I am not without suspicion of Its meaning more than the Generous purposes it professes. I should suppose that If the mode for Negociation which he points out, should be adopted, which I hope never will be thought of, that It ought to have been fixed and settled previous to any application of this sort, and at best that his conduct in this Instance is premature and Officious, & leading to consequences of fatal and Injurious nature to the rights of this Country.[82]

Lastly, what killed Drummond's attempts to achieve peace was the publication of the Prohibitory Act, for it affirmed many rebels' suspicions that the Ministry would only accept a peace by force. Although one of the provisions of the Prohibitory Act called for the sending of a peace commission, the terms essentially placed the colonies out of the protection of the Crown. The colonies' property, especially their commercial interests, was now capable of being exploited. The harsh provisions of the Prohibitory Act were nothing new in English maritime history. It had been common practice to impress crews and confiscate the naval property of criminals. Different rules applied to vessels belonging to other nations during times of war, but any Americans disobeying Parliamentary directives were viewed as nothing more than rebels or pirates. Therefore, the British government viewed privateering and the continuation of commerce without their consent as a course of piracy.[83] With many of the colonists' livelihood involved in commercial shipping, historian Olive Anderson points out that "no stronger policy was ever followed than that embodied in the Prohibitory Act."[84]

---

[82] Ibid, George Washington to John Hancock, February 14, 1776, 306.
[83] Olive Anderson, "British Governments and Rebellion at Sea," *The Historical Journal*, Vol. 3, No. 1 (1960), 56-64.
[84] Ibid, 61.

A Failed Peace

The peace commission appointed through the Prohibitory Act, or the "Act of Independency," as John Adams called it, did not fair any better than previous attempts by the Ministry.[85] When Major General Charles Lee heard the names of the potential commissioners to be appointed, he exasperated "what damned fools the Ministry are!"[86] The rebels enthusiastically welcomed peace negotiations, just not under the conditions the British intended on practicing. It was rumored the commissioners were not to negotiate peace with Congress, but only with the different colonies and local governments. On February 21 the *Pennsylvania Gazette* published an excerpt from an issue of the *London Gazetteer,* dated December 6, 1775. It reported, "Most of the American Governors will be appointed Commissioners (36) to America, is, to treat with each province separately about an accommodation, and so dispatch the business: - They are not to treat wit the Congress, as was first reported." A tactic that Washington described as "insulting."[87] James Warren called it a "Negro policy," arguing that Britain should not believe the colonies are "so stupid as to suppose that they will be able to avail themselves of the Advantage of getting different terms from different Colonies."[88] Warren used the term "negro" in a derogatory sense, since he and many other rebels viewed the Prohibitory Act as treating the colonists as criminals or slaves, not free men.[89] His wife, Mercy Otis, saw little hope of the success of an accommodation. She described the unfair attempt at peace as a "test" of the strength of the union of the colonies. She wrote to John Adams, that although "many among us are Ready to Flatter

---

[85] Taylor, *The Papers of John Adams*, Vol. 4, 57 n 2.

[86] Abbot & Twohig, *The Papers of George Washington*, Revolutionary Series, Vol. 3, Major General Charles Lee to George Washington, February 19, 1776, 340.

[87] Ibid, George Washington to Joseph Reed, February 26-March 9, 1776, 375.

[88] Taylor, *The Papers of John Adams*, Vol. 4, James Warren to John Adams, March 7, 1776, 45.

[89] Ibid, 46 n 3.

themselves that an Accommodation with Britain is Easey," we should have "Little Expectation that the Commissioners...will submit to such Humiliating Terms as the safety, the Happiness, and the justice of America Demands."[90]

Joseph Reed had received intelligence from Robert Temple that the peace commissioners were initially instructed "to get from us as much as they can," but if peace "can not be had on their Terms, to make it ours." He ruled such information to be "so inconsistent with all that we have seen," that he did "not believe a Word of it." Reed was "more afraid of these Commissioners than their General & Armies," since he feared their true mission was to divide the colonies.[91] Jonathon Trumbull held a comparable opinion when he wrote to Washington their "business is to divide our Councils and Exertions as much as possible," and to "hold out pardons to penitent Sinner...to those who are abject enough to take the guilt of Treason upon them and supplicate remission."[92]

The General agreed, believing the commissioners come with "invidious Intentions" to "distract, divide, & create as much confusion as possible."[93] Washington felt "no Man" wished for the "restoration of Peace more fervently than" he, but only upon "such terms as will reflect honour upon the Councils."[94] North Carolina's Provincial Congress was so concerned that the commissioners were planning on dividing the united colonial effort that they passed a resolve forbidding any locality from negotiating peace. This was reiterating what the Articles of Confederation had already adopted, which stated, "[T]he power and duty of Congress" to determine "war & peace, the entering into alliances, the reconciliation with Great Britain; the settling of

---

[90] Ibid, Mercy Otis Warren to John Adams, March 10, 1776, 51.
[91] Abbot & Twohig, *The Papers of George Washington*, Revolutionary Series, Vol. 3, Joseph Reed to George Washington, March 15, 1776, 476.
[92] Ibid, Jonathon Trumbull to George Washington, March 25, 1776, 540.
[93] Abbot & Twohig, *The Papers of George Washington*, Revolutionary Series, Vol. 4, George Washington to Joseph Reed, April 1, 1776, 11.
[94] Ibid.

all disputes...and the planting of new colonies when proper."⁹⁵ North Carolina's read:
> That if any Commissioner or Commissioners appointed by the King, according to the Act of Parliament, to come over from Great Britain to America, shall arrive in this Province, under any pretext whatever, unless such Commissioner or Commissioners shall produce a commission to treat with the Continental Congress, that the person or persons of such Commissioner or Commissioners shall be required to return immediately on board the vessel in which he or they arrive; and in case of refusal, or if such Commissioner or Commissioners shall at any time after be found on shore within this Province, the person or persons of such Commissioners be seized and immediately sent to the said Congress.⁹⁶

John Adams referred to the commissioners as "a Messiah that will never come."⁹⁷ He further added the "story of Commissioners is as arrant an illusion as ever was hatched in the brain of an enthusiast, a politician, or a maniack. I have laughed at it, scolded at it, grieved at it, and I do not know but I may, at an unguarded moment, have ripped at it. But it is in vain to reason against such delusions."⁹⁸ Adams even thought the peace commissioners were already in America. They were the "Governors, Mandamus Councillors, Collectors, and Comptrollers, and Commanders of the Army and Navy," and they were plotting to "receive submissions" from individual colonies, but, according to Adams, the colonies "are not in a very submissive mood."⁹⁹

Some preferred to just cut off ties with Britain altogether rather than negotiate any peace. Joseph Ward preferred to "Cut the

---

⁹⁵ Boyd, *The Papers of Thomas Jefferson*, Vol. 1, Articles of Confederation 1775, 177.
⁹⁶ Force, *American Archives*, Fourth Series, Vol. 5, 1323.
⁹⁷ Force, *American Archives*, Fourth Series, Vol. 5, 942.
⁹⁸ Ibid.
⁹⁹ Ibid.

Irreconcilable Grievances

Gordian knot, and the timid and wavering will have new feelings...and the determined faithful friends of their Country will kindle with new ardour, and the United Colonies increase in strength and glory every hour."[100] John Winthrop queried, "Is it possible to come to a reconciliation with people that have treated us with so much barbarity?"[101] He believed most people would gladly "throw off that dependence which has been the source of all evils we have suffered," because a return to British rule would "expect but a repetition of the same scene."[102] In the end, the Prohibitory Act drove some moderates, such as Robert Alexander, into the radicals' camp.

It did not however cause the members of Congress to lose all hope, for on May 6, Congress was still waiting on the possibility of the commissioners arriving to treat with them. It was even resolved "that General Washington be informed, that the Congress suppose, if commissioners are intended to be sent from Great Britain to treat of peace, that the practice usual in such cases will be observed, by making previous application for the necessary passports or safe conduct, and on such application being made, Congress will then direct the proper measures for the reception of such commissioners."[103] All the way up to the adoption of the Declaration of Independence, moderate and conservative members of Congress hoped the commissioners would arrive to finally work out a resolution to the conflict. That resolution never materialized though, leaving the rebels committed to the autonomy of a new nation.

Not all the colonies supported such an initiative. A number of inhabitants from New Jersey petitioned Congress to wait and work out reconciliation with England. They wrote:

---

[100] Taylor, *The Papers of John Adams*, Vol. 4, Joseph Ward to John Adams, March 23, 1776, 63.
[101] Ibid, John Winthrop to John Adams, April 5, 1776, 110.
[102] Ibid.
[103] Abbot & Twohig, *The Papers of George Washington,* Revolutionary Series, Vol. 3, 525 n 9. Also in Force, *American Archives,* Fourth Series, Vol. 5, 1227, 1696.

A Failed Peace

> To effect which desirable end, we apprehend the union of the Colonies was recommended; for which purpose alone was the Continental Congress delegated, and their authority hitherto submitted to; and upon the same hopes of peace and reconciliation, we are daily impatiently expecting Commissioners from his Majesty. From these considerations, gentlemen, we were convinced that sentiments of separation and independence must be not only highly impolitic, but may be of the most dangerous and destructive consequences...[104]

The King's peace commission was at a large disadvantage, mostly because they were not officially appointed until May 3, 1776. On that date Richard Howe and Major General William Howe were appointed as the commissioners, with Henry Strachy as their secretary.[105] What their powers exactly encompassed was the subject of much debate in Parliament. Even prior to the commissioners' appointments, the Duke of Grafton questioned their authority. He voiced his opinion, stating:

> I was in the country when this act first cam to my hands, and on comparing the King's speech with the clause, I must own I was astonished. What does the clause say? That Commissioners are to be appointed, and that is all. What are they to do? To receive submissions. Does it state what conditions, or, indeed, provide for any condition at all? Have the Commissioners the least shadow of power by this act to make any concession whatever? None; the alternative is resistance on one hand, till both or either party are destroyed; or that America shall instantly disarm, surrender, and submit.[106]

In May, General Conway, Edmund Burke, and Temple Luttrell would reiterate the argument, but Lord North would clarify exactly

---

[104] Force, *American Archives*, Fourth Series, Vol. 6, 789.
[105] Force, *American Archives*, Fourth Series, Vol. 5, 1176.
[106] Force, *American Archives*, Fourth Series, Vol. 6, 322.

Irreconcilable Grievances

what the powers the commissioners possessed. He stated:
> It gives a power of granting general and also special pardons; it empowers the Commissioners to confer with any of his Majesty's subjects, without exception; it authorizes and directs them to inquire into the state and causes of their complaints; it cannot offer any terms--no such have ever yet been settled by Parliament; nor has the Congress, nor any of the American, ever yet offered any which Parliament could listen to. These being the only powers of the commission, the instructions can give no power of agreeing upon or settling any terms of accommodation; they hold out no ultimatum; they make no concessions; they do not presume to bind Parliament-they cannot do that; they go to empowering the Commissioners not to treat, but to confer and to sound for grounds of peace; but all must be referred to Parliament.[107]

Upon arriving in the colonies to assume his duties, on June 20, 1776 Richard Howe issued the following proclamation to the inhabitants of Massachusetts regarding peace:
> It shall and may be lawful to and for any person or persons, appointed and authorized by his Majesty, to grant a pardon or pardons to any number of description of persons, by Proclamation, in his Majesty's name; to declare any County, Town, Port, District, or place, in any Colony or Province, to be at peace of Proclamation in any of the aforesaid Colonies or Provinces, or if his Majesty shall be graciously pleased to signify the same by his Royal Proclamation, then, and from and after the issuing of such Proclamation, then, and from and after to such Colony or Province, Colonies or Provinces, County, Town, Port, District, or place, shall cease, determine, and be utterly void...[108]

The proclamation confirmed Washington's fears regarding the

---

[107] Ibid, 382-83.
[108] Ibid, 1001.

A Failed Peace

peace commission. He would write to John Hancock, stating, "All that has been said about the Commissioners was illusory, and calculated expressly to deceive and unguarded, not only the good people of our own country, but those of the English nation that were adverse to the proceedings of the King and Ministry."[109] The King's speech, rejection of the Olive Branch Petition, and subsequent attempts of reconciliation by Parliamentary sympathizers were essential for the revolutionaries to legitimize the push for independence.

The actions confirmed a legal precedent set during the English Civil Wars of the seventeenth century, that the people are entitled to a law of redress against public oppression, and if a monarch broke the original contract between King and people, violating the fundamental laws of England, then the people had a right to revolt. According to Blackstone's *Commentaries on the Laws of England*, only "society itself" can make the decision that a monarch had abdicated the throne, since "there is not upon earth any other tribunal to resort to."[110] The colonies' declaring themselves independent of Great Britain was a radical step, viewed by the revolutionaries as, in some measure, the next legal redress according to English law. The King's failure to address the colonists' petitions allowed "the People" the right "to alter or to abolish" any "Form of Government" that becomes "destructive to these ends." Frederick County, Maryland reminded their delegates, "all just and legal Government was instituted for the ease and convenience of the People, and that the People have the indubitable right to reform or abolish a Government which may appear to them insufficient for the exigency of affairs."[111]

In many of the colonies' and localities' declarations of independence and instructions to the delegates regarding the vote for autonomy, the rejection of the Olive Branch Petition and King George's declaring the colonies in "open rebellion," were called attention to as a means to give them validity. The Cheraws

---

[109] Force, *American Archives*, Fifth Series, Vol. 1, 500.

[110] Maier, *American Scripture*, 72.

[111] Force, *American Archives*, Fourth Series, Vol. 6, 933.

Irreconcilable Grievances

District of South Carolina made sure to point out in their declaration that their "humble petitions styled insults," caused them to take "the only and last means of securing their own honor, safety, and happiness" by supporting independence.[112] The Virginia Convention began their list of grievances by stating Parliament's declaring of "all these Colonies…to be in rebellion and out of the protection of the British crown" as the principle for adopting their own "plan of Government as will be most likely to maintain peace and good order."[113] North Carolina similarly structured their declaration for independence when affirming that the "disregarding" of "their humble petitions for peace, liberty, and safety," forced them to seek autonomy.[114]

---

[112] Ibid, 514.
[113] Ibid, 461-2.
[114] Force, *American Archives*, Fourth Series, Vol. 5, 859-60.

Chapter Three

A Legal Independence

When in the Course of human events it becomes necessary for one people to dissolve the political bands...
            Declaration of Independence, July 4, 1776

Issues over taxation certainly caused continual friction between Great Britain and her colonies, but the legality of American separation rested primarily on the Whig interpretation of the English Constitution and colonial charters. In a debate with Thomas Hutchinson, Samuel Adams made sure to center his argument around this point. American Whigs were essentially insisting upon some sort of constitutional reform that would secure the same constitutional guarantees as Britons living at home. If Americans were guaranteed such rights, Adams believed, their loyalty to England would remain true and undiminished.[1]

In his March 22, 1775 plea for reconciliation, Edmund Burke held a similar opinion. Before Parliament, Burke held the opinion that if the colonists were given the "civil rights associated with your government," they "will cling and grapple to you; and no force under heaven will be of power to tear them from their allegiance." Burke also issued a political warning to his colleagues. He believed if Parliament continued to break "the spirit of the English Constitution" and deny America "this participation of freedom," the colonists will "break that sole bond, which originally made, and must still preserve, the unity of the Empire."[2] What Adams and Burke were both essentially referring

---

[1] Max Savelle, "Nationalism and Other Loyalties in the American Revolution," *The American Historical Review*, Vol. 67, No. 4 (July 1962), 905.
[2] Ibid, 902.

to was the idea of British nationalism. A strong nationalism towards the mother country had always existed in America. The colonists' actions were often glorified in the name of Britain especially during colonial wars such as the French & Indian War. It is not to say that Americans lacked their own nationalistic ideals, but they were certainly proud of their Briton heritage.

Historian Max Savelle points out that the Americans were extremely self-conscious that "they were a different sort of Briton living in a different "country."[3] A new American-British nationalism developed as the colonial governments began possessing more freedoms than any other citizens within the British Empire, including those living in England. Political, economic, and social freedoms aided the development of the American feeling of national "differentness" and "consciousness." In short, Americans believed they were a specially favored segment of British imperial society. Patriot John Trumbull commented on this distinctiveness, stating:

> America hath a fair prospect in a few centuries of ruling both in arts and arms. It is universally allowed that we very much excell in force of natural genius: And although but few among us are able to devote their whole lives to study, perhaps there is no nation in which a larger portion of learning is diffused through all ranks of people.[4]

Feelings of American superiority did not divide along political lines. Both loyalists and rebels shared this sense of distinctiveness. Where the two sides differed in opinion was on the issue of constitutional reform. Although most colonists agreed on the Whig interpretation of the British Constitution, the "American Whigs stood...against the policies and actions of what they took to be a series of misguided ministries;" while the "Tories clung to the old loyalty despite the policies of those same ministries, however misguided."[5]

---

[3] Ibid, 904.
[4] Ibid, 908.
[5] Ibid, 904.

A Legal Independence

To many of the revolutionaries, the current conflict seemed very similar to the Glorious Revolution of 1689. That revolution was a bloodless political maneuver that removed the Stuarts from the throne for a multitude of alleged constitutional injustices.[6] Even David Hartley, a member of the House of Commons, saw the connection, stating the Americans were "driven to resistance in

---

[6] Patriot Judge William Henry Drayton of South Carolina held a common American Whig interpretation of the Glorious Revolution. He believed the Glorious Revolution "became the foundation on which the Throne of the present King of Great Britain is built" and supported "the edifice of Government" the colonies "have erected." Force, *American Archives*, Fourth Series, Vol. 5, 1028. Although it is difficult to generalize for the entire empire, the majority of British subjects, at home and abroad, held a similar contention about the Glorious Revolution. So much so that even famed historian, philosopher, scientist, and political commentator David Hume received much criticism for interpreting the Glorious Revolution differently. Hume certainly agreed that the Revolution of 1688 had been advantageous to the nation, helping Britain enjoy the most perfect liberties known to mankind at that time. Where he received much criticism from Whig proponents, who were able to get their hands on his famed six volume *The History of England from the Invasion of Julius Caesar to the Abdication of James the Second, 1688*, was his refusal to depict the Stuarts as complete devils. Hume interpreted such writing as bad history, since it was not objective. John. M. Werner, "David Hume and America," *Journal of the History of Ideas*, Vol. 33, No. 3, (July-Sept, 1972), 442. Hume's analysis was essentially closer to what we know today as modern historical scholarship than that of any other writer up to that period. Regardless of our current admiration for his attempts to be more objective, many of his eighteenth century contemporaries did not. Later in their lives, John Adams and Thomas Jefferson wrote much about their discontent with Hume's Tory interpretation of the Glorious Revolution. For Hume believed the Stuarts had been "reasonable and forbearing monarchs who defended the traditional prerogatives of the crown and rightfully resisted the aggressive designs of their antagonists." Douglas L. Wilson, "Jefferson vs. Hume," *William and Mary Quarterly*, Third Series, Vol. 46, No. 1 (Jan., 1989), 51. Jefferson claimed to have taken fifty years to "eradicate the poison it had instilled" in his mind. Ibid, 49.

their own defence, and in support of those very claims for which we ourselves have successfully taken up arms in former times to rescue us from the violence and tyrannical pretensions of the House of Stuarts."[7] When the Boston Assembly gave instructions regarding the vote for independence, their representatives were reminded that they were on "the verge of a glorious Revolution."[8] In much the same light, Brunswick, Massachusetts legitimized their support for autonomy due to "their attachment to the system of legal Government established by the glorious Revolution."[9] Buckingham County, Virginia reminded its delegates regarding the vote for autonomy, that it was by the Glorious Revolution, "and the choice of the people, that the present royal family was seated on the throne of Great Britain." So it was that the Glorious Revolution came to be revered as the most important political ideal of American independence; when government becomes defective "or deviates from the end of its institution, and cannot be corrected, [be] that the people may form themselves into another, avoiding the defects of the former."[10] The American Revolution was far from bloodless, but when the patriots referred to the rights of their forefathers, they were undoubtedly including those British patriots who reaffirmed their constitutional rights with the Declaration of Rights in 1689 and the subsequent Bill of Rights.

The documents contained in Declaration of Rights are especially worthy of attention since they affirmed Parliament's law creating power, thus forever changing the role of the monarchy within the law making process. What had been the absolute power of the monarchy was now restricted. The monarchy could only maintain their power by maintaining the good graces of Parliament and the people.

Throughout the Glorious Revolution and through the English Civil Wars of the eighteenth century, this idea of a social contract

---

[7] Force, *American Archives*, Fourth Series, Vol. 6, 279.
[8] Force, *American Archives*, Fourth Series, Vol. 6, 556.
[9] Ibid, 604.
[10] Tarter & Scribner, *Revolutionary Virginia: the Road to Independence*, Vol. 7, Part One, 112.

A Legal Independence

between the people and their monarch or representatives had grown exponentially. Any infringement upon the people's ancient and constitutional rights could potentially be seen as a reason to usurp government if not redressed, but the precedents set by the Glorious Revolution did not give the people any justification to replace their ruler. Technically the King had to vacate the throne while subverting the constitution for that to take place.[11]

William and Mary of Orange were only legally able to take the throne of England because James II had fled to France, cancelled the writs for parliamentary elections, and tossed the Great Seal into the Thames. At least this is what the writers of the Declaration of Rights stated what constituted the legality behind granting William and Mary of Orange the throne. In actuality, radical members of Parliament had invited William to usurp the throne from James II. To convince conservative leaders of the grounds for the legality of such a move, while preventing another military dictatorship, as was created during the reign of Oliver Cromwell, the radicals had to promote the issue of James II's fleeing in conjunction with infringements upon their ancient liberties. Originally, the conservatives had justified James II's removal by stating it was God's will. Since their King had now fled, the radicals argued, the throne was again vacant, thus it was divine intervention that William and Mary had arrived to assume James' place on the throne.

Now, almost one hundred years later, King George III was in the throne, and was he wasn't planning on leaving it vacant during the American Revolution. Abdication was not deemed an option. But by 1776, political thought had evolved drastically. Bernard Bailyn has given the most insight on the birth of the ideological origins of the American Revolution. Bailyn's *Pamphlets of the American Revolution* and *The Ideological Origins of the American Revolution* have given historians invaluable knowledge as to what influenced the founding fathers' revolutionary ideas. As Bailyn and others have pointed out, the arguments the founding fathers made against England had evolved. Yet, the questioning of

---

[11] Maier, *American Scripture*, 72.

Parliament's sovereignty on several issues was not initially pointed out in their complaints over British administration of the colonies. It would take nearly a decade before their argument was directly implied.

Even Jefferson felt it necessary to model the precedent set in the Declaration of Rights--that of the King vacating the throne--in his draft preamble of the Virginia Constitution. It states that King George "has forfeited the kingly office" due to his "several acts of misrule." It was the King's actions that made it "absolutely necessary" to immediately dispose of all his "privileges, powers, & prerogatives."[12] Jefferson could not use the exact wording of the 1689 Declaration of Rights, since King George had not vacated the throne. Nonetheless, Jefferson certainly felt it necessary to address the issue to give the rebellion validity in the eyes of Englishmen. Pauline Maier points out that Jefferson's use of the word "forfeited" suggested the relationship between the ruler and his subjects was contractual. Any violation of that contract could potentially lead to the King's loss of authority.[13]

Judge Drayton also tried to incorporate the legal precedent of James II vacating the throne in his oration to the Charlestown Grand Jury. He stated the King had "abdicated the Government," causing the throne to "thereby" be "vacant." Drayton argued the fleeing of colonial governors legally withdrew royal authority in those said colonies. He believed the governor was the "King of Great Britain's representative," and "by the agency of" King George's "substitute," the withdrawing of the said governor meant "it will appear that George the Third hath withdrawn himself out of this Colony."[14] Drayton's loose connection was not legally justified but serves as pertinent evidence to just how important the principles of the Glorious Revolution were to the legitimacy of the American Revolution.

---

[12] Boyd, *The Papers of Thomas Jefferson*, Vol. 1, Jefferson's First Draft of the Virginia Constitution, 339.
[13] Maier, *American Scripture*, 56.
[14] Force, *American Archives*, Fourth Series, Vol. 6, 1030.

A Legal Independence

The Glorious Revolution's exemplification of replacing one king for another seemed logical to many since it had been done before, but some rebels must have queried about to whom this power was to be legally transferred in their given situation. Although the rebels felt they possessed the right to usurp rulers who interfered with their natural rights, they also believed the King was appointed by God, who ultimately answered to him. Transferring authority to elected assemblies, similar to what was vested in their charters seemed logical, but the question arose of who would prevent these officials from also subverting their rights?

A purely representative government with no higher or equal authority had never been attempted, leaving the future uncertain for most. Charlotte County, Virginia answered the question by "taking the God of Heaven to be our King."[15] This reasoning made sense to Buckingham, Virginia, too. They believed "Divine intention" would maintain good government, therefore putting the providence under the supervision of "the Ruler of the Universe."[16] When Buckingham instructed their delegates regarding the vote for independence, they stated "the Supreme Being hath left it in" their power "to choose what government we please for our civil and religious happiness."[17]

The idea seems to have been widespread in colonial declarations of independence and in the instructions to delegates regarding autonomy. Pennsylvania told their delegates the "Supreme Governour of the Universe" will decide not only the outcome of this "fatal controversy," but will also "implant" his "divine wisdom" in the "hearts of His creatures."[18] In short, it was implied that God's will would direct the people to the form of government they should establish. Much like "Almighty God" delivered the English in the Glorious Revolution "from popery and

---

[15] Ibid, 1035.
[16] Ibid, 1208.
[17] Tarter & Scribner, *Revolutionary Virginia The Road to Independence*, Vol. VII, Part One, 112.
[18] Force, *American Archives*, Fourth Series, Vol. 5, 755.

arbitrary power" and caused "letters to be written to the Lords Spiritual and Temporal being Protestants...in order to such an establishment as that their religion, laws and liberties might not again be in danger of being subverted," it was believed God would interfere to protect an independent America from future tyrannical government.

Pauline Maier's *American Scripture* draws many parallels between the drafting of the Declaration of Independence and the Declaration of Rights 1689 and probably gives the most detailed comparison between the two documents. Maier's assertions are undeniably correct, but there is a much broader connection between the grievances of the American colonists and those listed in the Declaration of Rights and Bill of Rights of 1689. This aspect of the American Revolution is virtually unexplored and unbeknownst to most readers, except for students of both the Glorious Revolution and the American Revolution. The two revolutions are in no way identical, but the former certainly influenced the latter.

Judge Drayton documented the connection, as viewed by many rebels, especially those with a legal background such as Jefferson or Adams, when he spoke to the grand jury of Charlestown, South Carolina on April 23, 1776. Drayton made sure to point out the reaffirmation of the principles of the Glorious Revolution of 1689, when in 1719 the "House of Brunswick" was called "for no other purpose than to preserve to a People their unalienable rights."[19] It was when the "King accepted the invitation" from the House that the King "thereby indisputably admitted the legality of that Revolution," and "in doing so, by his own act...vested in those our forefathers" a "clear right to effect another revolution, if ever the government of the House of Brunswick should operate to the ruin of the people."[20]

---

[19] Force, *American Archives*, Vol. 5, 1026.
[20] Ibid. Also found in Keith Krawczynski, *William Henry Drayton: South Carolina Revolutionary Patriot*, (Baton Rouge, LA: Louisiana State University Press, 2001), 221-4.

A Legal Independence

To the rebels, a right to effect a revolution had arrived, almost a year to the date of Drayton's speech, when the Battle of Lexington & Concord forced them "to take up arms in our own defence." "By surprise they drew the sword of civil war and plunged it into the breasts of Americans!"[21] Drayton followed his history lesson regarding the political rights of his English forefathers with a "catalogue of…oppressions, Continental and local."[22] What he was essentially doing was justifying the colonists' actions and South Carolina's establishment of new government until reconciliation could be adopted.

Drayton knew "of no change upon principles so provoking, compelling, justifiable" than the struggle which the colonists currently confronted. Although he referred to the Glorious Revolution as "inferior," Drayton knew of "no better authority than that illustrious precedent" and thought it best to "compare the causes of, and the law upon, the two events."[23] Drayton felt it would be "as clear as the sun in the meridian" that "George the Third has injured the Americans at least as grievously as James the Second injured the People of England." The only difference between the two rulers was that James II "did not oppress these in so criminal a manner as George has oppressed the Americans."[24]

Drayton's connection, though loose on some of the charges, provides interesting parallels between the two civil wars. Drayton only lists six of the thirteen articles found in the 1689 Declaration of Rights to draw comparisons between the American Revolution and the Glorious Revolution. Of those six, two warrant particular attention in contrasting the two events: 1) exercising the power to dispense and suspend laws, and 2) the maintenance of standing armies in times of peace.

---

[21] Force, *American Archives*, Vol. 5, 1027.
[22] Ibid, 1026.
[23] Ibid, 1028.
[24] Ibid, 1031.

Dispensing and Suspending Power

The 1689 Declaration of Rights contained thirteen articles, the most pertinent being the first and second, which stated "the pretended power of suspending of laws or the execution of laws by regal authority without consent of Parliament is illegal," and the "pretended power of dispensing with law...is illegal."[25] Although dispensing and suspending with the law seem similar, they held different meanings.

Suspending the law "was the power to set aside the operation of a statute for a time" but did not mean the power to repeal.[26] Meanwhile, *dispensing the law* was the "power to grant permission to an individual or corporation to disobey a statute."[27] Improper use of the dispensing and suspending power by the monarch could unbalance the government if unchecked, thus destroying the power of Parliament. Although these powers were never fully exploited by the Stuart monarchy, it was universally feared they intended to do so.

Both Charles II and James II attempted to bring relief to Britain's Catholic subjects through multiple acts. The monarchs' collective attempts to put Catholics on an equal footing with Protestants were deemed not only too radical for the majority but perpetuated a fear throughout England that the King intended to subvert Protestantism for Catholicism. The breaking point occurred when James II reissued the Declaration of Indulgence in 1688, which suspended penal legislation against Catholics. He and his father, Charles II, had issued such acts before but were retracted after unfavorable reaction by Parliament and the people.

---

[25] Lois G. Schwoerer, *The Declaration of Rights, 1689*, (Baltimore, MD: The Johns Hopkins University Press, 1981), 58.
[26] Ibid, 60.
[27] Ibid. Whether the monarchy had the authority to use the dispensing and suspending powers depends on the reference. Even today, scholars debate whether the Stuart Kings and preceding monarchies had the right to enact power. The question is significant when examining whether the Glorious Revolution was legally justified, but regardless, it was the strongest contributing factor in that said revolution.

A Legal Independence

What made this attempt more threatening than the preceding two was that James II required it be read by the Anglican clergy from their pulpits. What was further appalling to Parliament was the King's control over the judiciary. All judges were Crown appointees. Hence, if a judge did not side in favor of the King, he could easily be replaced by someone who was sympathetic to the King's agenda. Most importantly, if the King could suspend and dispense laws without being checked, Parliament's role was largely diminished.

The connection between King James II and King George III in the manner of suspending and dispensing the law rested primarily in concerns to the revocation of colonial charters. Judge Drayton cited the correlation in his address to the Charlestown grand jury, when he stated, "James the Second suspended the operations of laws: George the Third caused the Charter of Massachusetts-Bay to be in effect annihilated; he suspended the operation of the law which formed the Legislature in New-York, vesting it with adequate powers; and thereby he caused the very ability of making laws in that Colony to be suspended." In actuality, the King had the legal authority to revoke charters, which was even stated in the documents themselves. Where the inconsistency in the law rested was within the framework of the English Constitution. The constitution guaranteed every citizen the right to representation in Parliament through the House of Commons. Thus, at least technically, the colonists were virtually represented, but, as political thinking evolved, this form of representation was not a sufficient platform for American colonial affairs to be heard. For the rebel leadership believed neither Parliament nor the King could enact internal colonial legislation without the consent of a colonial "Legislative Assembly chosen by the personal election of that People over whom such doings were exercised."[28]

There were also objections regarding Crown appointed governors. Governors that were sent to the colonies were often thought to be "utterly unacquainted" with America's "local

---

[28] Force, *American Archives*, Fourth Series, Vol. 6, 1029.

interests, the genius of the people," and their laws.[29] Initially, colonial assemblies possessed checks over their governors, for example, control over their salaries. These checks would be removed by King George as the rebellion persisted, giving the people no redress if the governor "behaved ill."

The Declaration of Independence specifically cites the "taking away of our charters," "abolishing our most valuable laws, and altering fundamentally the forms of our governments" as justification for American autonomy. This grievance was also implied within Jefferson's first charge against the King. It stated, "He has refused his assent to laws the most wholesome and necessary for the public good." Although the charge is noticeably general in its language and can allow for multiple charges against the King, the choice of words was purposely intended. Declarations in English law were supposed to be plain and clear to satisfy the vast numbers of officials who were expected to approve it. The Declaration of Independence was no exception. The document was, indeed, so general that opponents such as Thomas Hutchinson and John Lind had a difficult time refuting it.

Standing Armies

The treatment of the issue of standing armies and the quartering of troops has been recognized by historical and constitutional scholars alike as another noteworthy point of similarity shared by the American Revolution and the Glorious Revolution. The issues weighed with great import on the minds of the revolutionaries and would help form the basis of the Third Amendment of the American Constitution. Before the Amendment was ever penned in the Constitution, though, Jefferson gave the matter substance in the list of grievances in the Declaration of Independence. Jefferson stated "He has kept among us, in times of peace, Standing Armies without the Consent of our legislatures," and charged the King with the quartering of "large bodies of armed troops among us."

---

[29] Ibid, 1031.

A Legal Independence

Although the two issues were listed separately, the quartering problem, by its history and nature, was intimately connected with the larger political issue of the standing army. Historians William Fields and Dave Hardy write that the two matters were actually "indistinguishable" and "products of a common experience," since their origins and development paralleled...at crucial junctures in both English and American history."[30] Moreover, the standing army grievance, coupled with the events of Lexington and Concord, was what Jefferson penned to be the cause for the colonies to have taken up arms in his *Declaration of the Causes and Necessity for Taking Up Arms,* and he even made the list of complaints in the First Continental Congress' initial petition, the Declaration of Rights and Grievances.[31]

The first documented grievances against the involuntary quartering and maintenance of standing armies in British history developed after the Norman Conquest in 1066. It would not be until 1130 that Henry I's London Charter enacted that "no one be billeted within the walls of the city, either of my household, or by force of anyone else." Henry II's London Charter of 1155 further provided, "that within the walls no one shall be forcibly billeted, or by the assignment of the marshall."[32] The Magna Charta, in 1215, did not specifically reference the "quartering of troops" but did include the two previous charters when it confirmed the "ancient liberties and customs" of London and other cities, boroughs, and towns.

The issue would turn out to be a crucial factor in aiding the nation towards a civil war. It began with Charles I, who was engaged in multiple foreign wars. Since Parliament would not adequately furnish him with revenue to support his armies, Charles resorted to the quartering of his soldiers in the private homes of his

---

[30] William S. Fields; David T. Hardy, "The Third Amendment and the Issue of the Maintenance of Standing Armies: A Legal History," *The American Journal of Legal History*, Vol. 35, No. 4, (Oct. 1991), 395.
[31] Boyd, *The Papers of Thomas Jefferson*, Vol. 1, 213-18.
[32] Fields; Hardy, "The Third Amendment and the Issue of the Maintenance of Standing Armies: A Legal History," *The American Journal of Legal History*, 399.

citizenry. The issue gained such notoriety and concern for Parliament that the matter made the 1628 Petition of Right, which stated:

> Whereas of late, great companies of soldiers and mariners have been dispersed into divers counties of the realm, and the inhabitants, against their wills have been compelled to receive them into their houses, and there to suffer them to sojourn, against the laws and customs of this realm, and to the great grievance and vexation of the people... And that your majesty would be pleased to remove said soldiers and mariners; and that your people may not be so burdened in time to come.[33]

The issue was never resolved, and the failure to do so contributed to the commencement of a civil war in 1642 whereby both sides would abuse the issue, quartering their armies within the civilian population. Nearly two decades after the Restoration, in 1679, Parliament officially enacted the Anti-quartering Act, which stipulated that "n[oe] officer military or civil nor any other person whatever shall from henceforth presume to place quarter or billet any souldier or souldiers."[34] The act was ignored by James II, the King's blatant disregard of the law greatly contributing to the Glorious Revolution of 1689. Although the quartering of soldiers was consequential to the King's indictment, the fact was curiously omitted within the Declaration of Rights. The omission in the declaration was, however, probably made for two important reasons. One, the issue of quartering might have been purposely left out since their new sovereigns, William and Mary of Orange, could also be charged with the offense. Second, and most importantly, the quartering of soldiers was lawfully an implied feature of the anti-standing army attitude. For article six of the Declaration of Rights did state the "raising or keeping a standing army within the kingdom in time of peace" without the consent of

---

[33] Ibid, 404.
[34] Ibid.

A Legal Independence

Parliament to be against the law.[35] As had been the case with Charles I, the quartering problem was implied to be directly related to the maintenance of standing armies.

Throughout the Middle Ages, England was slowly evolving into a military society based upon the unit of the citizen. The arming of the citizen class had the dual purpose of providing the nation with an instant army to defend against foreign aggressors and serving as a means to check the monarchy from sequestering the rights of the people. By the fifteenth century, Englishmen already regarded their militia as a vital component of their legal system.[36] Much like how the issue of quartering of troops became a pertinent issue of seventeenth century England, so did the issue of a standing army.

When Charles II was restored to the throne in 1660, a small standing army was kept and quartered within the civilian population. James II continued the tradition of his father, Charles II, by maintaining an army both in peace and in war. Up to that point, the monarchy's maintenance of standing armies had never been addressed by Parliament. No one had ever denied the King's right to have a standing army. It was not until 1674 that Parliament called a standing army a grievance, and not until 1679 was it called illegal and a grievance.[37]

Parliament only became infuriated when events such as the Popish Plot and the monarchy's policy of appointing Catholics as military officers brought the issue to the forefront. The two events, compiled with anti-standing army political argumentation from James Harrington and others, made the issue an article for the Declaration of Rights. Prior to this article, Parliament knew full well the King had the legal right to maintain or raise a standing army without parliamentary consent. Following the Glorious Revolution, this attitude drastically changed. The raising of an army was now viewed in similar terms to Parliament's right

---

[35] Schwoerer, *The Declaration of Rights of 1689*, 71.
[36] Fields; Hardy, "The Third Amendment and the Issue of the Maintenance of Standing Armies: A Legal History," 401.
[37] Schwoerer, *The Declaration of Rights of 1689*, 73.

to enact taxes. Since the army required large amounts of revenue from the state, it was now deemed within rightful parliamentary power as to whether such funds should be appointed to raise a military force.[38]

It is noteworthy that, although the standing army was largely rejected among English society following the accession by William and Mary of Orange, it was still held in favor by many who saw the standing army as a practical necessity. The Machiavellian principle that a militia was "necessary to a free State" remained entrenched in Whig ideology, but an army also had to be maintained in order to prevent James II and the Stuart line from reclaiming the Crown. Besides, William and Mary were currently in an unending conflict with Holland and France, meaning an army would be required until those wars ceased. A militia-based military was no longer thought to be an adequate fighting force against the trained professional armies of the European continent. William Blackstone logged in his commentaries:

> But, as the fashion of keeping standing armies…has of late years universally prevailed over Europe…it has also for many years past been actually judged necessary by our legislature for the safety of the kingdom, the defense of the possessions of the crown of Great Britain, and the preservation of the balance of power in Europe, to maintain even in time of peace a standing body of troops, under the command of the crown; who are, however *ipso facto* disband at the expiration of every year unless contained by parliament.[39]

Even with a standing army deemed as a necessity by the majority of Parliament, fundamental opposition to the idea persisted among some of the members. Algernon Sidney was one of these many spokesmen, borrowing from the radical Whig ideals of the militia and from Machiavelli and James Harrington. Sidney

---

[38] Ibid, 74.
[39] William Blackstone, *Commentaries*, 413-4.

A Legal Independence

argued against the maintenance of a standing army, not only because it infringed upon the civil liberties of the people, but because it perpetuated dependent relationships in society. It was up to the people to respond against any efforts to maintain a standing army and to demand the reestablishment of the militia. For if the citizenry failed to do so, then they, the people, must be corrupt, since they are unwilling to claim their "birthright to bear arms." Sidney believed citizen armies had greater military potential than and were far superior to any hired mercenary army. He attributed this combat success to the "quality of commanders and the courage of rank and file" a citizen army could bring and have superiority over any other form of military. For while mercenary armies were fighting for specie and plunder, a citizen army was fighting for much more--their national pride and property.[40]

Other prominent opponents of a standing army would publish their sentiments regarding the subject. Robert Viscount Molesworth used, for purposes of exemplification, the history of Denmark in his *Account of Denmark as It Was in the Year 1692* to show the effects of what happens when a freely-based militia system is overridden by an absolute monarch's standing army. Molesworth attributed Denmark's decline as a free nation to the moment when the citizenry failed to accept their civil responsibility in maintaining the militia. It was Denmark's inability to defend their liberties that led to rise of that country's absolute monarchy.[41] John Trenchard, John Toland, Walter Moyle, and Andrew Fletcher also published popular tracts regarding the unconstitutionality of a standing army. Like the writers before them, these radical Whigs pushed the idea that professional soldiers were an immediate threat to the constitutional balance of Britain.[42]

---

[40] Lawrence Delbert Cress, "Radical Whiggery on the Role of the Military: Ideological Roots of the American Revolutionary Militia," *Journal of the History of Ideas*, Vol. 40, No. 1 (Jan-Mar, 1979), 47.
[41] Ibid, 48.
[42] Ibid, 49.

Irreconcilable Grievances

Between 1730 and 1746, the writings of Francis Hutcheson, an Irish philosopher, had reached many readers and would help keep these ideals alive. Hutcheson was adamantly against professional soldiers and felt the best solution against it was that military service should be the obligation of every citizen in society, an idea that exists today in some nations, for example, in Norway and Israel. He felt a "sober virtuous people employed in arms for a few years, would in all intervals of military service be exercising some industrious arts, and would return to them with delight when their term expired." Above all, such a military institution not only protected the rights of the people but inspired similar virtues among the citizenry, forming strong nationalistic principles. Hutcheson believed "Such reputable virtuous citizens, many of them having valuable stakes in their country, would have both greater courage and fidelity than mercenaries for life, domestic or foreign, chosen or offering themselves out of the refuse of the people, even such as were unfit for any other occupation."[43]

Although the idea of a militia was slowly declining within England, the American colonies still found the institution extremely applicable to their needs. A militia system was not only cost efficient, but more capable than any other system could have been for the colonists. Their borders were too vast for the use of a standing army to be effective. It was clearly better, tactically speaking, for the colonists to incorporate the militia in their defense since it offered a rapid response force from every settlement. What's more, the initial, primary threat was not the encroachment of their land from European powers but from disputes with local Indian tribes and the internal threat of slave uprisings. As the European conflicts began to spread to the American frontier, more and more professional soldiers from all nations began building outposts to defend their economic interests. These armies usually did not interfere with British colonial America since the units generally operated outside colonial settlements. It was not until the mid 1700s that the practice of quartering of troops would grow into an issue affecting the

---

[43] Ibid, 52.

colonies. The Seven Years War had brought large bodies of British troops to America for the first time. Parliament preferred to build permanent barracks within cities, such as New York, to house the soldiers. The proposition of quartering received much disfavor from colonial assemblies because a permanent barracks would technically denote their acceptance of a standing army, an action in violation to the principles of the English Constitution. In multiple instances, the colonies only relented to allowing the troops to build quarters due to the threat from British officials who would only send more troops if their request was not complied with.[44]

Technically, Parliament was within its authority to push for the quartering of their troops within the American colonies. Shortly following the Glorious Revolution, Parliament had enacted the Mutiny Act, which had included a provision against the quartering of soldiers in the private homes of citizens without consent of the owner. Interestingly enough though, the act of prohibiting quartering did not stretch as far as the American colonies, allowing for the legality of one of the earliest grievances of the American Revolution, the Quartering Act of 1765. The act required that colonists swallow the cost of providing barracks and particular supplies for British soldiers. If these barracks could not adequately quarter the troops, the act also authorized the soldiers to be housed in livery stables, alehouses, or inns.[45] What was even more infuriating to the colonists was that the Stamp Act of 1765 was passed in order to provide the revenue to pay for these expenses. When British troops would arrive three years later, Andrew Eliot noted, "you cannot conceive of our distress, to have a standing army! What can be worse to a people who have tasted the sweets of liberty?"[46]

---

[44] Fields; Hardy, "The Third Amendment and the Issue of the Maintenance of Standing Armies: A Legal History," *American Journal of Legal* History, 413-15.
[45] Ibid, 415.
[46] Richard Frothingham, *Life and Times of Joseph Warren*, (New York, NY: De Capo Press, 1971), 75.

Irreconcilable Grievances

A standing army, in conjunction with the quartering of troops, was already seen as a basic infringement of property rights. Britain's sending of reinforcements, following their failed taxation policies, was not viewed as an attempt to restore order but as an attempt to turn freemen into slaves. A conspiracy theory existed among radicals that Parliament's goal had been to wait until the colonies flourished before taking the property themselves; they firmly believed England's elite had grown jealous of the colonists' holdings and freedoms. The maintaining of the British army is what only gave any credibility to the idea, even though such evidence was miniscule, and the theory preposterous.

Although Parliament was legally within their rights to sending professional troops to the colonies, even following the completion of the Seven Years War, the colonists interpreted the English Bill of Rights provision against the "raising or keeping a standing army within the kingdom in time of peace, unless it be with consent of Parliament" in their own way. The law specifically granted "Parliament" the authorization to send troops, but the colonial assemblies interpreted that such an act meant, in turn, that provincial assemblies also had to approve of it before such a measure could be fully enacted. Judge Drayton was sure to address the point when he compared James II's maintenance of a standing army "in time of peace" to King George's sending of troops "without" and "against the consent of the Representatives of the People among whom the army is posted."[47] The grievance was listed in Buckingham, Virginia's instructions to delegates regarding independence, demanding "that no standing armies whatever should be kept in time of peace."[48] The assembly of Scituate, Massachusetts also expressed to their delegates that the sending of a standing army "so repugnant to the nature of free Government, to fire and sword, to bloodshed and devastation," aided their decision in the vote for autonomy.[49]

---

[47] Force, *American Archives*, Fourth Series, Volume 5, 1029.
[48] Ibid, 1208.
[49] Force, *American Archives*, Fourth Series, Volume 6, 699.

A Legal Independence

These same inviolable principles were echoed six years earlier, on March 5, 1770, when the Boston Massacre occurred. Although the jury found all the soldiers not guilty of murder, and two guilty of manslaughter, radical Whig tracts against the maintenance of standing armies were distributed throughout the colonies. Despite the order for the immediate withdrawal of the regulars within Boston following the incident, the Boston Massacre affirmed the predictions of anti-standing army language.[50] Samuel Adams addressed the issue in his 1772 *List of Infringements and Violations of Rights,* stating, "Introducing and quartering standing Armies in a free Country in times of peace without the consent of the people either by themselves or by their Representatives, is, and always has been deemed a violation of their rights as freemen."[51]

An uneasy peace would continue to prevail from 1770 until the spring of 1774 when news arrived that the British army was returning to enforce the provisions of the Boston Port Act. Josiah Quincy Jr was so adamantly against the resending of troops, he penned the pamphlet *Observations on the Act of Parliament Commonly Called the Boston Port Bill: With Thoughts on Civil Society and Standing Armies* on May 14, 1774. Josiah Quincy Jr., who had been one of the defense lawyers, along with John Adams, for the British soldiers charged in the Boston Massacre, now felt it necessary to publish a lengthy tract expressing his opposing views against the maintenance of standing armies within the colonies. The pamphlet drew upon historical examples and precedents to argue his point. To Quincy "The greatest happiness of the greatest number being the object and bond of society, the establishment of truth and justice ought to be the basis of civil policy and jurisprudence." Such an establishment could not exist as long as "there exists a power superior to the civil magistrate," like that of a standing army.[52] He felt standing armies needed to be "an object

---

[50] Cress, "Radical Whiggery on the Role of the Military: Ideological Roots of the American Revolutionary Militia," *Journal of the History of Ideas,* 56.
[51] Cushing, *The Writings of Samuel Adams,* Vol. 2, 362.
[52] Josiah Quincy, *Memoir of the Life of Josiah Quincy,* (New York, NY: De Capo Press, 1971), 396.

of serious attention," since the "the history of mankind affords no instance of successful and confirmed tyranny, without the aid of military forces."[53] In particular, Quincy believed the soldiers of Great Britain were a real threat to the welfare of the colonies because they were "deprived of those legal rights" from the Mutiny Act, "which belong to the meanest of their fellow subjects, and even the vilest malefactor."[54] This lack of "rights and privileges which render Britons the envy of all other nations, and liable to such hardships and punishments as the limits and mercy of our known laws utterly disallow; it may well be thought they are persons best prepared wand most easily tempted to strip others of their rights, having already lost their own."[55] Quoting Barton Montesquieu, Josiah believed, "A slave living among freemen will soon become a beast."

In short, Josiah Quincy's belief that "an army in peace is worse than a militia," was a reiteration of Machaivelli, Harrington, Sidney, Trenchard, Gordon, and Molsesworth. The writings of these early opponents of standing armies were owned, by such notable revolutionaries as Benjamin Franklin, Jonathon Meyhew, James Otis, John Hancock, John Adams, Samuel Adams, George Mason, Thomas Jefferson, James Wilson, and John Dickinson. In addition, James Burgh's *Political Disquisitions* (1774-75), which was a reinstatement of Sidney and Harrington, was another popular publication shared by revolutionary leaders. Those who received Burgh's first edition available in America included John Adams, George Washington, Samuel Chase, John Dickinson, Silas Deane, John Hancock, Thomas Mifflin, James Wilson, and Thomas Jefferson.[56] Even the well-read David Hume believed "when the sword is in the hands of a single person, as in our constitution, he will always neglect to discipline the militia, in order to have a pretext for keeping up a standing army." When

---

[53] Ibid, 400.
[54] Ibid, 403.
[55] Ibid, 404.
[56] Cress, "Radical Whiggery on the Role of the Military: Ideological Roots of the American Revolutionary Militia," *Journal of the History of Ideas*, 54.

A Legal Independence

this occurred, "It is evident that this is a moral distemper in the British government; of which it must at last inevitably perish."[57]

The connection between radical Whig ideology against standing armies and its impact on the founding fathers becomes more evident in examining the first year in the life of the American Revolution. In responding to Lord North's Conciliatory Proposal, Congress conveyed their emphatic objections to the taxing of the colonies "for the purpose of undermining their civil rights" and diverting it "to the support of standing armies," because it was "inconsistent with their freedom and subversive of their quiet."[58] George Mason included the issue in his Virginia Declaration of Rights, with it being resolved that "a well regulated Militia, composed of the body of the people, trained to arms, is the proper, natural, and safe defence of a free State; that Standing Armies, in time of peace, should be avoided as dangerous to liberty; and that, in all case, the military should be under strict subordination to, and governed by, the civil power."[59] Provisions relating to the maintenance of standing armies would also be included in either declarations of independence or constitutions of Delaware, Maryland, Massachusetts, New Hampshire, North Carolina, Pennsylvania, and Vermont.[60]

The issue of standing armies influenced John Adams' *Thoughts on Government*. Adams was undoubtedly referring to the use of standing armies when he penned, "Fear is the foundation of most governments; but is so sordid and brutal of passion, and renders men, in whose breasts it predominates, so stupid, and miserable, that Americans will not be likely to approve of any political institution which is founded on it."[61] The "fear" Adams was referring to was Britain's use of their standing army to force its

---

[57] Quincy, *The Memoir of Josiah Quincy Jun.*, 412.
[58] Boyd, *The Papers of Thomas Jefferson*, Vol. 1, 231.
[59] Rutland, *The Papers of George Mason*, Vol. 1, 288.
[60] Fields; Hardy, "The Third Amendment and the Issue of the Maintenance of Standing Armies: A Legal History," *American Journal of Legal History*, 418.
[61] Taylor, *The Papers of John Adams*, Vol. 4, Thoughts on Government, 86-87.

colonial subjects into submission. With a militia, such an event would never occur since the government would not be able to force unpopular legislation upon its people if the citizens themselves were the enforcers of those rights.

The politics surrounding standing armies would also create difficulties in establishing the Continental Army. Now the rebels were confronted with a moral dilemma not unlike the situation England presented itself following the Glorious Revolution. A society which balked at the idea of a standing army was now about to create one? For each colony or locality to assemble their militia in defense of their rights was viewed as constitutionally viable, but creating a unified Continental Army might prove to be as, if not more, dangerous than the British army already stationed among them. Much like the radical Whigs who pushed aside their anti-standing army principles for the betterment of society in England, the American rebels were forced to do the same in order to maintain more important liberties.

To many radical Whig revolutionaries, the militia was the preferred manner to fight the British. John Adams preferred a militia-based society since "it is always a wise institution, and under "the present circumstances of our country" is "indispensable."[62] For General Washington, the militia was a plague. He considered their ranks undisciplined, improperly trained and equipped, and their enlistments lasted for only short periods. In an attempt to supersede the fragmented control over the armies at Cambridge by each colony, and to aid Washington, Congress submitted the Militia Bill to each provincial assembly. John Adams felt the bill was "so necessary, at this critical moment, for the publick service."[63] The bill would put the militia of the New England colonies under the direction of the Continental Congress, but the proposal was not viewed favorably for many reasons. Samuel Adams, for one, queried, "should we not be cautious of putting them under the direction of the

---

[62] Ibid, 91.
[63] Force, *American Archives*, Fourth Series, Vol. 3, John Adams to James Otis, November 28, 1775, 1653-4.

generals...at least until such a legislative shall be established over all America, as every colony should consent to?"[64] He hoped the militia would "always be prepared to aid the forces of the Continent in this righteous opposition to tyranny, but this ought to be done an application to the Government of the Colony." Until a strong Legislative could be formed, Samuel Adams thought it "dangerous to the liberties of the people to have an army stationed among them, over which they have no control."[65] He would write to James Warren on the matter:

> It is certainly of the last Consequence to a free Country that the Militia, which is the natural Strength, should be kept upon the most advantageous Footing. A standing Army, however necessary it may be at sometimes, is always dangerous to the Liberties of the People. Soldiers are apt to consider themselves as a Body distinct from the rest of the Citizens. They have their Arms always in their hands. Their Rules and their Discipline is severe. They soon become attachd to their officers and disposed to yield implicit Obedience to their Commands. Such a Power should be watchd with a jealous Eye. I have a good Opinion of the principal officers of our Army, I esteem them as Patriots as well as Soldiers. But if this War continues, as it may for years to come, we know not who may succeed them. Men who have been long subject to military Laws and inured to military Customs and Habits, may lost the Spirit and Feeling of Citizens. And even Citizens, having been used to admire the Heroism which the Commanders of their own Army have displayed, and to look up to them as their Saviors may be prevaild upon to surrender to them those Rights for the protection of which against Invaders they had employd and paid them. We have seen too much of this Disposition among some of our Countrymen. The Militia is composed of free Citizens. There is therefore no Danger of their making

---

[64] Cushing, *The Writings of Samuel Adams*, Vol. 3, Samuel Adams to Elbridge Gerry, October 29, 1775, 229.
[65] Ibid, 230.

use of their Power to the destruction of their own Rights, or suffering others to invade them. I earnestly wish that young Gentlemen of a military Genius...might be instructed in the Art of War, and at the same time taught the Principles of a free Government, and deeply impressed with a Sense of the indispensable Obligation which every member is under to the whole Society. These might be in time fit for officers in the Militia, and being thoro[ughly] acquainted with the Duties of Citizens as well as Soldiers, might be entrusted with a Share in the Command of our Army at such times as Necessity might require so dangerous a Body to exist.[66]

Elbridge Gerry agreed with Samuel Adams on this matter. He feared whichever General was in control of the militia "might forget his station and conceive himself its master." Gerry suggested that for a "Continental General" to assume control over all militia, he must gain approval through each colony's legislature. The revolutionaries believed many officers had already shown their thirst for power. For the colonies' security, the military had to be strictly regulated "to keep the military entirely subservient to the civil."[67]

The Militia Bill also incited privates of thirty companies, in the surrounding Philadelphia area, to petition their grievances to the Pennsylvania Assembly. These militiamen supported the principles of the revolution but disagreed on giving Congress control of the militia. The purpose of the militia was to ensure the safety of the colony and to be only called up in the event of an emergency. In their view, the Militia Bill undermined their own rights. They would now be subjugated to the martial laws of Congress instead of being regulated by their elected representatives from Pennsylvania. Men in the militia companies were also concerned about the length of their enlistments. If Congress assumed control of the militia, the men technically could

---

[66] Ibid, Samuel Adams to James Warren, January 7, 1776, 250-51.
[67] Force, *American Archives*, Fourth Series, Vol. 3, Elbridge Gerry to Samuel Adams, December 13, 1775, 255-6.

A Legal Independence

be assembled for an indefinite period of time. The petitioners proposed that they voluntarily offer their services for six-month periods. At the conclusion of this enlistment, each was to determine on their own whether they should "renew their enlistment or demand their discharge."[68]

Some viewed the current military structure differently. An anonymous author, under the pseudonym Caractacus, described the soldiers serving at Cambridge as mercenaries. In his essay entitled *Standing Armies*, he aimed "only to condemn...the practice of several of our Provincial Conventions in taking a number of Minute-Men into pay." Caractacus argued that paying troops to serve the cause takes away from the military spirit of the people. He felt it "impossible to subdue a country...where citizen is a soldier and every soldier is a citizen." He pointed to the ancient armies of Rome, Athens, Sparta, and the Republic of Switzerland as examples of citizen soldiers. Those citizens that do not stand up for their rights against Britain are "an enemy to his Country."[69]

On November 4, Congress initially granted Washington the authority to call upon any New England militia unit to support his army, but widespread dissatisfaction with the Militia Bill caused its removal. A new resolution allowed only Washington to assume control of New England militias when he had "obtained the consent of those officers in whom the executive powers of Government in those Colonies may be vested."[70] Thus, the politics of standing armies would figure strongly in the disintegration of the Continental Army during the winter of 1775. In writing to Joseph Reed, Washington assigned Congress some of the blame for when he wrote, "They (delegates of Congress) will

---

[68] Ibid, Correspondence and Proceedings of Pennsylvania Assembly, September 27, 1775, 821-2.
[69] Ibid, On Standing Armies, August 21, 1775, 219-21.
[70] Force, *American Archives*, Fourth Series, Vol. 3, Continental Congress, December 7, 1775, 1945.

prove the destruction of the army if they are not more attentive and diligent."[71]

The hotbed of politics regarding standing armies in Congress did not flare up with the Militia Bill, but with the appointment of Continental Officers in June 1775. The delegates were fully aware of what could transpire if the wrong military leader was elected. Monstrous images of Oliver Cromwell and other military dictatorships were certainly fresh in the delegates' minds during this crucial time. Horatio Gates or Charles Lee would have been the logical choice for Congress if one were to measure an officer's capability based on experience. Both of these astute military commanders were veterans of the French & Indian War and had served in the British army following that said conflict. John Adams confessed their "advice...might be of great advantage to us," but, what steered him away were "the natural prejudices, and virtuous attachment of our countrymen to their own officers."[72] Adams and other delegates were afraid the troops under men such as Gates or Lee would become more loyal to their commander than to the cause. This fear, along with other serious political considerations, confronted the rebels in their task of appointing the commander-in-chief of the newly formed Continental Army.

Many delegates expressed fears around the risk of giving over command. Two varying schools of thought existed among military commanders concerning the reach of their authority. On the one hand, it was believed a military leader must "assume responsibility in emergencies," and make decisions on the spot.[73] General Horatio Gates was a firm believer in this principle. The other school of thinking was that the commander was an 'agent in the field' to the civilian authority empowered over him. Washington strongly believed in this school of thought. Congressional delegates were acutely aware of the powers a

---

[71] Abott & Twohig, *The Papers of George Washington*, Revolutionary Series, Vol. 2, To Joseph Reed, November 28, 1775.

[72] Taylor, *The Papers of John Adams*, Vol. 3, John Adams to Elbridge Gerry, June 18, 1775, 25-26.

[73] Samuel White Patterson, *Horatio Gates, Defender of American Liberties*, (New York, NY: Columbia University Press, 1941), 22.

A Legal Independence

commander of standing armies could potentially impress. Since Washington believed in working in conjunction with the Continental Congress, and, therefore, appeared more in tune with republican sentiments, his appointment was well supported.

Although the politics of standing armies undoubtedly influenced Washington's selection as commander-in-chief, he was primarily and strategically chosen as a means to unify the Southern colonies with the New England colonies. John and Samuel Adams both nominated Washington to prevent any conflict with the South on future Congressional matters.[74] The deliberation took just two days. The immediate concern among some of the delegates was the removal of the current commander, Artemas Ward, who might cause some of the New England forces to implode.[75] Since Ward had undoubtedly earned the respect of his fellow New Englanders, what was to prevent this attachment to their commander to supersede their dedication to the revolutionary cause? It must be remembered that officer appointments were extremely political. Congress might have elected Washington with confidence, but he would write to Congress that he was not self-assured about his new appointment.[76] The General had never commanded a force so large, or possessed a command since 1755, where he was handily defeated by the French. He was ill-prepared for the task confronting him and well aware of that fact. Regardless of Washington's own doubts, and a Congress grown weary of putting control of their forces into the hands of one man, the General was, as history would bear out, the perfect choice. He understood the social concerns of establishing a standing army even under the stress of maintaining an efficient fighting force.

Thus, standing armies came to play a crucial role not only at the outbreak of hostilities, but also in the manner the war for independence would be fought. Even under the dire need for a

---

[74] Ibid, 48.
[75] John Ferling, *A Leap in the Dark: The Struggle to Create an American Republic*, (New York, NY: Oxford Press, 2003), 144.
[76] Abott & Twohig, *Papers of George Washington*, Revolutionary Series, Vol. 1, June 16, 1775.

uniform and more permanent fighting force, the colonies chose the traditional militia system over a standing army since they believed the latter would interfere with their civil liberties. The issue did not end there. The debate would continue after the war with rebellions such as Daniel Shay's, in 1786, which drew attention to the ineffectiveness of the state militia system. Because the Articles of Confederation had not provided authorization to the federal government to react to such emergencies, the debate around the standing army issue would once again surface in the process of drafting the Constitution.

Part Two:

To Turn Slaves Against Their Masters

Chapter Four

Dunmore's Proclamation and Domestic Insurrections

Hell itself could not of vomited anything more black than [Lord Dunmore's] design of emancipating our slaves; and unless he is cutoff before he is reinforced, we know not how far the contagion may spread.
    Extract of a Letter from Philadelphia, December 6, 1775

In American history, the issue of slavery involving a civil war has been traditionally associated with the nineteenth century conflict, and receives little acclaim for being one of the causes for the push for independence. In fact, if there was one issue historians could pinpoint as to what united more Southerners towards independence than any other expedient, the complicated inclusion of slaves in the Revolutionary War would be the answer. The final draft of the Declaration of Independence states, "He has excited domestic insurrections amongst us." From these words, many who research this particular era believe it is in reference to Lord Dunmore's Proclamation and the British Army's policy of harboring slaves. Also known as John Murray, Lord Dunmore, on November 7, 1775, drew up an order freeing the slaves of rebels and declared martial law throughout the Virginia colony. The order stated:

> As I have ever entertained Hopes that an Accommodation might have taken Place between GREAT-BRITAIN and this Colony, without being compelled by my Duty to this most disagreeable but now absolutely necessary Step, rendered so by a Body of armed Men unlawfully assembled, firing on His MAJESTY'S Tenders, and the formation of an Army, and that Army now on their March to attack his MAJESTY'S Troops and destroy the well disposed subjects of the Colony.

Irreconcilable Grievances

To defeat such treasonable Purposes, and that all such Traitors, and their Abettors, may be brought to Justice, and that the Peace, and good Order of this Colony may be again restored, which the ordinary Course of the Civil Law is unable to effect; I have thought fit to issue this my Proclamation, hereby declaring, that until the aforesaid good Purpose can be obtained, I do in Virtue of the Power and Authority to ME given, by His MAJESTY, determine to execute Martial Law, and cause the same to be executed throughout this Colony: and to the Peace and good Order may the sooner be restored, I do require every Person capable of bearing Arms, to resort to His MAJESTY'S STANDARD, or be looked upon as Traitors to His MAJESTY'S Crown and Government, and thereby become liable to the Penalty the Law inflicts upon such Offenses; such as forfeiture of Life, confiscation of Lands, &. &. And I do hereby further declare all indented Servants, Negroes, or others, (appertaining to Rebels,) free that are able and willing to bear Arms, they joining His MAJESTY'S Troops as soon as may be, foe the more speedily reducing this Colony to a proper Sense of their Duty, to His MAJESTY'S Crown and Dignity. I do further order, and require, all His MAJESTY'S Liege Subjects, to retain their Quitrents, or any other Taxes due or that may become due, in their own Custody, till such a Time as Peace may be again restored to this at present most unhappy Country, or demanded of them for their former salutary Purposes, by Officers properly to receive the same.

Unfortunately we can't be certain whether Dunmore's Proclamation is what the founding fathers were referring to when they accused the King of "exciting domestic insurrections amongst us," because following this statement it reads the King "has endeavoured to bring on the inhabitants of our frontiers the merciless Indian Savages, whose known rule of warfare is an undistinguished destruction of all ages, sexes and conditions." Therefore, this statement might have been referring strictly to the British employment of Indians on the frontier. In all probability, however, this is unlikely. In *Declaration for the Causes and Necessity for Taking up Arms,* Jefferson and Dickinson differentiate between exciting "domestic enemies" and "instigating...Indians." Thus, it can be logically deduced that "domestic insurrections" referred to slave revolts. Even if this statement solely implied the Indian threat, we know from Thomas Jefferson's first draft of the Declaration of Independence that slavery had much to do with influencing his opinion towards autonomy. It stated:

He has waged cruel war against human nature itself, violating its most sacred rights of life and liberty in the persons of a distant people who never offended him, captivating and carrying them into slavery in another hemisphere, or to incur miserable death in their transportation hither. this piratical warfare, the opprobrium of *infidel* powers, is the warfare of the *Christian* king of Great Britain. [determined to keep open a market where MEN should be bought and sold,] he has prostituted his negative for suppressing every legislative attempt to prohibit or to restrain this execrable commerce [determining to keep open a market where MEN should be bought and sold]: and that this assemblage of horrors might want no fact of distinguished die, he is now exciting those very people to rise in arms among us, and to purchase that liberty of which *he* had deprived them, by murdering the people upon whom *he* also obtruded them: thus paying off former crimes committed against the *liberties* of one people, with crimes which he urges them to commit against the *lives* of another.

In his statement, Jefferson clearly blamed the King for the institution of slavery within the colonies but made no mention of their emancipation.[1] Just two months earlier, the Virginia Convention attributed, that, in some measure, their formation of a revolutionary government was due to "a piratical and savage war

---

[1] Sidney Kaplan, "The 'Domestic Insurrections' of the Declaration of Independence," *The Journal of Negro History,* 61, (1976), 243-245.

against us tempting our Slaves by every artifice to resort to him and training and employing them against their masters."² In February 1772, the Virginia House had begun a debate on the importation of slaves, voting to petition the King from prohibiting their importation. Virginia was probably influenced by the non-importation proceedings of their neighbor, South Carolina. In August 1769, the *South Carolina Gazette* published a non-importation resolution, in which Article IV states, "we will not import, buy, or sell, any Negroes that shall be brought into this province from *Africa*; nor, after the 1ˢᵗ day of *October* next, any Negroes that shall be imported from the *West Indies*, or any other place."³ The petition stated two reasons why the importation of slaves must stop. First, it was believed the slave trade was too inhumane. The stories of slaves transported across the Atlantic had alarmed many people. The Virginia Convention was not the only legislative assembly to pronounce such a contention. Many colonies and abolition groups had petitioned England for the end of the slave trade, based on a similar argument. Secondly, the slave trade was unique to the Southern colonies and was undoubtedly the primary influence for the issuance of the petition. The address stated, "we have too much reason to fear [the continual importation of slaves] will endanger the very existence of your Majesty's American dominions."⁴ With an ever-growing slave population resulting from internal growth, Virginians were mindful of the distinct possibility of a surging slave uprising. Furthermore, the prevention of the importation of slaves would have a compounding effect. It would bring more security to the

---

² Tarter and Scribner, *Revolutionary Virginia: The Road to Independence*, Vol. 7, Part I, Proceedings of the Ninth Day of Session, May 15, 1776, 143.

³ William Henry Drayton, *The Letters of Freeman, Etc.,* (Columbia, SC: The University of South Carolina Press, 1977), 10.

⁴ William J. Van Schreevan, *Revolutionary Virginia: The Road to Independence*, Volume 1, (Virginia: The University of Virginia Press, 1973), Address to the House of Burgesses to the King in Opposition to the Slave Trade, April 1, 1772.

colony while raising the value of their current slaves. The sudden push for an end to the slave trade is particularly interesting, since just a decade earlier, the Southern colonies preferred to practice a much different system.

At that time, the Southern colonists supported the importation of slaves, seeking to acquire more Negroes because of the potential profits through labor. Regardless of the riches of the land, little wealth could be gained without a sufficient labor force.[5] The demand for Negro slaves remained high until the Proclamation of 1763, which prohibited colonial settlement beyond the Appalachian Mountains. Thus, with the inability to gain more land, colonists were provided with only two methods by which they could gain wealth. Either the price of their current property would have to appreciate or they would have to provide a product that was high in demand and that would bring large profits, which for most colonists was agriculture. Unfortunately, profit in the agricultural industry was difficult to achieve for the majority of farmers, particularly in certain Southern agricultural products. To make things worse, England had restricted the sale of most American goods to British markets. Thus, many colonists could never bring in any more money than the British market was willing to pay for their unfinished goods which, in most cases, was less than the cost it took to produce it.

The Proclamation of 1763 further affected the economy by restricting the acquisition of new land grants. The result was that, on the one hand, the land east of the Appalachian Mountains appreciated in value, but on the other hand, slavery began to depreciate in value for plantation owners with large slave populations.. This is because the continual importation of slaves flooded their markets with an overabundance of slave labor. It was this loss in property value that impelled many Southern slave owners to encourage the end of the slave trade to the American colonies. Little did the colonists know within a month of their

---

[5] W. Robert Higgins, "The Ambivalence of Freedom," *The Revolutionary War in the South, Power, Conflict, and Leadership*, (Durham, NC: Duke University Press, 1979), 48.

petition, the need for more slave labor was about to arise once again. This is because, from March 1772 to July 1774, eleven hundred and sixty four grants were made for 300,000 acres scattered from Princess Anne to Augusta County, Virginia. The new governor, Lord Dunmore, would even approve ten patents totaling 13,616 acres west of the line stipulated by the Proclamation of 1763. Lord Dartmouth instructed Dunmore to send a list of all these patents. Dunmore was severely reprimanded for permitting surveys and was prohibited from issuing "such claims until you shall have received further orders from the King."[6]

Fear of revolts also perpetuated slave owners to seek the end of the slave trade. Increasing slave populations caused many to hypothesize the increased likelihood of a successful slave revolt. The events of the Stono Rebellion, in fall of 1739, when one hundred slaves staged a rebellion at the Stono River, South Carolina, remained imbedded in their minds. The ranks of these rebels included white indentured servants, other poor whites, black slaves, and black indentured servants. The rebellion was quelled, but it undoubtedly created a palpable fear in hearts of slave owners; in response, there was an increase in slave legislation, slave patrols, and the refusal to allow blacks to take up arms. On December 1, 1774, the Southern slave owners temporarily got their way when the Continental Association forbade slave importation.[7] Samuel Hopkins' fears were put at ease when he wrote, "have we not reason to think this has been one means of obtaining the remarkable, and almost miraculous protection and success, which heaven has hitherto granted the united Colonies."[8] Hopkins thought the trading of slaves immoral and unconditionally approved the measure banning their importation.

---

[6] Isaac S. Harrell, "Some Neglected Phases of the Revolution in Virginia," *William and Mary Quarterly*, 2nd series, Vol. 5, No. 3 (July 1925), 159-160.

[7] Taylor, *Papers of John Adams*, Vol. 3, Samuel Hopkins to Samuel Cushing, December 29, 1775, 390 n. 2.

[8] Ibid, 389.

Dunmore's Proclamation and Domestic Insurrections

He wished Congress would go further and declare freedom to all the slaves, because by keeping them in bondage "have we not reason to fear he (God) will take his protection from us, and give us up to the power of oppression and tyranny...by refusing to let the oppressed go free and to break every yoke?"[9] In regards to Dunmore and his proclamation freeing rebel slaves, Hopkins wrote:

> Does not the conduct of Lord Dunmore, and the ministerialists, in taking the advantage of the slavery practiced among us, and encouraging all slaves to join them, by promising them liberty, point out the best, if not the way to defeat them in this, viz. granting freedom to them ourselves, so as no longer to use our neighbor's service without wages, but give them for their labours what is equal and just?[10]

Hopkins' proposal would formally take effect two days after he drafted this letter to Samuel Cushing. On December 31, George Washington wrote, "it has been represented to me that the free Negroes who have served this army are very much dissatisfied at being discarded...I have presumed to depart from the resolution respecting them, and have given license for their being enlisted. If this is disapproved by Congress I will put a stop to it."[11] Washington's request was granted when Congress replied by accepting those "who have served faithfully in the army at Cambridge...but no others."[12] The General was influenced in drafting the letter as a means to meet his troop quotas, but would have never supported such an initiative had it not been for the bellicose actions of Lord Dunmore.[13] Dunmore's Proclamation

---

[9] Ibid.

[10] Ibid.

[11] W.W. Abbot &Dorothy Twohig, *The Papers of George Washington*, Revolutionary War Series, Vol. 2 (Charlottesville, VA: University Press of Virginia, 1987), To John Hancock, December 31, 1775, 623.

[12] Ibid, 625 n. 5.

[13] Patrick Charles, *Washington's Decision: The Story of George*

significantly affected Washington, so much so, that he wrote:
> If my Dear Sir that Man is not crushed before Spring, he will become the most formidable Enemy America has--his strength will increase as a Snow ball by Rolling; and faster, if some expedient cannot be hit upon to convince the Slaves and Servants of the Impotency of His designs.[14]

Just two months earlier,, Washington had helped push for blacks' exclusion from the Continental Army. However, with his back against the wall regarding enlistments and the open employment of blacks by the British Army, the General would have a change of heart. The decision proved to be a crucial one. By the end of the war, black soldiers would form 5-10% of the Continental forces, most of them being slaves, once they were allowed to openly enlist in 1777.

Lord Dunmore's Proclamation was not the only subject of grievances the Virginian colonists had with the governor. In fact, the proclamation was not the first order to send a rift through the delegates of the Virginia Assembly. On March 28, 1775, the governor forbade the Virginia delegation from attending the Second Continental Congress.[15] The proclamation was not Dunmore's idea, but was, in fact, an order issued earlier that month by British Secretary of State William Legge, Earl of Dartmouth. The Virginia Assembly ignored the proclamation, elections were still held, and delegates were sent to Philadelphia on May 4. Because their actions were considered treasonous, in effect, the delegates were escorted by independent companies of armed men. In addition, Dunmore's threat of arresting anyone who attempted to attend the Congress was cause for concern.

Washington's Decision to Reaccept Black Enlistments in the Continental Army, December 31, 1775, (Charlestown, SC: Book Surge Publishing, 2006), 116-117.

[14] Abbot & Twohig, *The Papers of George Washington*, Revolutionary War Series, Vol. 2, George Washington to Colonel Richard Henry Lee, December 26, 1775, 610-613.

[15] Van Scrheevan, *Revolutionary Virginia*, Vol. 3, 29.

Dunmore's Proclamation and Domestic Insurrections

In the following month, the Virginia Convention passed a resolution ordering the "raising a body of armed Men in all the counties."[16] Dunmore, upon hearing the news, feared the rebels would overtake the armory. Complying with Lord Dartmouth's orders, he sent a detachment of British seamen to seize the local gunpowder.[17] Under the cover of night the sailors transported the gunpowder to *HMS Magdalen* "abreast Burwell's Ferry" in the James River. Unknown to the seamen, a spy had witnessed their mission and informed the revolutionary leaders. News of the event spread instantly. The following day "drums were beating, shouting citizens assembling, and the local independent company of gentlemen volunteers following into ranks."[18] The situation turned so violent that Peyton Randolph, the speaker of the Virginia assembly, had to intervene to restore order. He asked the mob to disperse so a governing body could be assembled to address the matter.

The assembly members argued that the absence of the gunpowder made the town vulnerable. A rumor had been circulating that a slave insurrection was afoot. Dunmore took advantage of the situation and stated that he, too, had heard of "an insurrection in a neighboring county."[19] He published that he heard of "an intended insurrection of the Slaves, who had been seen in large numbers in the night time about the Magazine."[20] He informed the assembly if they needed the powder it would be made available to them in half an hour. Dunmore's assurance that

---

[16] Ibid, 4.

[17] Ibid. Dartmouth's orders had called for "the most effectual measures for arresting, detaining, and securing any Gunpowder, or any sort of Arms or Ammunition which may be attempted to be imported into the Province under your Government, *see* Selby, *The Revolution in Virginia*, 19, Dartmouth to American Governors, October 19, 1774 and January 14, 1775.

[18] Van Schreevan, *Revolutionary Virginia*, Vol. 3, 5.

[19] Ibid.

[20] Force, *American Archives*, Fourth Series, Vol. 2, Dunmore Proclamation, May 3, 1775, 465.

he had only taken the gunpowder to prevent a possible slave revolt calmed down the colonists.[21] The incident is useful in demonstrating the colonists' apprehensions towards slave uprisings. Dunmore had played to the colonists' fears to justify his actions. The Virginians' acceptance of this excuse evinces to what degree southern colonists' feared blacks taking up arms.

Dunmore was not the only governor who took measures to disarm the revolutionaries. Governor Josiah Martin of North Carolina dismantled the pieces of cannon next to his residence on similar reasoning. Upon doing this, a group of inhabitants from New Bern confronted the governor since "the circumstance had caused alarm, because the Governor of Virginia had lately deprived the People of that Colony of their Ammunition."[22] Martin informed the body of men he had "dismounted the Guns...because the carriages were entirely rotten and unserviceable, and incapable of bearing the discharge of them on the King's birthday that was at hand."[23] The answer persuaded the men to disperse but even Governor Martin admitted it "was not really one of [his] motives."[24] The real reason Martin had the cannon dismounted was "to make the removal of them more difficult" since he had received "repeated advices of a design concerting ...to seize those guns by force."[25]

Governor Robert Eden of Maryland would have taken similar measures to secure his gunpowder stores had he "thought such a step to be expedient, had our powder been worth removing."[26]

---

[21] Selby, *The Revolution in Virginia*, 2.

[22] United States, Naval History Division, *Naval Documents of the American Revolution*, Vol. 1, Josiah Martin to Lord Dartmouth, June 20, 1775, 788.

[23] Ibid.

[24] Ibid.

[25] Ibid.

[26] Ibid, Robert Eden to William Eden, April 28, 1775, 243. Eden, unlike Dunmore or Martin, was still respected among the large majority of Maryland's Whigs. He had received instructions to secure the powder, but after consulting with his Council they agreed to surrender the arms,

Dunmore's Proclamation and Domestic Insurrections

Following news of Lexington and Concord reaching Annapolis, "six Gentlemen" approached the governor since "Apprehensions of some Attempt being made by the Servants or Slaves for their Liberty" was afoot.[27] The men wanted to be provided with arms and gunpowder to quell any slave revolt that might be brewing. Eden tried pleading with them to refrain from taking up arms because it would only "accelerate the Evil they dreaded from their Servants and Slaves." Eden gave in to the Council and permitted the distribution of 100 arms to each of four counties, making the total 400. Eden was no fool; he knew part of the reason the arms were requested was to protect themselves from the British. His assumptions were solidified, in turn, when the rebels "took away the Powder...except five barrels of mine in the Magazine."[28] Eden had the last laugh though: the rebels were seemingly unaware that the powder was "useless" since it had been there for twenty years.

Regarding the removal of the Virginia colonists' gunpowder, their fears only subsided for a couple of hours, because later that night, rumors began circulating that British troops were again coming to the city of Williamsburg. The seizure of munitions the day before had caused some to perceive it as a precursor to invasion.[29] The rumor spread throughout Williamsburg in a night. On the morning of April 23, William Pasteur reported that Dunmore had flown into a violent rage at an alderman about the issue. Dunmore went so far as to threaten to incite a slave insurrection against the colonists. From his mouth burst, "By the living God, if any insult is offered to me, or those who have obeyed my orders, I will declare freedom to the slaves and lay the town in ashes!"[30] Thomas Gage commented, "We hear by a

---

powder, stores to the colonels of the militia "under the ancient establishment." Bernard C. Steiner, *Life and Administration of Sir Robert Eden*, (Baltimore, MD: John Hopkins University, 1898), 90.
[27] Ibid.
[28] Ibid.
[29] Selby, *Revolutionary Virginia*, 3.
[30] Christopher Ward, *The War of the Revolution*, Vol. 2, (New York, NY: The MacMillan Company, 1952), 845, Force, *American Archives*,

private Letter that a Declaration his Lordship has made, of Proclaiming all the Negroes free who should join him, has startled the insurgents."[31] By July, this news had reached London. Count De Guines commented, "This threat made [the rebels] come to their senses; but is it not a pity that a Nation of Merchants be reduced to freeing slaves in order to protect its Colonies against its own Colonists!"[32] The news of Dunmore's outburst spread to a group of slaves who, late in April, went to the governor's house to volunteer their services. Dunmore had them dismissed but expressed to the Earl of Dartmouth, that, once supplied with arms and ammunition, he would be able to recruit enough Indians and slaves to assemble a force to quell any rebellion. Meanwhile reports continued to circulate about the gunpowder incident and the frightening words that came out of Dunmore's lips.[33]

When the news reached Fredericksburg about the removal of the gunpowder, their assembly became extremely concerned.[34] The similarity between Thomas Gage's attempt to seize Massachusetts' stockpile of arms at Lexington and Concord and Lord Dunmore's actions seemed too coincidental.[35] Both Gage and the governor's actions at the armory were significant since obtaining gunpowder was extremely difficult. Throughout the first two years of the revolution, maintaining sufficient gunpowder stocks haunted American commanders and would be a pertinent factor in convincing some towards seeking foreign alliances.

Regardless of the actions at the Williamsburg armory, the possibility of a settlement between the Virginia Assembly and Dunmore was possible. Unfortunately, during the first weekend the assembly met to work out reconciliation, a band of young men

---

Fourth Series, Vol. 2, Testimony by William Pasteur, June 15, 1775.

[31] United States, Naval History Division, *Naval Documents of the American Revolution*, Vol. 1, General Thomas Gage to William Legge, Lord Dartmouth, May 15, 1775, 338.

[32] Ibid, Count de Guines to Count de Vergennes, July 7, 1775, 1319.

[33] Selby, *The Revolution in Virginia*, 3.

[34] Van Schreevan, *Revolutionary Virginia*, Vol. 3, 6-7.

[35] Selby, *The Revolution in Virginia*, 4.

decided to break into the public magazine. Three were wounded when they tripped a spring that discharged a rigged shotgun. The colony erupted. The people of Williamsburg felt Lord Dunmore was personally to blame for the device that injured the intruders. The issue at hand was not that the young men were hurt, but that they were injured without any warning. No notice was posted either publicly or at the armory that the "life of anyone entering it would be endangered" if intruded upon.[36] The same day the young men were injured, a committee visited the governor to request the keys for the magazine. Dunmore burst into a violent rage and rejected their request "on the foolish ground that, since it was not written and did not identify the petitioners, he could not give the keys to people he did not know."[37] News immediately spread of Dunmore's outburst, and the following day a mob stormed the magazine.

On June 8, due to his belief his life was in mortal danger, Dunmore fled to the *HMS Magdalen*. Historian John Selby believes "the retreat proved worse for Dunmore than the attack…his flight polarized political opinion in Virginia even more than had his raid on the magazine."[38] The abandonment of his post was viewed as cowardly, but Dunmore might have retreated only as a "strategic withdrawal."[39] From his new post, Dunmore possessed more flexibility with his forces in case a rebellion would ensue. His post aboard the *HMS Fowey* also prevented him from being held prisoner or used as leverage against the British.

Although Dunmore fled, the Virginia Convention requested his return to the assembly. Dunmore responded that he would only return if certain conditions were met. His terms were precise: he requested the individuals who raided the magazine must return the arms they stole and be "brought to punishment."[40] The Virginia

---

[36] Ibid.

[37] Ibid, 42-3.

[38] Ibid.

[39] Van Schreevan, *Revolutionary Virginia*, Vol. 3, An Introductory Note, 17.

[40] Force, *American Archives*, Fourth Series, Vol. 2, Dunmore to the

Convention promised to return the arms but would not prosecute the individuals responsible. Dunmore further requested that they reopen the courts, disarm all "independent companies," and reinstate the full powers of his office.[41] The Virginia Assembly debated the proposal and informed the governor, "With pain and disappointment...we cannot, my Lord, close with the terms of that Resolution."[42]

While the Virginia Convention was supporting the aims of the Continental Congress in the months to come, Dunmore ended up taking command of a small contingent of British men and Virginian loyalists. With such small numbers, he did not pose a large threat to the colony but, just the same, remained a nuisance to the Virginians. Dunmore was such a nuisance that all three *Virginia Gazettes* perpetually tracked the governor's whereabouts to inform their readers of any possible threat which may be posed. On September 30, Dunmore struck back when his 14 sailors & Marines, and 8 grenadiers from *HMS Mercury* marched through the streets of Norfolk and seized the printing press. He reasoned that the printer was encouraging "treason and rebellion against his majesty's crown and government."[43]

On October 17, Dunmore attacked Kemps Landing, ten miles southeast of Norfolk, to dispose of the arms and gunpowder of the rebels.[44] Fortunately, for the rebels, the gunpowder had been removed. In November, Dunmore would be successful in attacking Great Bridge and Kemps Landing once more. One of the townspeople from Norfolk wrote Dunmore "finds a defenseless place, he lands, plunders the plantations, and carries off the negroes."[45] There was nothing the rebels would have

---

Virginia House of Burgesses, June, 10, 1775, 122-3.
[41] Ibid.
[42] Ibid., Virginia House of Burgesses, June 12, 1775, 1204.
[43] Van Schreevan, *Revolutionary Virginia*, Vol. 4, An Introductory Note, 6.
[44] Ibid.
[45] Wheeler, *Letters on the American Revolution*, Extract of a letter from Norfolk, Virginia, October 28, 1775, 221.

desired more than to see "the traitor" Dunmore captured.

Whether the colonists were aware that Dunmore was seriously considering his threat of freeing the slaves is debatable. In the summer of 1775, Maryland Governor Robert Eden complained, "The governor of Virginia [Dunmore], the captains of the men of war, and mariners have been tampering with our Negroes; and have nightly meetings with them; and all for the glorious purpose of enticing them to cut their masters' throats while they are asleep...Gracious God! That men noble by birth and fortune should descend to such ignoble base servility."[46] In June, James Madison wrote, "our Governor has been tampering with the Slaves & that he has it in contemplation to make great Use of them in case of a civil war in this province."[47] By early August, Dunmore had already initiated an unofficial policy of employing slaves. The Virginia Convention noted early that month the governor had carried away a number of slaves not belonging to him. George Mason made a note of it when he drafted *An Ordinance for Establishing a General Test Oath*. The resolve did not pass, and such a measure would not until 1777, but Mason remarked, "Lord Dunmore...by and unexampled & wanton suspension of the Law of the Land & Institution of that horrid Supporter of Tyranny, Law Martial, by seising, and imprisoning and transporting the persons of our peaceable Citizens, by declaring our Servants and Slaves free and inviting & arming them to assassinate their Masters, our innocent Wifes and helpless Children."[48] Historian Benjamin Quarles believes Dunmore was waiting for the perfect timing to employ his strategy. He had already written the order on

---

[46] Force, *American Archives*, Fourth Series, Vol. 3, Extracts of a Letter from a Clergyman in Maryland to His Friend in England, August, 2, 1775, 10.

[47] William T. Hutchinson, *The Papers of James Madison*, Vol. 1, (Chicago, IL: The University of Chicago Press, 1962), To William Bradford, June 19, 1775, 153.

[48] Robert A Rutland, *The Papers of George Mason: 1725-1792*, Vol. 1, (Chapel Hill, NC: The University of North Carolina Press, 1970), An Ordinance for Establishing a General Test Oath, August 19, 1775, 246.

Irreconcilable Grievances

November 7, 1775, but was waiting for that "auspicious moment."[49] Dunmore found it following his mid-November skirmish at Kemp's Landing. Upon entering the village victorious, the support of the surrounding Tories aided the governor in making his decision to officially free the slaves of rebels. John Page wrote to Thomas Jefferson on the subject, "Our late Governor, as we now call him, was so ela[ted] with this Victory, that he erected his Standard, pub[lished] the Proclamation you will see in our Papers, which he had before printed in the Press he had taken from Norfolk, and marched about making Prisoners of a Number of People, and administering an Oath of his own Framing," denouncing Congress and the other revolutionary governments.[50] Dunmore wrote to Lord Dartmouth his reasoning behind the proclamation, stating:

> These overt acts of rebellion [particularly the repulsion of the British at Hampton, Virginia] determined me to Issue the inclosed Proclamation, which however I postponed as long as possible, in hopes of having Instructions from your Lordship for my Conduct, in this as well as in many other matters I have so often prayed to be instructed in, for many Months past, but not one line have I had the Honor to receive from your Lordship since yours of the 30th of May. God only knows what I have suffered since my first embarking, from my anxiety of mind, not knowing how to at in innumerable instances that occur every day, being one moment deffident of my own judgment (and not having one liveing Soul to advise with) and then on the other hand fearing if I remained a Tame Spectator and permitted the Rebels to proceed without any interuption, that they would by persuasion, threats, and every other art in their power, delude many of His Majesty's well disposed Subjects to their party, then again it occurred to that should I be able to prevail on only a

---

[49] Benjamin Quarles, "Lord Dunmore as Liberator," *William and Mary Quarterly*, 15, (October 1958), 498.
[50] Boyd, *The Papers of Thomas Jefferson*, Volume 1, From John Page, November 24, 1775, 265.

Dunmore's Proclamation and Domestic Insurrections

few to espowse His Majesty's Cause (with the very small force I had to support them) I should only involve them in inevitable ruin.[51]

Lord Dunmore's Proclamation was initially a psychological threat more than a physical one.[52] The numbers of slaves that originally escaped to the former governor has been disputed but 300 is a fair estimate. This number doubled Dunmore's strength to roughly 600 men. Although the proclamation did not bring many slaves to Dunmore's lines, it did inspire them to run away from their masters and show up in British camps.[53] By the end of the war it is estimated that 12,000 of Georgia's 15,000 slaves and 25,000 of South Carolina's 110,000 ran away to British lines.[54] Dunmore's Proclamation primarily affected the South, but rumors soon spread of possible freedom behind British lines, thus impelling slaves from all thirteen colonies to attempt escape. The proclamation's purpose was not to disrupt the security of the North, but that of the Southern rebels. For two preceding centuries, the South's greatest fear had been a massive slave insurrection. Their fear had finally come true. Thomas Jefferson was so struck by the Proclamation he wrote to his wife Patty a proposition to keep her and his friends "at a distance from the alarms of Lord Dunmore."[55] More importantly, Dunmore felt that instituting a perpetual fear of slave revolts within the minds of revolutionaries would prevent many from taking up arms against

---

[51] United States, Naval History Division, *Naval Documents of the American Revolution*, Vol. 2, Lord Dunmore to Lord Dartmouth, December 6, 1775, 1309-1311.
[52] Sylvia Frey, *Water from the Rock*, (Princeton, NJ: Princeton University Press, 1992), 63.
[53] Benjamin Quarles, *Negro in the American Revolution*, (Chapel Hill, NC: The University of North Carolina Press, 1961), 18-32.
[54] James & Lois Horton, *The Making of Slavery in America*, (New York, NY: Oxford University Press, 2005), 60.
[55] Boyd, *The Papers of Thomas Jefferson*, Vol. 1, To Francis Eppes, November 21, 1775, 264.

the King's standard. He hypothesized that the revolutionaries' concerns with their own property and livelihood would overcome any ambition they had in entering the conflict.

News of the Proclamation spread quickly, causing local governments, Congress and the people mobilize in order to defend themselves both physically and psychologically. The slave codes had been the primary means to keep slaves from insurrection but now proved useless once a slave learned of Dunmore's proclamation. To the slaves, the proclamation was their chance at freedom. Several newspapers printed an incident in Philadelphia in which a woman was walking on a "narrow" sidewalk when she crossed paths with a black man. The black man refused to step aside into the muddy street even when the woman asked him to. The black man replied to the woman, "stay, you white…bitch, till Lord Dunmore and his black regiment come, and then we will see who is to take the wall."[56] The task at hand was difficult, but the "military preparation of the colonists was matched by their promptness in adopting "home front" measures to prevent slaves from joining the governor."[57] Local patrols were doubled, main roads were vigilantly watched, and owners of small naval vessels were warned of the dangers they faced. Regardless of these measures and of the slave codes, blacks were willing to exchange the possibility of punishment, even death, for freedom.

Whether Dunmore's Proclamation freeing the slaves was expected by Virginians, is debatable since many of the colonists were shocked upon hearing the news of it. As with any major event in history, there are those who anticipate it and those that do not. The same was true for this event. There were Virginians who expected it, while there were others that believed it would never happen to them. Those who anticipated the proclamation knew Dunmore had threatened to "declare freedom to the slaves and lay

---

[56] Raphael, *A People's History of the American Revolution*, 321, Pennsylvania Evening Post, December 14, 1775.
[57] Quarles, "Dunmore as Liberator," *William and Mary Quarterly*, 15 (October, 1958), 498.

the town in ashes!"[58] Many Virginians had not put it past Dunmore to participate in such an act. Before the issuance of Dunmore's Proclamation, even Benjamin Franklin accused the Governor of inciting the slaves. When Franklin wrote a list of grievances in September, one of them blamed the Ministry of "encouraging our Blacks to rise and murder their Masters."[59] He was referring to Governors Dunmore and Martin's "steps towards...exciting an Insurrection among the Blacks."[60] Dunmore's character was not highly viewed among the colonists following his actions earlier that year. Even John Page, a former member of Dunmore's Council, perceived the governor to be nothing more than a poor loser.[61] Following the flight of the governor in June, Page gave his services to the Virginia Convention and Virginia Committee of Public Safety. Lord Dunmore, in Page's view, did not take criticism well and at times would leave his advisors so he may have "a free and unbiased discussion."[62]

Peyton Randolph and the Virginia Convention should not have been surprised since they had received intelligence months prior regarding slaves' excitement upon seeing British warships, and the possibility of redcoats being deployed in the region. William Davies of Norfolk had informed the Convention on July 21 that "bad effects have arisen among the blacks from the neighborhood of the men of war, which we have great reason to believe will be very much increased by the arrival of these troops."[63] Also, Holt's

---

[58] Ward, *The War of the Revolution*, Vol. 2, 845.

[59] William B. Willcox, *The Papers of Benjamin Franklin*, Vol. 22, (New Haven, CT: Yale University Press, 1982), Benjamin Franklin to Jonathan Shipley, September 13, 1775, 200.

[60] Smith, *Letters of the Delegates to Congress 1774-1789*, Vol. 1, Benjamin Franklin to Jonathan Shipley, July 7, 1775, 607.

[61] Van Schreevan, *Revolutionary Virginia*, Vol. 3., New Kent County Committee, May 3, 1775, 85-6 n. 2.

[62] Ibid.

[63] United States, Naval History Division, *Naval Documents of the American Revolution*, Vol. 1, Committee of Norfolk to Peyton Randolph,

Virginia Gazette reported:
> This town and neighborhood have been much disturbed lately with the elopement of their negroes, owing to a mistaken notion which has unhappily spread amongst them, of finding shelter on board the men of war in this harbor, notwithstanding the assurances given by the commanding officers, that not the least encouragement should be shewn them.[64]

The *Virginia Gazette* report triggered officers of the volunteer companies in Williamsburg to petition the Virginia Convention. The officers requested some form of instructions be passed regarding the incident; otherwise it "might precipitate their countrymen into unnecessary calamities."[65] Since the governor had carried off a number of their slaves, the officers felt "it high time to establish the doctrine of reprisal."[66]

Upon news of the Proclamation, newspapers rushed to publish it as a means to alert slave owners.[67] Pinckney's *Virginia Gazette* went as far to publish the response of a black man described as an "honest negro." Caesar, the famous barber of York, "being asked what he thought of Lord Dunmore's setting the negroes free, said, that he did not know any one foolish enough to believe him, for if he intended to do so, he ought first to set his own free."[68] The credibility of this journalism is questionable. It is possible it was published purely to discredit the effects of Dunmore's Proclamation.

Besides increased security measures to deter runaways, many psychological arguments were also posed and distributed among

---

July 21, 1775, 947.

[64] Ibid, Holt's "Virginia Gazette," August 2, 1775, 1048.

[65] Ibid, Journal of the Virginia Convention, August 3, 1775, 1056.

[66] Ibid.

[67] Quarles, *The Negro in the American Revolution*, 23.

[68] United States, Naval History Division, *Naval Documents of the American Revolution*, Vol. 3, Pinkney's Virginia Gazette, December 9, 1775, 25.

the slave population. The most circulated rumor was Dunmore's Proclamation was a means for the British to finance their war against the colonists. They were told upon reaching Dunmore or British lines, they would be told they would be receiving their freedom, but then boarded on a ship and resold into slavery in the West Indies.[69] This was untrue, but there is evidence the revolutionaries truly believed this. Edmund Pendleton, in letter to Thomas Jefferson, wrote about Dunmore's Proclamation, "his slave scheme is also at an end, since it is now Public that he has sent off a sloop load to the West Indies, which has made others use every endeavor to escape from him."[70] George Washington truly believed the slaves were falling into a trap when he wrote to Richard Henry Lee if "that Man is not crushed before Spring, he will become the most formidable Enemy America has…if some expedient cannot be hit upon to convince the Slaves and Servants of the Impotency of His designs."[71] Reports of Dunmore's sloops carrying off slaves, along with multiple reports of his whereabouts most likely caused many revolutionaries to hypothesize their property was being resold. Not to mention, the Virginia convention had gone through great lengths to ensure coastal supplies were well out of Dunmore's reach. Selling slaves for goods seemed highly probable to them.

Some slave owners argued it was better for slaves to stay with their owners, who would protect them from this exploitation. Henry Laurens gathered his brother's slaves, while he was away, to convince them not to flee. Laurens informed the slaves of the great peril that lay in front of them if they chose to accept false offers of freedom, and reasoned he could protect them from this assured exploitation by Lord Dunmore and the British. According to Laurens, the slaves promised to follow his advice and to do

---

[69] Quarles, "Dunmore as Liberator," *William and Mary Quarterly*, 499.

[70] Boyd, *The Papers of Thomas Jefferson*, Vol. 1, Thomas Jefferson to Edmund Pendleton, November 16, 1775, 261.

[71] Abbot & Twohig, *The Papers of George Washington*, Revolutionary Series, Vol. 2, George Washington to Richard Henry Lee, December 26, 1775.

anything to continue in the service of their master. Slave owners "preferred to envision themselves as purveyors of freedom, the British engineers of slavery."[72] This was not true, and most slaves were aware of this. Even five of Henry Laurens slaves, who had pledged their allegiance to their master, joined the British on August 14, 1776.

Laurens felt a different course of action was necessary regarding a group of slaves who had fled to British protection at Tybee Island, Georgia. Their presence was seen as a nuisance since it provided another haven for slaves to escape. Rather than try to retake the island, Laurens agreed with Stephen Bull, who made a bold proposition he preferred to not be read "to so large a number of People, but to be only to the Council, for no one does at least ought to know." The plan called for the "Negroes on Tybee Island...to be shot if they cannot be taken." Bull preferred to see such human property murdered rather than be "carried away, and converted into money," since "the Public is obliged to pay for them." [73] Laurens agreed, but first thought proper encouragement should be given to "induce Proper Persons to seize" their property. If this could not be done, Laurens felt the Indians ought to be employed to take out the "Rebellious Negroes."[74]

It is not clear as to whether the Georgia Council of Safety was influenced by these recommendations, but action was taken against the British and the runaway slaves on Tybee Island. The attack took place on March 25 by Archibald Bulloch. A force consisting of Georgia militia and thirty Creek Indians burned most of the houses, killed a British Marine, and wounded three others. The British condemned the action, claiming the militiamen disguised themselves as Indians, and joined the Creeks in conducting "signs of the most savage barbarity" that "exceeded the ferocity of the Indians."[75]

---

[72] Raphael, *A People's History of the American Revolution*, 322-23.
[73] Chesnutt, *The Papers of Henry Laurens*, Vol. 11, Stephen Bull to Henry Laurens, March 14, 1776, 163.
[74] Ibid, Henry Laurens to Stephen Bull, March 16, 1776, 172.
[75] Ibid, 173 n.7.

Dunmore's Proclamation and Domestic Insurrections

Robert Carter, a southern slave owner and one of the wealthiest Virginians, gathered his slaves to give them a "history lesson" about the hostilities between Britain and the colonies. British warships were sailing nearby, and Carter feared some might attempt to take Lord Dunmore up on his offer of freedom. He told them what they might have heard about Dunmore's Proclamation was false, and informed them there had been slaves who had responded to the offer who were being sold to the West Indies.[76] He then had them take an oath of allegiance to him and the "13 United Colonies."[77] None of his slaves left the plantation. In February 1778, British ships sailed down the Potomac once more. Many slaves gathered to meet Dunmore, including three of George Washington's own, but none left Carter. It was possibly quite common for slave owners to denounce Dunmore's Proclamation, reason with their slaves, and administer oaths of allegiance to prevent their slaves from running away, but Carter's plea to his slaves is rare since he was truly looking out for the best interests of his slaves. Following the Revolution, in 1791, Carter would free all of his slaves. The legality of manumissions fluctuated in Virginia. Just prior to the Revolution, freeing a slave would have been illegal, but after the war the Virginia Convention was so "inspired by the revolutionary tide of opinion turning against slavery" that they authorized private manumissions.[78] Thousands of slaves were set free in the following years, Robert Carter and his uncle, Landon Carter, being two of the most notable slave owners to do so. Carter is a unique case, because most slave owners used scare tactics to prevent slaves from leaving. Masters meeting with their slaves in reaction to Lord Dunmore's

---

[76] Philip D. Morgan, Slave *Counterpoint: Black Culture in the Eighteenth Century Chesapeake and Low Country*, (Chapel Hill, NC: University of North Carolina Press, 1998), 283-4.

[77] Andrew Levy, *The First Emancipator: The Forgotten Story of Robert Carter the Founding Father Who Freed His Slaves*, (New York, NY: Random House, 2005), 76-7.

[78] Gary Nash, *Race and Revolution*, (Madison, WI: Madison House Publishers, 1990), 115.

proclamation were probably common, but Carter's appeal was rare in that he used political argumentation to persuade his slaves.[79]

Some slave owners that mentioned Dunmore's Proclamation warned their slaves only of the penalties that would occur if escape were attempted. On April 11, 1776, South Carolina's General Assembly passed an act that offered death to slaves that intended "to join any land or naval force raised or to be raised or sent by Great Britain."[80] Except those who served as laborers and defended batteries, South Carolina specifically bound blacks aiding the British. The act ensured the possibility of blacks taking up arms for the rebel cause was not affected, but the delegates had no immediate desire to use this to their advantage. It stated, "nothing in this Act contained shall be constructed or taken to prevent the good people of this Colony from arming slaves or negroes, for the better defense of this Colony, against all enemies whatsoever, who shall invade or attack the same, or endanger the safely thereof."[81]

Many psychological arguments against Dunmore's Proclamation were published. One unknown individual argued, "to none...is freedom promised, but such as are able to do Dunmore service." The main point of this argument was the women, children, elderly, and injured would not receive their freedom since they were unable to bear arms. These slaves were to "remain the property of their masters," and in some cases this did occur. [82] Due the persistent shortage of supplies, the British could only clothe, feed, and arm so many slaves, thus they were forced to turn away many.

The same author made sure to address Dunmore's labeling of the Americans as "rebels." In the opinion of the author, the

---

[79] Levy, *The First Emancipator: The Forgotten Story of Robert Carter the Founding Father Who Freed His Slaves*, 76-7.

[80] MacGregor & Nalty, *Blacks in the United States Armed Forces*, Vol. 1, Act of the General Assembly of South Carolina, April 11, 1776, 40.

[81] Ibid.

[82] Force, *American Archives*, Fourth Series, Vol. 3, Correspondence from Virginia, Williamsburg, November 23, 1775, 1387.

Dunmore's Proclamation and Domestic Insurrections

Americans were not the rebels, Dunmore was. It was Lord Dunmore who wrote "false and inflammatory letters to the Ministry of State" took "from us our powder," set a trap at the armory, and "withdrew himself from the seat of Government."[83] Dunmore had their towns attacked, "seized upon" Virginia's inhabitants, and now "presumes to insult our understandings."[84] The Virginia leadership did not believe they were rebels because, in their view, they were protecting the rights that "nature" and the British Constitution gave them. The natural rights they referred to was not an idea that was created during the Revolutionary War. These "natural rights" were one of the main causes of the English Civil War, which set up the governmental structure of eighteenth century England. One Virginian argued they (the rebels) had "an undoubted right to" take up arms "in defense of the British Constitution." Technically, this argument was accurate. The principles of the Glorious Revolution and the British Constitution authorized English citizens to defend against unjust rulers. From the American colonists' point of view, especially Virginians, Lord Dunmore's Proclamation was direct evidence of the tyrannical rule they had been claiming. It was stated, "The King and his Governors are bound by the laws, as much as his subjects."[85]

In some instances, slave owners threatened either to sell or execute other slaves on the plantation if anyone should attempt to escape. On Thursday, December 14, 1775 the Virginia Convention issued a declaration in response to Dunmore's Proclamation stating:

> Whereas, Lord Dunmore, by his Proclamation...may induce a necessity of inflicting the severest punishments upon those unhappy people...by an act of the General Assembly...it is enacted, that all negro or other slaves conspiring to rebel or make insurrection; shall suffer death and be excluded all benefit of clergy: We think it proper to declare, that all

---

[83] Ibid, 1385-86.
[84] Ibid, 1386.
[85] Ibid, Correspondence from Virginia, Williamsburg, November 30, 1775, 1385-6.

slaves, who have been, or shall be, seduced by his Lordship's proclamation or other arts, to desert their masters' service, and take up arms against the inhabitants of this Colony, shall be liable to such punishments as shall hereafter be directed by the General Convention.[86]

In January 1776, the Virginia Convention passed legislation ordering any slave found in arms with the British be sold to the West Indies or the Bay of Honduras. For each slave that was to be sold, the owner received the net value of the slave, and any remaining money was used to procure arms for the colony. Those slaves that had neither bore arms or reached Dunmore were to be returned to their owners. Run away slaves that refused to submit their owners name upon capture or slaves that were not claimed by their owners were sold at auction.[87]

Congress would not learn about Dunmore's Proclamation until nearly two weeks after it was issued. Patrick Henry sent a copy of the Proclamation to Congress writing it "is fatal to the public safety."[88] He asked Congress to use "every possible exertion, in your power."[89] Congress's response would become historically significant towards Virginia's push towards independence. Congress resolved that the inhabitants of Virginia should "resist to the utmost the arbitrary Government intended to be established therein by their Governor."[90] Furthermore, it was recommended to the Virginia Convention to establish a "liberal form of government...during the continuance of the dispute."[91] It was

---

[86] Force, *American Archives*, Fourth Series, Vol. 4, Declaration by Virginia Conference, December 17, 1775, 258-9.

[87] Ibid, Virginia Convention, January 17, 1776, 128.

[88] Kaplan, *The Black Presence in the Era of the American Revolution* Patrick Henry Circular Letter, November 20, 1775, 75.

[89] Ibid.

[90] Force, *American Archives*, Fourth Series, Vol. 3, Continental Congress, December 5, 1775, 1941.

[91] John Drayton, *Memoirs of the American Revolution as Relating to the State of South Carolina*, Vol. 2, (New York, NY: Arno Press, 1969), 147.

Dunmore's Proclamation and Domestic Insurrections

Lord Dunmore's declaration of martial law which occasioned Congress to express their determination in this matter.

The Virginia Convention reacted by issuing its own declaration in response. The declaration was to be distributed throughout the colonies and published in the newspapers. On December 13, the declaration was complete. It provided a legal argument against the validity of Dunmore's proclamation, questioned his character, derided the tyranny of Britain's Parliament in allowing this to occur, and sent a message to loyalists that retaliation would ensue if they helped the enemy.[92]

The legal argument claimed that Dunmore's proclamation was "in direct violation of the Constitution, and the laws of this country, to declare martial law in force." The Virginia Convention declared Dunmore's authority null and void. They argued that Dunmore claimed to have powers that "the King himself cannot exercise." What Dunmore had done, in their view, was destroy the fabric of society itself. They asserted that they were the "guardians of the lives and liberty of the people, our constituents, conceive it to be indispensably our duty to protect them against every species of despotism, and to endeavor to remove those fears with which they are so justly alarmed." The declaration also appealed to the colonists by reminding them of Lord Dunmore's well-known actions in Virginia. It stated, "His Lordship can be traced as a source of innumerable evils," and his behavior "can be considered only as a repetition." The Virginia Convention informed the people that they were not rebels, but good citizens standing up against Britain's tyranny.[93] The argument the Virginian delegates wanted to make clear was that there was a social contract between the government and its people. When a government or ruler breaks that contract, the people must restore the state to justice. It was argued:

The assemblage of horrors might want no fact of

---

[92] Continental Congress, *Virginia Convention*, December 13, 1775, Declaration in response to Lord Dunmore's proclamation, (National Archives: Washington, DC), 81-82.
[93] Ibid.

distinguishing die, he is now exciting those very people to rise in arms among us, and to purchase that liberty which he has deprived them, by murdering people upon whom he also obtruded them. Thus paying off former crimes committed against the liberties of one people, with crimes which he urges them to commit against the lives of another.[94]

The Virginia Convention also warned loyalists that if any "shall be found in arms, or continue to give assistance to our enemies, we shall think ourselves justified, by the necessity we are under, in executing upon them the law of retaliation."[95] Moreover, the Convention passed a separate declaration, later that day, offering pardon to slaves who returned ten days after the declaration in response to Dunmore's Proclamation was drafted. This was their way of offering the slaves a peaceful resolution by promising they would not be punished if they returned on their own.[96]

Dunmore's Proclamation is the most frequently cited attempt by the loyalists and the British to rally the slaves to their cause, but the idea was not new. In fact, the probability of the British employment of slaves to keep the colonies in line was hypothesized my many. Some British officers and colonial governors had even already unofficially enrolled slaves to their cause prior to Dunmore's Proclamation. What is significant about the latter is it was not only published, but the first large scale attempt to recruit the negro slave.

---

[94] Carl Becker, *The Declaration of Independence: The Study in the History of Political Ideas*, (New York: Harcourt Brace & Company, 1922), 174-84.

[95] Continental Congress, *Virginia Convention*, December 13, 1775, Declaration in response to Lord Dunmore's proclamation, (National Archives: Washington, DC), 81-82.

[96] Ibid, 81-82.

Chapter Five

Alternate Contributions

Things are now come to a Crisis, that we must avail ourselves of every resource to raise the Negroes, on our cause.
        Thomas Gage to Lord Barrington, June 12, 1775

Lord Dunmore was not the only individual conjuring up ideas of employing slaves for the conflict, because in early 1775, General Thomas Gage had mentioned the strategy in a letter to John Stuart, the British Indian Superintendent of the Southern District in Charleston. Gage wrote, "It is to be hoped for your own Sakes that the Delegates you send to Philadelphia will be moderate People, but you Carolinians are as hot as your climate--however it is well known that if a Serious Opposition takes place, you can do but little--You have too much to take care and think of, but should you proceed greater lengths it may happen that your Rice and Indigo will be brought to market by negroes instead of white people."[1] Because of the high concentration of slaves within the colonies, it seemed possible to many that a social revolution among slaves might be brewing behind any political revolution that occurred.[2] The South Carolina Provincial Congress so feared that Stuart would incite slaves and Indians against them that it dispatched two members to pursue him. The British Ministry addressed the event in a report a year later. It

---

[1] Peter H. Wood, "Taking Care of Business" in Revolutionary South Carolina: Republicanism and the Slave Society, Jeffrey Crow, Editor, *The Southern Experience in the American Revolution*, (Chapel Hill, NC: The University of North Carolina Press, 1978), 280.
[2] Ibid.

stated, "The news papers were full of Publications calculated to excite the fears of the People--Massacres and Instigated Insurrections, were Words in the mouth of every Child--The pretended Discovery of an intention to Instigate Insurrections of the negroes and bring down the Indians was the pretence for tendering an Instrument of Association to every Person in the Province."[3]

In June 1775 Gage even considered the possibility of employing a regiment of freed slaves.[4] He wrote, "things are now come to that Crisis, that we must avail ourselves of every resource even to raise the Negroes, on our cause."[5] The British possessed few troops in Boston during this time, and Gage persistently feared the Americans would overtake his position. Although intelligence informed him that the American camps could easily be taken, he remained cautious. Gage wrote to Lord Barrington, "I wish this cursed place was burned, the only use is its harbour...but in all other respects it's the worst place either to act Offensively from, or defencively."[6] Evidence suggests Gage considered arming blacks for three reasons: (1) he did not possess sufficient troop strength, (2) he had observed them being enlisted within the rebel army, and (3) he was not receiving the support from Tories as he had hoped.

Tory support was, for the most part, nonexistent. In April, a

---

[3] Ibid, 281.

[4] Kaplan, *Blacks Presence in the Era of the American Revolution*, 17.

[5] Ibid. *See also* Clarence Edwin Carter, *The Correspondence of General Thomas Gage with the Secretaries of State, and with the War Office and the Treasury*, Vol. 1, Thomas Gage to Lord Barrington, June 12, 1775, (Archon Books, 1969), 684. On June 12, Gage also wrote to Lord Dartmouth requesting the use of Indian auxiliaries in the conflict and issued his proclamation declaring martial law. Some event or mindset must have influenced Gage on this day. By this point, he most assuredly saw the war no longer as a argument over Parliamentary policy. He now viewed the conflict as a war for independence.

[6] Carter, *The Correspondence of General Thomas Gage with the Secretaries of State, and with the War Office and the Treasury*, Vol. 1, Thomas Gage to Lord Barrington, June 26, 1775, 687.

number of Tories had indicated to the General their intentions of taking up arms, but nothing became of it. His feelings on support of the "Friends of Government" were expressed in a letter to Lord Barrington. Gage wrote the Tories "are passive Friends, quietly wishing to promote Peace and Tranquility, the Opposers active and violent, and overturn all Moderate Men."[7] Gage had no intentions on starting a racial social revolution by considering the inclusion of blacks within the British army. He had seen their inclusion at the Battles of Lexington, Concord, and Bunker Hill. Regardless, Gage took no action towards implementing the idea. Although he supported Lord Dunmore in his efforts in Virginia, and had made a mention of their employment to John Stuart, he took no action to secure the aid of blacks.[8]

In August, the colonists of North Carolina foiled a potential plot to incite a slave revolt. The governor of the colony, Josiah Martin, was charged with "giving encouragement to the slaves to revolt from their masters."[9] Governor Martin was willing to encourage this "when every other thing to preserve the King's Government should prove ineffectual."[10] The New Bern (North Carolina) Committee had found his letter which stated:

> I beg leave to make you my acknowledgements for your communication of the false...of my having given encouragement to the negroes to revolt against their masters; and as I persuade myself you kindly intended thereby to give me an opportunity to refute so infamous a charge...that nothing could ever justify the design falsely imputed to me, of giving encouragement to the negroes, but the actual and declared rebellion of the King's subjects, and the failure of

---

[7] Ibid, Thomas Gage to Lord Barrington, May 13, 1775, 678.

[8] John Richard Alden, *General Gage in America Being Principally A History of His Role in the American Revolution*, (Baton Rouge, LA: Louisiana State Univ. Press, 1948), 259-60.

[9] Force, *American Archives*, Fourth Series, Vol. 3, Newbern North Carolina Committee, August 2, 1775, 8.

[10] Ibid.

Irreconcilable Grievances

all other means to maintain the King's Government.[11]

The committee ordered the letter to be published as an alarm "against the horrid and barbarous designs" against their colony.[12] Jonathan Trumbull, Governor of Connecticut, feared Martin would "succeed too well in his attempts to divide that Province." He thought the employment of slaves was a "cruel, wicked, detestable policy." Only the "Savages are merciful compared with our enemies."[13] Most likely, the governor was not intending to use slaves against his colonists. He had written to Lord Dartmouth a week later, "as a most infamous report had lately been propagated among the People, that I had formed a design of Arming the Negroes and proclaiming freedom to all such as should resort to the King's Standard."[14] From this statement it can be determined the letter the colonists intercepted was taken out of context.[15] Martin was not the only North Carolina loyalist charged with inciting a slave insurrection.

In July 1775, the Committee of Safety of Wilmington, North Carolina, accused Captain John Collet of inviting slaves to take up arms against their country.[16] The Committee acted upon hearing a

---

[11] Ibid, Letter to Lewis H. De Rossett, June 24, 1775, 8.

[12] Ibid.

[13] *Collections of the Massachusetts Historical Society*, Fifth Series, Vol. 10, "Trumbull and Washington Letters," (Boston, MA: Massachusetts Historical Society), John Trumbull to George Washington, March 25, 1776, 12.

[14] United States, Naval History Division, *Naval Documents of the American Revolution*, Vol. 1, Josiah Martin to Lord Dartmouth, June 30, 1775, 790.

[15] Martin's attempt to organize the Highlanders has evidentiary support, but the rumor of his intent to incite the Indians and slaves does not. The rumors about Martin changed the military landscape in North Carolina. Slave patrols were created to find slaves that did not possess a pass from their master or were carrying any firearms. See Vernon O. Stumpf, *Josiah Martin: The Last Royal Governor of North Carolina*, (Durham, NC: Carolina Academic Press, 1986), 125-27.

[16] United States, Naval History Division, *Naval Documents of the*

Alternate Contributions

report from the inhabitants Brunswick. They deemed Collet guilty of "cruelly and illegally" detaining the property of individuals, and "frequently solicited...his base encouragement of Slaves eloped from their Masters, feeding and employing them, and his atrocious and horrid declaration that he would excite them all to an insurrection."[17]

Following Lexington and Concord, Collet was assigned to protect Fort Johnson's artillery pieces from falling into enemy hands. In dire need of men, supplies, and powder to defend the outpost, he resorted to any means necessary to support the garrison. He informed Governor Martin of his situation and the possibility that he might have to dismantle the "14 eighteen Pounders, 16 nine do and 20 swivels."[18] The revolutionary North Carolinians had no problem collecting a "great many volunteers" to remove Collet from the fort. Collet escaped while "about 500 men marched to the Fort, and burnt and destroyed all the Houses & c., in and about the same; demolished as far as they could, the back part of the Fortification, and effectually dislodged that atrocious Freebooter."[19] The slaves were "recovered by their several owners," and as for Collet's treachery, they burnt down his house and all his valuables.[20]

An unaddressed letter from London to a revolutionary in Philadelphia discussed the rumor of the Ministerial Army possibly employing the slaves to revolt against the colonists. The author of the letter wrote:

The Ministry have thoughts of declaring all your negroes

American Revolution, Vol. 1, Minutes of the Committee of Safety of Wilmington, North Carolina, July 21, 1775, 947-8.

[17] Ibid, "The People" to Josiah Martin, Governor of North Carolina, July 16, 1775, 898.

[18] Ibid, Captain John Collet to Captain Francis Parry, May 20, 1775, 373, Captain John Collet to General Thomas Gage, July 8, 1775, 844.

[19] Ibid, Minutes of the Committee of Safety of Wilmington, North Carolina, July 21, 1775, 948.

[20] Ibid, Minutes of the Committee of New Bern, North Carolina, August, 7, 1775, 1091.

free, and to arm them; but I told them negroes could not read proclamations, and that the Americans would march them back, and perhaps arm them all that they could trust: pray this matter before the Congress requesting the negroes; you know the great numbers in the Southern Provinces; if got in arms against you, it would much embarrass you. I told the gentlemen if the Ministry act in that way they would be worse than barbarians.[21]

The author of the letter must have been unaware that some blacks could read. Some slaves had been taught to read the Bible since many slave owners wanted their slaves to convert to Christianity. In some instances, slave owners used the Bible as a means to justify the peculiar institution itself. Although the literacy rate of blacks in colonial America was low, word of mouth spread quickly among slaves. Historian Sylvia Frey writes this was particularly true "in a period of history when written communication was still hindered by undependable mail service and a paucity of printers and publishers."[22] The slave community also possessed the ability to maintain their African oral tradition. Slaves and poor whites lived mostly in communal quarters comprising of ten or more people. Communication between them was very common, and in some cases, complex. Those slaves that were employed as attendants or musicians would relay the conversations they overheard to the other slaves.[23]

James Madison mentioned the possibility as far back as November 1774 when he referred to the possibility that the British would employ slaves to subdue the colonists. He conveyed his sentiments to William Bradford about the rumors spreading among the slaves that if they swarmed to the British they would be granted their freedom. Madison wrote:

---

[21] Force, *American Archives*, Fourth Series, Vol. 3, Extract of a Letter Received in Philadelphia, Date London, August 24, 1775, 256.
[22] Frey, *Water from the Rock*, (Princeton, NJ: Princeton University Press, 1992), 50.
[23] Ibid.

Alternate Contributions

If america & Britain should come to an hostile rupture I am afraid an Insurrection among the slaves may & will be promoted. In one of our Counties lately a few of those unhappy wretches met together & chose a leader who was to conduct them when the English Troops should arrive-which they foolishly thought would be very soon & that by revolting to them they should be rewarded with their freedom. Their Intentions were soon discovered & proper precautions taken to prevent the Infection. It is prudent such attempts should be concealed as well as suppressed.[24]

In September, John Adams wrote in his diary concerning a discussion he had with two delegates from Georgia. The delegates had told Adams that if a thousand regular British troops came to the shores of either South Carolina or Georgia they could easily take control of the South. All these troops would have to do is "proclaim freedom to all the Negroes" and "twenty thousand...would join it from the two provinces in a fortnight."[25] The delegates believed this event was unlikely, since "all the King's friends and tools of government have large plantations and property of Negroes; hence the slaves of the Tories would be lost, as well as those of the Whigs." Their assumption turned out to be wrong. Dunmore would announce his proclamation before notifying Parliament or the King. Dunmore believed it necessary that he take the initiative and act quickly. He had been waiting for instructions from the ministry, but, following the acclaim he received from Tories after his victory at Kemp's Landing, he had changed his mind.[26] Therefore the plan was not revealed to Parliament until it was too late to reverse it.

---

[24] Hutchinson, *The Papers of James Madison*, Vol. 1, To William Bradford, November 26, 1775, 130.

[25] *The Negro in the Military Service of the United States Collection*, Extract from a Diary of John Adams, September 24, 1775, an interview with Mr. Bullock and Mr. Houston of Georgia, Works of John Adams, Vol. 2, 428.

[26] Selby, *The Revolution in Virginia*, 64.

Irreconcilable Grievances

South Carolina was in as much dismay as Virginia over the possibility of slave revolts. Historian Robert A. Olwell compiled a strong case of how the issue of slavery drove South Carolina from a state of "disgruntled loyalty to one of militant rebellion."[27] Christopher Gadsden even described South Carolina as a "very weak Province...and [the] great part of our weakness (though at the same time tis part of our riches) consists in having such a number of slaves amongst us."[28] The colony's law required one white male for every twenty-five slaves, but the reality, in many localities, was there were but few white overseers. Consequently, the white colonists of South Carolina were in perpetual fear of slave insurrections due to their demographic makeup. The South Carolina Association would even list it as a reason for their martial action:

> The actual commencement of hostilities against this continent, by the British troops, in the bloody scene on the 19 of April last, near Boston-the increase of arbitrary impositions from a wicked and despotic ministry-and the dread of instigated insurrections in the colonies-are causes sufficient to drive an oppressed people to the use of arms...[29]

Throughout the eighteenth century, harsh penalties were handed out to any slaves who committed a violent crime or were convicted of plotting to revolt. In these instances, slaves were put to death in public spectacles. One slave woman, in 1769, was accused of poisoning her master. To set an example for her treachery, she was "burned at the stake on the Charleston green." Caesar, for trying to lead a group of runaway slaves, was hung,

---

[27] Robert A. Olwell, "Domestick Enemies: Slavery and Political Independence in South Carolina, May 1775-March 1776," *The Journal of Southern History*, Vol. 55, No. 1, (Feb., 1989), 21-48.
[28] Ibid, 22.
[29] W. Robert Higgins, "The Ambivalence of Freedom: Whites, Blacks, and the Coming of the American Revolution in the South," *The Revolutionary War in the South: Power, Conflict, and Leadership*, (Durham, NC: The Duke University Press, 1979), 63.

then placed in chains in the town for all the Negroes to view passing by. The ideology behind this form of Justice was that it would "deter other Negroes from committing such Insolencies and Crimes for the future."[30]

The problem the American Revolution posed to South Carolina slave owners actually threatened the entire South. It was thought that any animosity or division among whites might cause slaves to pursue their own self-interests. Any internal or external division severely hindered the white minority's ability to punish, so that a revolt might become an alternative for slaves to lash out against their masters. As political divisions developed between rebels and Tories, heightened fears developed over potential slave revolts or that "dissident whites might ally with blacks in order to gain power."[31] Their fears were realized when Peter Hinds, of Charleston, was accused of "entertaining and admitting Negro Preachers in his House and on his grounds, where they deliver doctrines to large Numbers of Negroes, dangerous to and subversive of the Peace, Safety, and Tranquility of this Province." Another resident wrote Charleston slaves "entertained ideas that the present contest [with Britain] was for obliging us to give them liberty." This belief was solidified once Arthur Lee's report from London was distributed throughout the colonies, informing them the Ministry might grant freedom to slaves who desert their masters. On May 29, the *South Carolina Gazette* printed an extract of a letter from London to which the author claimed:

> There is gone down to Sheerness, seventy-eight thousand guns and bayonets, to be sent to America, to put into the hands of [negroes], the Roman Catholics, the Indians and Canadians; and all the...means on earth used to subdue the Colonies.[32]

Whether or not the rumors were true did not matter. Once one rumor was proved false, another would arise, causing the cycle to

---

[30] Ibid, 24.
[31] Ibid, 26.
[32] Ibid, 29-30.

continually repeat. The case of a free black harbor pilot, Thomas Jeremiah, might have been caused by one of these rumors. Unfortunately for Jeremiah, he would not escape the death penalty. From the testimony of slaves he was found guilty of conspiring to arm slaves to fight against the rebels of South Carolina. Governor William Campbell was "convinced there was not the least ground" for his sentencing.[33] Even the court itself was reluctant to execute him, but the records do not show whether this was done because they truly felt Jeremiah was guilty or because it was a ploy to persuade him to name his accomplices. Governor Campbell sympathized with Jeremiah, since he, too, was falsely accused of conspiring to arm slaves against their masters. Upon the Governor's arrival, it was reported that 14,000 stands of arms were aboard his sloop, the *Scorpion*, to accomplish this task. Campbell expressed his compassion for Jeremiah when he wrote to Lord Dartmouth:

> Your Lordship will I am sure excuse myself to acquaint You, that Yesterday under the colour of Law, they hanged, & burned, an unfortunate Wretch, a free Negroe of considerable property, one of the most valuable, & useful Men in his way, in the Province, on suspicion of instigating an Insurrection, for which I am convinced there was not the least ground. I could not save him my Lord! The very reflection Hollow my Soul! I have only the comfort to think I left no means untried to preserve him.[34]

Governor Campbell wanted to revoke the sentence but knew if he did he "would raise a flame all the water in Cooper River could not extinguish." Once news of his feelings on the matter became public, it "raised such a clamor amongst the people as is incredible...they openly and loudly declared if I granted the man a

---

[33] United States, Naval History Division, *Naval Documents of the American Revolution*, Vol. 1, William Campbell to Lord Dartmouth, August 19, 1775, 1184.

[34] Ibid.

pardon they would hang him at my door."[35] Although the early expectation of a British slave alliance was unfounded with little to no evidence, it was dually shared by slaves and masters.[36] The calling up of the local militias, increased security measures, and the colonies' administration of justice would quell the fears of most colonists through the summer of 1775. Anything that could have been done to deter slaves from revolting had been initiated. A cloud would surround Governor Campbell until the day he fled aboard the *Tamar*. His desire to interfere in the Thomas Jeremiah case brought about a persisting fear he might "seek to ally himself with the low country whites' domestic rivals."[37]

Campbell's flight to the *Tamar* would have a strong effect on the slave population located within the vicinity of Charleston. Two governments were claiming to be the rightful protectors of the colony. There was the rebel government that controlled the continent, and the authority of the governor, that lay abreast within the harbor. Sullivan's Island was also within the control of the governor. The island had historically introduced blacks to the horrors of slavery upon their receipt from slave ships. Now it offered the complete opposite--freedom. It was around this time that Dunmore's Proclamation was issued. Whether it encouraged slaves to seek asylum on Sullivan's Island is unknown, since the South Carolina papers did not publish it. The *South Carolina Gazette* did publish a false account that Dunmore was selling slaves to the West Indies, therefore, meaning word of the proclamation most likely reached the colony at this time. By mid-December 1775, nearly 500 slaves had accumulated on Sullivan's Island.[38] The situation on the island not only threatened the Southern way of life, but armed parties of slaves were committing

---

[35] Olwell, "Domestick Enemies: Slavery and Political Independence in South Carolina, May 1775-March 1776," *The Journal of Southern History*, Vol. 55, No. 1, 38.
[36] Ibid, 34.
[37] Ibid, 39.
[38] Ibid, 42.

"several robberies and depredations" upon the colony.[39] As with other large slaveholding colonies, the threat of slave revolts would propel South Carolina towards independence. With no end to the conflict with the Mother Country in sight, the rebel governments could no longer afford a "prolonged challenge to their authority."[40] The time to establish good order had arrived.

Potential plots of slave insurrection had actually been a part of Britain's American policy and always a factor in the relations with her Southern colonies.[41] Just two weeks prior to Dunmore's Proclamation, October 26, 1775, William Henry Lyttleton, former governor of South Carolina (1755-1760) and of Jamaica (1760-1766), issued "a proposal for encouraging the negroes in that part of America to rise against their masters, and for sending some regiments to support and encourage them, in carrying the design into execution."[42] Since the "Southern Colonies...were weak, on account of the numbers of negroes in them," Lyttleton "intimated if a few regiments were sent there the negroes would rise, and embrue their hands in the blood of their masters."[43] A debate ensued until 4:30 A.M., but the motion was handily defeated by a vote of 278 to 108. The plan was thought of as being "too black, horrid and wicked to be heard of, much less adopted by a civilized people."[44] Lord North, during the debate over his Prohibitory Bill, reiterated the point when he declared "there never was any idea of raising or employing the negroes or Indians."[45] News of Dunmore's Proclamation was not the first account Parliament

---

[39] United States, Naval History Division, *Naval Documents of the American Revolution*, Vol. 3, Minutes of the South Carolina Council of Safety, December 16, 1775, 135.

[40] Olwell, "Domestick Enemies: Slavery and Political Independence in South Carolina, May 1775-March 1776," *The Journal of Southern History*, Vol. 55, No. 1, 48.

[41] Frey, *Water from the Rock*, 56.

[42] Ibid, 67.

[43] Force, *American Archives*, Fourth Series, Vol. 6, 21.

[44] Frey, *Water from the Rock*, 67.

[45] Force, *American Archives*, Fourth Series, Vol. 6, 187.

received regarding the employment of blacks. General Carleton's employing of blacks arrived in England roughly around the same time Dunmore was issuing his proclamation. Lord North assured Parliament that Carleton had only recruited them since "the Americans themselves had first applied to them."[46] This statement was correct since blacks had participated on the American side in every engagement until their temporary exclusion in October 1775. Even in this circumstance, blacks were allowed to finish their terms of enlistment until they were reinstated by Washington on December 31, 1775.

Slave soldiers would remain an issue of debate among British officials until informed of Dunmore's Proclamation. Once news reached England, it was not universally accepted.[47] Edmund Burke, a Member of Parliament, believed "horrible consequences might ensue from constituting 100,000 fierce barbarian slaves to be both judges and executioners of their masters."[48] Lord North, the British Prime Minister, believed "Dunmore's Proclamation should be tabled, awaiting further information and discussion."[49]

Proposals to arm slaves did not fair any better with many English citizens. Merchants and traders from London and Bristol condemned the idea.[50] The slave trade was centered from these ports, and in a petition they expressed "indignation and horror" at the idea of arming slaves against "our American brethren."[51] Raising slaves was deemed as an improper manner for carrying out the war. Despite slave labor applied in a military capacity having been common among European powers since the seventeenth century, its practice was only used in circumstances where shortages of manpower forced colonial nations to do so. Historical precedents for employing slaves in a military capacity reach as far back as ancient societies. These slaves, however,

---

[46] Ibid.
[47] Horton, *Slavery and the Making of America*, 59.
[48] Frey, *Water from the Rock*, 76.
[49] Horton, *Slavery and the Making of America*, 60.
[50] Frey, *Water from the Rock*, 69.
[51] Ibid.

played only a secondary or subordinate role. In these situations, the arming of slaves was only used in desperation. This was partly due to a fear that the slaves would turn their arms against their masters. It was also due to ideological factors. According to tradition, military duties were only to be prescribed to those of higher social status. The highest classes were given the most important obligations, while slaves were normally excluded from military service.[52]

Burke feared such an act "deeply wounded" Britain's national honor and dishonored "our character as people."[53] To him, the issue was a moot point since it is just "as hard to persuade slaves to be free as it is to compel freeman to be slaves."[54] In addition, would not "an offer of freedom from England would come rather oddly," since it was coming "from that very nation which has sold them to their present masters?"[55]

Parliament was also fearful of retaliation. What would prevent the Americans from marching the slaves back and arming all those they could trust? Burke warned "when we talk of enfranchisement, do we not perceive that the American master may enfranchise too; and arm servile hands in defense of freedom?"[56] Governor Johnstone expressed similar sentiments when he addressed the House of Lords regarding King George's speech declaring the Americans goal to be independence. Arming the slaves did not seem logical. He believed "Roman history fully confirms" the slaves' situation "rather strengthens fidelity and attachment" to their master. During the "corruptions of that Government, the slaves were seldom or ever unfaithful to his master," since the "principle lies in human nature."[57] Johnstone

---

[52] Ibid, 70.
[53] Force, *American Archives*, Fourth Series, Vol. 3, Extract of a Letter Received in Philadelphia, August 24, 1775, 256.
[54] Edmund Burke, *Speeches and Letters on American Affairs*, (London, England: J.M. Dent & Sons Ltd, 1956, 102-3.
[55] Ibid.
[56] Frey, *Water from the Rock*, 71.
[57] Ibid.

Alternate Contributions

added, "Where mankind are deprived of the means of getting subsistence, where they are accustomed to look up to another for food, raiment and protection, they insensibly forget the original injury they sustained and become attached to their master." "In general," he felt, "masters are kind to their slaves," and slaves "will not prove unfaithful" to "men of this temper." [58] His assumption was, however, wrong, since a substantial amount of slaves would, indeed, answer the call.

In all fairness to Dunmore, he was not deviating from the orders Lord Dartmouth had distributed to the governors of all the Southern colonies stating that the "most vigorous Efforts should be made, both by Sea & Land, to reduce his Rebellious Subjects to Obedience."[59] Governors Wright, Eden, Martin, and Dunmore had all received instructions to "exert every Endeavor & employ every means in your power to aid & support him [Thomas Gage] and Admiral Graves, in all such operations as they may think proper to undertake for carrying the King's orders into full execution, and restoring the Authority of his Majesty's Government."[60]

Dunmore's proclamation played an important factor in justifying the revolution, especially to those individuals who questioned whether the use of military force was the real answer. Sylvia Frey, author of *Water from the Rock: Black Resistance in a Revolutionary Age*, believes, "In the end the British strategy of manipulating conflict between the races became a rallying cry for white southern unity and impelled the South toward independence."[61] Count de Guines, writing from London, felt royal officials promoting slave rebellions would cause "an

---

[58] Force, *American Archives*, Fourth Series, Vol. 6, 29.

[59] United States, Naval History Division, *Naval Documents of the American Revolution*, Vol. 1, Lord Dartmouth to Lord Dunmore, July 5, 1775, 1312.

[60] Ibid, Lord Dartmouth to Josiah Martin, Lord Dunmore, Robert Eden, July 5 1775, 1310-1312.

[61] Frey, *Water from the Rock*, 45.

insurmountable obstacle to any conciliation."[62] Edward Rutledge believed that the Proclamation tended "more effectually to work an eternal separation between Great Britain and the Colonies...than any other expedient which could possibly been thought of."[63] Ralph Izard, in writing to Henry Laurens, believed the danger the Proclamation posed "should unite all our Countrymen...even those of the most discordant opinions."[64] Laurens felt a British policy of employing slaves as "What meanness! What complicated wickedness! Oh England, how changed! How fallen!"[65] Richard Henry Lee felt that "Lord Dunmore's unparalleled conduct in Virginia has, a few Scotch excepted, united every Man in that Colony. If Administration had searched thro the world for a person the best fetted to ruin their cause, and procure union and success for these Colonies, the could not have found a more complete Agent than Lord Dunmore."[66]

Archibald Cary wrote to Richard Henry Lee, "The Proclamation from Ld D[unmore] has had a most extensive good consequence--Men of all ranks resent the pointing a dagger to their throats, thro the hands of their Slaves--nothing cou'd be more unwise than a declaration of that nature which involved his friends as well as others in the general danger. We have, however, no apprehensions on that score--yet proper precautions will not be neglected."[67] Maryland thought Dunmore's Proclamation so

---

[62] United States, Naval History Division, *Naval Documents of the American Revolution*, Vol. 1, Count de Guines to Count de Vergennes, August 4, 1775.

[63] Quarles, *The Negro in the American Revolution*, Rutledge to Ralph Izard, December 8, 1775, 20 n. 3.

[64] Chesnutt, *The Papers of Henry Laurens*, Vol. 10, Henry Laurens to Ralph Izard, December 20, 1775, 578.

[65] Ibid, Vol. 2, Henry Laurens to John Laurens, August 14, 1776, 224.

[66] James Curtis Ballagh, *The Letters of Richard Henry Lee*, Vol. 1, (New York, NY: De Capo Press, 1970), Richard Henry Lee to Catherine Macaulay, November 29, 1775, 162.

[67] United States, Naval History Division, *Naval Documents of the American Revolution*, Vol. 3, Archibald Cary to Richard Henry Lee,

dangerous that all communication between Virginia and the colony was prohibited by "Land or Water."[68] A July 15, 1776 diary entry by Landon Carter shows just how much Dunmore was despised in Virginia. Carter was witnessing the illumination of the sky and queried, "What can be the Joy?" He knew there was no scheduled celebration but was certain "some great victory was obtained." He wondered whether "Clinton's defeat is true or it may be Dunmore killed in the late engagement…or it may be George 3d is [dead]."[69]

If Dunmore's Proclamation was so important, one might wonder, "Why did it not make the final draft of the Declaration of Independence?" There is no definitive answer as to why it did not, but historians have been left a few clues as to why such a grievance was not listed. David Hawke believes the debate of the charge "must have been long and rancorous."[70] Although the entire passage was struck, the opening clause of the twenty seventh charge carried on the charge, stating, "He has excited

---

December 24, 1775, 227.

[68] Ibid, Governor Eden to Lord Dartmouth, January 25, 1775, 981. On December 22, 1775, Dartmouth wrote to Eden, "it may have very important consequences to the colony under your government, and, therefore, you will do well to consider of every means by which you may, in conjunction with Lord Dunmore, give facility and assistance to its operations." From Eden's response on January 25, it can be inferred that Eden did not agree with the measures Dunmore had taken to free the slaves. Eden's letters were intercepted in April 1776. Although the Continental Congress and Charles Lee wanted the governor arrested, Maryland's Assembly hesitated because no evidence existed that Eden was collaborating with Dunmore. Their borders had, for the most part, been secure from the effects of the conflict with Great Britain. They saw no reason to arrest and usurp their current government "on suspicion only." For more, see Steiner, *Life and Administration of Sir Robert Eden*, 106-128.

[69] Jack P. Greene, *The Diary of Colonel Landon Carter of Sabine Hall, 1752-1778*, Vol. 2, (Charlottesville, VA: The University Press of Virginia, 1965), 1058.

[70] Hawke, *A Transaction of Free Men: The Birth and Course o the Declaration of Independence*, 192.

domestic insurrections amongst us." It was too controversial for many of the southern delegates (and for some contradictory, with their involvement in slavery), so they moved to have the word "slavery," and the charges of the institution itself stricken from the document. The indirect charge against King George III satisfied Jefferson. Although he had written the charge, Jefferson may have seen the error of his ways. To be specific on the charge "would have called attention to American slavery...an embarrassing topic whose keynote was human freedom."[71] What's more, the assertion that the *"Christian* King" of England was solely responsible for the slave trade was unwarranted. The contradiction between colonial principle and practice was easily recognizable. No one wanted to draw attention to the "persistence of the slave trade and to the anomaly of American slavery."[72]

The contradiction between the institution of slavery and the colonists' demands for freedom was recognized just months prior by the Virginia Convention. On May 15, 1776 they voted to prepare a Declaration of Rights "as will be most likely to maintain peace and good order in this colony."[73] George Mason's first draft stated "all men are born equally free and independent and have certain inherent natural Rights."[74] But Robert Carter Nicholas objected to the wording because it insinuated that freedom would also be granted to all the slaves. The statement implied their "black chattels were their political and social equals."[75] The issue would not be solved until the first week of June when it was

---

[71] Kaplan, "The "Domestic Insurrections" of the Declaration of Independence," *The Journal of Negro History*, 245.

[72] Maier, *American Scripture* 146-7.

[73] Tarter & Scribner, *Revolutionary Virginia: The Road to Independence*, Vol. 7, Part 1, Proceeding of the Ninth Day of Session, May 15, 1776, 143.

[74] Rutland, *The Papers of George Mason*, Vol. 1, First Draft of the Virginia Declaration of Rights, 277.

[75] Tarter & Scribner, *Revolutionary Virginia: The Road to Independence*, Vol. 7, Part 1, Proceedings of the Twentieth Day of Session, May 29, 1776, 302 n. 6.

decided it should read "all men are by nature equally free and independent of which they enter into a state of Society."[76] The proposal seemed to "admit the equality of all white men, while avoiding an admission of the equality of masters and slaves."[77] The words "state of Society" was interjected into the draft by Edmund Pendleton since "slaves being no part of the society to which the declaration applied and the masters having control over when those outside should enter."[78]

In Jefferson's notes on the passage of the Declaration of Independence, referred to the deleted passage:

[T]he clause too, reprobating the enslaving the inhabitants of Africa, was struck out in complaisance to South Carolina & Georgia, who had never attempted to restrain the importation of slaves, and who on the contrary still wished to continue it…our Northern brethren also I believe felt a little tender under those censures; for tho' their people have very few slaves themselves yet they had been pretty considerable carriers of them to others.[79]

The charge was probably too malicious for those delegates whom, even though they were voting on independence, still saw the probability of reconciliation. The Georgia and South Carolina delegates frowned upon Jefferson's attack on the slave trade but could not dispute the fact the British had been responsible for propagating slave revolts. It has been hypothesized the term "domestic insurrections" might have been referring to a Loyalist counter-revolution. Unfortunately, although there was also a widespread fear a loyalist uprising could occur at any moment, the revolutionary governments had effectively prohibited their

---

[76] Rutland, *The Papers of George Mason*, Vol. 1, Final Draft of the Virginia Declaration of Rights, 287.

[77] Tarter & Scribner, *Revolutionary Virginia: The Road to Independence*, Vol. 7, Part 2, Proceedings of the Thirty Second Day of Session, June 12, 1776, 454 n. 16.

[78] Ibid, taken from memo of H. Carrington, September 9, 1851.

[79] Boyd, *The Papers of Thomas Jefferson*, Vol. 1, 314-315.

organization. Through verbal and physical threats, legislation, economic blackmail, property infringement, propaganda, and even the sentence of death, revolutionary interim governments had checked Tory unification. Sidney Kaplan believes the "domestic insurrections" charge was "an indictment of the monarch for stirring up an enslaved and an oppressed people to seek their freedom from freedom-seeking revolutionaries, the Declaration is perhaps doubly flawed."[80]

Kaplan's assertion is well supported when examining the declarations of independence from states and localities. In North Carolina's instructions to their delegates regarding independence, one of their grievances state, "That Governors in different Colonies have declared protection to slaves who should imbrue their hands in the blood of their masters."[81] Charlotte County, Virginia, informed its delegates of Britain's "likewise encouraging, by every means in their power, our savage neighbors, and our more savage domesticks."[82] Maryland listed "slaves" as being "proclaimed free, enticed away, trained and armed against their lawful masters" as a reason for autonomy.[83] By contrast, none of the northern colonies, or their localities, which contained considerably low slave populations, would list slave insurrections as a grievance to the British Crown. This gives us another possible reason to explain why Jefferson's first draft on the grievance was struck from the Declaration of Independence.

---

[80] Kaplan, "The "Domestic Insurrections" of the Declaration of Independence," *The Journal of Negro History*, 253.
[81] Force, *American Archives,* Fourth Series, Vol. 5, 860.
[82] Ibid, 1034.
[83] Force, *American Archives*, Fourth Series, Vol. 6, 1018.

Part Three:

Fire From The Sea

Chapter Six

The Most Horrid Devastations Upon the Country

This is savage and Barbarous in the highest stage...What more can we want to Justifie any Step to take, Kill, and destroy, to refuse them any refreshments, to Apprehend our Enemies, to Confiscate their Goods and Estates, to Open our Ports to foreigners, and if practicable to form Alliances.
James Warren to John Adams, October 20-22, 1775

    The British war from the sea was a strong contributing factor in swaying the Continental Congress towards independence. Although the disruption of colonial commerce helped to form the rebels' organized political resistance, it had only a minute effect on the decision to seek full-fledged independence. It was the British bombardment of coastal towns during the first year of the conflict that swayed public opinion to the revolutionaries' side. The tales of this alleged barbarity circulated throughout the colonies, portraying the British as oppressors from the sea and the rebels as protectors of freedom.

    The impact of the British Navy on American independence is evident since it is featured in many of the colonies' grievances against the throne. It was also documented in a multitude of state and local declarations of independence, including Jefferson's Congressional draft. North Carolina's delegates charged "that the British Fleets and Armies have been, and still are, daily employed in destroying the people, and committing the most horrid devastations upon the country," and the "ships belonging to America are declared prizes of war...many of them...violently seized and confiscated."[1]

    The Virginia Convention considered the British Navy's

---

[1] Force, *American Archives*, Fourth Series, Vol. 5, 860.

"piratical and savage warfare" as a reason for their desire for "total separation from...Great Britain."[2] The Connecticut Assembly charged the ministry with invading the "said Colonies with fleets and armies, to destroy our towns" and "shed the blood of our countrymen."[3] It was seeing their "towns plundered, burnt, and destroyed" that convinced Charles County, Maryland to vote for separation.[4] New York accused the British Navy of burning "[our] towns, seizing our vessels, and murdering our precious sons of liberty," and wrote that New Yorkers would "not become their slaves."[5]

Judge William Henry Drayton even included the actions of the British Navy in his infamous address to the Grand Jury of Charleston, South Carolina. He felt the "ruins of Charlestown, Falmouth, and Norfolk (towns not constructed for offence or defence), mark the humane progress of the Royal arms," and compared it to the ruins of "Carthage, Corinth, and Numantium," which "proclaimed to the world that justice was expelled from the Roman Senate!"[6]

The British Navy's main strategy had been to prevent the importation of supplies to the colonies. Lord Dartmouth believed "Conquest by land is unnecessary, when the country can be reduced first by distress and then to obedience by our Marine totally interrupting all commerce and fishery, and even seizing all the ships in the ports, with very little expense and less bloodshed."[7] The Ministry particularly wanted to limit the importation of any supplies that could be used for war. As early as October 1774, Dartmouth called for the "most effectual measures for arresting, detaining, and securing Gunpowder, or any sorts of Arms or Ammunition which may be attempted to be imported into the Province" of Massachusetts.[8]

---

[2] Force, *American Archives*, Fourth Series, Vol. 6, 461.
[3] Ibid, 867-68.
[4] Ibid, 1018.
[5] Ibid, 614-15.
[6] Force, *American Archives*, Fourth Series, Vol. 5, 1027.
[7] Allen, *A Naval History of the American Revolution*, Vol. 1, 19.
[8] Selby, *Revolutionary Virginia*, 19, Lord Dartmouth to American

The Most Horrid Devastations Upon the Country

King George and his advisors were also concerned with the colonies being supplied with arms by either the French or Spanish. If the British Navy could prohibit all forms of illicit munitions trade, it was believed the rebel army might not have enough military provisions to last the winter. Lord Dartmouth instructed each colony's royal governor to take the necessary measures to prevent military stores and provisions from reaching the hands of rebel armies. Thomas Gage, Lord Dunmore, Josiah Martin, and Robert Eden all took what actions they could to adhere to this order.

However, Vice Admiral Samuel Graves, headquartered in Boston, had little success in implementing the Ministry's plans. In May 1775, he admitted, "I am extremely mortified that notwithstanding [the fact that] the King's Ships and Vessels have been very active this Winter, no seizures of any Consequence have been made."[9]

Although initially the main mission of the British Navy was to halt illicit gunpowder and munitions traffic, it served other purposes as well. One of the Coercive Acts called for the prevention of all commerce, both to and from Boston harbor. Once the British learned that the rebellion extended past the colony of Massachusetts, they needed to take measures to prevent other coastal towns from supplying and aiding the rebel cause. Not only were many of these port towns aiding the enemy, but in many cases, they were going to great lengths to prevent the re-supply of British vessels. This is significant since the British Navy received most of their military supplies from the mother country, but relied upon the colonies' port towns for fresh provisions and water. This made the British Navy an essential part in the survival of the British Army in Boston. Gage even wrote to Dartmouth he had to "depend on them for our Subsistence."[10]

Governors, October 19, 1774.
[9] Neil R. Stout, *The Royal Navy in America 1760-1775*, (Annapolis, MD: Naval Institute Press, 1973), 162-63.
[10] Carter, *The Correspondence of General Thomas Gage with the Secretaries of State, and with the War Office and the Treasury*, Vol. 1, Thomas Gage to Lord Dartmouth, 1775, 403.

Irreconcilable Grievances

Ironically, the coastal towns upon which the British forces so heavily relied had become havens for rebels seeking to collect intelligence about British troop movements and plans. This task was made particularly easy for the rebels since the only British garrison in the colonies, through 1775 and up to March 1776, had been Boston. No other large troop garrisons had been established. With only one harbor properly defended, the British military commanders were limited in how far they could reach into the interior of the continent without overextending their already thin lines. Reinforcing Boston was definitely not the answer either. The Continental Army, although poorly equipped and manned, had led the British to believe a frontal attack on Charlestown Neck would be futile. Thus, the British began to consider other locations for attack.

To curb the burgeoning colonial resistance, the refusal to adhere to British demands, and sporadic fire from coastal towns, Vice-Admiral Graves began to recommend to his subordinate naval officers a more ruthless form of warfare. Graves ordered Lieutenant Henry Mowat to "lay waste burn and destroy such Seaport Towns as are accessible to his Majesty's Ships."[11]

Graves took command of the North American station in July 1774 when Admiral John Montagu was relieved of his duties. Graves' mission was far from simple. He had been charged with preventing the "landing and discharging, lading or shipping, of goods, wares, and merchandise" in Boston as a means to cripple

---

[11] United States, Naval History Division, *Naval Documents of the American Revolution*, Vol. 2, Vice Admiral Samuel Graves to Lieutenant Henry Mowat, October 6, 1775, 324. This coupled with the other naval tribulations has caused many American historians to label Graves a poor administrator, lacking both organization and honor. William Fowler wrote Graves "was not a man, and to him must be assigned a generous share of the blame for the Navy's lackluster performance." William Fowler, *Rebels Under Sail: The American Navy During the Revolution*, (New York, NY: Charles Scribner's Sons, 1976), 31. In actuality, Graves, like Thomas Gage and subsequent military commanders within the American colonies, were ill equipped and informed to accomplish the mission set forth by their superiors.

Massachusetts' economy.[12] Graves knew the tasks in front of him were difficult since "notwithstanding the utmost attention I find that our Numbers are too few to guard all the small Channels, and that many Vessels pass unseen and supply the Town and neighborhood with smuggled and other Goods..."[13]

How was Graves expected to accomplish these tasks? He lacked adequate supplies, was short on able-bodied seamen, and most importantly, was forced to operate with little to no direction from the ministry. The British Navy or Army had never been trained to respond to the types of situations they encountered in Boston and throughout the colonies. Internal colonial disputes fueled by guerilla tactics were a far cry from a battle at sea. Moreover, the Navy had strict guidelines regarding the engagement of enemy ships, but there were no directions regarding the types of conflict Graves faced. In short, Graves was doing the best he could with that which he was outfitted. Early in the conflict he was "equally desirous in chastising the Rebels," but could only "heartily wish" he was "empowered to act."[14]

In September 1774, he conveyed his belief that "an effectual interposition of Military Power" was "the only means left to restore these deluded people to the right Use of their reason."[15] During the Battle of Lexington and Concord, Graves expressed a desire to use his fleet to harass the towns believed to be the center of the rebellion, but such words were more likely propagated by

---

[12] John Andrew Tilley, *The Royal Navy in North America, 1774-1781: A Study in Command*, Unpublished Dissertation, (Columbus, OH: The Ohio State University, 1980), 32.

[13] Ibid, 34.

[14] United States, Naval History Division, *Naval Documents of the American Revolution*, Vol. 1, Vice Admiral Samuel Graves to Captain James Wallace, May 19, 1775, 363. Graves was not the first naval officer to make such comments. In late 1774, Captain James Wallace had stated, "I hope in God," to Admiral Graves, "to make them pay dear for their frolick." Wallace was writing since he was frustrated over repeated attempts to capture his ship, the *Rose*. See Steiner, *The Royal Navy In America 1760-1775*, 163.

[15] Tilley, *The Royal Navy in North America*, 40.

frustration over that day's events than anything else.[16] He actually teetered on the idea of using force. In multiple instances, he hoped to be given the opportunity to use his power to make the rebels "just and obedient." Although a sufficient amount of evidence confirms this, Graves still seemed to have persistent doubts about executing such a plan without being compelled to do so by a higher authority.[17]

It was not until October 4, 1775 that Graves received the orders he had been waiting for, "upwards of four months at his own peril."[18] The home government authorized the seizure of colonial merchant vessels, permitting him to "employ to the full such power as his little fleet might exercise."[19] They stated that Graves could "carry on such operations upon the sea coasts of the four governments in New England as he should just most proper for suppressing the rebellion now openly avowed and supported in those colonies."[20] Lastly, he was ordered that:

> All such Seaport towns as were accessible to the kings ships that if any violences should hereafter be offered therein to officers of the Crown or peaceably disposed subjects, or bodies of men raised & armed or military works erected, or attempts made to seize or destroy the public magazine of

---

[16] Ibid, 134.
[17] Yerxa, *Admiral Samuel Graves and the Falmouth Affair*, 106-07.
[18] United States, Naval History Division, *Naval Documents of the American Revolution*, Vol. 2, Narrative of Vice Admiral Graves, October 4, 1775, 292-3. These orders were dated July 6, 1775. Donald Yerxa asserts Graves was initially influenced in bombarding the coastal towns due to the pressures from superiors such as Lord Sandwich. This is inaccurate. These dispatches were dated July 30 and August 25 respectfully. This means they would have arrived with the July 6 orders or some time after. It was the orders from the Lord Commissioners of the Admiralty that primarily influenced Graves. Yerxa, *Admiral Samuel Graves and the Falmouth Affair*, 104-05.
[19] W.M. James, *The British Navy in Adversity: A Study of the War of American Independence*, (New York, NY: Longmans, Green and Co. Ltd., 1926), 30-1.
[20] United States, Naval History Division, *Naval Documents of the American Revolution*, Vol. 1, July 6, 1775, 292.

The Most Horrid Devastations Upon the Country

arms ammunition or other stores, it would be the duty of the commanders of each of the Squadrons after such signification to proceed by the most vigourous methods against the said town as in open rebellion.[21]

Graves was essentially following these orders when he wrote Henry Mowat:

My Design is to chastize Marblehead, Salem, Newbury Port, Cape Anne Harbour, Portsmouth, Ipswich, Saco, Falmouth in Casco Bay, and particularly Mechias where the *Margueritta* was taken, the Officer commanding her killed, and the People made Prisoners, and where the *Diligent* Schooner was seized and the Officers and Crew carried Prisoners up the Country, and where preparations I am informed are now making to invade the Province of Nova Scotia.[22]

According to Graves, the New England port towns had "been daring enough to make Seizures of several of his Majesty's Ships and Vessels...and also have fired upon killed and wounded many of the Kings Subjects serving on board his Majesty's Ships...and of their determination to cut off and destroy his Majesty's Subjects serving in his Fleet and Army whenever it is in their Power."[23]

The colonists viewed Graves as a tyrant; ironically, many of his

---

[21] United States, Naval History Division, *Naval Documents of the American Revolution*, Vol. 2, Narrative of Vice Admiral Graves, October 4, 1775, 292-3.

[22] Ibid, Vice Admiral Samuel Graves to Lieutenant Henry Mowat, October 6, 1775, 324.

[23] Ibid. Graves was referring to many events different many coastal towns, but he wanted Mowat to first pay a visit to Gloucester, MA. Preceding his orders to "chastise" the New England port towns, Graves wrote, "that town having fired in the month of August last upon his Majesty's Sloop Falcon, wounded her people, and taken many prisoners; you are to burn, destroy and lay waste the said town together with all vessels and craft in the harbour that cannot with ease be brought away." Ibid; Also see Joseph E. Garland, *The Fist and the Falcon: Gloucester's Resolute Role in America's Fight for Freedom*, (Charleston, SC: History Press, 2006), 128.

superiors in England and fellow administrators in the colonies saw him as incompetent.[24] His removal, like most commanders who were replaced in the American colonies, was probably unwarranted. He was improperly equipped, exposed to warfare techniques more befitting pirates and guerillas than British gentlemen, and only received instructions from superiors once the instructions were no longer pertinent. The distance intelligence had to travel to England and back severely hindered British commanders' ability to effectively fight the war. Historians of the American Revolution often pinpoint this as one of the key reasons the rebels won. While Graves and Gage waited an average of two months for a response to their dispatches, George Washington only had to wait two weeks, at most, for guidance from the Continental Congress.

The leaders of the revolutionary movement felt Graves' conduct served as just another indication that England was attempting to subjugate the colonies to a state of slavery. How could reconciliation be worked out if the British government was practicing total war against its very own people? Viewing the situation from the rebels' perspective, it is easy to see why a push towards independence seemed imperative.

What frustrated the British the most was not that the rebels made them look foolish, but that many of the port towns were acting under a cloak of secrecy. Until October, when the order was issued to bombard New England port towns, many localities' governments disavowed any involvement in aiding the rebel movement. Graves was well aware of what was truly transpiring. He wrote to Captain Andrew Barkley, "I can draw no other Conclusion that the…People are as perfectly disposed for Rebellion as those of Massachusetts Bay, and that they will endeavor by force or stratagem to drive you or destroy you."[25]

At first, the rebellion was thought to have been limited to

---

[24] James, *The British Navy in Adversity: A Study of the War of American Independence*, 32.
[25] United States, Naval History Division, *Naval Documents of the American Revolution*, Vol. 1, Vice Admiral Samuel Graves to Captain Andrew Barkley, June 23, 1775, 742.

The Most Horrid Devastations Upon the Country

Massachusetts. The British leadership had been naïve to the possibility that thirteen different colonies could unite in a common cause. Their reasoning made sense since the home government often had to mediate disputes between the colonies over territories and trading, but their assumption was wrong. Following the events of Lexington and Concord, the New England colonies were able to mobilize quickly, putting Graves and Gage at a huge disadvantage. Colonial port towns' commercial vessels were quickly retrofitted into men-of-war to limit British military operations, as well as prevent the re-supply of the Redcoats stationed in Canada and Boston.

An example of this occurred at Conanicott, Rhode Island. Captain James Wallace, whom some historians have inaccurately accused of terrorizing the coast, had stationed his small fleet in the area because he "had information of this Colony's fitting out Arm'd Vessels from Providence to attack the King's Ships." Wallace split his two-sloop force "out different ways to reconnoitre" the Narragansett Bay.[26] Unfortunately a rebel armed sloop took advantage, being equipped with "50 Men and Carriage Guns and a dozen swivels" and met the crew of the *Rose*.[27] An engagement ensued just before sunset with the two ships exchanging fire for nearly an hour. Although the exchange did not damage either vessel, another rebel armed sloop approached the British man-of-war from its rear, pinning it in between two fields of fire. The engagement lasted another half hour until "By Accident the Swivel Catrages" exploded and "the musquet catridges near expended."[28] As a result, the British man-of-war ran ashore at Conanicott, with the Captain and his crew fleeing for their lives. For a whole day, the British sailors hid on the island until they attempted a bold escape. The men had convinced a ferryboat man they were fisherman, but after "sailing some Distance seized the ferryman, took helm and came round the So.

---

[26] Ibid, Captain James Wallace to Vice Admiral Samuel Graves, June 19, 1775, 720.
[27] Ibid, Diary of Ezra Stiles, June 15, 1775, 686.
[28] Ibid, Journal of His Majesty's Ship *Rose*, Captain James Wallace, June 16, 1775, 695.

End of Conanicott to the Men o' War."²⁹

The British and rebel accounts regarding the incident are vastly different. As will be seen with each of these events, the rebels left out pertinent details in their accounts, in all probability to convince undecided colonists of the worthiness of their cause. Propaganda was masterfully utilized by the rebel leadership. Newspapers that sympathized with the British, portraying them in any other light than dastardly villains, were shut down by rebel mobs. Only two loyalist presses were published through the majority of the war, leaving most colonists to gather their information purely from rebel sources.

In the case of the incident at Conanicott, the *Providence Gazette* reported the British tender was already "piratically seized and detained by Capt. Wallace" and "was...in Quest of Plunder, as usual." It was the British who came in contact with "an armed sloop, fitted out by the Colony for the Protection of its Trade, whose Commander not answering in a Tone sufficiently submissive, was fired upon by the Tender; the Compliment was returned with such Effect as to put the Pirates into some Confusion."[30] The *Pennsylvania Evening Post* also reported that upon the rebels aboard the ship "not answering in a tone sufficiently submissive, was fired upon."[31] The *Newport Mercury* stated Wallace was "obliged to turn tail [to] while the *Rose* was "probably...delivered to her proper owner." The same publication reported that one of the men-of-war fired "a number of musket-balls...into the town, one of which entered a closet window of a house on Gravelly-point...by which one or two persons narrowly escaped being killed or wounded."[32]

The British witness account is much different. Savage Gardner reported the *Rose* was hailed by the rebel sloop, which "told Us to bring to or she would sink Us immediately and directly fired a shot

---

[29] Ibid, Diary of Ezra Stiles, June 16, 1775, 695.
[30] United States, Naval History Division, *Naval Documents of the American Revolution*, Vol. 1, *Providence Gazette*, June 17, 1775, 705.
[31] Ibid, Extract of a Letter from Newport, Dated Monday, June 19, 1775, *Pennsylvania Evening Post*, July 1, 1775, 723.
[32] Ibid, *Newport Mercury*, June 19, 1775, 722.

which we returned with Small Arms and Swivels and kept a smart fire on both Sides for near half an hour." Upon Gardner's running the *Rose* ashore, the British sailors were pursued by "a Number of Men from the Vessels of whale Boats who closely pursued and fired at" the men. The terrified sailors thought it necessary to "separate and conceal" themselves until "a proper Opportunity offered of joining the Ship which was accomplished the next day without the loss of one Man."[33]

It is significant that what really happened at Conanicott was only known by the individuals who were involved. The colonists were led to believe whatever the rebels wanted them to know. Abraham Whipple's testimony stating "...the first Shot was fired on Water in defiance of the British Flag" was inaccurate.[34] The first shot fired "in defiance of the British" was fired four days before in Machias.

But the act of rebellion that infuriated Graves the most was unquestionably the saga of the *Margaretta*. It was the only event Graves described in detail to Henry Mowat when he gave the order authorizing the "chastising" of the coast.

Captain James Moore, in charge of the *Margaretta*, had orders from Graves to "take under your Convoy the five Vessels belonging to Mr. Ichabod Jones...and proceed with them to Mechias, where you are to remain for their Protection."[35] Jones had been commissioned by Gage to supply the Boston garrison with fuel and lumber. Such a measure had to be taken since word had leaked out that the rebels planned to destroy Jones' supply vessels.

Much like many New England port towns, Machias was short on provisions, especially since they were active participants in the Association, which forbade the import of any British goods and export of any colonial goods to England. Machias deviated from this and caved in to Gage, opting to allow Jones to supply the

---

[33] Ibid, Mr. Savage Gardner's Report to Captain James Wallace, 721-2.
[34] Ibid, note 2, Abraham Whipple's petition.
[35] United States, Naval History Division, *Naval Documents of the American Revolution*, Vol. 1, Vice Admiral Samuel Graves to James Moore, 537.

British with fuel and lumber in exchange for unnamed but apparently acutely-needed provisions. The town's inhabitants assembled on June 6 and "seemed so averse to the measures proposed" that Jones allegedly had the *Margaretta* anchored so close to the town "that her Guns would reach the Houses." It was under this duress that Jones allegedly attempted to "proceed in his Business as usual without molestation," allowing the town's individuals to "purchase the provisions brought into the place and pay him according to Contract." What moved the inhabitants to retaliate, according to Chairman James Lyons, was that Jones "distributed his provisions among those only, who voted in favour of his carrying Lumber to Boston." Lyons testified:

> This gave such offence to the aggrieved party, that they determined to take Capt Jones, if possible, & put a final stop to his supplying the kings troops with any thing; Accordingly, they secretly invited the people of Mispecka & Pleasant River to join them.[36]

This threat was acted upon, forcing Jones to hide in the woods, fearing for his life, unable to be located by the inhabitants of the town. Jones was not the only person sought out by the rebels that day. Captain Moore and Mr. Stillinsfleet had been ashore at the meeting house, attending the Sunday morning service, when Moore heard "a Bustle, looked out of the Window & saw a Number of People Armed making towards the House."[37] Luckily for the both of them, they were able to make their escape to the *Margaretta*.

Up to this point, the incident as described by both sides is relatively consistent. Now, however, it splits into two widely divergent tales. According to the rebel James Lyons, Moore then sent an express to the inhabitants of Machias, stating that "he had…orders to protect Capt Jones; that he was determined to do his duty whilst he had life; & that, if the people presumed to stop

---

[36]

[37] Ibid, Pilot Nathaniel Godfrey's Report of Action Between the Schooner *Margueritta* and the Rebels at Machias, June 11, 1775, 655. Tilley, *The Royal Navy in North America, 1774-1781*, 87.

The Most Horrid Devastations Upon the Country

Capt Jones's vessels, he would burn the Town."[38] Jabez Cobb gave similar testimony, stating, "Capt Moore replied he would defend his Vessel as long as he lived and would fire on the Town...unless they desisted and delivered up Jones's Vessel."[39] The information distributed throughout the colonies was to this effect. John Thaxter wrote to John Adams, "the tender threatned instant Demolition to the Town if there was not immediate Resignation of them."[40]

This was vastly different from the British account. According to pilot Nathaniel Godfrey, the *Margaretta* was told to "strike to the Sons of Liberty" and turn over Ichabod Jones. Upon Moore's refusal, later that evening, the rebels overtook one of Jones' provision vessels. Moore attempted to retake the vessel, but "was hailed on Shore by the Rebels, once more desiring him to strike to the Sons of Liberty, threatening him with Death if he resisted."[41] Moore had not even replied to the threat when the mob fired a volley of small arms, which was returned with "Swivels and Small Arms." Thomas Flinn gives an identical account, stating, "they first Desired Capt Moore to strike to the sons of Liberty and come on shore; but on his refusing they fired upon him and he Return'd it."[42]

Failing to capture the *Margaretta* in their first attempt, the rebels decided to load a number of men aboard boats and canoes in an attempt to surprise the British crew in the middle of the night. The rebels' plan was soon discovered and they were "beat off by a brisk fire...and obliged to quit their Boats."[43] The rebel account

---

[38] Ibid, James Lyons, Chairman of the Machias Committee, To the Massachusetts Provincial Congress, June 14, 1775, 676.
[39] Ibid, Deposition of Jabez Cobb Regarding the Loss of the Schooner *Margaretta*, June 26, 1775, 757.
[40] Ibid, John Thaxter to John Adams, June 28, 1775, 768.
[41] Ibid, Pilot Nathaniel Godfrey's Report of Action Between the Schooner *Margueritta* and the Rebels at Machias, June 11, 1775, 655.
[42] Ibid, Deposition of Thomas Flinn, Master of the *Falmouth Packet*, July 10, 1775, 848.
[43] Ibid, Pilot Nathaniel Godfrey's Report of Action Between the Schooner *Margueritta* and the Rebels at Machias, June 11, 1775, 655.

states the men had rowed to the *Margaretta* in order to demand her surrender. If this was truly their intent, the British were inclined to believe otherwise. Assuming that a rebel mob ran one of their supply vessels ashore, instigating an hour-long engagement, why would they now send armed men sneaking over in the middle of the night to politely request the British vessel's surrender? The situation would not have made sense to any military commander. It was at this point a British sailor allegedly cried "fire and be damn'd" and the crew of the *Margaretta* immediately discharged their firearms upon the men in the small boats.

The rebels were beaten back once again, but they would have the last laugh. Early the next morning, the mob was able to seize two vessels, allowing them to pursue the *Margaretta*. In response, Moore and his crew retreated down the river, constructing wooden barricades aboard to protect themselves from small arms fire as they sailed. During the passage they were "continually fired at from the Shore" until a sudden gust of wind caused them to run aground on a sandbank.

The rebels, once again, told the crew to "strike to the Sons of Liberty," this time promising to treat them well, but if any resistance was attempted, "they [would] put us to Death."[44] Moore "seeing there was no possibility of getting clear" decided to engage the rebels. He "threw some Hand Grenades" and ordered his men to board the rebel ship. The move would prove fatal, for Moore would receive "two Balls, one in his right Breast, the other in his Belly." He was carried to Machias for medical attention, which would prove futile. When he was asked "why he did not strike when they hailed him," Moore replied, "he preferred Death before yielding to such a sett of Villians."[45] The British would lose not only Moore but five marines. The rebels only lost Robert Avery, killed by a ball in the head. Their casualties were limited since they too had built breastworks in their vessels, screening

---

[44] Ibid. Tilley, *The Royal Navy in North America, 1774-1781*, 88.

[45] United States, Naval History Division, *Naval Documents of the American Revolution*, Vol. 1 Pilot Nathaniel Godfrey's Report of Action Between the Schooner *Margueritta* and the Rebels at Machias, June 11, 1775, 655.

them from any enemy fire.

The killing of Captain Moore elated the rebel cause. The end result did not surprise John Thaxter when he wrote, "our Men, as usual, proved victorious."[46] In the end the inhabitants of Machias would capture "three Tenders, and two Sloops taken from Jones...28 prisoners," one of which was "Old Ichabod Jones."[47]

The death of six men in the *Margaretta* skirmish infuriated Graves. Not only was it an embarrassment to the mightiest navy in the world, but solidified Graves' belief that the rebellion was not limited to Massachusetts Bay. The Admiral felt an example should be made of the rebels once he received orders permitting him to do so.

The rebels' attempts to withhold needed provisions from the British were not limited to sea operations. On land, rebels worked in unison, moving cattle away from the coast and burning agricultural stores. One such incident occurred at Grape Island.[48] In May 1775, a contingent of 300 British troops landed there to forage supplies. The island's inhabitants feared the troops were going to march upon the town, but in fact their mission was only to procure hay. Lacking boats, the local rebel contingent could not stop this from occurring, but their small arms fire prevented "their getting [any] more than 3 ton of Hay." Later when the rebels were able to access the island, they set fire to the barn, relegating "80 ton tis said" to the flames.[49]

On Deer Island, the rebels partook in an expedition to recover 500 sheep that were in British hands. They accomplished their mission, taking nine prisoners to boot.[50] Abigail Adams wrote to her husband, John, about a "little Expidition" to Long Island. Captain Benjamin Tupper had gathered 300 men on whale boats to

---

[46] Ibid, John Thaxter to John Adams, June 28, 1775, 768.

[47] Taylor, *Papers of John Adams*, Vol. 3, James Warren to John Adams, August 9, 1775, 114.

[48] Allen, *A Naval History of the American Revolution*, Vol. 1, 4-6.

[49] L.H. Butterfield, *Adams Family Correspondence*, Vol. 1, (Cambridge, MA: The Belknap Press, 1963), Abigail Adams to John Adams, May 24, 1775, 204.

[50] Ibid, Eunice Paine to Abigail Adams, June 4, 1775, 210-11.

bring off "70 odd Sheep, 15 head of cattle, and 16 prisoners, 13 of whom were sent by Simple Sapling to mow the Hay which they had very badly executed." The rebels operated under cover of night, undetected by their enemies. The next night 125 men revisited the island in order to "set fire to the Buildings and Hay." The fire alarmed the British men-of-war nearby, who then surrounded the rebels with "bullets flying in every direction."[51] As the rebels fled, the British continued to fire upon them, killing one of their men, Mr. Clarke of Stoughton.

On July 18, at Nantasket, Massachusetts, a similar incident occurred when a party of rebel soldiers were employed to land on Long Island and strip it of all its ripe grain. They did not stop there, returning the next evening to set fire to the lighthouse. The fire alerted nearby British men-of-war, who chased the rebels back to Nantasket. "A Hot Fire" ensued between the sides for nearly an hour as the rebels tried to draw the British on shore, but "the men-of-Wars-men seem'd evidently afraid to come near them; and at last put off so as to be out of the reach of our Musquetts."[52] The lack of an immediate British reprisal led Abigail Adams to believe "they will burn the Town down as soon as our forces leave it."[53] The British did take immediate measures to repair the lighthouse, but on July 31 the rebel Captain Tupper would take his turn raiding the island, wrecking it again and capturing a detachment of British Marines.[54]

The first New England town to be bombarded by British warships was Charlestown during the Battle of Bunker Hill. Prior to this, few thought the British capable of committing such acts. That event changed everything. Revolutionary leaders now presumed retaliation upon the coasts could occur at any moment. The town of Malden, Massachusetts included the incident as a reason to "support and defend" Congress if they chose to declare America "a free and independent Republick." Their declaration of independence stated the "defenceless towns have been attacked

---

[51] Ibid, Abigail Adams to John Adams, July 16, 1775, 248.
[52] Ibid, Richard Cranch to John Adams, July 24, 1775, 258-9.
[53] Ibid, Abigail Adams to John Adams, July 25, 1775, 261.
[54] Ibid, Richard Cranch to John Adams, July 24, 1775, 258-9, note 1.

The Most Horrid Devastations Upon the Country

and destroyed; the ruins of Charlestown, which are daily in our view, daily remind us of this."[55] John Adams wrote, "every Year brings us fresh Evidence, that We have nothing to hope for from our loving Mother Country, but Cruelties more abominable than those which are practiced by the Savage Indians."[56] Cotton Tuft, following Charlestown's burning, described the British as "those Vermin that float on the Watre and spit out their Venom, Fire and Rage at us."[57]

The events leading up to and including Charlestown led Mercy Otis Warren to comment that the seas are "being made Miserable by the Depredations of the once formidable Navy of Briton Now Degraded to a level with the Corsairs of Barbary."[58] The revolutionaries believed the British set fire to Charlestown in retaliation for the colonists' opposition to British tyranny. Just days before, on June 12, Gage's Proclamation had been issued, offering "his most gracious pardon to all persons who shall forthwith lay down their arms, and return to the duties of peaceable subjects."[59] The rebels thought that Charlestown's destruction was due to their refusal to accede to Gage's demand and his declaration of martial law. The Redcoats' grim situation within the Boston Neck even caused Abigail Adams to predict, "Necessity will oblige Gage to take some desperate steps."[60] The revolutionaries' view that British set fire to Charlestown in a spirit of retaliation was false. Regardless, it was firmly believed in revolutionary circles and was a strong rallying cry in the call for independence a year later.

Following Lexington and Concord, Admiral Graves had

---

[55] Force, *American Archives*, Fourth Series, Vol. 6, 603.
[56] Butterfield, *Adams Family Correspondence*, Vol. 1, John Adams to Abigail Adams, July 1, 1775, 241.
[57] Ibid, Cotton Tufts to John Adams, July 3, 1775, 235.
[58] Taylor, *The Papers of John Adams*, Vol. 3, From Mercy Otis Warren, July 5, 1775, 56.
[59] Vaughn, *Chronicles of the American Revolution,* Gage's Proclamation, June 12, 1775, 178-181.
[60] Butterfield, *Adams Family Correspondence*, Vol. 1, Abigail Adams to John Adams, June 16, 1775, 217.

become obsessed with responding to the rebels by force. Graves told Gage that the war for the colonies had started and they needed to begin devising plans to protect their naval and military assets. He viewed both Charlestown and Roxbury as threats to their position in Boston. His recommendations to Gage included the evacuation and burning of Charlestown and Roxbury, coupled with the seizure and fortification of Bunker Hill and Dorchester Heights.

Even though Lexington and Concord had upset Gage as well, he chose not to act on any of Graves' recommendations. Not only was he was reluctant to treat the colonists as enemies, but he thought such a scheme would stretch his already thin lines to the breaking point. Graves would later reassert his belief that Charlestown and Roxbury should be destroyed. He believed the towns offered a strategic vantage point to attack his ships by land, and advised building a battery on Cobb's Hill. With Gage's permission, four 24-pound guns were erected and pointed directly at Charlestown.[61]

On June 17, the rebels had accomplished what the British thought unthinkable: they built a series of breastworks and fortifications along Breed's Hill in a single night. The position afforded the rebels the opportunity to bombard the British position in Boston. The following morning Gage sent 2,000 regulars to Charlestown. According to rebel Captain Elijah Hyde, the Redcoats "plundered the town of all its valuable effects & then set fire to it in ten different places at once."[62] Hyde was correct that the British set fire to Charlestown, but not to exact revenge or plunder the town. The fire started between 2 and 4 p.m., depending on the account. As the British regulars approached the rebels on Breed's Hill, General Howe observed that the left wing was sustaining heavy rebel fire from concealed positions in Charlestown. Graves asked Howe "if he wished to have the place burned". Howe answered in the affirmative, allowing Graves to

---

[61] Tilly, *The Royal Navy in North America, 1774-1781*, 75-6.
[62] United States, Naval History Division, *Naval Documents of the American Revolution*, Vol. 1, Captain Elijah Hyde's Account of the Battle of Bunker Hill, 699.

"immediately send to the ships to fire red hot balls" at the town.[63]

Whether Graves took advantage of Gage's absence in this instance is questionable. The evidence suggests that the Admiral never informed Howe that two months prior Gage had denied his request to destroy the town.[64] In his defense, Graves had received permission from Gage to construct the battery on Cobb's Hill for dilemmas such as this. There can be little doubt that under the circumstances, Gage would have affirmed the order to burn Charlestown to aid in minimizing troop casualties.

Charlestown's demise can also be partly attributed to rebel Colonel William Prescott, who used the walls and fences of Charlestown to protect his right flank. William Heath, in his memoirs, wrote that Charlestown posts were "essential, and contiguous thereto" for the defense of Breed's Hill.[65] Therefore, it made perfect military sense for Howe to remove the threat to his left if he was to employ the whole of his force upon Prescott's fortification.

---

[63] Ibid, Narrative of Samuel Graves, June 17, 1775.
[64] Tilly, *The Royal Navy in North America, 1774-1781*, 98.
[65] William Heath, Memoirs of Major-General Heath Containing Anecdotes, Details of Skirmishes, Battles and other Military Events During the American War, (Boston, MA: I. Thomas and E.T. Andrews, 1798), 12. Following Lexington & Concord, Graves had actually warned the inhabitants of Charlestown that he would destroy the town if the inhabitants attempted to erect batteries that could be used to annoy his vessels. Donald Allan Yerxa, *Admiral Samuel Graves and the Falmouth Affair: A Case Study in British Imperial Pacification, 1775*, (Orono, ME: Thesis for University of Maine, 1974), 71.
[65] Historian William Goold states Graves order to bombard Falmouth was "in consequence of representations of" Captain Henry Mowat and Samuel Coulson. He cites the diary of Dr. Deane which reads "Capt. H. Mowatt...obtained, by his most urgent solicitation, an order from Graves, &c." William Goold, *The Burning of Falmouth: By Captain Mowatt, in 1775*, (Boston, MA: 1873), 11. There is no direct evidence that Mowat coerced Graves to bombard Falmouth. Although Graves was unhappy with the events that took place in Falmouth during the late spring of 1775, he was motivated by multiple events as is evidenced in his orders to Mowat on October 6.

Irreconcilable Grievances

The tragedy of Charlestown was more a casualty of warfare than a British attempt to unleash their anger upon the rebels. Although the British stationed at Boston had little affection for the rebels after months of skirmishes and standoffs, the evidence does not point to revenge as the primary motive for Charlestown's demise.

The destruction of Falmouth was a different matter.[66] On September 1, Graves requested Gage's permission to "lay Waste such Sea Port Towns in the New England Governments as are not likely to be useful to His Majesty's Stores and to destroy all Vessels within the Harbours."[67] Gage responded by wishing "that

---

[66] Historian William Goold states Graves order to bombard Falmouth was "in consequence of representations of" Captain Henry Mowat and Samuel Coulson. He cites the diary of Dr. Deane which reads "Capt. H. Mowatt...obtained, by his most urgent solicitation, an order from Graves, &c." William Goold, *The Burning of Falmouth: By Captain Mowatt, in 1775*, (Boston, MA: 1873), 11. There is no direct evidence that Mowat coerced Graves to bombard Falmouth. Although Graves was unhappy with the events that took place in Falmouth during the late spring of 1775, he was motivated by multiple events as is evidenced in his orders to Mowat on October 6.

[67] United States, Naval History Division, *Naval Documents of the American Revolution*, Vol. 1, Vice Admiral Samuel Graves to General Thomas Gage, September 1, 1775, 1281. Graves wanted Mowat to "burn, destroy, and lay waste" to Gloucester, MA first, but Mowat deviated from these orders. Mowat first experienced troubles with northward winds, but arrived within range of Gloucester on October 11. Mowat wrote, "Upon viewing the Town, Mr. Grant the Artillery Officer, gave it as his opinion, that the houses stood too scattered to expect success...On considering the ill consequences of a disappointment in the first attempt of this expedition...I passed this port." Garland, *The Fish and the Falcon*, 129. It is uncertain as to whether Mowat would have executed Graves' orders on Gloucester. Would he have issued the same proclamation he did to Falmouth's inhabitants? Since the act never occurred, historians can only speculate. Historian Joseph Garland insinuates Mowat would have burned the town based on his letter to Graves, but Mowat was a subordinate officer. The rank and file etiquette in the British Navy was extremely strict. Deviation or failure to complete a superior's orders were damaging to a naval officer's career. Even

The Most Horrid Devastations Upon the Country

something of this kind has been proposed at an earlier Period, when it would have been more" in his "Power to have furnished the Supplys you demand, however I shall do all I am able in the present Moment."[68] Graves had finally gotten Gage on board with his plans to deliver a decisive blow to the rebels. However, it would take nearly a month before the fleet was properly supplied to attempt the mission. Coincidentally, just as the Admiral was about to send Captain Henry Mowat to accomplish this task, orders arrived from England giving Graves permission to destroy the city of Falmouth. Although Graves distributed these orders, Mowat deviated from them, giving the inhabitants of Falmouth an opportunity to save their town.[69]

The bombarding and burning of Falmouth was not the town's first run-in with the British Navy. As early as April 1775, Captain

---

though Mowat knew this, he gave Falmouth's inhabitants an opportunity to save their town. An opportunity that Mowat knew could cost him his commission. Yerxa, *Admiral Samuel Graves and the Falmouth Affair*, 119-20. When he wrote to Graves about the burning of Falmouth, he made sure to only include those events the Admiral wanted to hear. To do otherwise might danger his career. George Washington had a similar problem as is evidenced with his correspondence to John Hancock and the Continental Congress. Washington often told his true sentiments to his friends such as Richard Henry Lee and Joseph Reed. When writing to Congress, Washington had a different tone in his letters, telling Congress what they wanted to hear. Part of being an effective military officer is being a good politician and telling your superiors what they want to hear.

[68] United States, Naval History Division, *Naval Documents of the American Revolution*, Vol. 2, General Thomas Gage to Vice-Admiral Graves, September 4. 1775, 7-8.

[69] Goold was the first to write in detail on the subject, and seems to have influenced many that Mowat "had a grudge upon the town, and…was too glad to execute the orders he had solicited from" Admiral Graves. Goold, *The Burning of Falmouth*, 5. Goold's research is only supported by the journals to two rebel ministers, but does offer some insight into the events that took place from their perspective. Goold wrote similar insights in his *Falmouth Neck in the American Revolution*, (Portland, ME: Thurston Print, 1897).

Irreconcilable Grievances

Henry Mowat and the *Canceaux* were lying in the harbor to protect the interests of a known loyalist, Captain Coulson.[70] Coulson had lived in the colony for three years and was involved in the shipbuilding business. Upset that the town's Committee of Inspection had refused to allow him to land some "rigging, sails, and stores which he had just imported for a ship he was building here," Coulson procured the assistance of Mowat to rig his ship.[71] Coincidentally, while Coulson was irritating the town by inviting the sloop of war *Canceaux*, news of Lexington and Concord reached Falmouth.[72] On April 23, a town meeting was held in which the assembly authorized the purchase of powder, the mobilization of the local militia, and the dispatch of a company to aid the people of Boston. The day after these proceedings, two more tenders arrived, which the inhabitants assumed were "intended to reinforce Mowat and enable him to pursue offensive measures."[73] The outraged citizens considered destroying Mowat's ship, but were dissuaded from doing so due to the dangerous consequences that could arise from such an action.[74]

Rebel Colonel Samuel Thompson of Brunswick thought otherwise. Unbeknownst to the inhabitants of Falmouth, Thompson's fifty-man company seized Mowat, his surgeon, and the Reverend Mr. Wiswell while they were walking upon a hill.[75]

---

[70] In late March 1775, Graves was informed there "were great disturbances at Falmouth," and sent the *Canceaux*. He hoped "her presence will be some Check to the common disturbers." Henry Wahll, *Henry Mowat: Voyage of the Canceaux 1760-1776*, (Bowie, MD: Heritage Books, 2003), 259-60.
[71] William Willis, *The History of Portland*, (Somersworth, NH: New Hampshire Publishing Company, 1972), 506.
[72] Goold, *The Burning of Falmouth*, 8.
[73] Willis, *The History of Portland*, 508. These apprehensions proved to be unsupported, since these vessels were returning from Penobscot, where they had been dismantling a fort.
[74] According to General Preble, in a letter to the Provincial Congress, British Lieutenant Hogg threatened to fire the town if Mowat was not returned before six o'clock, and even fired two blank shots as warnings. Goold, *The Burning of Falmouth*, 8.
[75] Willis, *The History of Portland*, 509.

The Most Horrid Devastations Upon the Country

Some of the primary leaders of Falmouth attempted to persuade Thompson to give up the prisoners, but to no avail. Fearing there would be reprisal by the British, Colonel Phinney of Gorham sent for his regiment to protect the town. It was only under this persistent pressure that Thompson finally gave in and paroled Mowat, who immediately violated his parole and boarded the *Canceaux* at his earliest possible convenience.[76]

Since the arrival of Colonel Thompson's regiment, Falmouth had been living under martial law. Thompson's board of war, acting upon the news of Mowat's departure, immediately seized persons suspected of being disloyal to the rebel cause. Mr. Wyer, Mr. Wiswell, and Captain Jeremiah Pote were the main Tories summoned and ill-treated. In addition, Captain Pote was forced to supply a bond of two thousand pounds and give account of his conduct before the provincial Congress.

To the disgust of Falmouth's inhabitants, the rebel soldiers regularly behaved in a riotous manner. They vandalized Captain Coulson's house, using it as their personal barracks, and indulged themselves in his liquor cellar. One soldier, Calvin Lomard, even went to the waterside, discharging his musket at the *Canceaux*. Lastly, the soldierly mob seized Coulson's boat, disassembled it and hauled it through the streets of the town. The same act was committed again thar day to another suspected Tory vessel. Mowat, rightfully disturbed by the events occurring in town, ordered the rebel soldiers' removal or he would fire upon the town.[77] The citizens, however, pleaded to Mowat that the

---

[76] The inhabitants were also fearful if Thompson detained Mowat, they would be prevented from receiving several vessels laden with corn and flour. Goold, *The Burning of Falmouth*, 9.

[77] On May 2, 1775, Mowat had received support for his station in Falmouth by a group of 18 loyalists. They wrote to him, stating, "since the Arrival of His Majesty's Ship under your command, we have been relieved by your Spirited Conduct from those Anxieties natural to Persons who are obnoxious to the Enemies to our happy Constitution; and by your courteous and kind behavior to all the Friends of Government, flattered Ourselves with the pleasing Prospect of a continuance of your Protection; but those agreeable Sensations are

disturbances were out of their control. The chairman of the town's committee of safety remarked, "Good God! Give us a regular government or we are undone."[78]

Thompson's rebel soldiers stayed in Falmouth until May 13, when the inhabitants were finally successful in convincing them to leave. Mowat remained uneasy until this was accomplished. He had heard rumors that cannon were being brought from the country to be employed against his ship. Mowat sent a letter to the town's leaders, making clear that if he was fired upon, the town would be considered in a state of rebellion and the act would be reciprocated. The drama came to an end, for the time being, once it was assured the rebel soldiery had departed.[79] Mowat's patience and tact paid off, since he was able to avoid any serious incident from occurring. However, his involvement in this coastal drama would play a large part in the way he executed Graves' orders to destroy the town five months later.

There is ample evidence to suggest that Mowat would have preferred not to destroy the town of Falmouth at all. The respectful treatment he received while temporarily incarcerated there, coupled with the townspeople's past compliance with his orders to discharge the rebel force, compelled Mowat to give Falmouth plenty of opportunity to prevent its own destruction. All eyewitnesses who gave detailed accounts of the incident mention

---

entirely vanished, and we are reduced to the last degree of despair, by your information, that when Captain Coulson's ship will be ready for Sea, you are immediately to leave this place – and consequently us, a prey to the Sons of rapine and lawless Violence. We therefore entreat you will remain with us till we can make known our deplorable situation to General Gage, which we shall do without delay..." Wahll, *Henry Mowat: The Voyage of the Canceaux 1760-1776*, 263. Mowat wrote to Graves about this "deplorable" situation in detail. See Ibid, 263-264.
[78] Willis, *The History of Portland*, 510-11.
[79] Ibid, 512. Mowat left Falmouth on May 15, 1775. See Wahll, *Henry Mowat: The Voyage of the Canceaux 1760-1776*, 266-67. One inhabitant never thought Mowat would fire upon the town, stating "he has not fired yet, and here I sit writing at my desk in the old place, being fully convinced that Mowatt never will fire on the town in any case whatsoever." Goold, *The Burning of Falmouth*, 10.

The Most Horrid Devastations Upon the Country

the process by which Mowat bargained with inhabitants, and his demands were hardly impossible to meet. Graves' orders were very specific. They stated:

> You are to go to all or to as many of the above named Places as you can, and make the most vigorous Efforts to burn the Towns, and destroy the Shipping in the Harbours. And as the Number of Marines you carry in the Vessels are too few to land and maintain any Post, you are to be careful not to risqué their Lives or the Lives of any of your People by attempting where there is not great probability of Success, but to content yourself with falling upon the Rebels, doing what you can with [the] Expedition and coming away before they can assemble to cut off your Retreat, and never risqué your Ships aground or where you cannot put to Sea at all times of Trade, Wind permitting.

Mowat undoubtedly understood these orders, but was willing to give more weight to the concluding passage, which provided a way out. Graves wrote, "Whenever you can distinguish the persons or property of those who have taken no part in the rebellion and have given proofs of their Attachment to the Constitution by refusing to concur in the unwarrantable measures that have been adopted to subvert it, you are to protect and defend them to the utmost of your power."[80]

On October 15, the inhabitants of Falmouth spotted the *Canceaux* off Cape Elizabeth. The ship was engaging a small rebel schooner, which would end up escaping to Falmouth's harbor. The event was "gazed [upon] by hundreds," causing these people to be "immediately thrown into a furious agitation...and vow[ing] revenge with the utmost menace and caution." The Committee of Safety reacted by ordering a company of guards "to secure cattle...intimidate Tories and to observe the motions of the enemy."[81]

---

[80] United States, Naval History Division, *Naval Documents of the American Revolution*, Vol. 2, Vice Admiral Graves to Lieutenant Henry Mowat, H.M. Armed Vessel *Canceaux*, October 6, 1775, 324-326.

[81] Ibid, Letter from Reverend Jacob Bailey, October 16, 1775, 471.

Irreconcilable Grievances

The event was particularly disturbing to Falmouth's inhabitants since similar events had occurred at Gloucester, Massachusetts just two months prior. On August 9, the sloop of war *Falcon*, commanded by Captain John Linzee, had pursued two schooners, but was only able to detain one at sea.[82] Acting on orders to prevent all commercial shipping to and from the New England colonies, Linzee intended on confiscating the other schooner, which had anchored in the harbor. Linzee dispatched two barges of 15 men each, as well as a whale boat manned by a Lieutenant and six privates. The local militia immediately responded, firing on the British as they were boarding the vessel through the cabin windows. Linzee initially fired on the rebels to provide cover for his small boarding party, but the rebel fire "continued very heavy [on] in the Schooner," and Linzee took a bold step to distract them away from his men. He "made an Attempt to set fire to the Town of Cape Anne" by setting a keg of powder alight inside the town. The plan failed. The keg "set fire...before it was properly placed," killing one of the men.[83] The rebels won a decisive victory that day, but the uncanny similarity between the preceding events at Gloucester and the actions of the *Canceaux* alarmed the Falmouth inhabitants. They felt they must take all the necessary measures to prevent the *Canceaux* succeeding where Linzee's *Falcon* had failed.[84]

---

[82] Allen, *A Naval History of the American Revolution*, Vol. 1, 14.
[83] United States, Naval History Division, *Naval Documents of the American Revolution*, Vol. 1, Captain John Linzee to Samuel Graves, August 10, 1775, 1110-11. Ibid, Journal of His Majesty's Sloop, *Falcon*, August 8, 1775, 1093. Donald Yerxa writes an interest anecdote about the publication of the event in colonial circles. He writes, "According to colonial propaganda, the British officer took 'diabolical pleasure to see what havock his cannon might make [stating]...Now my boys, we will aim at the damn'd Presbyterian church...one shot more and the house of God will fall before you." Yerxa, *Admiral Graves and the Falmouth Affair*, 85-86.
[84] For a narrative history of the *Falcon* and Gloucester, see Garland, *The Fish and the Falcon*, 107-117. Garland narrates the incident from the rebel perspective. Although the documents Garland used are easily accessible, he gives the most detailed account to date.

The Most Horrid Devastations Upon the Country

When the *Canceaux* arrived, many of the town's inhabitants had strong anti-British leanings, but felt more at ease once they learned Mowat, whom they trusted, was commanding the small fleet. Daniel Tucker, for instance, held the opinion the fleet was coming with "hostile intentions," but his friend, Paul Little, informed him, "Captain Mowatt had the command and there was no danger."[85] It was thought Mowat would "shew some favor to the Town" since he "was under particular obligations to some Gentn in Falmouth, for the Civilities shewn him when in Captivity amongst them."[86] Finding the people "so disposed," Mowat wrote the town a letter, stating:

After so many premeditated Attacks on the legal Prerogatives of the best of Sovereigns. After repeated Instances you have experience in Britain's long forbearance of the Rod of Correction; and the Merciful and Paternal extension of her Hands to embrace you, again and again, have been regarded as vain and nugatory. And in place of a dutiful and grateful return to your King and Parent state; you have been guilty of the most unpardonable Rebellion, supported by the Ambition of a set of designing men, whose insidious crews have cruelly imposed on the credulity of their fellow creatures, and at last have brought the whole into the same Dilemma ; which leads me to feel not a little for the Innocent of them, in particular on the present occasion, having it in orders to execute a just Punishment on the Town of Falmouth: In the name of which Authority I previously warn you to remove without delay the Human Species out of the said town; for which purpose I give you the time of two hours, at the period of which, a Red

---

[85] United States, Naval History Division, *Naval Documents of the American Revolution*, Vol. 2, Narrative of Daniel Tucker, October 17, 1775, 488. Graves approved of Mowat's "Officerlike Conduct at Falmouth" back in May 1775, when he handled the situation of Coulson's masts and Colonel Thompson's military occupation without incident. Wahll, *Henry Mowat: The Voyage of the Canceaux 1760-1776*, 268.

[86] Ibid, Pearson Jones' Certificate Concerning the Burning of Falmouth, October 24, 1775, 590-592.

pendant will be hoisted at the Maintopgallant Masthead with gun: but should your imprudence lead you to shew the least resistance, you will in that case free me of that Humanity...I also observe that all those who did upon a former occasion fly to the King's Ship under my Command for Protection, that the same door is now open and ready to receive them...[87]

The letter was read before a large number of the inhabitants. Upon its completion, "there was a profound silence, and it was desired to be read a second time." The deliverer of the note, Mr. Fraser, "seeing such a general distress increase," offered the people a chance to make a proposal to Mowat. A committee was sent to wait on the Captain, requesting to know the "nature of the chastisement, and to request longer time be allowed them." Mowat informed them he was under no obligation to show any leniency, but if they would deliver up all their "Arms and Ammunition...I would...put off destroying the Town."[88]

Mowat stipulated that the arms, including the "Five Guns...to be on Carriages," should be assembled by eight o'clock the next morning. The committee returned before eight that evening with ten stands of arms as a pledge of faith that they intended on delivering more. It was made clear to the men, however, that if Mowat's demand was not "fully complied with by nine the next morning as it would be impossible to clear the town of the women and children before that hour," the threat to destroy the town would be carried out. Mowat also assured them that "if any person should presume to escape by water during the night," the town would be laid waste.[89]

That morning the committee was punctual, but had neither delivered any more arms or convinced the townspeople to evacuate. The rebel account contends the inhabitants found the

---

[87] Ibid, Lieutenant Henry Mowat to the People of Falmouth, October 16, 1775, 471.
[88] Ibid, Lieutenant Henry Mowat to Vice Admiral Samuel Graves, October 19, 1775, 513-14.
[89] United States, Naval History Division, *Naval Documents of the American Revolution*, Vol. 2, 488.

The Most Horrid Devastations Upon the Country

swearing of allegiance to "his majesty King George the third...inadmissible," and therefore the "town was sacrificed to the cause of Liberty and Patriotism, as there was no other alternative."[90] This makes a great story, but is erroneous since the town had been working with Mowat to prevent its destruction just an evening ago. An outside factor must have prevented the committee from delivering on their promise to Mowat.

One account contends the Sons of Liberty dispatched messengers, relaying the gravity of Falmouth's situation. Companies of armed rebels entered the town before midnight, directing that "if any compliance or submission was made, they would burn [the town] to ashes." Rebels from "30 miles round" were "beating drums, firing alarms, and mustering under arms."[91]

This provides a sensible explanation of the reason Falmouth was not evacuated during the night.[92] The inhabitants had to choose between either being immediately torched by the rebels, or taking their chances in the morning with Mowat, whom they hoped would show compassion. It was under this predicament the Falmouth committee met with Mowat at nine o'clock in the morning. They requested time to return ashore to ensure the women and children were removed from the town, which was granted, and they bestowed "expressions of thankfulness for the

---

[90] Ibid, Narrative of Daniel Tucker of Falmouth, October 17, 1775, 489.
[91] United States, Naval History Division, *Naval Documents of the American Revolution*, Vol. 2, 488.
[92] There are conflicting accounts as to when the majority of Falmouth's inhabitants began evacuating the town. Some accounts state some had been evacuating the night before, while some claim much later. Both should be given credit. There would have been inhabitants that thought their best option was to leave right and away, while others felt no danger was posed to them because they planned on complying with Mowat's request for the five cannon. Lastly, there were inhabitants that decided not to leave at all. Mowat reported to Graves that none of the inhabitants had assembled the morning of October 18, and the town was in the greatest confusion. Many inhabitants chose not to leave, including many loyalists. They feared the looting and destruction of their property by the rebels, especially by the militia force that had arrived the night before. Yerxa, *Admiral Samuel Graves and the Falmouth Affair*, 121-23.

lenity that had been shown."⁹³ As for the loyalists, William Tyng thought Mowat "was so kind to offer us (those I mean who had formerly fled to him for Protection), a Passage to Boston, but it was impracticable to get on board -- tho we wished to, for had we been discovered in the Attempt, we shou'd have been shot from the Shore by the Rebels -- nor could we have carried the least Article."⁹⁴

The bombardment of Falmouth started at forty minutes after nine, arguably granting plenty of extra time for the people to disperse. But this did not occur. The streets were jammed with people gathering their belongings in an attempt to rescue as much property as possible. With the streets "replete with people, oxen and horses," Mowat's first volleys were fired over the town in an attempt to compel the inhabitants to hastily leave. The barrage "struck the multitude into instant alarm and amazement" causing the oxen to run over rocks, "dashing everything into pieces, and scattering large quantities of goods about the streets."⁹⁵ Despite the cannonading, parties "of armed men" stayed behind, putting out the fires as soon as they sparked. This led Mowat to send a small contingent of Marines to land and "set fire to the vessels, wharfs, storehouses, as well as to many parts of the town that escaped from the shells."⁹⁶

The mission was no easy task, for the marines faced repetitive small arms fire, but they were able to accomplish the job "without the loss of a man and only one slightly wounded."⁹⁷ Some rebels

---

⁹³ United States, Naval History Division, *Naval Documents of the American Revolution*, Vol. 2, Lieutenant Henry Mowat to Vice Admiral Samuel Graves, October 19, 1775, 515.
⁹⁴ United States, Naval History Division, *Naval Documents of the American Revolution*, Vol. 3, 1312-14.
⁹⁵ United States, Naval History Division, *Naval Documents of the American Revolution*, Vol. 2, Letter from Reverend Jacob Bailey, October 18, 1775, 500.
⁹⁶ Ibid, Lieutenant Henry Mowat to Vice Admiral Samuel Graves, October 19, 1775, 515.
⁹⁷ Ibid, Master's Log of H.M. Armed Vessel *Canceaux*, October 18, 1775, 501-502. For British journal entries and other information

were upset with the town's inhabitants for not quashing such a small force. Jacob Bailey wrote "about a thousand men in arms attended this scene of devastation...without attempting any repulsion."[98] Daniel Tucker argues it was not within their ability to do that, since "there was not a canon mounted in town...and there was a great scarcity of powder."[99] Major General Charles Lee disagreed, believing they acted with extraordinary "cowardice," since they had "two hundred fighting Men and powder enough for a battle [yet] cou'd suffer with impunity twenty-five marines to land and set their Town in flames."[100]

Word of the incident at Falmouth spread just as fast as the fire that set the town ablaze.[101] Washington described it as an "Outrage exceeding in Barbarity & Cruelty every hostile Act practiced among civilized Nations."[102] Benjamin Franklin remarked sarcastically, "such is the Government of the best of Princes!"[103] Nathanael Greene responded to the news by writing to Rhode Island Governor Nicholas Cooke "Fight or be slaves! Is the American motto."[104] Greene would also write to Samuel

---

regarding the burning of Falmouth see Wahll, *Henry Mowat: The Voyage of the Canceaux 1760-1776*, 310-20.

[98] Ibid, Letter from Reverend Jacob Bailey, October 18, 1775, 500.

[99] Ibid, Narrative of Daniel Tucker of Falmouth, October 18, 1775.

[100] Taylor, *The Papers of John Adams*, Vol. 3, Charles Lee to John Adams, November 19, 1775, 312.

[101] The destruction of Falmouth received wide coverage among the American press. Throughout the colonies, editors copied and printed two or three accounts of the event. The most vicious account referred to Mowat as a "execrable Monster" and stated, "May heaven protect an innocent, distressed People; and may their implacable cruel Enemies perish in the Fire they kindling for others...no Mercy is to be expected form our savage Enemies." Yerxa, *Admiral Samuel Graves and the Falmouth Affair*, 142.

[102] Abbot & Twohig, *The Papers of George Washington*, Revolutionary War Series, Vol. 2, Washington to John Hancock, October 24, 1775, 227-28.

[103] Smith, *The Letters of the Delegates to Congress 1774-1789*, Vol. 2, Benjamin Franklin to Richard Bache, October 24, 1775, 246.

[104] Richard K. Showman, *The Papers of Nathanael Greene*, Vol. 1,

Ward, "Will not this brutal conduct rouse a spirit of indignation throughout America?"[105] Major General Charles Lee illustrated it as "inhuman bus[i]ness," acted out by "hell hounds of an execrable Ministry."[106] Brigadier General John Sullivan believed such "Havock and Destruction" fills the British "with delight" in "deducing to ashes the most Elegant and populous towns."[107] James Warren commented, "This is savage and Barbarous in the highest stage...What more can we want to Justifie any Step to take, Kill, and destroy, to refuse them any refreshments, to Apprehend our Enemies, to Confiscate their Goods and Estates, to Open our Ports to foreigners, and if practicable to form Alliances."[108]

Warren was not alone in his suggestion to take the revolution to the next step in response to Falmouth. Joseph Ward wrote, "The late infernal conduct of the Pirates at Falmouth, I apprehend is a full answer to all American Petitions, and in its consequences will, I conceive, be the best answer we have received." Ward had heard that the Continental Congress had "resolved to offer free trade to all Nations" and to cut their ties with Britain until they have "repaired the injuries." "If this news is not true," he added, "I hope it is a forerunner to such proceedings."[109]

While the burning of Falmouth sparked thoughts of independence in some members of the Continental Congress, it

---

(Chapel Hill, NC: The University of North Carolina Press, 1976), Greene to Deputy Governor Nicholas Cooke of Rhode Island, October 24, 1775, 142-43.

[105] United States, Naval History Division, *Naval Documents of the American Revolution*, Vol.1, Brigadier General Nathanael Greene to Samuel Ward, October 23, 1775, 576.

[106] United States, Naval History Division, *Naval Documents of the American Revolution*, Vol. 2, Major General Charles Lee to Colonel Alexander McDougall, October 26, 1775, 607.

[107] Ibid, Orders of Brigadier General John Sullivan, November 1, 1775, 832-33.

[108] Taylor, *The Papers of John Adams*, Vol. 3, James Warren to John Adams, October 20-22, 1775, 222.

[109] Ibid, Joseph Ward to John Adams, November 4, 1775, 275-76.

also fostered a fear that such tactics could disintegrate the Continental Army. Reports circulated among the soldiers of Washington's army that the British intended on destroying every seaport between Falmouth and Boston. A Committee of Conference made up of Thomas Lynch, Benjamin Harrison, and Benjamin Franklin believed "it is easy to conceive what Effects this must produce in this Camp." Those soldiers whose families and friends resided around Falmouth were asking for "leave to go and take care of" them "and to find a place for them" for the upcoming winter. Such requests could not be refused because they were "too reasonable." The circumstances caused the Committee to fear "shoud the Same Fate fall to the share of many such Towns, tis easy to fortell what must happen to the Army" especially "shoud it happen before the new Army is inlisted."[110]

Falmouth was not the only New England town to be set afire in early October. Throughout the first week of October, New England rebel bands were working hard to prevent colonists from providing supplies to British scavenging parties. While James Wallace, Captain of the *Rose*, was in New York requisitioning supplies, loading transports, and sending them off to Boston, he was informed that "Governor Cooke of Providence raised the Country" and "sent down 1500 Men to Newport" to prevent Wallace and the British from completing their mission. Despite the rebels' "utmost efforts," however, the British "got all that

---

[110] Smith, *The Letters of the Delegates to Congress 1774-1789*, Vol. 2, Committee of Conference to John Hancock, October 24, 1775, 244. Washington would later use his soldiers' fears and emotions concerning Falmouth to his advantage. With the army disintegrating around him at the end of 1775, the General appealed to honor telling them of the "great Cause" they were engaged in. Moreover, he reminded them of the "innocent Women & Children" and "our towns" that needed their protection from their "barbarous Designs." These words did not inspire everyone to remain with the army, but it serves not only as an example of the genius of Washington as a motivator of troops, it also shows how severe the burning of Falmouth resonated. See John Ferling, *Almost a Miracle*, (New York, NY: Oxford University Press, 2007), 79.

could be got notwithstanding."¹¹¹ Consequently, the rebels decided to go to Brenton's Neck, where the residents had been assisting the British in gaining provisions. There the rebels "took all away, not leaving a Chicken for the Women." The *Newport Mercury* reported the rebels got off about "1000 sheep and between 40 and 50 head of cattle, sheep, and hogs on two farms belonging to Jaheel and Benjamin Brenton."¹¹²

To further prevent the supplying of their "inveterate enemies," the rebels once again raided the Bretons' farms on October 5, taking nearly the all of what remained. Wallace, infuriated by this action, ordered the town to send the rebels away or it would otherwise become his "Duty to destroy them and the town" of Newport. Wallace would have preferred not to act on his threat "because it seemed that many of them could not help the Irruption from the Banditti."¹¹³

Meanwhile, the rebels had been assembling arms to counter the threat Wallace posed to Newport. Even many of the townspeople "moved part or all their effects out." There were so many carts, chaises, riding chairs, and trucks clogging the streets that almost all the "streets and roads were blocked up with them."¹¹⁴

To counter the rebels' efforts, and perhaps teach them a lesson in the rules of war, Wallace departed the town and anchored off Bristol. The rebels' accounts state Wallace requested that the town provide him with 300 head of sheep or he would destroy it. It was upon the town's refusal to meet this demand "they began an heavy fire...upwards of an hour."¹¹⁵ Historian David Lovejoy's

---

¹¹¹ United States, Naval History Division, *Naval Documents of the American Revolution*, Vol.1, Captain James Wallace to Vice Admiral Graves, October 14, 1775, 451.
¹¹² Ibid, *Newport Mercury*, October 9, 1775, 375.
¹¹³ Ibid, Captain James Wallace to Vice Admiral Graves, October 14, 1775, 451.
¹¹⁴ Ibid, *Newport Mercury*, October 9, 1775, 375.
¹¹⁵ Ibid, this also includes the accounts of David Cobb to Treat Paine (October 10, 1775, 388), Letter from Bristol, RI to a New York Correspondent (October 12, 1775, 420-1), and Thomas Greenleaf to Robert Treat Paine (October 15, 1775, 463).

The Most Horrid Devastations Upon the Country

Rhode Island Politics portrays a similar account, writing, "Defenseless Bristol was raked with cannon fire for refusing to satisfy Wallace's demands."[116] Unfortunately Lovejoy, like many American historians researching this subject, only uses revolutionary sources. His tale of the series of events that rocked the Rhode Island coast lacks objectivity. For a truly accurate depiction of what happened, both the revolutionary and British accounts must be explored.

Captain James Wallace paints a different picture from that of the rebels, implying that the threat to fire upon the town might not have been initially issued, and stating that he offered to pay for the sheep but the town never responded to his offer. From reading all the accounts, Wallace's seems the most accurate. Certainly the continual driving of cattle away from the coastline annoyed Wallace to no end; he even mentions this in his summary of events. This may have inclined him to fire upon Bristol.

Following the cannonade, a committee was sent to wait upon the Captain to prevent any further destruction. Wallace queried why the town had not answered his initial summons, given that 'my intentions [were] friendly, that I only came to purchase Stock for the King's forces." He even offered to pay for whatever "quantity of Stock" they could supply after setting fire to the town. The committee "hesitated and prevaricated much," insisting the "country people had drove [the livestock] off."[117] Wallace rebutted with a demand of fifty sheep and a promise not to harm Newport, which was agreed to by the committee. The saga did not end there, for the entire time the British were loading the sheep, the rebels were firing several shots at them. In response to this retaliation, Wallace therefore saw fit, once he set sail, to destroy the Bristol ferries.

Following this, a rebel contingent led by Colonel Hopkins arrived on the scene, but were told by the inhabitants their

---

[116] David S. Lovejoy, *Rhode Island Politics and the American Revolution 1760-1776*, (Providence, RI, Brown University Press, 1958), 185.
[117] United States, Naval History Division, *Naval Documents of the American Revolution*, Vol.1, Captain James Wallace to Vice Admiral Graves, October 14, 1775, 451.

presence would lead to another attack by Wallace. Hopkins informed them of a new measure that will "probably...be adopted with respect to all the sea-port Towns in America." They were given orders "to prevent the pirates from landing or receiving supplies from the shore; and that instead of being intimidated from defending their property by fear of the Town being fired upon, they might be assured he [Hopkins] would destroy the Town, rather than the pirates should land in or draw supplies or advantage from it."[118]

This plan did not take effect as the rebel leadership might have hoped, since Newport, Rhode Island continued to supply Wallace through that winter. Newport's leadership even gained discretionary Congressional permission to do so since they feared Wallace "may cannonade and even burn the Town."[119]

Newport's fears were well-founded since it was common knowledge in December 1774 that the inhabitants had participated in the assault of the island fortress guarding that town, hauling off forty-four cannon. In addition, while Wallace was sent to Newport in response to this attack, he received information that a mob was coming for him while he attended a social function at the home of George Romes. The inhabitants' alleged intent was to tar and feather the two men. Wallace was determined to defend himself "like an Officer and an Englishman," and summoned his crews to assist in barricading the house. Although the mob never materialized, Wallace vented his frustration to Rhode Island Governor Wanton, arguing that his "behaviour and Character entitle [him] to" "the Countenance and Protection of You and the Laws," "whether it is War or Peace."[120]

Much like Falmouth, word about Bristol spread quickly through individual correspondence, provincial proceedings, and newspaper circulation. The *New York Journal* described Wallace as a pirate and his naval colleagues as "Free-Booters," stating,

---

[118] Force, *American Archives*, Fourth Series, Vol. 3, 1109.

[119] United States, Naval History Division, *Naval Documents of the American Revolution*, Vol.3, Governor Nicholas Cooke to George Washington, January 21, 1775, 901.

[120] Tilley, *The Royal Navy in North America, 1774-1781*, 45.

"Wallace...in cowardly dependence on his lawless force, to demand the property of the inhabitants, and like other Robbers, threaten[ed] them with destruction in case of refusal, which threat he inforced, by murderously and treasonably firing a number of shot against the town of Bristol."[121]

The significance of the burning of Bristol and Falmouth is broad and far-reaching. First, these incidents established a perpetual fear among coastal towns they could be attacked at any time. Secondly, they solidified New England's revolutionary governments' push for the establishment of a Continental Navy.[122] Lastly, they led to the fortification of coastal towns, aiding the British military leadership in making the decision to relocate their forces to New York and extending the warfront to the Southern colonies.[123]

---

[121] United States, Naval History Division, *Naval Documents of the American Revolution*, Vol.1, *New York Journal*, October 19, 1775, 524.

[122] The burning of Falmouth also propagated Congress to encourage privateering to protect their coasts. See Force, *American Archives*, Fourth Series, Vol. 3, 1927-28.

[123] On July 13, 1776, Congress would also use the burning of Falmouth and Charlestown to persuade the St. John's and Mickmac Indian tribes to join the cause. It was stated to the tribes, "they burnt the town of Charlestown, consisting of several hundred houses, taking away everything valuable they could find there; and several of their ships-of-war went and destroyed a great part of the town of Falmouth...burning near two hundred houses there, with many things of value in them." Force, *American Archives*, Fifth Series, Vol. 1, 842.

Chapter Seven

Portsmouth and the Tragedy of Norfolk

Does it not call for vengeance from both God and Man?
Colonel Robert Howe to the Virginia Convention, January 2, 1776

In the month of December 1774, the town of Portsmouth, New Hampshire was foremost in the minds of the revolutionaries. Only a few weeks earlier, in late October, the British Navy had inflicted devastation on the neighboring coastal towns of Falmouth, Massachusetts and Bristol, Rhode Island. Leading up these events, New Hampshire had had a tumultuous relationship with the Crown. Portsmouth lay within the Piscataqua River, neighboring both Newcastle and Fort William and Mary. Guarding the entry to Portsmouth's port was the province's only permanently manned British military installation, Fort William and Mary. In the dead of night on December 15, 1774, Major John Sullivan and a band of rebels assaulted the fort. Some historians speculate that it was this moment the Revolutionary War truly began. The arms and ammunition they captured, which might have been used against the port and the city, were used instead in the Battle of Bunker Hill. The fort was only defended by "five effective men," and since its stores contained large quantities of ammunition, arms and supplies, it was deemed an easy target.[1] At "three o'clock" the fort was surrounded by four hundred rebels. Captain Cochran, British commander of the fort, warned the attackers to enter "on their peril." He ordered "three four-pounders to be fired" on the rebels, followed immediately by small arms fire. Defense of the fort proved futile. Sullivan and his army

---

[1] Nathaniel Bouton, D.D., *Documents and Records Relating to the Province of New Hampshire, From 1764 to 1776*, Vol. VII, Captain Cochran to Governor Wentworth, December 14, 1775, (New York, NY: AMS Press, 1866), 420.

"stormed on all quarters," securing the fort and making prisoners of the small British troop contingent.[2] Captain Andrew Barkley of the *Scarborough* arrived just in time to prevent the carrying of no more than "18 Guns of different sizes," saving 53 cannon.[3] This attack is significant not only for the reason that it occurred before Lexington and Concord, but also because it was the direct cause of that skirmish.[4] General Thomas Gage had ventured to Concord in order to retake these stolen munitions, but fortunately for the revolutionaries the armaments had been moved prior to the engagement.

In May 1775, the British were frustrated even further with Portsmouth's inhabitants once intelligence was received that the port town had become a haven for the assembling of rebel ships. Tension mounted when Captain Barkley informed Admiral Graves of a group of 300 men that had carried away a "Quantity of Masts" for such a purpose. Barkley was unable to prevent the act because "if such a thing was attempted they would immediately cut them to pieces."[5] Reports of the destruction and seizure of British supplies were widely known at this time. The same day the masts were stolen, news of rebels in Halifax, Nova Scotia had destroyed hay stores also arrived. Graves already "heartily wish[ed]" he was empowered to act, since he was "equally desirous of chastising the Rebels."[6] With what power was afforded him by the ministry,

---

[2] Ibid, 420-21.
[3] Ibid, Captain Andrew Barkley to Vice Admiral Graves, December 20, 1774, 38. Samuel Graves wrote to Philip Stevens on the subject, "It is however certain that those who committed the late outrage are skulking about there Country, and are only prevented by the King's Ships in the River from being as insolent & troublesome as ever." Wahll, *Henry Mowat: The Voyage of the Canceaux 1764-1776*, 257.
[4] Stark, *The Loyalists of Massachusetts and the Other Side of the American Revolution*, (Boston, MA: W.B. Clarke Co., 1910), 51.
[5] United States, Naval History Division, *Naval Documents of the American Revolution*, Vol.1, Captain Andrew Barkley to Vice Admiral Graves, May 19, 1775, 362.
[6] Ibid, Vice Admiral Graves to Captain James Wallace, May 19, 1775, 363.

Portsmouth and the Tragedy of Norfolk

Graves issued orders to his subordinates to "stop and send to Boston all Vessels loaded with Provisions."⁷ Graves was fully aware the rebellion was not limited to the Boston neck. Lacking the capability to deploy a physical presence in all these hot areas, he thought it best to prevent the supply of port towns as a means to draw out the rebels. To make matters worse, the persistent attack on British stores forced Graves to acquire supplies by any means necessary.

Portsmouth's suspected involvement in the attack on Fort William & Mary, along with the seizure of masts, caused Graves to enact a blockade upon Falmouth's inhabitants. Barkley would carry out the orders, confiscating "two vessels laden with corn, Pork, Flower & other Provisions."⁸ It was act that caused Governor Wentworth and his Council to fear "consequences of which will be most probably very fatal to his Majesty's service."⁹ A town committee assembled but was unsuccessful in their petition for the release of the needed provisions.¹⁰ The rebels then took matters into their own hands, measures they deemed necessary by assembling "three or four hundred" men to throw up an entrenchment "and getting cannon ready there to fire on the Ship."¹¹

---

⁷ Ibid, Captain Andrew Barkley to Vice Admiral Graves, May 30, 1775, 567.
⁸ Ibid, Memorial of Portsmouth Merchants to John Wentworth, Governor of New Hampshire, May 29, 1775, 555.
⁹ Bouton, *Documents and Records Relating to the Province of New Hampshire, From 1764 to 1776*, Vol. VII, Meeting of his Majesty's Council, May 29, 1775, 375.
¹⁰ Ibid, 376-377.
¹¹ United States, Naval History Division, *Naval Documents of the American Revolution*, Vol.1, Captain Andrew Barkley to Vice Admiral Samuel Graves, June 1, 1775, 583. Also see Bouton, *Documents and Records Relating to the Province of New Hampshire, From 1764 to 1776*, Vol. VII, May 30, 1775, 376. In this document it states "the inhabitants of this and the neighboring Towns were greatly alarmed, and, next morning, between five and six hundred men, in arms, went down to the battery called *Jerry's Point*, the whole that were there, weighing four thousand eight hundred pounds each, and brought them up to this Town.

Irreconcilable Grievances

Barkley knew the threat this posed to his small fleet and informed Graves of the cannon the rebels intended to mount against him. He took what preventative measures were necessary by removing the "forty or fifty Tons of Shot" from the fort, and hoped he "shall have Instructions how to act, against those people."[12] He even "warn'd them to desist in such treasonable proceedings, for they might be assured that the moment a Shot was fired either from the Cannon or Musquetry" he would "instantly batter down...and destroy all the Vessels and Craft belonging to that part and likewise make prisoners of every Man...met with."[13] The town pleaded with the Captain, stating they were not affiliated with any of the rebel element that had taken firm control of the countryside. Barkley took them on their word, even later writing to Graves he thought to be on "pretty good term with the People of the Town."[14] It was a definite dilemma, since Governor Wentworth assured the town meant no harm, all the while Barkley could see the townspeople evacuating in unison, as numbers of armed men assembled. From their movements, the Captain suspected that the town had "some intention of putting their threats into execution." So much so, Fort William and Mary was abandoned.

Barkley's intuition was right, for on the morning of June 3 his "Guard-boat" was fired upon "by about forty Men who lay concealed."[15] Although Governor Wentworth assured him they

---

While they were taking off the cannon, the Canceaux, with a tender, set sail with the two provisions vessels for Boston. The next day the Town was full of men from the country in arms."

[12] Ibid, Captain Andrew Barkley to Vice Admiral Samuel Graves, May 31, 1775, 574.

[13] Ibid, Captain Andrew Barkley to Vice Admiral Graves, June 5, 1775, 612. See also, Bouton, *Documents and Records Relating to the Province of New Hampshire, From 1764 to 1776,* Vol. VII, Letter from H. Wentworth to Matthew Thornton, May 31, 1775, 377.

[14] Ibid, Captain Andrew Barkley to Vice Admiral Graves, June 16, 1775, 689.

[15] Ibid, Captain Andrew Barkley to Vice Admiral Graves, June 5, 1775, 612.

were in no way connected with this event, Barkley reacted by impressing local fisherman. Wentworth would plea with Barkley, requesting their release because he thought such an act would be "very powerful Evidence that his Majesty's Servants are ever ready and disposed to lead by Acts of kindness to the re-establishment." Barkley reluctantly complied, once it was assured he would "be supplied as usual and the intercourse no way interrupted."[16] All would remain calm until June 13 when Colonel Fenton, a loyalist and member of the local assembly, was arrested by the town. Fenton had been onboard the *Scarborough* for three weeks to ensure his safety. Upon receiving notice that the assembly was to meet, he went ashore to attend. The "populous hearing of his coming to Town assembled in a large body to seize him." Fenton sought shelter in Governor Wentworth's house, but surrendered when he was immediately surrounded and threatened with "two pieces of Cannon planted against the Door."[17] The event compelled Wentworth to inform General Gage:

> Seeing every idea of the respect due to his Majesty's Commission so far lost in the frantic rage and fury of the people as to find them to proceed to such daring violence against the Person of his Representative, I found myself under the necessity of immediately withdrawing to Fort William and Mary, both to prevent as much as may be a Repetition of the like insults and to provide for my own security.[18]

In the meantime, through Graves' orders, Barkley possessed only the authority of cutting off any supplies to Portsmouth. Graves would not have Barkley "begin a war upon any Account," but if attacked it was instructed "to defend the King's Ships and do

---

[16] Ibid, Governor John Wentworth to Captain Andrew Barkley, June 3, 1775, 600.

[17] Ibid, Captain Andrew Barkley to Vice Admiral Graves, June 16, 1775, 689.

[18] Bouton, *Documents and Records Relating to the Province of New Hampshire, From 1764 to 1776*, Vol. 7. Governor Wentworth to General Thomas Gage, June 15, 1775, 381.

your utmost to destroy the Enemy, Pirate or Rebel."[19] Upon hearing news of the firing on the guard boat, the organization of rebel forces, and the seizure of Fenton, Graves concluded "the New Hampshire People are as perfectly disposed for Rebellion as those of Massachusetts Bay." He knew a "few good thinking People...no doubt naturally disavow such Outrages...but what are their feeble Efforts opposed to a whole Province under the worst influence?"[20]

The crisis in Portsmouth would finally boil over in early July when the rebels seized the treasury. As early as December 1774, Barkley had informed Governor Wentworth of the possible rebel confiscation of the Customs House Treasuries. No such precautionary action had been taken though, allowing the Continental Congress ample opportunity to order its removal. A Congressional Committee arrived "in great Triumph," confiscating "from sixteen hundred to two thousand Pounds...without the least hindrance or Molestation to the Astonishment of every Person who wished well to Government."[21] In addition, Barkley lost a sloop and schooner "laden with wood, Spars and mercantile fish" to the rebels in that same week. His attempts to prosecute the individuals proved ineffectual. Every legal mind in the town knew the taking of the case to the local Vice Admiralty Court would risk their "life and property." Graves thought these events proved there is "no reason to hope Order and good Government will for some time be restored."[22] Barkley could do nothing more than continue to stop all the shipping headed to Portsmouth.

This positioned the members of Portsmouth Committee of Safety in a dangerous situation, compelling them to cut off all communication with the *Scarborough,* while ordering the

---

[19] United States, Naval History Division, *Naval Documents of the American Revolution*, Vol.1, Vice Admiral Graves to Captain Andrew Barkley, June 3, 1775, 601.
[20] Ibid, Vice Admiral Graves to Captain Andrew Barkley, June 23, 1775, 742.
[21] Ibid, Captain Andrew Barkley to Vice Admiral Graves, July 7, 1775, 833.
[22] Ibid, Vice Admiral Graves to Captain Andrew Barkley, July 15, 1775.

armament of the town. Surprisingly, the move did not provoke an attack. Governor Wentworth and his family would join the British off the harbor, and the fleet would sail for Boston on August 23 without incident. Although there was no confrontation, the rebel authority was well aware that a reprisal could come at any moment. Even prior to learning the news of Bristol and Falmouth, Washington did not put it past the British to attack a coastal town, particularly Portsmouth. When he was informed a "64 Gun Ship a 20 Gun & 2 Sloops with 2 Transports of Soldiers" had departed Boston, Washington wrote the Portsmouth Committee of Safety their design "is probably to batter some Town on the Coast."[23] The Committee had already taken measures to physically secure the town against a potential British naval attack, but it took Washington's warning even more seriously. The Committee was not "without great suspicion that the enemy have an intention upon this Town."[24] They requested "a Number of men" be "properly officered & equipped (We think 200 may be sufficient)," and more batteries constructed.[25]

Following the news of Falmouth and Bristol in October, the Portsmouth Committee received the aid of Washington and Congress in fortifying the coast. Brigadier-General John Sullivan, a New Hampshire native, was given the task of repelling "any attacks upon this or upon any other sea-port in this Quarter."[26] Sullivan was not one of the most experienced officers within Washington's Council of War but his familiarity with the region and his local popularity made him the perfect candidate for the

---

[23] Abbot & Twohig, *The Papers of George Washington*, Revolutionary Series, Vol. 2, To the Portsmouth Committee of Safety, October 5, 1775, 113-14.
[24] United States, Naval History Division, *Naval Documents of the American Revolution*, Vol.2, Portsmouth Committee to the New Hampshire Committee of Safety, October 7, 1775, 332.
[25] Bouton, *Documents and Records Relating to the Province of New Hampshire, From 1764 to 1776*, Vol. 7, 620
[26] United States, Naval History Division, *Naval Documents of the American Revolution*, Vol.2, Brigadier General John Sullivan to the New Hampshire Committee of Safety, October 27, 1775, 616.

job. The Committee of Safety of Hillsborough County, New Hampshire had told him he should ever be remembered as one of "our heroes of 1775" for his part in the assault on William and Mary.[27] Sullivan would not disappoint them this time around either. He took all the necessary measures on land and on sea to prevent a potential British invasion. Sullivan had heard and firmly believed Captain Mowat's mission was to "burn all the sea-ports east of Boston." Sullivan expected him "daily but, in case he does not arrive in a few days, shall despair on his coming."[28]

By October 31 the threat of attack seemed to have subsided. Washington requested that Sullivan return to Cambridge because the Council of War believed the British had "laid aside their design" on Portsmouth for the moment.[29] Although he was leaving, Sullivan wanted to ensure the town was prepared for any attack that may occur. He, like Washington, used the events of Charlestown, Falmouth, and Bristol to inspire and remind Portsmouth's inhabitants of what they were fighting for:

As the barbarity of our Cruel and inveterate enemies has in many instances exceeded that of the more Savage Barbarians, as they have fully proved that neither the tears of the aged or the cries of the Tender infant can have the least effect upon them, as Havoc and Destruction Seemes to give them Pleasure and deducing to ashes the most Elegant and populous towns fills them with Delight...The General therefore calls upon his Distressed Countrymen...to quit themselves like men to meet those melicious enemies with a becomming fortitude inspired with a just resentment deal to them that Destruction which their unnatural and Cruel

---

[27] Otis Hammond, *The Papers of John Sullivan*, Vol. 1, (Concord, NH: New Hampshire Historical Society, 1930-39), Committee of Safety of Hillsborough County, N.H. to John Sullivan, July 19, 1775, 69.

[28] Bouton, *Documents and Records Relating to the Province of New Hampshire, From 1764 to 1776*, Vol. VII, General Sullivan to George Washington, October 29, 1775, 635-36.

[29] Hammond, *The Papers of John Sullivan*, Vol. 1, Horatio Gates to John Sullivan, October, 31, 1775, 120.

Portsmouth and the Tragedy of Norfolk

Conduct so justly merits."[30]

Portsmouth was never attacked, but the immediate reaction by the Continental Congress and the Continental Army to aid the town is evidence of the fear perpetuated by the attacks of Charlestown, Bristol, and Falmouth. Fear of coastal attacks influenced Washington to write to Sullivan, "I...desire that you will delay no time in causing the seizure of every officer of Government at Portsmouth" and Tory, "who have given pregnant proofs of their unfriendly disposition to the cause we are engaged in."[31]

The creation of a Continental Navy in October 1775, can be, in part, attributed to British reprisals upon coastal towns. The idea of a navy did not originate from these events, but it was further propagated in response to them. As early as June 1775, Christopher Gadsden of South Carolina had been a proponent of the idea, sharing his opinions on the matter with John Adams. Gadsden, earlier in his career, had gained much insight into the operations of the British Navy when he served on one of His Majesty's men-of-war. He was confident that he knew their tactics inside and out. Gadsden's scheme was to entrap some of the smaller British vessels when they were at their greatest risk-- away from the protection of the larger men-of-war. His plan essentially amounted to a campaign of of piracy (guerrilla warfare) by way of the sea. By isolating and attacking British ships, the rebels could gradually chip away at the British fleet until they were too vulnerable to conduct any significant operations.[32] The plan did not receive any acknowledgment by his congressional colleagues, though, and was apparently not even brought to the floor.

But John Adams, excited by Gadsden's proposal, forwarded the

---

[30] Ibid, John Sullivan's General Orders, November 1, 1775, 123.
[31] Bouton, *Documents and Records Relating to the Province of New Hampshire, From 1764 to 1776*, Vol. 7, George Washington to General Sullivan, November 12, 1775, 652.
[32] William M. Fowler, *Rebels Under Sail: The American Navy During the Revolution*, (New York, NY: Charles Scribner's Sons, 1976), 42-3.

idea to his friends in Massachusetts. James Warren had already been working on a similar plan, but more information to help the cause was appreciated. The issues revolving around the plan to create a navy were far more complicated, however. As historian William Fowler points out, "It was one thing to appoint a commander in chief over a rabble in arms surrounding "ministerial butchers" in Boston...that could be justified on strictly defensive grounds, but a navy was another matter, for the mobility and striking capability of armed vessels give them an inherent offensive character."[33] Most importantly, a navy would denote sovereignty, which would misconstrue to the Ministry that their rebellion over constitutional and institutional issues was a push for autonomy.[34]

This concern would have been unnecessary if the rebels would have only known King George was already in the opinion they were "collecting a naval force." He had made a note of it in his famous speech to the House of Lords on October 26, 1775. It was the same speech in which it was stated, "the purpose" of the rebellion was to establish "an independent empire."[35] Lastly, there was much concern over the high cost a navy would pose. John Adams knew the "Expence would be very great," but felt "perhaps the Profits and Benefits to be obtained by it, would be a Compensation." He was conscious their fleet would not be capable of performing traditional naval warfare, but thought "it might destroy small Concerts or Fleets of those like Wallaces at R. Island and Lord Dunmores at Virginia."[36] The cost a Continental Navy presented was at a price most New England colonies were willing to pay; however, their Southern counterparts initially believed they would not see any return on such an investment.

As early as July 18, Congress began to loosen its restrictions on

---

[33] Ibid, 42.
[34] Nathan Miller, *Sea of Glory: The Continental Navy Fights for Independence 1775-1783*, (New York, NY: David McKay Company, 1974), 40.
[35] Force, *American Archives*, Fourth Series, Vol. 6, 1.
[36] Taylor, *The Papers of John Adams*, Vol. 3, John Adams to James Warren, October 19, 1775, 214.

naval operations for the war. It was resolved that, "each colony, at their own expense, make such provisions by armed vessels or otherwise...for the protection of their harbors and navigation on their coasts."[37] These same vessels would soon harass Graves and his fleet in the early goings of the war. Washington also commissioned a small navy consisting of the *Hannah*. Historian William Fowler asserts that Washington did not need much convincing to commission naval vessels for his dispense. Fowler believes the perpetual intelligence the General received regarding British naval maneuvers made the decision to create a navy an easy one.

It is true a small naval fleet would invaluably aid American operations, but much like the members of Congress, Washington was fully aware of the political issues a navy created. Washington would not turn down the opportunity to add a navy to his arsenal, but he chose to not inform Congress of the operations until two months later, on October 5. Washington's disclosure of this information might have only occurred due to instructions he received from Congress the day before. On October 4 he received orders allowing John Glover and Stephen Moylan "to equip to armed Vessels" for service.[38] It must have been the ideal time for the General to disclose his secret operations. Washington was so careful about the operations of the *Hannah* that he gave precise instructions to the crew: Captain Nicholson Broughton was only to attack those vessels and men who were directly involved in supplying the ministerial army.[39] The order allowed Washington to keep his operations secret from Congress, since they were "still not certain about the nature of the hostilities" and did not want to prevent any possibility of reconciliation.[40]

---

[37] Fowler, *Rebels Under Sail: The American Navy During the Revolution*, 45. See also *Journals of the Continental Congress*, Vol. 2, 189.
[38] Abbot & Twohig, *The Papers of George Washington*, Revolutionary Series, Vol. 2, Instructions to Colonel John Glover and Stephen Moylan, October 4, 1775, 90-1.
[39] Fowler, *Rebels Under Sail: The American Navy During the Revolution*, 25.
[40] Ibid, 26.

Rhode Island was the first colony to bring the idea of a Continental Navy before the floor of the Continental Congress. British Captain James Wallace's patrolling of the Narragansett Bay had propelled the Rhode Island delegates to explore the issue. Their primary concerns were the stoppage of trade within the harbors, and the alleged unwarranted harassing and threatening of the colony's inhabitants. On August 26, the colony forwarded to Congress, "that the building and equipping [of] an American fleet, as soon as possible, would greatly and essentially conduce to the preservation of the lives, liberty, and property of the good people of these Colonies and therefore instruct their delegates to use their whole influence at the ensuing congress, for building at the Continental expense a fleet of sufficient force for the protection of these colonies."[41] The proposal provoked many questions from the Congressional delegates. They had already been debating the possibility of opening their ports to foreign trade, but how would all this be perceived? How would Great Britain react? What harm would the British navy pose? How could they protect themselves from such a threat?

When the Rhode Island proposal came to the floor on October 7, it was not quickly dismissed as such ideas had been in the past. Samuel Chase of Maryland called it the "maddest Idea in the World to think of building an American Fleet." Even proponents of a navy did not show their support for the Rhode Island plan. There seemed to be no substance to it, no actual plan, just the vague proposal to build a navy. Edward Rutledge asked to know the number of ships that would be requested before making a decision, but in the end the proposal was laid aside for future consideration.[42] Surprisingly, the first commissioned Continental vessels would not come about from a physical threat to American shipping or their coasts, but rather as a means to prevent the re-supplying of the British. On October 5, John Barry had passed an intelligence report to Congress that detailed the sailing of two

---

[41] Ibid, 48. Also in John R. Bartlett, *Records of the Colony of Rhode Island and Providence Plantations in New England*, (Providence, 1856-65) Vol. 7, 368-69.
[42] Ibid, 49.

supply vessels laden with munitions and headed for Quebec. If the Americans could quickly dispatch two vessels to intercept these two brigs--both ships unarmed and without convoy--a significant blow could be delivered to Gage's army at Boston. The news led to the eventual commissioning of the *Andrew Doria* (originally named *Defiance*) and *Cabot*, the first two vessels of the Continental Navy.

Over the next month, more naval initiatives would pass with the support of the Southern Colonies. The Southern delegates were brought into line with their New England brethren once they received reports of Lord Dunmore's actions in the Chesapeake. They were so appalled with the ease the former governor was able to successfully forage their coasts, that the Southerners soon made the issue of naval security a priority. As far back as August, Edmund Randolph reported to Thomas Jefferson of Dunmore's "Robberies, and other Violations of private Property." He further wrote Dunmore "plunders Custom-Houses, and reviews his Body-Guard at Gosport, unarrested."[43] Dunmore's seizure of the printing press at Norfolk caused great concern for the Southern delegates, especially the Virginian Convention. On September 30, fourteen marines and sailors and seven grenadiers went ashore, carrying away John Holt's *Virginia Gazette* press and bringing it aboard the *Otter*.[44] What was even more appalling to the rebels was that such a small force was capable of landing, marching through the streets of Norfolk and carrying away the press without the least bit of resistance. Not one individual made an attempt to challenge the British contingent, an aura of indifference so prevalent that it caused most rebels to believe the town was a Tory-infested haven.[45] And if this was the case, most rebels

---

[43] Boyd, *The Papers of Thomas Jefferson*, Vol. 1, From Edmund Pendleton, August 31, 1775, 243.
[44] Eller, *Chesapeake Bay in the American Revolution*, Alf J. Mapp, "The Pirate Peer," 73.
[45] Purdie's *Virginia Gazette* spun the event to give rebels hope. The newspaper's argument was all the rebels were out of town that day, thus, Dunmore was successful in capturing the press. The article read, "Let no Tory plume himself on lord Dunmore's success at and in the

believed Virginia's physical security was significantly challenged internally.

The rebel leadership in Virginia was jumping to conclusions without taking the incident and conflict into context. In reality, the majority of colonists preferred to avoid conflict whenever possible. Historians disagree on the exact percentage of neutrals that existed in the conflict, but there is a consensus that non-partisans made up a large portion of the population. Moreover, why would Norfolk's inhabitants, firmly pro-revolutionary, act in this instance? Dunmore was not attacking a town but carrying away a press. If their lives were not in imminent danger, why risk them to save a press?

Reports of the seizure of the Norfolk press were so prominent that an account would be indirectly referenced in George Mason's Virginia's Declaration of Rights. The final draft stated, "That the freedom of the Press is one of the greatest bulwarks of liberty, and can never be restrained but by despotic Governments."[46] Edmund Pendleton described the situation as "degrading and mortifying."[47] Richard Henry Lee wrote to George Washington, "You will, no doubt, have heard the disgraceful conduct of our Norfolk...It happened when the good men of that place were all aw[a]y, and none but Tories & Negroes remained behind."[48] Congressional

---

neighborhood of Norfolk. The situation of Norfolk and Portsmouth was very different from that of any other place in Virginia. The inhabitants were almost to a man merchants and mechanicks, and a majority of them Scotchmen and rank Tories; the towns are full of slaves; ready for an insurrection at the beck of their leader; two men of war always prepared to fire on them; the inhabitants had little or no ammunition, and were badly furnished with arms...But with all these advantages, the great exploit of seizing the printers was achieved when many of the most spirited gentlemen were out of town; and the soldiers stole away the cannon in the night, not daring to venture so far from their ships in the day. " *Virginia Gazette,* Purdie, October 27, 1775, page 2, column 1.
[46] Rutland, *The Papers of George Mason*, Vol. 1, Final Draft of the Declaration of Rights, June 12, 1775, 288.
[47] Eller, *Chesapeake Bay in the American Revolution*, Alf J. Mapp, "The Pirate Peer," 75.
[48] Ballagh, *The Letters of Richard Henry Lee,* To General George

delegate Thomas J. Nelson wrote the feelings of his Congressional colleagues on the matter, stating:
> Is it possible, says one, that they would suffer such a thing? Why you see it is possible, says another; for they have suffered it. Well, says a third, I would not have such a disgrace upon my colony for the whole world. Can you conceive a more unhappy state for a man of feelings? A man who has the honour of his country at heart? I tell them that the chief of the inhabitants are tories: Then why do you suffer such wretches stay among you![49]

The Williamsburg newspapers also questioned Norfolk's character, stating, "whether they acted in this affair becoming the character of freemen or whether pusillanimity had not too great a share of their conduct."[50] Dunmore had not seized the press without provocation. Throughout the revolution, control of the presses belonged to the rebels. The Tories could only control a limited number of publications and found themselves incapable of getting much of their information widely circulated, leaving the majority of information in the hands a rebel press. Holt's *Virginia Gazette* was no exception. For months, the publication had slandered Captain Matthew Squire of the *HMS Otter* and the governor. On September 6, Holt's *Gazette* published, "Is it not a melancholy reflection that men who effect on all occasions to style themselves 'his Majesty's servants' should think the service of their Sovereign consists of plundering his subjects and in committing such pitiful acts of rapine as would entitle other people to the character of robbers?"[51] Squire would address Holt in a message stating:

Sir,
> You have in many papers lately taken the freedom to mention

---

Washington, October 22, 1775, 152.
[49] Eller, *Chesapeake Bay in the American Revolution*, Alf J. Mapp, "The Pirate Peer," 76.
[50] Ibid, 75.
[51] Ibid, 71. From John Hunter Holt's *Virginia Gazette or, the Norfolk Intelligencer*, September 6, 1775.

my name, and thereto added many falsities. I now declare, if I am ever again mentioned therein with any reflections on my character, I will most assuredly seize your person and take you on board the *Otter*.[52]

Holt responded by printing the letter in its entirety, with the note it "needs no comment" and it was "very extraordinary." He further stated:

> The Printer cannot forebear to say that he has always endeavored to keep an open and liberal press, as free for Captain Squire as for anyone else. If there have been any mistakes, the have been the result of the popular voice, and although it would always have given the Printer pleasure to be in any degree instrumental to the strictest harmony between his Majesty's subjects in this colony and the gentlemen of the navy, yet he does not conceive that his press is to be under the direction of anyone but himself, and while he has the sanction of the law, he shall always pride himself in the reflections that the liberty of the press is one of the grand bulwarks of the English Constitution.[53]

Holt's assertion that the press was "open and liberal" was far from the truth. The lack of objectivity within the revolutionary presses was intended to gain support for the rebel cause. There were pamphleteers and newspapers which supported the stance of the British government, but these were not as well organized as those of the rebels, not to mention, many loyalist presses that were forced out of business. John Mein, editor of the *Boston Chronicle*, was beaten up by a mob and forced out of Massachusetts for his criticism of non-importation.[54] James Rivington's *Gazetteer* press was smashed by a Patriot group on November 25, 1775, and the type was carted off to Connecticut where it was forged into ammunition. In most instances, Patriots pressured citizens not to

---

[52] Ibid.
[53] Ibid.
[54] Potter, *The Liberty We Seek: Loyalist Ideology in Colonial New York and Massachusetts*, 32.

read or subscribe to Loyalist publications.[55] The revolutionary intolerance of loyalist views was appalling when compared to the freedom of speech afforded in Britain. It was ironic to some loyalists that those in Great Britain who supported America's stance were not silenced and free to express their dissenting views.[56]

In January 1776, Azor Betts was summoned to the New York Committee of Safety for "denouncing Congresses and Committees, both Continental and Provincial as a set of damned rascals, who acted only to feather their own nests."[57] He was ordered to close confinement, but finally released in April upon penitence, paying a fine, and taking an oath of allegiance. Thomas Robinson of Delaware was ordered to stand trial for allegedly stating the Whig Committees "were a pack of fools for taking up arms against the King, that our charters were not annihilated, changed, or altered by the late acts of Parliament" and "the present Congress were an unconstitutional body of men, and also, that the great men were pushing on the common people between them and all danger."[58] In 1775, Leonard Snowden had written letters to England that were abusive towards the Whig cause, and, once found by the rebel authorities, he was consequently arrested.[59] A loyalist in Delaware, only described by the initial "C," was inspected for cursing Congress. Upon his trial, the audience called for the charge of treason, but the inspection committee called only for recantation. Following the proceeding, the crowd was not satisfied and pushed for a "coat of tar and feathers; but after some hesitation, and much persuasion, were prevented from using any violent measures."[60] Benjamin Butler of Connecticut was arrested

---

[55] Ibid, 32-33.
[56] Ibid, 30.
[57] Sabine, *Biographical Sketches of Loyalists of the American Revolution*, Vol. 1, 227.
[58] Sabine, *Biographical Sketches of Loyalists of the American Revolution*, Vol. 2, 231.
[59] Ibid, 322.
[60] Vaughn, *Chronicles of the American Revolution*, "A Loyalist Encounters Delaware Justice: A Letter from Samuel M'Masters of

for defaming the Continental Congress. Butler was deprived of bearing or wearing arms, and forbidden to hold public office.[61]

Holt did not desist in voicing his "liberal" opinion. He continued charging Squire of capital crimes and soon would include Dunmore in his personal criticisms. The reminder that the governor's father rebelled against the Crown in 1746 was suspected to have caused Dummore's reprisal. Squire again reminded Holt to cease and desist one more time on September 30, but Dunmore had seen enough. Dunmore wrote to Lord Dartmouth stating:

> The public prints of this little dirty Borough of Norfolk, has for some time past been wholly employed in exciting, in the minds of all Ranks of People the spirit of sedition and Rebellion, by the grossest misrepresentations of facts, both, public & private; that they might do no further mischief, I sent a small party on shore...and brought off their press.[62]

Dunmore's seizure of the press, permitting runaway slaves to board his ships, and foraging parties were all abusive policies that impelled the Southern delegates to support the establishment of a naval force. Nonetheless, a large naval force was not yet desirable, since establishing such a large institution might be construed by the British as a gesture towards independence. This judgment would soon change once news of Dunmore's Proclamation spread, and Norfolk would become the dramatic epicenter of even more appalling events.

In the Declaration of Independence it states, "He has plundered our seas, ravaged our coasts, burnt our towns, and destroyed the lives of our people." This statement was broad enough to incorporate the long list of naval grievances the rebels held the

---

Lewes, Delaware, to Dr. James Tilton of Dover, November 14, 1775," 206.
[61] Sabine, *Biographical Sketches of Loyalists of the American Revolution*, Vol. 1, 281.
[62] H.S. Parsons, "Contemporary English Accounts of the Destruction of Norfolk in 1776," *William and Mary Quarterly*, Second Series, Vol. 13, No. 4, (October 1933), 223.

Portsmouth and the Tragedy of Norfolk

British accountable for. With the words "burnt our towns," Jefferson was undoubtedly referring the events of Bristol, Falmouth, and Charlestown, but if there was one town Jefferson could have denounced with disrepute it would have been Norfolk. Throughout the colonies, the rumors regarding the burning of Norfolk circulated the news that the British had heartlessly fired upon the town. Pinkney's *Virginia Gazette* reported with "the wind being favorable to their [British] design, the flames spread with great rapidity, and when the fire had run to a great extent, and our enemies imagined they had spread confusion and terror amongst our young troops."[63] In Williamsburg it was believed rebels should "rejoice that half the mischief of our enemies can do us, is done already," when the British "destroyed one of the first towns in America."[64] The event led George Woolsey of Baltimore to believe "we have all the Reason in the world to think he intends for this in the spring."[65]

For Washington, his greatest fears were realized. A month earlier, he had intercepted intelligence which laid out Dunmore's entire "devious" plan along the Chesapeake. Before the papers could be confiscated, neither Congress nor Washington knew anything except what Dunmore had released to the newspapers and the private correspondence they had received from fellow rebels in Virginia. The plan showed an organized attack on Alexandria, which was within eight miles of Washington's home, Mount Vernon. The General was even more disturbed by this fact, because, just months earlier he had also received reports that Dunmore threatened to kidnap his wife, Martha Washington. It can be speculated this might have been the cause of Washington's request to hasten Martha to join him earlier that fall. Although Martha would be at his side when information of Norfolk was

---

[63] United States, Naval History Division, *Naval Documents of the American Revolution*, Vol.3, Pinkney's Virginia Gazette, January 6, 1776, 661.

[64] Force, *American Archives*, Fourth Series, Volume 4, 539.

[65] United States, Naval History Division, *Naval Documents of the American Revolution*, Vol.3, George Woolsey to George Salmon, January 26, 1776, 1000.

received, he must have felt Dunmore was capable of any atrocity.[66] Washington would write to his good friend Joseph Reed:

> I hope my Countrymen (of Virginia) will rise superior to any losses the whole Navy of Great Britain can bring on them, & that the destruction of Norfolk, & threatned devastation of other places, will have no other effect than to unite the whole Country in one indissoluble Band against a Nation which seems to be lost to ever sense of Virtue, and those feelings which distinguish a Civilized People from the most barbarous Savages. A few more of such flaming Arguments as were exhibited at Falmouth and Norfolk, added to the sound Doctrine, and the answerable reasoning contain (in the pamphlet) Common Sense, will not leave numbers at a loss to decide upon the Propriety of Separation.[67]

Washington's opinion was largely influenced by Paine's pamphlet, but John Hancock had written similar sentiments to the General. Hancock wrote, "Lord Dunmore has endeavored to exercise the same barbarity against the defenceless town of Norfolk, as was exercised against Falmouth...these repeated instances of inhumanity so contrary to the rules of war and so long exploded by all civilized nations."[68]

It is intriguing to see the similarity, yet evident inaccuracy in the accounts of both the senior-ranking rebel officers at Norfolk. Only some of the facts were reported. On the one hand, Colonel Robert Howe wrote to the Virginia Convention, "Under cover of their guns they landed and set fire to the town in several places near the water, though our men strove to prevent them all in their power," stating the purpose of the bombardment was to "throw us

---

[66] Charles, *Washington's Decision: The Story of George Washington's Decision to Reaccept Black Enlistments in the Continental Army, December 31, 1775*, 68-70.

[67] Abbot & Twohig, *The Papers of George Washington*, Revolutionary Series, Vol. 3, To Lieutenant Colonel Joseph Reed, January 31, 1776, 225-29.

[68] Ibid, From John Hancock, January 6-21, 1776, 42-45.

Portsmouth and the Tragedy of Norfolk

into confusion." He further stated the women and children had to run through a "crowd of shot to get out of the town, some of them with children at their breasts; a few have, I hear, been killed."[69] Colonel William Woodford, on the other hand, would only divulge to Colonel Thomas Elliott of the seven-hour cannonade, the landing of the British, and the "Nine tenths of the town" which were destroyed.[70] Both these Sons of Liberty were leaving out a very pertinent part of the story. The fact was that the rebels were responsible for the destruction of nine-tenths of the town, not the British.

According to the October 1777 report of the commissioners to inquire into the losses at Norfolk, Lord Dunmore was responsible for the destruction of nineteen buildings at a cost of 1,616 pounds, while the rebels were accountable for 863 houses valued at 110,807 pounds. Much like Falmouth, Charlestown, and Bristol the destruction of Norfolk was in no way a cut and dry case of the British being at fault for its destruction. In fact, an overwhelming amount of evidence proves the rebels were responsible for the town's demise. Colonel Howe used his distorted rebel version of the story to pose the question to the Virginia Convention, "Does it not call for vengeance from both God and Man?"[71] Historian Pauline Maier writes, "Norfolk…with the burning of Charlestown, Massachusetts…and the destruction of Falmouth, Maine…seemed to show how harshly George III was prepared to repress his American subjects."[72] How was truth of such an event covered up to the majority of the public? Williamsburg falsely reported the town had to be destroyed in order to "prevent our enemies taking shelter in them."[73] It was further stated:

---

[69] United States, Naval History Division, *Naval Documents of the American Revolution*, Vol.3, Colonel Robert Howe to the President of the Virginia Convention, January 2, 1776, 579-80.
[70] Ibid, Colonel William Woodford to Colonel Thomas Elliott, January 4, 1776, 617.
[71] Ibid, Colonel Robert Howe to the President of the Virginia Convention, January 2, 1776, 579-80.
[72] Maier, *American Scripture*, 27.
[73] Force, *American Archives*, Fourth Series, Vol. 4, 946-47.

> Thus, in the course of five weeks, has a town which contained upwards of six thousand inhabitants, many of them in affluent circumstances, a place that carried on an extensive trade and commerce, consequently affording bread to many thousands, been reduced to ashes, and become desolate, through the wicked and cruel machinations of Lord North and the junto, aided by their faithful servants, my Lord Dunmore, with his motley army, and the renowned Captain Bellew, Commodore of his Britannick Majesty's fleet in Virginia...[74]

Landon Carter, the wealthy Virginia landowner, initially heard "the town was burnt and fired upon" because Col. Howe would not give them "Provisions and necessaries."[75] These clearly misrepresented and slanted versions of events, or some form of them, are what was believed to have occurred. Not until nearly sixty years later were these accounts finally publicly disavowed. It would take another hundred years for historians to find and note the fact.

Since the seizure of the printing press back in October, Norfolk was suspected as a haven for Tories. One rebel blamed the removal of the press due to the town's large majority of "merchants and mechanicks, and a majority of them Scotchmen and rank Tories." The author further added that Dunmore's success "has but served to increase that resentment which has been suppressed for some time past."[76] Many of the prominent rebels concurred. Colonel Scott described Norfolk as "the most horrid place I ever beheld."[77] In October, Richard Henry Lee hoped "to hear of the demolition of that infamous nest of Tories."[78] These

---

[74] Ibid.
[75] Jack P. Greene, *The Diary of Colonel Landon Carter of Sabine Hall, 1752-1778,* Vol. II, (Charlottesville, VA: The University Press of Virginia, 1965), 968.
[76] Force, *American Archives,* Fourth Series, Vol. 3, 1191.
[77] Ibid, Vol. 4, Colonel Scott to Captain Southall, December 17, 1775, 292.
[78] Ballagh, *The Letters of Richard Henry Lee,* Vol. 1, To George

Portsmouth and the Tragedy of Norfolk

opinions undoubtedly reached Norfolk, since the remaining inhabitants expressed concern that the rebels had designs of firing the town. Lord Dunmore also rightfully speculated "a large body of the Rebel Army" intended to destroy Norfolk "because its inhabitants had professed their loyalty to Government."[79]

The confiscation of the printing press was one of many events that severely upset the rebel leadership. In his campaign of foraging and raiding, Dunmore would be successful in taking Kemp's Landing twice. He then began a series of raids on October 12, which purpose was to capture the rebels' cannon and gunpowder stores. For the most part, the raiding party landed unopposed, but it was unsuccessful in capturing the gunpowder. To meet the threat, the rebels deployed Colonel William Woodford, who was chosen over Patrick Henry to lead the expedition. He was given the following orders:

> You are to use your best endeavors for protecting and defending the persons and properties of all friends to the cause of America, and to this end, to attack, kill, or captivate all such as you shall discover to be in arms for the annoying of those persons, as far as you shall judge it prudent to engage them. You will use every means in your power for stopping all communication of intelligence and supplies of provisions, to the enemies of America in Norfolk or Portsmouth... There may be many persons in these towns, or near them, who may be afraid in their present situation, exposed to the vengeance of the Navy, to declare their real sentiments. We think, therefore, that all those who will continue peaceable, giving no assistance or intelligence to our enemies, nor attempting to annoy our troops, or injure our friends, may for the present remain unmolested; those Tories and others who take an active part against us, must be considered as enemies; your own humanity and discretion will, however, prevent the wanton damage or destruction of

---

Washington, October 22, 1775, 152-53.
[79] United States, Naval History Division, *Naval Documents of the American Revolution*, Vol.3, Extract of a Letter from a Gentleman, Dated Ship William, December 25, 1775, 242.

any person's property whatsoever...We will wish you to be attentive to the force and motions of the enemy, and act offensively or defensively, as your prudence may direct for the good of the common cause...[80]

Woodford would be distracted from reaching Norfolk due to the threat the British posed in nearby Hampton, Virginia. The rebels would come out of that engagement victorious, causing Governor Dunmore to issue his proclamation declaring martial law and freeing the slaves "that are able and willing to bear arms." He drafted the document on November 7 but would not publish it until the success of his second raid upon Kemp's Landing. These events, accompanied with the oath of allegiance the inhabitants of Norfolk took to "his sacred Majesty George III," angered the large majority of rebels.[81] Following the news of Kemp's Landing, the rumor concerning the intended rebel burning of the town reached Norfolk's inhabitants.[82] In one instance, Doctor Archibald Campbell had heard from Colonel Woodford that Norfolk "was to be plundered then burnt." Unhappy with Woodford's remark,

---

[80] Eller, *Chesapeake Bay in the American Revolution*, Alf Mapp Jr., "The Pirate Peer," 78.
[81] Force, *American Archives*, Fourth Series, Vol. 3, 1671.
[82] Anthony Warwick from Portsmouth, Virginia wrote to his friend in Glasgow: "It is now certain that the provincials are on their march from Williamsburg for this place, or Norfolk; it is uncertain which, though it is generally believed they come with a professed intention of destroying both by fire. Their number cannot be ascertained. It is said they only set off from Williamsburg with 600, but expected to be increased to 1500 before they got to this place; which I dare say will be the case, as the whole country are anxious to have these towns destroyed, as they think them places for refuge for those that are inimical to what they call the liberties of America....I am satisfied there will be bloody work when these forces come down, as the governour, even with the small number he has, and may be able to raise in that country, is determined to attack them; and if they succeed in their intention of destroying these towns, he is determined to lay waste the whole country that can be come at with a tender or barge. *Virginia Gazette*, Purdie, December 29, 1775, page 1, column 1.

Portsmouth and the Tragedy of Norfolk

Campbell informed him "they were to act to avoid such calamities."[83] Woodford told him to make an application to the Virginia Convention, and, coincidentally at around this same time, Campbell was charged with aiding Lord Dunmore. Campbell's reputation was now on trial because he had conveyed his adverse sentiments towards Woodford's wanting to burn Norfolk.

The Virginia Committee of Safety took the alleged threat to burn Norfolk very seriously. Edmund Pendleton issued the following denial:

> Whereas divers reports have been propagated, that the army destined to guard and protect the inhabitants of the counties of Norfolk and Princess Anne, and the parts adjacent, were empowered and directed to destroy the houses and properties of particular persons in some of the towns in those parts, who have been justly alarmed by such false and malicious reports: In order, therefore, to do justice to the publick in general, and to satisfy all private persons in particular, the Committee of Safety think it necessary to declare, in the most solemn manner, that the above mentioned reports have been propagated without having the least foundation in truth, it having been determined, and the army aforesaid being instructed, particularly to support and protect the persons and properties of all friends to America, and not wantonly to damage or destroy the property of any person whatsoever.[84]

Some have insinuated that Dunmore simply began cannonading Norfolk in response to the rebel occupation of the town, but such an allegation portrays the story neither accurately nor objectively. Due to the embarrassing loss of the Battle of Great Bridge,

---

[83] Force, *American Archives*, Fourth Series, Vol. 4, 86.
[84] Eller, *Chesapeake Bay in the American Revolution*, Alf Mapp Jr., "The Pirate Peer," 82. John Page had also made note to Thomas Jefferson that, "The People at Norfolk are under dreadful Apprehensions of having their Town burnt by this Detachment. They know they deserve it, but we seem to be at a Loss what to do with them." Boyd, *The Papers of Thomas Jefferson*, Vol. 1, John Page to Thomas Jefferson, November 11, 1775, 258.

Irreconcilable Grievances

Dunmore had lost the capability to effectively supply his forces. He organized a strategic withdrawal to the British men-of-war and harbored off the coast of Norfolk while the rebels retook the town. Even all of Norfolk's loyalists went aboard with Dunmore, "with their whole families, and their most valuable Effects, some in the Men of War, some in their own Vessels." The rebels were also able to take a British supply brig loaded with salt which was stationed a "Musquet Shot of the Town," arrested the two officers on board, and "burnt her when they had taken out but a Small portion of the Salt." Later that day, a group of rebels went down to the bay to fire "twelve or fifteen Shot at the *Otter* Sloop of War," an action not condoned by Colonel Woodford.[85]

An interesting facet of the rebel recapture of Norfolk was how the event was portrayed in the newspapers. Pinkney's *Virginia Gazette* reported:

> A correspondent, upon whose information we may depend, informs us that our soldiers shewed the greatest humanity and tenderness to the wounded prisoners. Several of them ran through a hot fire to lift up and bring in some that were bleeding, and who they feared would die, if not speedily assisted by the surgeon. The prisoners expected to be scalped, and called out, For God's Sake, Do Not Murder our men, was answered by him, put your arm around my neck, and I'll she you what I intend to do. Then taking him...he walked slowly along, bearing him up wit great tenderness to the breast-work. Captain Leslie seeing two of our soldiers tenderly removing a wounded regular from the bridge, on which he lay, stepped up to the platform of the fort, and bowing with great respect, thanked them for their kindness. These are instances of a noble disposition of foul Men who can act thus must be invincible.[86]

Whether this "noble" incident actually took place is debatable,

---

[85] United States, Naval History Division, *Naval Documents of the American Revolution*, Vol.3, Lord Dunmore to Lord Dartmouth, December 6-17, 1775, 140-42

[86] Ibid, Pinkney's Virginia Gazette, December 23, 1775, 220.

but the account was probably propaganda since no other information exists concerning the humane treatment of prisoners. Physical reprisals upon Tories were extremely common, making the notion of such sympathy rather dubious. Thomas MacKnight, a known Norfolk Tory, wrote of having to "avoid being assassinated" for the threat his loyalist ideals held towards the "raising of a strong party...in favour of Government."[87] The Virginia Convention had passed on to Woodford, "all such Tories, taken by him, who shall...appear to have born arms against this colony be sent to the city of Williamsburg."[88] The rebel army, which had allegedly showed such "noble disposition," would do much more than just send the prisoners to Williamsburg. With "upwards of 100 of them" in their guard, one loyalist remarked, those "who fall into their hands, they treat with the greatest cruelty, chaining them to Negroes."[89] The rebels degraded the white Tories in this fashion to serve as a lesson since Dunmore had issued his proclamation offering freedom to slaves.

Following the Battle of Great Bridge, Dunmore was already short on provisions, but his situation would turn even more desolate because he lacked the supplies to adequately feed his troops and the loyalists under his protection. He sent Captain Squire ashore under a flag of truce to request "His Majesty's forces to be supplied with fresh provisions."[90] The request was rejected, but Captain Bellew of the *Liverpool* would make another attempt. The Virginia Convention answered his request, resolving, "that his Convention are fully sensible of the hardships many innocent persons on board his majesty's ships may be exposed to, for want of regular supplies of fresh provisions, which we would not wish to withhold, unless compelled by the duty we

---

[87] Ibid, Thomas MacKnight to Reverend Dr. MacKnight, December 26, 1775, 260.
[88] Ibid, Journal of the Virginia Convention, December 14, 1775, 103.
[89] Ibid, Colonel William Woodford to Edmund Pendleton, December 17, 1775, 139. Second quotation taken from Ibid, Extract of a Letter from a Gentleman Off Norfolk, Virginia, December 25, 1775, 243-44.
[90] Ibid, Lord Dunmore to Lord Dartmouth, December 6-17, 1775, 140-42.

owe to the country, loudly calling upon us to use every exertion for the defence of its inhabitants." The rebels would not supply any ships unless it could be proven they "come to Virginia on a friendly errand."[91]

Knowing would be incapable of caring for the Norfolk inhabitants aboard any of his fleet, Dunmore allowed them to petition Colonel Woodford, "desiring they might have leave to return, as their wives and children are greatly distressed." The colonial officer replied that women and children may return with full protection as long as they were "not to be at liberty to return or give intelligence to the enemy." The men, if they wished to return, "should have no violence offered to them than to remain prisoners till they could be fairly and impartially tried by their country."[92] It was upon hearing this impudent answer, compounded by the prevention of their supply, that Dunmore and Captain Squire reached a full-blown state of distress. Their patience would run out on December 31, when "1500 Rebels...began to insult us, by firing at us, and particularly attempting to shoot" Dunmore.[93]

On January 1, 1776 Captain Bellew would fire the first shots from the *H.M.S. Liverpool*. He was sparked to fire "a few Shot" upon discovering the rebel army was "parading in the Streets," an act deemed an insult. Bellew's example was followed by cannonading from the rest of the men-of-war. Dunmore then ordered the firing of the warehouses near the shore since they had been "continually annoyed by firing from the Rebels out of that part of the town."[94] The fire was intended to only destroy that quarter of the town which posed a threat to the fleet. In truth, it was the rebels, as soon as the "Men of War ceased fireing," that set "fire to every House," and "burnt many houses on both sides of the River, the property of individuals who have never taken any

---

[91] Ibid, Journal of the Virginia Convention, December 29, 1775, 295.
[92] Ibid, Journal of the Virginia Convention, January 2, 1776, 579.
[93] H.S. Parsons, "Contemporary English Accounts of the Destruction of Norfolk in 1776," *William and Mary Quarterly*, Second Series, Vol. 13, No. 4, (October 1933), 221.
[94] Force, *American Archives*, Fourth Series, Vol. 4, 540-41.

Portsmouth and the Tragedy of Norfolk

part of this contest."[95] "The country around, for several days, was illuminated with the fires of houses" the rebel forces burnt.[96]

The identity of the rebel officer who gave the order to fire Norfolk remains unknown. It has been speculated the rebel army might have acted independently of their officers. It is of common opinion that Norfolk was nothing more than a "nest of Tories," hence it is fathomable that the rebel army took advantage of the confusion. The buildings could have been looted and set afire since it would not be possible to establish which were set afire by the British or by her defenders.

Prior to the bombardment of Norfolk, Colonel Howe wrote to the Virginia Convention with a proposal for the town's destruction. He recommended its destruction due to the ease by which the British could defend the region. The mouth of the James River served to complement Britain's naval superiority and it was believed the town's ample number of buildings would "conveniently barrack almost any number of troops."[97] Howe pointed out to the Virginia Convention's delegates, "Norfolk cannot be maintained with any troops you can place there…In short, thought this is a situation extremely desirable to your adversaries who have shipping, it will ever remain in the kind of war we are waging a place disadvantageous and dangerous to you."[98] The request was denied, but his words point suspiciously to Howe, himself, as the orchestrator of the burning of Norfolk.

The fact was that neither Howe nor Woodford held the inhabitants of Norfolk in high regard. Their acceptance of Dunmore had angered the majority of Virginia rebels. Regarding the burning of Norfolk Virginia patriot John Page simply felt its inhabitants "deserve it," and was "at a Loss" with what to do with them. Page felt many of them "deserve to be ruined and hanged,"

---

[95] United States, Naval History Division, *Naval Documents of the American Revolution*, Vol.3, Lord Dunmore to Lord Dartmouth, January 4, 1776, 617-18.
[96] Force, *American Archives*, Fourth Series, Vol. 4, 540-41.
[97] Eller, *Chesapeake Bay in the American Revolution*, Alf Mapp Jr., "The Pirate Peer," 86.
[98] Ibid.

but knew some were only acting for "Want of Protection."[99] Howe was actually disappointed his army "met with no resistance" because "he could not treat it as it deserved," as traitors and enemies to their country. He queried, how "could a colony so truly Respectable as this in every other Part, could have belonging to it, so contemptible a lot of wretches." Colonel Scott described Norfolk as "the most horrid place I ever beheld."[100]

In essence, Norfolk was nothing more than a casualty of war, and more importantly a casualty for the rebel cause. The town's destruction would serve both as an example to those colonists who wanted to remain loyal to the Crown and as a rallying call for the rebel leadership. Williamsburg reported:

They have done their worst, and to no other purpose than to harden our soldiers, and learn them to bear, without dismay, all the most formidable operations of war, carried on by a powerful and cruel enemy, to no other purpose than to give the world specimens of British cruelty and American fortitude, unless it be to force us to lay aside that childish fondness for Britain, ant that foolish, tame dependence on her.[101]

News of the event at Norfolk spread quickly, reaching Baltimore in less than a week, but not reaching the London newspapers until April. The news affirmed the seriousness of the situation and was not well received by many in Britain. One Englishman believed "the Americans will be neither discouraged nor subjugated, in spite of the care taken by the Ministry to frighten them with our so-called hostile intentions towards them."[102] He was correct. In effect, the rebel account of the event advanced the revolutionary argument against the tyranny of

---

[99] Boyd, *The Papers of Thomas Jefferson*, Vol. 1, John Page to Thomas Jefferson, November 11, 1775, 258.

[100] Ivor Noel Hume, *1775: Another Part of the Field*, (New York, NY: Alfred A. Knopf, 1966), 445.

[101] Force, *American Archives*, Fourth Series, Vol. 4, 539.

[102] United States, Naval History Division, *Naval Documents of the American Revolution*, Vol. 4, 956.

Portsmouth and the Tragedy of Norfolk

Britain. The news of Norfolk itself had a minimal effect in England compared to news of Falmouth' destruction. Count De Vergennes, advisor to French King Louis XVI, at first could not to believe the news. He wrote to Count De Guines:

> I can hardly believe this absurd as well as barbaric procedure on the part of an enlightened and civilized nation, more especially as the perpetrators of this terrible crime allegedly declared that the order had been given to burn all maritime towns from Boston to Halifax. If the English had resolved to abandon America to its own and to cut the last threads binding them to their brothers, one could see in this resolution the effect of furious and boundless despair. But in view of the intention the Government seems to have to carry a large army to America it seems inconceivable to destroy the places for shelter and storehouses. If it is the plan on the part of the British to turn the coast into a desert, how will they penetrate the country where will they establish their magazines?[103]

Neither did the event make much sense to some members of the British Ministry. A small investigation into the matter was conducted, when in January, the Lord Commissioners had forwarded to Germain two letters from Graves concerning the accounts of Falmouth and Machias.[104] Germain wrote to General William Howe in order to obtain more factual information regarding the incidents. It would not be until the summer that Howe confirmed Germain's request for a "more explicit Account of the Expedition of Falmouth."[105] Confusion over the matter only helped to confirm the October decision to remove Admiral Graves

---

[103] United States, Naval History Division, *Naval Documents of the American Revolution*, Vol. 3, Count De Vergennes to Count De Guines, December 31, 1775, 467.

[104] Ibid, Lords Commissioner to Lord George Germain, January 3, 1776, 471.

[105] United States, Naval History Division, *Naval Documents of the American Revolution*, Vol. 4, Major General William Howe to Lord George Germain, May 7, 1776, 1435-7.

from command, at least those who were unhappy with the handling of the conflict. Surprisingly, Falmouth was not a factor in Graves' dismissal. News of the British Navy's attack arrived months after the decision to remove him had already been made. In fact, an incident like Falmouth might have aided in his remaining in command. In June, Philip Stevens had written to the Admiral, "their Lordships very much approve" of his conduct.[106] The Earl of Sandwich recommended to Graves, "to exert yourself to the utmost towards crushing the daring rebellion that [has] now extended itself almost over the whole continent of America...you may be blamed for doing too little, but can never be censured for doing too much."[107]

As far back as July 1775, the King let his sentiments about Admiral Graves be known to Lord North, when he wrote, "I do think the Admiral's removal as necessary if what is reported is founded."[108] Subsequently to the date he wrote this, news arrived, that in September 1774, Graves had been beaten with his own sword at Boston by Customs Commissioner Benjamin Hallowell. Their disagreement originated over the distribution of some hay, where Graves had both of his eyes blackened.[109] The King would change his stance, late in August, when he wrote to Lord Sandwich, "The letters from Vice-Admiral Graves seem to convey his being attentive to his duty."[110] This positive attitude would not last long. Count De Guines wrote back to France, "the entire Council of the King...does not seem to be favorably disposed to"

---

[106] United States, Naval History Division, *Naval Documents of the American Revolution*, Vol. 1, Philip Stevens to Vice Admiral Samuel Graves, June 24, 1775, 491.
[107] Tilly, *The Royal Navy in North America, 1774-1781*, 116.
[108] W. Bodham Donne, *The Correspondence with King George III to Lord North 1768-1783*, (New York, NY: De Capo Press, 1971), Letter 304, July 28, 1775, 256-7.
[109] Stout, *The Royal Navy in America 1760-1775*, 162. For the most detailed account of this affair, see Yerxa, *Admiral Samuel Graves and the Falmouth Affair*, 77-78.
[110] United States, Naval History Division, *Naval Documents of the American Revolution*, Vol. 2, King George III to Lord Sandwich, 687.

Graves and Gage, causing him to form the opinion, "they will lose their commands because they have been made responsible for all the defeats."[111] Lord Rochford, Secretary of State for the Southern Department would inform Grave's friend and political ally, the Earl of Sandwich, "The King...has authorized me to tell you that he does not see, after every letter laying such blame on him [Graves], how the command can any longer be left in such improper hands."[112] On September 17, Sandwich would write to Graves he had "received his Majesty's commands for your returning home at the close of the year."[113]

The unremitting reception of bad news concerning the administration of the conflict in the colonies, coupled with information that Graves and Gage disputed between one another over many issues, including the acquisition of supplies, the distribution of the British Marines, and the carrying out of the conflict, all these points of complaint helped push the decision to an inexorable and unfavorable end. Lord Rochford would forward to Lord Sandwich the "bitter complaints" of "Officers of distinction" who had "written a state of facts that cannot be contradicted." The accounts of vessels being taken, "officers killed, men made prisoners," the plundering of islands "under the protection of our ships," and the burning of a lighthouse "almost under the guns of two or three men of war" was too much. The complaining officers wondered what excuse could be found "for not enforcing instant restitution and reparation, or laying the towns in ashes" in response to the conduct of the colonists?[114] They would get their wish in October, but by then it was too late, as the decision to remove Graves had already been made. Other complaints regarding the Admiral would be made, even following his orders for chastising the coastal towns of New England. One commented since his arrival here, Graves has been "good for

---

[111] Ibid, Count De Guines to Count De Vergennes, August 18, 1775, 679.
[112] Tilly, *The Royal Navy in North America, 1774-1781*, 152.
[113] United States, Naval History Division, *Naval Documents of the American Revolution*, Vol. 2, Lord Sandwich to Vice Admiral Graves, September 17, 1775, 721.
[114] Ibid, Lord Rochford to Lord Sandwich, September 8, 1775, 708.

nothing."[115] Another criticized:
This vigilant officer, instead of sending his squadron to protect the store-ships and transports from England, has, with the utmost prudence, ordered the ships of war in this harbour to be secured with bombs all around, to prevent their being boarded and taken by the Rebel whale-boats; and for some time past he has never sent a single ship to cruise off Cape Ann, because the Rebels have had some cannon mounted upon it: no doubt the Parliament will thank him on his glorious return for so effectually preserving his Majesty's ships.[116]

Jonathan Sewell held a similar opinion on Graves actions, stating, "he is cursed as hard upon this Side of the Water, as he can be on yours...he has now no Advocate here, & I believe will scarcely find a Friend in England upon his return."[117] Graves would not learn of his removal until Rear Admiral Molyneux Shuldham arrived in December. One loyalist wrote, "It must be a change for the better, for so much Ignorance, Stupidity, Pride, Avarice & whatever You have a mind to add in the same Strain, never centered in one Commander of a Fleet in the British Navy since the Flag was hoisted, as in one Commander of a Fleet in the British Navy since the Flag was hoisted, as in one that is unknown among us."[118] The news was a shock to Graves, especially since Shuldham was a junior ranking officer, "who had not had a Flag when the Vice Admiral was appointed to the American command." His narrative states:
Nothing could be more unexpected or extraordinary than this Recall: for it bore the 29 of September, and he [Admiral Shuldham] had Letters from the Board of the entire Approbation of his Conduct down to the 6th of the same

---

[115] United States, Naval History Division, *Naval Documents of the American Revolution*, Vol. 3, Extract of a Letter from Boston, December 13, 1775, 84-86.
[116] Ibid, Letter from an Officer in Boston, December 21, 1775, 194.
[117] Ibid, Jonathan Sewall to Edward Winslow, January 10, 1776, 495-6.
[118] Ibid, N. Taylor to Joseph Taylor, January 16, 1776, 811.

Month. Nevertheless he [Vice Admiral Graves] betrayed no Emotion or Resentment either at the thing itself or the manner of it, concealed all Indignation, and was manly enough to avoid even taking the least notice of the hardness of his Usage in any Dispatch.[119]

Shuldham had been initially sent to be Graves' second in command. Following news of Lexington and Concord arriving in England, it was believed the task of administrating the navy for the entire American continent was too much of a burden for one man. Thus, while the Admiralty was working to increase Graves' fleet, it was believed Shuldham "would be a very able rear-admiral to command under" him.[120] Graves was informed that this would be the case but was surprised when he came on board the *Preston* and learned otherwise.

Not everyone blamed Graves for the misfortunes of the British Navy in America. In the House of Commons it was stated, "Will the noble lord declare that admiral Graves has ever received positive orders that he did not execute."[121] The statement was in fact correct. Graves had never disobeyed or deviated from any orders he had received from the Ministry. The naval problems primarily rested with the Ministry's assumptions. Lord Dartmouth held the sentiments of most of Parliament, when he wrote, "The Colonies will in a few months feel their distress; their spirits, not animated by any little success on their part or violence of persecution on ours will sink; they will be consequently inclined to treat, probably to submit to a certain degree."[122] As history would bear out, their assumptions would have dire consequences for both Britain and Graves.

Moreover, it is intriguing that the events at Charlestown, Falmouth, Bristol, or Norfolk were not the reason for his

---

[119] Ibid, Narrative of Vice Admiral Graves, December 30, 1775, 300.
[120] Tilly, *The Royal Navy in North America, 1774-1781*, 116.
[121] United States, Naval History Division, *Naval Documents of the American Revolution*, Vol. 3, Debate in the House of Commons on the Navy Estimates, November 1, 1775, 335-8.
[122] Allen, *A Naval History of the American Revolution*, Vol. 1, 19.

dismissal. It was, indeed, the intelligence Graves had received and not acted on that frustrated the King. As a consequence, it can be argued that if the Admiral had only acted more rashly and bombarded the towns, without the consent of Ministry, he might have kept his command. Also, Parliament was well informed that its current naval fleet was not sufficient to complete the operations at hand. Once they had learned the rebellion was no longer limited to Massachusetts, it had become "necessary to augment our navy." Only after Graves' removal was it determined that "the stronger the Navy was, the more effectual measures would be." It was therefore recommended, by the Duke of Grafton, they should raise the naval force to "seventy vessels, which would be such a force...as would render it impossible for the Americans either to resist, keep together, or subsist."[123]

In effect, viewing the British as tyrannical oppressors from the sea is a generalization and, for the most part, unfair. It cannot be said that intended violence was never committed, but such a policy was not universally practiced, especially among the subordinate naval officers. The King, his advisors, and his supporters did support harsh reprisals, but such actions were not mindlessly obeyed. The evidence shows that during the early operations of the war British officers in America acted as diplomatically as any could in an armed conflict, in an effort to work out reconciliation with the colonies. In observing Admiral Graves' conduct, it is safe to say that he did what he could with what was afforded him. Lacking an adequate fleet to achieve his objectives frustrated him greatly. Undoubtedly, by October 1775, after months and months of feeling hindered, he had lost his professional composure. As events progressed, he had stopped viewing the conflict as a police action and more as a war. What's more, he had orders permitting him to do so. He wrote, "Every appearance of Accommodation between Great Britain and her Colonies is vanished; the latter have made their Election in War."[124] It cannot be said that Graves did

---

[123] Force, *American Archives*, Fourth Series, Vol. 6, 7.
[124] United States, Naval History Division, *Naval Documents of the American Revolution*, Vol. 2, Vice Admiral Samuel Graves to Captain Edward Le Cras, October 18, 1775, 503.

not think about the possible consequences of chastising the rebels. In September, he wrote to Philip Stephens, "If I am erring in pursuing...severe measures against his Majesty's rebellious Subjects, I hope it will appear they have not been hastily adopted."[125] With the rebellion not limited to just Massachusetts and "diffusing itself through the whole Continent," Graves queried to Captain Edward Le Cras:

> What then becomes our Duty but with all possible Dispatch and Spirit to carry his Majesty's Commands into Execution by making the most vigorous Efforts to punish this ungrateful people and lay Waste their Country on the Sea Coast?[126]

It must be remembered Graves did what was essential to ensure his Majesty's troops were well supplied, while trying to accomplish his mission to prevent the importation of arms to the rebel army. Any other military leader would have taken similar measures to ensure mission accomplishment and troop welfare, including most of the colonial officers. Although this is evident today with our ability to look at all the information objectively, it was not viewed that way by the rebels. The rebels pushed the idea that Graves' mission was "to proceed" and destroy all "of the seaport towns and places being accessible to the king's ships, in which any troops shall be raised or military works erected."[127] Graves figured prominently in the American Revolution since his actions spurred the colonies' push for autonomy. The push began with the creation of a Continental Navy and the authorization of each colony to do the same. It was because "the good people of these colonies" had been "sensibly affected by the destruction of their property, and other unprovoked injuries," Congress would resolve the "fitting out of armed vessels and ships of force" in order to "procure some reparation for the same."[128] It would be

---

[125] Ibid, Vice Admiral Graves to Philip Stephens, September 26, 1775, 213.
[126] Ibid, Vice Admiral Samuel Graves to Captain Edward Le Cras, October 18, 1775, 503.
[127] Ibid, Journal of the Continental Congress, November 25, 1775, 1131.
[128] Ibid.

this objective, coupled with the rebel memory of burning coastal towns which helped convince the Congressional delegates to vote for the resolution of the Declaration of Independence.

Part Four:

The Inclusion Of Indian Auxiliaries

Chapter Eight

The "Savage" Threat from the Frontier

He has excited...the merciless Indian Savages whose known rule of warfare, is an undistinguished destruction of all ages, sexes and conditions.
                    Declaration of Independence, July 4, 1776

The Indian contribution to the American Revolution often goes overlooked or forgotten even in modern historical works covering the period.[1] Excluding those revolutionary historians who have made the subject a focal point of their research, the Indian is, for the most part, relegated to but a paragraph or footnote. Although their early contribution to the Revolutionary War was miniscule, their employment as auxiliaries was instrumental in gaining support for the rebel cause—helping to legitimize the colonies' push for autonomy. For the Declaration of Independence specifically accuses King George of exciting "domestic insurrections amongst us," and endeavoring "to bring on the inhabitants of our frontiers, the merciless Indian Savages whose known rule of warfare, is an undistinguished destruction of all ages, sexes and conditions." The declaration was published

---

[1] The western frontier of the thirteen colonies consisted of a multitude of tribes and federations, and not all will be addressed. Although some historians do not kindly look upon the assemblage of the different tribes of the indigenous people within North America, there will be certain instances within this chapter that will address them as such. This is not intended to diminish the diverse history of the different indigenous tribes that existed during the American Revolution or disgrace the impact of each tribe, but to, in some instances, explain either the British or Rebels' policy regarding their inclusion within the conflict itself. For both sides addressed their inclusion of the Indians broadly rather than on a tribe by tribe basis.

throughout Europe, and Congress made another note of the Indian grievance in their address to the people of Ireland.

The language regarding the Indians in these documents served the purpose of casting the British as oppressors, while portraying the revolutionaries as victims and defenders of liberty. Much like many of the other grievances in the Declaration of Independence, its word-for-word interpretation makes false implications. By way of information dissemination, through rebel-controlled newspapers and correspondence, most colonists only received biased reports of the British use of Indians against the colonists. Therefore, early in the conflict, many rebels truly felt the British had overstepped the boundaries of gentlemanly warfare by using the "savage" Indians against their own people. Much like the politics behind each side's employment of blacks, free or slave, who was initially responsible for instigating the use of Indians in the Revolutionary War is complex. While most historians believe Indian warfare was brutal, there is disagreement over who instigated this form of combat. Were the British to blame, or did the rebels instigate their employment? It is a difficult question to answer, but in all likelihood the inclusion of the Indians in the conflict would have occurred even without the solicitation of the white man.[2]

There was even disagreement in Parliament as to which side first employed the indigenous tribes. The competing political factions held different sentiments on the issue. When Parliament was debating the Olive Branch Petition, the Earl of Shelburne chastised the current administration for attempting to employ Russians, Hessians, Canadians, Irish Roman Catholics, and Indians. He believed the "Indians had been tampered with" as a means to "let the savages…loose on the Provincial Subjects of Great Britain." He thought such a measure "barbarous" and the attempt to employ them "cowardly."[3] Lord North defended against such allegations when he presented his Prohibitory Bill to

---

[2] Jack M. Sosin, "The Use of Indians in the War of the American Revolution: A Re-Assessment of Responsibility," *Canadian Historical Review*, (1965), 101.

[3] Force, *American Archives*, Fourth Series, Vol. 6, 133.

the House of Commons. North "declared there never was any idea of employing the negroes or the Indians, until the Americans themselves first applied to them."[4] This argument was not effective in persuading men like Edmund Burke, who felt they were "not fit allies for your Majesty in a war with your people."[5] Arguably, either the Americans or the British could be held liable for the inclusion of the Indians, but just like the employment of blacks, their use would have been, in all likelihood, inevitable.

Before the events of Lexington and Concord, evidence strongly asserts that the British were not planning on using their influence over the different indigenous tribes and federations against the rebels. If anything, the initial correspondence of British officials suggests they intended on keeping the indigenous people outside any potential conflict that might ensue. Up to his death in July 1774, Sir William Johnson was the Superintendent of Indian Affairs. He had earned quite a reputation as a skilled diplomat. Johnson was well respected by the colonists and indigenous people alike, and contributed substantially to maintaining peace within the frontier.

During the tumultuous summer of 1774, Johnson was such an able political tactician that he was able to prevent the Shawnee Indians from attacking the backcountry of Pennsylvania and Virginia. A series of murders had been committed by both the Shawnee and the colonists along the frontier. Apparently instigated by a party of colonists out surveying land within Shawnee territory, a skirmish resulted with eight Indians and eight colonists having perished, including a boy from the latter party.[6] It was reported to John Connolly that the Shawnee responded by declaring:

> Their intention of going to war with the white people, to revenge the loss of some of their Nation who have been killed; that they had scalped one of the traders, and detained

---

[4] Ibid, 187.

[5] Burke, *Speeches and Letters on American Affairs*, 169.

[6] Force, *American Archives*, Fourth Series, Vol. 1, Williamsburg, VA, June 2, 1774.

all the rest who were in their towns; that it was expected the Cherokees would join them, as they had sent a belt last fall to the Northern Nations to strike the white people, which had been received by the Shawanese and Wabash Indians; and that there is soon to be a Grand Council in the Lower Shawanese town, where about seventy Cherokees, and a number of other Indians are to attend, on the subject of going to war with the English.[7]

Such an alarm arose among the frontier colonists, that John Penn, Governor of Pennsylvania, would write to Johnson informing him of "a great Part of the Settlers" that "fled from their Habitations, and…the Panic is daily increasing, to such a Degree that there is just Reason to apprehend a total desertion of that Country."[8] Generally, conflict between the two sides arose mainly over colonial encroachments on the indigenous tribes' lands. Whether it was individuals who were trying to lay a claim or interference from land speculation companies, many tribal territories were being illegally taken into possession. This threat upon their lands was certainly not supported by the English government or its officials.[9] Following the French and Indian War, the Proclamation of 1763 had made the situation plain and clear, stating:

> And whereas great frauds and abuses have been committed in the purchasing lands of the Indians, to the great prejudice of our interests, and to the great dissatisfaction of the said

---

[7] Ibid, 404.

[8] Alexander C. Flick, *The Papers of Sir William Johnson*, Vol. 8, John Penn to William Johnson, June 28, 1774, (Albany, NY: The University of the State of New York, 1933), 1182.

[9] In 1763, a London newspaper reported a letter that stated, "if we search into the beginning of some of the late Indian wars, we shall find they have taken rise from some of our colonists over-reaching them in their treaties, and getting possession of the hunting and fishing grounds, without which they [the Indians] cannot possibly subsist." Quoted in Linda Colley, *Captives: Britain, Empire, and the World 1600-1850*, (New York, NY: Anchor Books, 2004), 33.

The "Savage" Threat From the Frontier

Indians; in order therefore to prevent such irregularities for the future, and to the end that the Indians may be convinced of our justice and determined resolution to remove all reasonable cause of discontent, we do, with the advice of our Privy Council, strictly enjoin and require that nor private person do resume to make any purchase from the said Indians of any lands reserved to the said Indians within those parts of our Colonies where we have thought proper to allow settlement; but that if at any time any of the said Indians should be inclined to dispose of the said lands, the same shall be purchased only for us, in our name, at some public meeting or assembly of the said Indians, to be held for that purpose by the Governour or Commander-in-chief of our Colonies respectively within which they shall lie...[10]

William Johnson faced endless threats from the colonists in response to the Proclamation of 1763, severely affecting the peace and security of British relations with the indigenous people. Johnson attributed much of the dispute to squatters. These were individuals who hoped to gain an advantage of the western land restrictions by settling the land before grants could be issued, thus hoping to gain possession adversely. John Stuart, the Indian Superintendent of the Southern Department, "knew of nothing so likely to interrupt and disturb our tranquility with the Indians as the incessant attempts to defraud them of their land by clandestine purchase."[11] Johnson wrote to Thomas Gage the "Irregularities committed on the Frontiers...were indeed so many & increased so fast that they alone would be sufficient to bring on a War." He credited it to the numbers of "Ruffians" that are "not contented with Settlements, or too lazy to cultivate Lands, but live by the Cha[s]e & thereby interfere more with the Indians." These "ruffians" relied on the "impotence" of the government in order to lay claim to these restricted lands. To secure these holdings, Johnson accused the individuals "guilty of Robberies &

---

[10] Force, *American Archives,* Fourth Series, Vol. 1, 172-75.

[11] Calloway, *The American Revolution in Indian Country*, 23.

Murders."[12] The situation was so serious it required the utmost exertion of Johnson's influence. Even with his abilities, Johnson feared even his "Schemes & endeavors for preserving or restoring tranquility are frequently defeated by the gross Irregularities of our worst Enemies the Frontier Banditti."[13]

Johnson's concern was warranted, but his efforts were once again successful in ensuring peace within the Northern frontier. He had kept the Six Nations from forming an alliance to retaliate on the Western colonial settlements. Unfortunately, Johnson died before seeing the success of his labors. On July 11, 1774, he died in the middle of negotiations between him and the Six Nations. The purpose of the meeting was to inquire into the violent incidents that had been reported to Johnson, for the Six Nations "to Assure him of their inclination to preserve peace," to "put a stop to the irregularities & Murders committed by our People," and "remedy the abuses of which" the Six Nations "so often Complained."[14] William's son-in-law, Guy Johnson, would be successful in finishing the negotiations, but Sir William's loss was grieved by many. Gage especially missed the late Superintendent, attributing the peace of the frontier to Johnson's talents, when he wrote to Lord Dartmouth that it was his "skill in managing them" that "restrained" the Indians "from taking Revenge."[15]

Although the meeting with the Six Nations was successful, Guy Johnson inherited the problems of his predecessor. Grievances by the Indians were unendingly laid before him. Continuing acts by settlers on the frontier propagated Johnson to remind Gage the Six Nations "may have occasion to Act should hostilities continue, or on any other occurring matter."[16] In August, another dilemma

---

[12] Milton W. Hamilton, *The Papers of Sir William Johnson*, Vol. 12, William Johnson to Thomas Gage, July 4, 1774, (Albany, NY: The University of The State of New York, 1957), 1115.

[13] Ibid, 1116.

[14] Ibid, Guy Johnson to Thomas Gage, July 12, 1774, 1122.

[15] Flick, *The Papers of Sir William Johnson*, Vol. 8, Thomas Gage to the Earl of Dartmouth, July 18, 1774, 1185.

[16] Albert B. Corey, *The Papers of Sir William Johnson,* Vol. 8, Guy

The "Savage" Threat From the Frontier

presented itself when Johnson got word the Ottawa's village in Detroit was being "surveyed & laid into Lots, to which many persons have set up Claims."[17] It seemed, one after another, individuals or surveyors insisted on violating the provisions of the Proclamation of 1763.[18]

The largest threat to the security of the frontier would come from what is known as Lord Dunmore's War. What began as a border dispute over the Pittsburg region developed into a small Indian war. It started when Virginia land speculators claimed the land to be theirs, but Pennsylvania had never relinquished it. To prevent hostilities, the Pennsylvania government was willing to surrender a portion of the territory. Dunmore replied that such a proposal amounted "in reality to nothing" and "could not possibly be complied with."[19] He then took the step of assembling his own militia to take control over the region. He did this even with the expressed dissatisfaction of Lord Dartmouth and Sir William Johnson.

John Connolly was Dunmore's agent in this war. The Pennsylvania inhabitants had been frustrated with Connolly's

---

Johnson to Thomas Gage, July 26, 1774, 642-43.

[17] Ibid, Guy Johnson to Thomas Gage, August 11, 1774, 667.

[18] Throughout the 1770's colonists trespassed on Indian Territory that was protected by the Proclamation of 1763. Sometimes it involved individuals who could not afford title to land and therefore settled beyond the colonial borders. In other instances, squatters thought they might be able to obtain title on the right of preoccupancy, or what we know today as adverse possession. These individuals hoped when the Proclamation of 1763 was lifted, they would have an advantage in claiming title to the land. Lastly, there were schemes by founding fathers such as Thomas Jefferson and George Mason to lift the proclamation, but they all proved ineffective. See Woody Holton, *Forced Founders: Indians, Debtors, Slaves, & the Making of the American Revolution in Virginia*, (Chapel Hill, NC: University of North Carolina Press, 1999) 28-31.

[19] Clarence Monroe Burton, "John Connolly, A Tory of the Revolution," *Proceedings of the American Antiquarian Society*, (Worchester, MA: The Davis Press, 1909), 75.

"extremely oppressive and tyrannical" conduct. What feared them the most was "his military operations may have a dangerous tendency to involve the colonies in a general Indian War."[20] In fact, much of the damage, had been, mitigated through efforts by Johnson in securing promises of neutrality with most tribes. Regardless, fear reasonably surfaced when Connolly sent a small military force to the Ohio River, which clashed with some Shawnee Indians. On June 25, 1774, the Pittsburg inhabitants wrote to Governor John Penn, "The distressed inhabitants of this place have just cause to charge their present calamity and dread of and Indian War entirely to the tyrannical and unprecedented conduct of Doctor Connolly, whose design, as we conceive, is to better his almost desperate circumstances upon the distress of the public, and ruin of our fortunes."[21]

On July 12, Dunmore further dispatched Colonel Andrew Lewis to attack the magazines of the Shawnee Indians and distress them in every way.[22] In the end, Lord Dunmore's War was a success for its supporters, with Lewis winning the crucial battle at Point Pleasant on October 10.[23] The Governor was quick to enter into a treaty with the Shawnee, which terms proved very generous to the latter. The negotiations with the Shawnees were to continue a year later and would have a significant effect on the Indian threat to the Virginia frontier during the American Revolution.

During the early 1770's many of the tribes became acutely aware of the disagreements that were taking place between the American colonies and the British government. Although British officials did their best to refrain from discussing these matters with the indigenous people, nothing could prevent the spread of information from the Indians' contact with traders. In early July 1774, William Johnson's brother, Joseph, conveyed his sentiments to William in regards to explaining the disputes to the indigenous tribes. Joseph was worried the "day of Trial" between the British

---

[20] Ibid.
[21] Ibid, 77.
[22] Ibid, 79.
[23] Selby, *The Revolution in Virginia, 1775-1783*, 17.

government and the colonists was "approaching, and perhaps is very nigh." Such an event would certainly try the hearts of the "Several Tribes Bordering the Sea Shore." The sight of "Christian People bleeding" grieved him much, but it grieved him much more when he sees "a Brother, taking up arms against a Brother...and a Brother bleeding to death before a Brother...is this the fruits of Christianity?" He wondered, "what will the heathen Nations say?" Because of these uncertainties, Joseph thought it "highly Necessary that a word of Caution be given to the New England Indians" concerning the disputes between the colonists and the government. His advice to William was "to advise the Indians to keep Still, or to be Nutrils." He felt that, if such advice was conveyed by William, he'd be saving "many lives and would be noticed and kindly accepted as a token of real Love."[24] Lastly, Joseph believed it necessary because the "Poor Indians" are "too easily captivated," worrying that many tribes could be easily coerced to join the rebels. William probably never received this letter because he died only three days after it was drafted. However, Guy Johnson certainly did receive it and held similar sentiments on the subject.

It is important to note that although Guy Johnson was loyal to the British government, he sincerely hoped that the meeting of the First Continental Congress would "rather be productive of harmony than disunion."[25] Once "Weak persons in this Country" had informed the Indians of the internal disputes that were taking place, he wrote to Gage about the dangerous situation it afforded. He felt it was "extremely dangerous" for Indian tribes to have knowledge of "Internal disputes" because "it may encourage disaffected Tribes...to seize opportunity for doing Mischief."[26] Johnson's chief concern was that the colonists would convince the

---

[24] Hamilton, *The Papers of Sir William Johnson*, Vol. 12, Joseph Johnson to William Johnson, July 8, 1774, 1117-18.

[25] Flick, *The Papers of Sir William Johnson*, Vol. 8, Guy Johnson to John Blackburn, September 12, 1774, 1199-1200.

[26] Hamilton, *The Papers of Sir William Johnson*, Vol. 13, Guy Johnson to Thomas Gage, November 10, 1774, 691.

tribes the King's intent was to take away their lands. Gage assured Johnson not to worry over such a matter. He was confident that Johnson will "explain these Matters to them [the tribes], and to show how little they affected them."[27] Johnson did just that, communicating to the tribes that the internal disputes "would soon be over," but reminded Gage they are "inclined to Watch our Motions, & therefore particular care is necessary to prevent their being led into any idle measures during the ensuing Season."[28] Thus, events began to be set in motion that would involve the tribes in the conflict.

Johnson's feelings on the matter gave Gage a cause to write to John Stuart, warning him "that ill affected people" were attempting to alienate the affections of the indigenous tribes from the King.[29] Stuart, in turn, wrote to his deputies warning "against any attempts of the like nature to debauch the Indians in their respective Districts."[30] By this time, the rebel elements of the Southern colonies had already developed a conspiracy theory involving the Indians. It was believed the King's restriction on sending arms and powder to the colonists had an underlying purpose. This was to leave the Southern colonies defenseless to either the slaves, Indians, or both. With this thought in the back of many rebels' minds, word spread of Gage's correspondence with Stuart. Although the rumor was false, rebel circles believed Stuart had received instructions to unleash the Indians against any opponents of British policies.

The Northern colonies were just as fearful that the ministry's underlying purpose was to incite indigenous tribes to attack frontier settlements. After Lexington and Concord, rebels shared the tactical fear that if a quick end was not brought to the contest,

---

[27] Ibid, Thomas Gage to Guy Johnson, November 28, 1774, 698.

[28] Ibid, Guy Johnson to Thomas Gage, December 14, 1774, 701.

[29] Philip M. Harmer, "John Stuart's Indian Policy During the Early Months of the American Revolution," *The Mississippi Valley Historical Review*, Vol. 17, No. 3 (Dec., 1930), 353.

[30] Ibid.

the natives would be employed as auxiliaries by the British.[31] Even prior to the outbreak of hostilities, rebel leaders fearful of the British government's strong influence over the tribes began contemplating methods to acquire their own alliances.[32] Evidence suggests the rebels would be the first of the two sides to attempt to incorporate indigenous tribes as auxiliaries. They understood that if the conflict was to extend to Canada it would only be a short matter of time before the Indians would be incorporated.[33] It began nearly three weeks before Lexington and Concord, when the Stockbridge Indians joined the Massachusetts Minutemen. In response, the Massachusetts Provincial Congress began to draft a letter to the Chief of the Mohawk Indian tribes.[34] The letter was nothing more than propaganda to persuade the Mohawk's to their cause, but adequately depicts the early rebel attempts to recruit the Indians to their side. It read:

Our Fathers in Great Britain tell us our Lands, and Houses, and Cattle, and Money, are not our own; that we ourselves are not our own men, but their servants; they have endeavored to take away our Money without our leave, and have sent their great Vessels and a great many Warriors for that purpose...We used to send our Vessels on the Great Lake, whereby we were able to get Clothes, and what we needed for ourselves and you; but such has lately been their conduct, that we cannot; they have told us we shall have no more Guns, no Powder to use and kill our Wolves and other game, nor to send to you, for you to kill you victuals with, and to get Skins to trade with us to buy you Blankets, and

---

[31] Andrew McFarland Davis, "The Employment of Indian Auxiliaries in the American War," *English Historical Review*, Vol. 2, No. 8(Oct., 1887), 709. Smith, *Letters of the Delegates to Congress 1774-1789*, Vol. 1, Richard Henry Lee to Francis Lightfoot Lee, May 21, 1775, 367.

[32] Jack M. Sosin, *The Revolutionary Frontier*, (Holt, Rinehart, and Winston, 1967), 88.

[33] Davis, "The Employment of Indian Auxiliaries in the American War," *English Historical Review*, 713.

[34] Force, *American Archives*, Fourth Series, Vol. 1, 1347.

what you want. How can you live without Powder and Guns? But we hope to supply you soon with both of our own making...They have made a law to establish the religion of the Pope of Canada, which lies so near to you. We much fear some of your children induced, instead of worshipping the true only God, to pay his due to images made with their own hands...These and many other hardships we are threatened with, which, no doubt, in the end, will equally affect you; for the same reason they would take our Lands, they will take away yours. All we want is, that we and you may enjoy that liberty and security which we have a right to enjoy, and that we may not lose that good Land which enables us to feed our wives and children. We think it our duty to inform you of our danger and desire you to give notice to all your kindred; and as we fear they will attempt to cut our throats, and if you should allow them to do that, there will nobody remain to keep them from you, we therefore earnestly desire you to whet your Hatchet, and be prepared with us to defend our liberties and lives.[35]

The Massachusetts rebels and Provincial Congress were operating on intelligence they had received on March 29, that reported the Caughnawaga Indians "say they have been repeatedly applied to, and requested to join with the King's Troops to fight Boston."[36] It was further informed that they "peremptorily refused" to join the British standard since "they are a very simple, politick people, and say that if they are obliged, for their safety, to take up arms on either side, that they shall take part on the side of their brethren, the English in New-England."[37] Thus, although the rebels were the first to incorporate Indian auxiliaries within their

---

[35] Ibid, 1349-50.

[36] Force, *American Archives*, Fourth Series, Vol. 2, 241.

[37] Ibid. There was speculation as to whether the Caughnawaga tribe would join Guy Carleton. See Smith, *The Letters of the Delegates to Congress 1774-1789*, Vol. 1, Connecticut Delegates to Jonathan Trumbull, June 26, 1775, 542-43.

The "Savage" Threat From the Frontier

forces, they did so on the false premise that the British were already doing the same.

The Massachusetts inclusion of the Stockbridge Indians brought the rebels more than just reinforcements. Captain Solomon Unhaunauwaunmut, the Chief Sachem of the Moheconnuck Indians, offered his services as an interpreter and diplomat to gain the support of other regional tribes. He wrote to the Massachusetts Congress about this and other matters, stating:

> Whenever I see your blood running, you will soon find me about you to revenge my brothers' blood. Although I am low and very small, I will grip hold of your enemy's heel, that he cannot run so fast and so light, as if he had nothing at his heels...You know I am not so wise as you are, therefore I ask your advice in what I am now agoing to say. I am thinking before you come to action, to take a run to the Westward, and feel the minds of my Indian brothers, the Six Nations, and know how they stand, whether they are on your side, or for your enemies. If I find they are against you, I will try to turn their minds. If I find they will listen to me; for they have always looked this way for advice concerning all important news that comes from the rising of the sun. If they hearken to me you will not be afraid of any danger from behind you. However their minds are affected, you shall soon know by me. Now I think I can do you more service in this way, than by marching off immediately to Boston, and stay there (it may be) a great while before blood runs. Now, as I said you are wiser than I, I leave this for your consideration, whether I come down immediately, or wait till I hear some blood is spilled....I would not have you think by this that we are falling back from our engagements; we are ready to do any thing for your relief, and shall be guided by your counsel....One thing I ask of you if you send for me to fight, that you will let me fight in my own Indian way. I am not used to fight English fashion, therefore you must not expect I can train like your man.[38]

---

[38] Force, *American Archives*, Fourth Series, Vol. 2, 315-16.

Irreconcilable Grievances

On May 24, Colonel Ethan Allen took Unhaunauwaunmut on his word, using the assistance of the Stockbridge Indians to dissuade the indigenous tribes in Canada from joining the British. The diplomatic tactics were largely successful, with seven Canadian tribes stating their plans to remain neutral "and [to] have nothing to do with this quarrel."[39] The Stockbridge Indians sent identical letters to the Hohnogwus, Swagaches, Canesadaugans, and Saint Francis tribes. Each read:

And as King George's soldiers killed our brothers and friend in time of peace, I hope, as Indians that are good and honest men, you will not fight for King George against your friends in America, as they have done you no wrong, and desire to live with you as brothers...I want you to have your warriors come see me, and help me fight the King's Regular Troops...if will, I will give you money, blankets, tomahawks, knives, paint, and any thing that there is in the army...You know it is good for my warriors and Indians...to kill the Regulars, because they first began to kill our brothers in this Country without cause...but if you our brother Indians do not fight on either side, we will still be friends and brothers...[40]

The letters were certainly not a request for neutrality but rather an attempt to gain military allies. In one instance, the Stockbridge Indians were not welcomed when they fell upon some members of the Six Nations and British regulars. The Stockbridge Indians were "taken and bound" by the British to be hanged. The British were well aware of the Stockbridge Indians' dealings to turn the indigenous tribes against them. Although the Canadian tribes were supporting the British, they were angry that the British were attempting to hang the diplomats. Some told the British in the "strongest terms" that they would take the place of the Stockbridge Indians rather than see them hang. The incident ended with the Canadian tribes releasing the Stockbridge Indians, stating to them,

---

[39] Ibid, 1002-03.
[40] Ibid, 714.

"now we shall know whom are our enemies." They also informed the Stockbridge Indians "that if they did fight at all, they would fight against the Regulars, for they did not like them."[41]

The Massachusetts Congress made another attempt to recruit Indian allies when it sent Captain Land to deliver a letter to the Eastern indigenous tribes in Nova Scotia. On May 15, it asked the tribes to "consider what may be best for you and ourselves…to get rid of the slavery designed to be brought upon us."[42] The main argument the Massachusetts Congress wanted to make was that the British intended to "make you and us their servants." Furthermore, the colonists blamed the British for the lack of guns and powder to trade with the tribes. The British governmental policy of preventing the exportation of powder or guns to the colonies had severely hindered the colonists' ability to trade with the tribes. The Massachusetts Congress made sure to convey to them it was not their fault and informing them that "we will do all for you we can" to "supply you as fast as we can," but they would have to do so with "guns and powder of our own making."[43] The rebels were already having a difficult time procuring arms for their own forces, so much so that the breastworks at Cambridge were defended with pikes. For them to provide supplies for the indigenous tribes on the Massachusetts frontier would be nearly impossible. Lastly, and most importantly, the letter's purpose was to recruit military auxiliaries. Congress hoped that the tribes would remain neutral by not "join[ing] with our enemies" but preferred they follow the example of "our good brothers," the Stockbridge Indians, and join their forces.[44]

On June 28, the New York Congress similarly addressed the Oneida and Tuscarora Indians. They conveyed to the tribes that the rumors to harm Guy Johnson were false and informed them the provisions they received were actually provided by them, not Johnson. According to the statement to the Oneida and Tuscarora

---

[41] Ibid, 1060-61.
[42] Ibid, 610-11.
[43] Ibid.
[44] Ibid.

Indians, the purpose of the current meeting was "purely on the account of the old friendship which has so long been kept up between us," not from any "unfriendly thoughts." Congress then appealed to the tribesmen's egos, stating, "we look to you, particularly, to be men of more understanding than others, by the benefits you have received in learning." The rebels wanted to convey to these tribes that only men of their skills could convince the "other Tribes and Nations" the error of joining the British.[45]

When promises failed to win over the Indians, the rebels resorted to bribes and intimidation. On June 23, Colonel Bailey addressed the Northern Indians. Bailey stated, "You are as much threatened as we; they want you to kill us; and then they will kill you, if you do not serve them." He offered those who would join the rebels "a good coat and blanket...and forty shillings per month," but delivered a warning to those who might choose to oppose him. He stated, "If you...or any other Indians, fight against us, we know your country, and shall be troublesome to you."[46] Benedict Arnold also made efforts to enlist the support of the indigenous tribes. In May, his initial reports suggest he was fearful the British army and Indians had already joined in an alliance to wreak havoc on the frontier around Ticonderoga, as well as retake the fort and Crown-Point.[47] By mid-June, he had changed his outlook, becoming optimistic that the Indians would side with their cause. Arnold then sent an Indian interpreter to Montreal to consult with some Canadian tribes "to know their Intentions in the present dispute." He received good news that these tribes were "disgusted with the Regulars," and "determined not to assist the King's Troops against us, & have made a Law, that if any one of their Tribe shall take up Arms for that purpose, he shall immediately be put to death."[48]

---

[45] Ibid, 1125.

[46] Ibid, 1070.

[47] United States, *Naval Documents of the American Revolution*, Vol. 1, Colonel Benedict Arnold to the Continental Congress, May 29, 1775, 561-62.

[48] Ibid, Colonel Benedict Arnold to Continental Congress, June 13, 1775,

The "Savage" Threat From the Frontier

In the meantime, the British government adopted a policy of keeping the indigenous tribes neutral. Although this policy was what most British officials practiced, not all agreed with it, and some made their own attempts to recruit the indigenous tribes as military auxiliaries. The rebels did not, however, place much trust in the policy, and interpreted the situation much differently. They viewed the British meetings with the indigenous tribes as attempts to turn the "savages" upon them. Yet, the evidence certainly does not support such speculation, and there is no evidence to support the rebels had any accurate intelligence to point to any such British dealings with the indigenous tribes. The rebels were purely speculating the motives for the meetings.

An example of this occurred in New York when the rebels felt compelled to enlist Indian support as a result of a series of controversial events that occurred in Tyron County.[49] A political battle was waging for the support of the local indigenous tribes between Colonel Guy Johnson, the acting Superintendent of Northern Indian Affairs, and the local rebels. The latter had been spreading reports among the Oneidas and Mohawks that the "King is set against the American Indians."[50] In addition, while the Mahicans, Narragansetts, Montauks, Pequots, and Niantics were en route to begin the settlement of lands procured for them through Johnson, another disturbing event occurred. The New England colonists were doing everything they could to prevent this migration, including threats and their refusal to pay debts owed to the tribes. Overall, the colonists' plan would prove quite effective in limiting the amount of new settlers among the Six Nations.[51]

671-72.

[49] *War of 1775-76*, Guy Johnson to Lord Dartmouth, October 12, 1775, 345-46, and Account of Guy Johnson's Indian Transactions by Frans Le Maistre, 347-50.

[50] Paul Lawrence Stevens, *His Majesty's "Savage" Allies: British Policy and the Northern Indians During the Revolutionary War. The Carleton Years, 1774-1778*, Vol. 1, (Ann Arbor, MI: University Microfilms International, 1984), 263.

[51] Ibid, 295.

Although Johnson was fully aware of rebel attempts to intervene in British-Indian affairs, he would not realize the full extent of their plans until he visited New York City in April 1775. During his visit, Guy Johnson intended on settling the late William Johnson's estate, attending the sessions of the local assembly, and procuring much needed supplies for his dealings with the indigenous tribes. The colonists' discontent with Britain's policies was evident, but what was truly disturbing was that Johnson's communications from Gage were already opened. Sending classified reports regarding to Boston would now prove difficult. Moreover, Johnson had heard the accounts of "the dreadful doings at Boston," but in spite of all these facts, still hoped the Indians would remain nonpartisan.[52]

Upon returning home, Johnson found that the local radicals had taken advantage of his absence. They had assembled the Mohawk Valley's committees of safety to convince them to take a stand against the British government. On May 11, Johnson replied by riding in on 300 rebels, who were assembled to raise a liberty pole nine miles west of Guy Park. With his party armed with pistols, he dispersed the crowd and even horsewhipped one inhabitant. Johnson felt his hold was slipping but believed he could redeem the situation with proper reinforcements. He wrote to royal officials about his optimism. To Gage, he wrote, "I foresee many difficulties, but I still hope to surmount them, especially if there can be any means of affording some support to this County or the Communication; half a Battalion in time might preserve peace & order."[53]

While Johnson was doing his best to minimize rebel influence on the Indians, including putting the rebel patriot Samuel Kirkland on house arrest, a body of New Englanders had formulated a plan to capture him. False reports had circulated that Johnson had the intention to turn the Six Nations against the colonists. Despite the colonists' fears, there is no evidence to suggest Johnson had any intention of employing the Six Nations as auxiliaries. Johnson

---

[52] Ibid, 296-97.
[53] Ibid, 297-98.

The "Savage" Threat From the Frontier

wrote a letter to the magistrates of Palatine reminding them that the "highest importance" is to "promote peace amongst the Six Nations, and prevent their entering into any such dispute."[54] Although he meant no harm to the colonists, he did warn "if the Indians find their council fire disturbed, and their Superintendent insulted, they will take a dreadful revenge."[55] The drama did not end there. Johnson, with the aid of the Mohawks, tried enlisting the support of the Oneida tribe to further prevent his being captured.[56] The letter to the Oneidas was intercepted, but five Indian envoys reached the tribe with a verbal bidding to join Johnson. The Oneidas ultimately decided to turn down the entreaties. The envoys ventured forth on their recruiting mission, asking for support in protecting Johnson, but the Oneidas had also given messages to the envoys. The messages informed the other tribes to wait until the Oneidas could inform them of the "truth of the matters."[57]

Although he did not receive any assistance outside of loyalists and Mohawks, Johnson allegedly had five hundred men surrounding his house to protect him and his family. The Committee in Tryon County saw Johnson's response as "very alarming" and "highly arbitrary, illegal, oppressive, and unwarrantable, and confirms us in our fears, that his design is to keep us in awe, and oblige us to submit to a state of slavery."[58] The Committee further hypothesized that Johnson's control rested on the tribes' fear of what reprisal might occur if they refused to come to the Colonel's aid. The Committee recommended sending a couple of men "well acquainted with the Indian language" to

---

[54] Force, *American Archives*, Fourth Series, Vol. 2, 661.

[55] Ibid. Smith, *Letters of Delegates to Congress 1774-1789*, Vol. 1, Eliphalet Dyer to Joseph Trumbull, June 3, 1775, 439.

[56] Ibid, Letter from the Mohawks to the Oneidas, May 1775, 665.

[57] Stevens, *His Majesty's "Savage" Allies: British Policy and the Northern Indians During the Revolutionary War. The Carleton Years, 1774-1778*, Vol. 1, 302.

[58] Force, *American Archives*, Fourth Series, Vol. 2, Resolutions of the Committee of Tyron County, New York, May 21, 1775, 665.

"dissuade" them from coming to help Johnson.[59] They were confident these Indians were "not satisfied with Colonel Johnson's conduct." The Tyron Committee then applied to the Albany committee to send two men to explain to the Six Nations the actual manner of the dispute. Just as mistrustful, the Albany committee complied with the request and enlisted support of the missionary, Samuel Kirkland.

In spite of all these events, on May 25, Guy Johnson played host to a rebel committee intended on convincing the Six Nations to remain neutral. In the end, the committee's work proved effective, with the Six Nations determined to not interfere in the white man's conflict. Even so, the Indians suspected that the committees had prevented the delivery of their gunpowder and other goods. They reminded the committee, "The love we have for the memory of Sir William Johnson and the obligations the whole Six Nations are under to him, must make us regard and protect every branch of his family."[60] The outcome of the meeting was actually applauded by the rebel-influenced Committee of Tyron County. They wrote to Guy Johnson thanking him for performing his duty, reminding him to use his "endeavors with the Indians to dissuade them from interfering in the dispute."[61] The committee was aware Johnson "may differ with us in the mode of obtaining a redress of grievances," and reminded him he held "large estates in the Country." In effect, the rebels were reminding the Superintendent that if he were ever to do anything distasteful, such as recruit Indian auxiliaries for the British, he would lose his property.[62] Johnson again would reply to such accusations against his character, writing:

I trust I shall always manifest more humanity than to promote

---

[59] Ibid, Committee of Palatine District, Tyron Committee to Albany, May 21, 1775, 666.

[60] Stevens, *His Majesty's "Savage" Allies: British Policy and the Northern Indians During the Revolutionary War. The Carleton Years, 1774-1778*, Vol. 1, 305.

[61] Force, *American Archives*, Fourth Series, Vol. 2, 889.

[62] Ibid.

The "Savage" Threat From the Frontier

the destruction of the innocent inhabitants of a Colony to which I have been always warmly attached a declaration that must appear perfectly suitable to the character of a man of honour and principle who can on no account neglect those duties that are consistent therewith however they may differ from sentiments now adopted in so many parts of America.[63]

The rebel majority did not take Johnson on his word. Once Washington was forwarded Johnson's response, he wrote to Philip Schuyler:
I think it evident from the Tenor and Spirit of Col. Johnson's Letter, that no art or Influence will be left untried by him, to engage them [Indians] in such an Enterprize. Should he once prevail on them to dip their Hands in Blood, mutual Hostilities will most probably ensue, and they may be led to take a more decisive Part.[64]

It was such actions taken by the New England governments, particularly the Massachusetts Provincial Congress, that led Thomas Gage and Guy Johnson to seriously consider the employment of Indians as auxiliaries. Up to mid-June, the armies surrounding Gage's forces at Boston were primarily controlled by the Massachusetts Congress. It was in charge of the operation, maintenance, and supply of the ragtag force. The Continental Congress only officially took charge of the entire operation once Washington arrived in early July. Though the Continental Congress had not approved of the use of Indians as auxiliaries, the Massachusetts Congress' actions had already set certain events in motion.

Gage certainly was not loathe to the possibility of using the Indians in any potential conflict. In the fall of 1774, he queried to Guy Carleton as to "what measures would be the most efficacious to raise a body of Canadians and Indians, and for them to form a

---

[63] Abbot & Twohig, *The Papers of George Washington*, Revolutionary Series, Vol. 1, 131 n.3.
[64] Ibid, George Washington to Philip Schuyler, July 28, 1775, 188.

junction with the king's forces in this province."[65] Gage, always thinking militarily, was preparing for the worst. What propagated Gage's inquiry about the possible inclusion of the Indians was the Powder Alarm of September 1774. The mustering of thousands of militia against his redcoats had sobered him to the desperation he would face if disputes turned to armed conflict.[66] It is uncertain as to how far Carleton went to prepare the tribes, but he did inform Gage, "The Savages of this Province, I hear, are in very good humor, a Canadian Battalion would be a great Motive, and go far to influence them, but you know what sort of People they are."[67]

Gage even commented to Secretary of War, Viscount Barrington, about the potential use of the tribes as a deterrent against the Middle and Southern colonies joining New England in any potential conflict. He stated that the colonists "talk every night," but "they can do nothing, their numerous slaves in the bowels of their country, and the Indians at their backs will always keep them quiet."[68] Gage was doubly aware of the repercussions such a move would provoke, thus he did not mention his early thoughts to Guy Johnson, nor did he make any further mention on the topic until he was surrounded on the Boston Neck by over 20,000 rebels. Gage actually did not consider the topic again until May 1775. His concern was that of the majority of British officials, maintaining the neutrality of the indigenous tribes. As late as July, Lord Dartmouth had only ordered Guy Johnson to "keep the Indians in such a state of affection and attachment to the king that his majesty may rely upon their assistance in any case in

---

[65] Davis, "The Employment of Indian Auxiliaries in the American War," *English Historical Review*, Vol. 2, No. 8(Oct., 1887), 724. See also Perry Eugene Leroy, *Sir Guy Carleton as a Military Leader During the American Invasion and Repulse in Canada, 1775-1776*, Vol. 1, (Columbus, OH: Dissertation for Ohio State University, 1960), 18.
[66] Stevens, *His Majesty's "Savage" Allies: British Policy and the Northern Indians During the Revolutionary War. The Carleton Years, 1774-1778*, Vol. 1, 259.
[67] Ibid, 260.
[68] Ibid, 264-65.

The "Savage" Threat From the Frontier

which it may be necessary."⁶⁹ Meanwhile, Gage was undoubtedly receiving reports of Indians killing his troops, most likely by the Stockbridge Indians. On June 21 John Kettel, a resident of Charlestown, reported that two Indians killed four British Regulars. On June 26, a British sentry was killed by two Indians. On August 7, the *Boston Gazette* reported "Parties of riflemen together with some Indians are constantly harassing the enemy's advanced guards, and say they have killed several of the regulars within a day or two."⁷⁰

Gage first makes mention of his notice of the rebel employment of Indian auxiliaries on June 12 in a letter to Lord Barrington. He believed the rebel attack on Fort Ticonderoga and their "excurtions to the Frontiers of Montreal" justified Carleton "in raising all the Canadians and Indians in his power to Attack" the rebel forces.⁷¹ He further vindicated this new Indian policy, since "the Rebels have shewn us the Example, and brought all they could down upon us here."⁷² Gage was so frustrated by the rebel tactics he even proposed the hiring of the "Hanoverians, Hessians" and "perhaps Russians."⁷³ He wrote similar sentiments to Lord Dartmouth, adding no less than 32,000 men should be assembled to combat the rebels, "a large part of which, should be good Irregulars, such as Hunters, Canadians, Indians & c."⁷⁴ Dartmouth

---

⁶⁹ Davis, "The Employment of Indian Auxiliaries in the American War," *English Historical Review*, Vol. 2, No. 8 (Oct., 1887), 724.

⁷⁰ Ibid, 715.

⁷¹ Carter, *The Correspondence of General Thomas Gage with the Secretaries of State, and with the War Office and the Treasury 1763-1775*, Vol. 2, Thomas Gage to Lord Barrington, June 12, 1775, 684.

⁷² Ibid. Guy Johnson agreed with these sentiments. He perceived "that the different Colonies were about to follow the example of Massachusetts Bay and finding that various measures were taking by New England Missionaries and others to alienate the affections of the Indians and Spirit them up to bad purposes." *War of 1775-1776*, 347.

⁷³ Ibid.

⁷⁴ Carter, *The Correspondence of General Thomas Gage with the Secretaries of State, and with the War Office and the Treasury 1763-*

approved Gage's employing of Indians, writing, "The Steps which you say the Rebels have taken for calling in the Assistance of the Indians...leave no room to hesitate upon the propriety of our pursing the same Measure." In addition, Dartmouth enclosed a letter for Guy Johnson "containing His Majesty's Commands for engaging a body of Indians."[75] It read:

> The unnatural Rebellion now raging there, calls for every Effort to suppress it, and the Intelligence His Majesty has received of the Rebels having excited the Indians to take a part, and of their having actually engaged a body of them-in Arms to support their Rebellion, justifies the Resolution His Majesty has taken of requiring the Assistance of his faithful adherents the Six Nations. It is therefore His Majesty's pleasure that you do lose no time in taking such steps as may induce them to take up the Hatchet against His Majesty's Rebellious Subjects in America...[76]

Although Gage refers to the rebel employment of Indians auxiliaries as a reason for the British to also procure their enlistment, historians have suggested Gage was considering their employment before he had such knowledge. Coincidentally, while Guy Johnson was working to move his camp westward into Canada, as a means to maintain communication with the tribes, a secret communication arrived from Gage regarding Indian recruitment. Johnson had relocated because the rebels were doing their utmost to impede his relations with tribes; hoping that decamping would allow him to maintain British relations with them. Gage's letter informed Johnson of Lexington and Concord, the difficulty in relaying further intelligence, and most importantly, the rebels' intention to attack Fort Ticonderoga. Unbeknownst to either Gage or Johnson, Ethan Allen and

---

1775, Vol. 1, Thomas Gage to Lord Dartmouth, June 12, 1775, 403-4.

[75] Carter, *The Correspondence of General Thomas Gage with the Secretaries of State, and with the War Office and the Treasury 1763-1775*, Vol. 2, Lord Dartmouth to Thomas Gage, August 2, 1775, 204.

[76] *War of 1775-76*, Lord Dartmouth to Guy Johnson, July 24, 1775, 345.

The "Savage" Threat From the Frontier

Benedict Arnold had been successful in taking the fort over a month prior to Gage even writing the dispatch. In addition, Gage wrote to Johnson to:
> Immediately to inform General Carleton of the State of Affairs here, and the threats against Ticonderoga, and the Point, and to concert with him the Assembling of Indians and the proper means to be taken for the support of that part of the Country, and otherwise to act as His Majesty's Service shall require.[77]

Gage wrote a similar letter to Colonel Caldwell, the Niagara commandant, asking him to work with Johnson and Carleton, stating:
> I would have you immediately cultivate the friendship of the Indians as much as possible. Have them ready to detach on the first notice, and in the me[a]n time have scouts out to get what Intelligence you can. It is said the Rebels intend attacking Ticonderoga, if so, a body of Indians may be of great use there, and to act with the 7th Regiment (ordered there) on the Frontiers of this Province. Coll. Johnson will give you all the Assistance he can with the Indians, and likewise what Intelligence he can gather.[78]

Moreover, Gage encouraged Carleton to enlist "a number of Canadians and Indians," since they "would be of great use on the Frontiers in the Province of Massachusetts Bay, under the command of a Judicious person."[79] Although Gage was encouraging the use of the Northern Indian tribes, he did not write

---

[77] Stevens, *His Majesty's "Savage" Allies: British Policy and the Northern Indians During the Revolutionary War. The Carleton Years, 1774-1778*, Vol. 1, 306. Cited as Thomas Gage to Guy Johnson, Boston, May 10, 1775, Gage Papers, Am. Series, Vol. 129.

[78] Ibid, 306-7. Cited as Thomas Gage to Lt. Col. John Caldwell, May 10, 1775, Gage Papers, Am. Series, Vol. 128.

[79] Ibid, 307. Cited as Thomas Gage to Gen. Guy Carleton, April 21-27, 1775, Gage Papers, Am. Series, Vols. 127 and 128.

such letters to the specific British officials in charge of the Western tribes. Gage only went so far as to encourage that these officers would "do well to cultivate the Friendship of the Indians on all Occasions, as they may be wanted for his Majesty's Service."[80]

None of these letters made any mention of the rebel employment of Indian auxiliaries, thus it can be inferred that Gage was unaware of it until June 12. This means that Gage was considering employing Indian tribes as auxiliaries only after the rebels had decided. Therefore, Gage's reception of the rebel employment of Indians has been viewed as nothing more than a well-timed coincidence giving justification for his actions.[81] Yet, such a scenario is unlikely. Evidence shows that Lieutenant Frederick Mackenzie of the Royal Welsh Fusiliers makes note of the rebel employment of the Stockbridge Indians on April 30.[82] Surely Mackenzie would have relayed this information to Gage. This negates the assertion that Gage was acting to employ the Indians without being induced by the rebels' actions. By late April, Gage only corresponded on the Indian issue with the intelligence that the rebels had taken the first steps. In addition, no evidence suggests he planned on using the tribes as anything more than auxiliaries to counter the rebel efforts. He never had any intention of turning them on the frontier settlers. Gage meant their employment to be a purely combative one, one where the British officers could control their "savage" ways.

Gage's intent was simple: he was intending on employing only the Indian tribes from Canada and the Six Nations as a means to relieve the military pressure surrounding Boston. Ideally, a western military front would pin the rebel army between two military forces. The plan failed. It would not be until the fall of

---

[80] Ibid, 308. Cited as Thomas Gage to Gen. Guy Carleton, Lt. Col. John Caldwell, to Capt. Richard B. Lernoult, and to Capt. Arent S. De Peyster, May 20, 1775, Gage Papers, Am. Series, Vols. 129 and 130.
[81] Ibid, 309.
[82] Frederick Mackenzie, *Diary of Frederick Mackenzie*, Vol. 1, (Cambridge, MA: Harvard University Press, 1930), 32.

The "Savage" Threat From the Frontier

1775 that Gage would consider employing Indians from the other military fronts. His expansion on the inclusion of Indian auxiliaries would be the result of three major factors; 1) the rebellion was not limited to Massachusetts and was manifested within all thirteen colonies, 2) he was proposed these plans through individuals such as Lord Dunmore and John Connolly, and, 3) the ineffectiveness in obtaining the affirmed loyalties within the Northern Indian tribes.

It is interesting that, although Gage had become an advocate for the strategic use of the tribes under certain circumstances, his subordinates, Carleton and Johnson were having little success in implementing the plan. The large majority of the Six Nations preferred to keep their neutrality throughout the early goings of the conflict, of which the rebels were fully aware. In fact, until 1777, no whole Six Nation tribe made a full commitment to participate in the war. Up until then, only individual tribesmen made a commitment to either side.

The tribes of the Six Nations preferred not to participate for many reasons, but primarily because the conflict seemed to be very unnatural and confusing. The Indians had experienced wars between the French and the English, but seeing Englishmen facing off against one another was a situation where many were uncertain what would happen if they became involved. Eventually, the majority of tribes—from the Northern frontiers of Massachusetts and New York to the Southern frontier of Georgia and South Carolina—would have to decide with whom they would lend their support.

In mid-July, Guy Johnson arrived in Montreal with what Indians would follow. Immediately, he and Guy Carleton differed over what use, if any, the Indians should be put.[83] Johnson preferred that the Indians be assembled at once to prevent the rebels from taking Ticonderoga, Lake Champlain, and he warned of their intent of taking Canada, since it was an "essential

---

[83] Barbara Graymont, *The Iroquois in the American Revolution*, (Syracuse, NY: Syracuse Univ. Press, 1972), 66.

object."[84] Carleton disagreed wholeheartedly. He felt Quebec should base its defense on Canadian militiamen; the Indians should only be used in the defense of the providence. Carleton's greatest fear was that the Indians, if let loose, would commit such atrocities that "the innocent might have suffered with the guilty."[85]

The rebels were always fearful of the threat the Indians posed to their security. As early as July 1775, Benjamin Franklin believed "Governor Carleton...has been very industrious in engaging the Indians to begin their horrid Work."[86] According to George Woolsey, the whole reason behind their pre-emptive maneuver at Ticonderoga was to prevent "General Carleton's Joining the troops with some Indians & Cannadiens..."[87] John Trumbull, Governor of Connecticut, felt strongly about maintaining the security of the frontier since it "becomes daily more evident from the reiterated Intelligence we receive of the

---

[84] Ibid, 67.

[85] Ibid. See also *War of 1775-76*, Guy Johnson to Lord Dartmouth, October 12, 1775, 346. In August 1775, Carleton rejected the assistance of the Indians, except for a small detachment that was retained to defend Canada against any invading forces. By the summer of 1776, even with the increasing hostilities, Carleton did not allow the Indians to operate outside of Canada, and refused to let them loose on the frontier. Sosin, "The Use of Indians in the War of the American Revolution: A Re-Assessment of Responsibility," *Canadian Historical Review*, 109-10.

[86] William B. Wilcox, *The Papers of Benjamin Franklin*, Vol. 22, (New Haven, CT: Yale University Press, 1982), Benjamin Franklin to Jonathan Shipley, July 7, 1775, 97. Franklin would later write in a short list of grievances that the British were guilty of "Exciting the Savages to fall upon our innocent Outsetlers, Farmers, (who have no Concern in, and from their Situation can scarce have any Knowledge of this Dispute) especially when it is considered that the Indian Manner of making War, is by suprizing Families in the Night, and killing all, without Distinction of Age or Sex!," Ibid, Benjamin Franklin to Jonathan Shipley, September 13, 1775, 200. This statement was later incorporated in Franklin's "Proposed Preamble to a Congressional Resolution," Ibid, Benjamin Franklin to Robert Morris, December 30, 1775, 323.

[87] United States, *Naval Documents of the American Revolution*, Vol. 1, George Woolsey to George Salmon, May 22, 1775, 506.

The "Savage" Threat From the Frontier

Plan...to distress us by Inroads of Canadians and Savages from the Province of Quebec."[88] After taking Ticonderoga, Benedict Arnold wrote to Congress about his fear that "400 regulars" were expected to be "joined by a number of Indians" to retake the fort."[89] The threat, though purely speculative at the time, was believed to be real. Their fears should have subsided once reports from their agents in Canada and Ticonderoga reported very positive news.

By late May 1775 the intelligence began to change in the rebels' favor. Ethan Allen wrote to Congress the "Indians and Canadians were more inclined to join with the British, but he had prevented it. He believed the Canadians and Indians "appear at present to be very friendly to us, and it is my humble opinion the more vigorous the Colonies push the war against the King's Troops in Canada, the more friends we shall find in that Country."[90] In addition, he reported that he had been successful in making much headway with the local tribes, stating the "Indians have been to visit us, and have returned to their Tribes to sue their Influence in our favr."[91]

Congress also received good news from Benedict Arnold regarding the Indian tribes. Arnold had sent his interpreter to Montreal to "know their Intentions in the present dispute." He returned with favorable news that "the Indians are determined not to assist the Kings Troops against us, & have made a Law, that if any one of their Tribe shall take up Arms for that purpose, he shall immediately be put to death."[92] Arnold also reported, the tribes "press very hard for our Army to march into Canada, being much

---

[88] Ibid, John Trumbull to Massachusetts Provincial Congress, May 25, 1775, 526-28.
[89] Ibid, Journal of the Continental Congress, May 31, 1775, 580.
[90] Ibid, Colonel Ethan Allen to Continental Congress, May 29, 1775, 563-64.
[91] Ibid, 564.
[92] Ibid, Colonel Benedict Arnold to Continental Congress, June 13, 1775, 671-72.

disgusted with the regulars."[93] Ethan Allen held similar sentiments, writing that if a war were directed there, it "would unite and conform the Canadians and Indians in our interest."[94] John Lane was struck by the willingness of the Northern indigenous tribes to aid the rebels, writing to the Massachusetts Congress, "I could not have thought that they had been so hearty in the cause, and are very ready to assist us."[95]

Throughout much of the early summer of 1775, rebel officers in Canada sent positive reports to Congress regarding the indigenous tribes. Ethan Allen, Benedict Arnold, and James Easton all believed a show of force would attach the Northern indigenous tribes to their interest.[96] Congress and the provincial assemblies were not as optimistic as their military representatives. Rebel governments received just as much bad news about Indian recruitment as they received good news. In late June, it was reported the British were "continually inviting the Indians to join with them and fight." They "offer them money to take up arms" but the Indians "utterly refuse it."[97] Similar intelligence was received from the Albany Committee, where it was reported the French Caughnewaga Indians "had taken up the hatchet."[98] Eleazer Wheelock gave a more moderate explanation of the Indians within Carleton's camp. He stated the Caughnewaga Indians had only joined the British "to save themselves from being distressed," and the "fullest evidence" shows it is only an issue of "self-preservation."[99]

By July, reports persisted about Carleton's attempts to persuade

---

[93] Ibid.
[94] Ibid, Colonel Ethan Allen to Provincial Congress of Massachusetts, June 9, 1775, 642.
[95] Force, *American Archives*, Fourth Series, Vol. 2, 942.
[96] Ibid, 919, 939.
[97] Ibid, 1042.
[98] Ibid, 1319.
[99] Nathaniel Bouton, *Documents and Records Relating to the Province of New Hampshire From 1764 to 1776*, (Nashua, 1873), 547-48.

The "Savage" Threat From the Frontier

the Canadian tribes to the British cause.[100] One account falsely claims Carleton threatened the tribes with the loss of their land if they did not fight against the colonists. They were forced to be "reduced to the disagreeable necessity either of relinquishing everything they held dear in life" or complying with Carleton's demands. The witness of this account claims this fear, coupled with Carleton's "presents of provisions and ammunition," persuaded the tribes to take up the hatchet against the rebels.[101] Not all accounts were so definitive or clear-cut. Philip Schuyler teetered in his beliefs as to whether Carleton could even recruit the Indians. Though Schuyler did not put it past Carleton to employ them, he did not know which intelligence report to trust. Regardless, just in case Carleton was successful, he hoped "to be a little more decently prepared to receive him."[102] Schuyler would later write to Washington that although he did not believe Carleton "will have any Success with the Canadian tribes," he is "Joined by some of the more remote Indians." It was this alliance that prompted Schuyler to "not hesitate one moment" in employing "any Indians that might be willing to join us."[103] Rumors were so rampant, and intelligence so uncertain, that the Massachusetts Provincial Congress resolved to make an application to the Continental Congress to handle the Indian affairs of the Northern colonies.[104]

On July 13, 1775, the Continental Congress responded by forming three Indian Departments; the Northern, Southern, and Middle. The commissioners of these departments, led by Samuel

---

[100] Showman, *The Papers of Nathanael Greene*, Vol. 1, Nathanael Greene to Henry Ward, September 30, 1775, 128.

[101] Force, *American Archives*, Fourth Series, Vol. 2, 1594-96.

[102] Abbot & Twohig, *The Papers of George Washington,* Revolutionary Series, Vol. 1, Philip Schuyler to George Washington, July 18, 1775, 130.

[103] Ibid, Philip Schuyler to George Washington, August 27, 1775, 367-68.

[104] Force, *American Archives*, Fourth Series, Vol. 2, 1395.

Kirkland,[105] had the duties of; 1) using their influence on the tribes to gain their assistance in the cause, 2) watching the conduct of the British Superintendents, and 3) arresting any "person whatsoever" who is "active in stirring up or inciting the Indians...to become inimical to the American Colonies."[106] On the subject of including the indigenous tribes within the conflict, Congress would take a more moderate stance. While many Provincial assemblies, localities, and officers had been actively procuring the assistance of the indigenous tribes, Congress desired that they "remain at home, and not join on either side."[107] In effect, Congress was taking a more diplomatic approach. Their primary objective was reconciliation with Great Britain, not arming every person who was willing to join the cause. To ensure the exclusion of the Indian auxiliaries, which otherwise would prove detrimental to peace negotiations, Congress ordered "Indians be not employed as soldiers in the armies of the United Colonies...without express approbation of Congress."[108] Unbeknownst to Congress, the inclusion of the Indians in the conflict had already begun.

---

[105] Samuel Kirkland was successful in persuading the Oneida Indians to declare neutrality in May 1775, and also obtained similar declarations from the Six Nations with the aid of the Oneidas. Kirkland would keep the Oneidas friendly throughout the war and employed their scouts to obtain British intelligence. Abbot & Twohig, *The Papers of George Washington*, Revolutionary Series, Vol. 2, 61 n.1.

[106] Ibid, 1879.

[107] Force, *American Archives*, Fourth Series, Vol. 2, 1882.

[108] Force, *American Archives*, Fourth Series, Vol. 5, 1634. On March 6, 1776, Richard Smith preferred the inclusion of Indians in the war, and commented in his diary "this appeared very absurd and impolitic." See Edmund C. Burnett, *Letters to the Members of the Continental Congress*, Vol. 1, (Washington, DC: Carnegie Institution of Washington, 1921), 382. On July 21, 1775, Benjamin Franklin preferred including the Six Nations in a "perpetual Alliance offensive and defensive" in his draft of the Articles of Confederation. The Articles were read in Congress, but not put on the record. Franklin's proposed articles were too radical, and were asked to be left off the Congressional Journal. Willcox, *The Papers of Benjamin Franklin*, Vol. 22, 121-24.

The "Savage" Threat From the Frontier

Massachusetts had already taken the initial steps to making an alliance inevitable, and by coincidence Gage and Lord Dartmouth had also engaged the support of the Indians on their side.

Chapter Nine

Choosing Sides

The proofs you have of the Ministry's intention to engage the Savages against us are incontrovertible.
     Philip Schuyler to George Washington, December 15, 1775

The rebels were operating on the false intelligence that Carleton had employed the Canadian tribes, though, in fact, he had received little, if any, assistance. Those Indians that did side with him during the early hostilities were only used for defensive purposes. This is because Carleton did not find it proper to employ Indians in an offensive capacity.[1] Regardless of these facts, Congress and the provincial governments were unaware of Carleton's true intent. They continuously received varying reports of Carleton's employment of the Indians. One eyewitness would testify that there were over five hundred Indians employed, while another would guess no more than "thirty or forty."[2] Patriot Edward Bancroft gave little consideration to these reports when making his determination whether the British would employ the Indians. He felt as long as the British prosecute the war "that endeavors will be used to excite the Indians of America."[3]

On August 3, the Massachusetts Provincial Assembly heard a report from an examination of one of the Chiefs of the Caughnawaga tribe. The assembly was informed that "the several Tribes of Indians" were invited to take up arms against them. The Chief further testified that the warriors only agreed to "take up

---

[1] Sosin, *The Revolutionary Frontier*, 89.
[2] Force, *American Archives*, Fourth Series, Vol. 3, 12-14, 26.
[3] Willcox, *The Papers of Benjamin Franklin*, Vol. 22, Edward Bancroft to Benjamin Franklin, August 7, 1775, 152.

arms and defend" themselves, not to "seek people to quarrel with them."[4] Similar intelligence was received from the St. Francis Indians, who affirmed Carleton was pressuring tribes to join the British through duress. They were ready to afford the rebels' assistance, "if wanted," and would "heartily" assist General Schuyler if he chose to "proceed into Canada."[5] The rebels became acutely aware of the situation at hand—they must now use whatever means necessary to gain the loyalty of the majority of the indigenous tribes.

At first, many tribes preferred to stay neutral in the contest. On August 11, fifty Indians of the Six Nations informed the rebels they were not going to "take up the hatchet on either side," and they trusted the rebel leadership to fill the vacancy left by the fleeing of the Guy Johnson.[6] Repeatedly, at meetings or conferences held by the Congressional Indian Superintendents, the tribes conveyed their intent to stay neutral in the conflict.[7] One report even informed Congress that many of the tribes, whom had taken up the hatchet against them, now wanted it to be buried. Moreover, the tribes even offered to capture Guy Johnson and bring him to the rebel committee at Albany.[8]

Through the first year of hostilities, the correspondence of Southern rebels portrays the Indian threat on the Southern frontier far more serious than anything the Northern colonies were facing. In reality, this threat became critical, coincidentally, at around the same time the Northern colonies were growing fearful of Guy Carleton's Canadian Indian allies. It took shape following Lord Dunmore's War, when the Governor had returned to Virginia to cheers and popularity. However, this popularity did not last long once Dunmore disassembled the Virginia Assembly, confiscated the town's gunpowder, and threatened to "declare freedom to the

---

[4] Force, *American Archives*, Fourth Series, Vol. 3, 301-2.
[5] Ibid, 340.
[6] Ibid, 86.
[7] Ibid, 625.
[8] Ibid, 1372.

slaves and lay the town in ashes!"[9] On May 1st, Dunmore wrote to the Ministry that, if he had a sufficient "supply of arms and ammunition," he could raise "such a force from among Indians, negroes, and other persons, as would reduce the refractory people of this colony to obedience."[10] This is the first documented threat to incite the indigenous tribes on the rebels. Whilst Southern rebels had, in all probability, already hypothesized that such a threat was possible, no physical, historical evidence of any Indian war plot would surface until August 1775, with the colonists remaining unaware of any conspiracy until November.

In early July 1775, Connolly had received word that Dunmore had been forced to flee to his ship and was instructed to persuade the Indians to join the cause of Great Britain. It has been argued that it was at this point Connolly began raising an Indian force to attack the western frontiers. However, there is no evidence to support this claim. Examination of the correspondence of John Connolly from May up to August 1775, suggests the contrary. Although many rebels did not believe Connolly was working out negotiations with the Shawnee who fought in Lord Dunmore's War, it seems likely that Connolly was performing the task he was instructed to perform—keep the tribes neutral in the conflict. On July 4, 1775, exactly one year prior to the Declaration of Independence, Connolly stated to the tribes present:

> As some foolish people of both sides have found means of getting into their possession Warlike Weapons with which they destroyed one another. We now take them out of their hands in behalf of the great Man of Virginia who proceeded into your country last year with this design and after thus convincing them of their folly, he then buried them deep in

---

[9] Charles, *Washington's Decision: The Story of George Washington's Decision to Reaccept Black Enlistments in the Continental Army, December 31, 1775*, 34.

[10] Ibid, 35. For Lord Dartmouth's response, *see* Force, *American Archives*, Fourth Series, Vol. 3, 6. Holton, *Forced Founders: Indians, Debtors, Slaves & the Making of the American Revolution in Virginia*, 148.

the earth.[11]

The Shawnee were deeply concerned with the continuation of trade with Dunmore. They were particularly concerned with ammunition and powder, since it "is so dear and Game become so scarce that it is out of our power to provide ourselves with that article."[12] Connolly responded he "would be extremely glad to everything in" his "power to but the Great Man of Virginia is much engaged in Business of Importance."[13] Throughout the peace negotiations, Connolly never encouraged the aid of the indigenous tribes in the conflict with the colonies.[14] He even stated he would do his utmost to protect the rights of the Shawnee and expected "the same brotherly friendship from" them by not "interfering in any of our disputes."[15] Just like Guy Johnson, Connolly was doing what was necessary to ensure peace on the American frontiers.

For all his wishes, Connolly was not about to delude himself with hopes of recruiting the Shawnee away from the rebels. The Virginia Assembly had sent their own committee which Connolly believed was to "impress upon the minds of the Indians, the justice of the hostile proceedings against this country."[16] Connolly was correct; Captain James Wood journal shows there was lobbying by both political factions to gain the interests of the Shawnee in their

---

[11] "Correspondence of Dr. John Connolly, May-August 1775," *Virginia Magazine of History and Biography*, Vol. 14, (1906-07), 69.

[12] Ibid, 72.

[13] Ibid.

[14] No documented historical evidence has been found proving Connolly initially intended to recruit the Indians as auxiliaries. All primary documents that state to that affect are from patriot sources and are based on hearsay, not evidentiary proof.

[15] Scribner and Tarter, *Revolutionary Virginia: The Road to Independence*, Vol. 3, 266.

[16] *The Narrative of the Transactions Imprisonment and Sufferings of John Connolly an American Loyalist and Lieutenant Colonel in his Majesty's Service*, (London, England), 6.

favor.[17] In the end, Connolly left with Shawnee promises to stand by the British government as "his Majesty's most faithful friends and auxilliaries," while being dually successful in "secretly frustrat[ing] the machinations" of the rebels plan to recruit the Shawnee to their aid. Connolly never informed the Shawnee of the disagreements between the colonies and Britain, and was offended by the rebel "prejudice" to his character, depreciating the value of his "publick services." He believed the accusations of him recruiting the Shawnee against the colonists "bespeak the care of the Government which I have faithfully served, & must therefore silent effectually, the slanderous tongues of the ungenerous."[18]

Could the rebels have offended Connolly to the breaking point? He felt affronted by many who thought he was nothing more than a "Ministerial Tool" ready to support "every measure which Lord Dunmore might recommend to me." He felt such insinuations were "malicious, & far foreign to truth."[19] It is unknown as to what exactly caused Connolly to plan a scheme to employ the indigenous tribes against the rebels, but his narrative gives us some insight. The idea seemed to gain favor while he was traveling from Fort Pitt to meet Lord Dunmore in Norfolk. His narrative states he was encouraged by the "unanimity of opinion" among his men, and "ventured to predict, that nothing less than independency, and total revolution, were intended by the leaders" of the rebels.[20] It was at this point Connolly chose to inform his men of the scheme to employ the Indians as auxiliaries and

---

[17] Scribner and Tarter, *Revolutionary Virginia: The Road to Independence*, Vol. 3, 275.

[18] "Correspondence of Dr. John Connolly, May-August 1775," *Virginia Magazine of History and Biography*, Vol. 14, John Connolly to George Rootes, August 1, 1775, 78-9.

[19] Ibid, 79.

[20] *The Narrative of the Transactions Imprisonment and Sufferings of John Connolly an American Loyalist and Lieutenant Colonel in his Majesty's Service*, 8.

"execute it at the hazard of life and fortune."[21]

In July, Connolly began his journey to meet up with Dunmore. Upon arriving, he proposed to raise a force among the loyalists and Indians. His plan included joining forces with Dunmore next Spring, severing Virginia from the Northern colonies, thus, forcing Virginia's early surrender.[22] Dunmore had no problem affirming the proposal inasmuch as had already written to Lord Dartmouth requesting such an employment just three months earlier. Dunmore had not heard any response to his letter, though. Therefore it seemed logical to advance such a plan to the next person in the chain of command, Thomas Gage. Dunmore immediately sent Connolly to Boston in order to gain Gage's approval.[23] Connolly delivered the plan to Gage, proposing 1) to prepare the Ohio Indians to act in concert, 2) travel to Detroit to procure ordnance, and 3) penetrate through Virginia and meet up with Dunmore in Alexandria.[24] Gage had no qualm approving the plan, since Lord Dartmouth had recently authorized the use of Indian auxiliaries. Both Gage and Dartmouth felt the rebel inclusion of the Stockbridge Indians at Cambridge, coupled with rebel interference with British Indian affairs, was evidence sufficient enough that the race to recruit the Indian warrior was afoot.

Once Connolly gained the approval of Gage, he set off to

---

[21] Ibid.
[22] Selby, *The Revolution in Virginia, 1775-1783*, 57. Abbot & Twohig, *The Papers of George Washington*, Revolutionary Series, Vol. 1, 31-32 n.3.
[23] Carter, *The Correspondence of General Thomas Gage with the Secretaries of State 1763-1775*, Vol. 1, Thomas Gage to Lord Dartmouth, September 20, 1775, 415.
[24] Burton, "John Connolly, A Tory of the Revolution," *Proceedings of the American Antiquarian Society,* 85-6. See also, Scribner and Tarter, *Revolutionary Virginia: The Road to Independence*, Vol. 4, Introductory Note, 14-15. Smith, *Letters of the Delegates to Congress 1774 to 1789*, Vol. 1, 227. For copy of plan see Scribner and Tarter, *Revolutionary Virginia: The Road to Independence*, Vol. 4, 82.

Choosing Sides

Portsmouth, Virginia to meet up with Dunmore once again.[25] On November 13, a day before the infamous publication of Lord Dunmore's Proclamation offering freedom to rebel slaves, Connolly left for Detroit to procure arms for his plan. Connolly's scheme never materialized though. He was seized by rebels at Hagerstown, Maryland. Unbeknownst to Connolly, he had been betrayed by John Gibson, to whom he had sent intelligence of his plan.[26] Gibson had been instructed to convey the plan to Captain White Eyes of the Shawnee, but instead turned it over to the local rebel authorities. In mid-October, Washington had also received similar intelligence from William Cowley. He learned the entirety of Connolly's plan to "go into the Indian Countrys to raise the Indians & French."[27]

Thus, while Connolly thought he was traveling under a cloak of safety, he was in fact a wanted criminal. Although his plan began unraveling in September and October, Virginia would not learn of it until late November, when the plans were forwarded to the Virginia Committee of Safety. It was General Washington who found the plans when he intercepted one of Dunmore's ships in mid-December. The ship contained much of Dunmore's correspondence, confirming what Philip Schuyler had already written to Washington. Schuyler had informed the General that the Six Nations presented a war belt that had been given to them by Guy Johnson, showing "sufficient proof that the Ministry attempted to engage the Savages, to fight against us."[28] The evidence prompted Washington respond to Schuyler, "The proofs you have of the Ministry's intention to engage the Savages against

---

[25] Ivor Noel Hume, *1775: Another Part of the Field*, (New York, NY: Alfred A Knopf, 1966), 389.

[26] *The Narrative of the Transactions Imprisonment and Sufferings of John Connolly an American Loyalist and Lieutenant Colonel in his Majesty's Service*, 16-17. See also, Scribner and Tarter, *Revolut\ionary Virginia: The Road to Independence*, Vol. 4, 41-42.

[27] Abbot & Twohig, *The Papers of George Washington*, Revolutionary Series, Vol. 2, William Cowley to George Washington, October 12, 1775, 67.

[28] Ibid, Philip Schuyler to George Washington, December 15, 1775, 554.

us are incontrovertible."[29]

Although Connolly was captured, Dunmore had received word from Lord Dartmouth authorizing him to raise a force "among the Indians, negroes, and other persons." Dartmouth had shipped the supplies and arms that Dunmore had requested in May and left it to his "Lordship's discretion to use this leave of absence or not, as you shall see occasion."[30] This particularly helped Dunmore because he was not receiving the British reinforcements he requested, but with supplies, he had the capability of raising a racially diverse force that the rebels feared would tear society apart.[31]

The situation in Virginia was similar to that of the Northern colonies with accusations and rumors rampant. Another threat allegedly stemmed from John Stuart. Much like Guy Johnson, Stuart was perpetually accused of attempting to alienate the affections of the Indians. In January, he had received correspondence from Thomas Gage informing him of the "ill-affected People" in the Northern colonies that were trying to gain the support of the Six Nations. Gage requested Stuart to warn his deputies "against any attempts of the like nature to debauch the

---

[29] Force, *American Archives,* Fourth Series, Vol. 4, 449. Abbot & Twohig, *The Papers of George Washington,* Revolutionary Series, Vol. 2, George Washington to Philip Schuyler, December 24, 1775, 600.

[30] Force, *American Archives*, Fourth Series, Vol. 3, 6.

[31] Captain James Wood was placed in charge of maintaining peace with the Shawnee, Delaware, Seneca, Wynandot, and Tawa tribes. Wood would often report his dealings with these tribes back to the Committee of Pittsburgh and the Virginians. What he informed them must have been alarming. According to Wood, through agents of Dunmore, the tribes had been informed that "all the people, except the Governour [Lord Dunmore], were determined on war with the Indians; that the Governour was for peace" and all the "white people were preparing for war."[31] Wood assured his superiors he had settled the matter and the tribes "appeared entirely satisfied." Wood assured his superiors he had settled the matter and the tribes "appeared entirely satisfied." Ibid, 76-78.

Indians in their respective Districts."[32] Stuart responded by affirming the safety of his district to Lord Dartmouth, stating that nothing in his power should "be omitted to keep all the Indians firm in their love & attachment to the King, & in a temper to be always ready to act in His Service."[33]

Accounts of Indian plots against colonists spread far and wide, arousing fears, but none of the stories had any real merit. Much like the fear of slave revolts, the stories were fictional hearsay based on the colonists' insecurities.[34] Meanwhile, British restrictions on munitions further sparked rebel fears of insurrection from slaves and indigenous tribes. The preventative measures established to prevent the procuring of munitions and weapons brought special reason for concern for the rebels that the British might enlist Indian support through generous gifts. It was dually believed these restrictions were also an attempt to leave the Southern colonies defenseless against slave revolts.[35] Stuart was the unfortunate benefactor of these fears when, on May 11, news of Lexington and Concord arrived. In an air of excitement, rebels oppressed Tories and other friends to the British government with ridicule, tarring and feathering, and forcing them to take oaths of allegiance. Rumors immediately began circulating that Stuart had sent orders to the Catawba and Cherokee Indians for an attack on the frontier settlements. Although there was no evidence to support such assertions, rebels regarded every message or action by which Stuart conducted his influence over the Indians as a threat against American interests.[36]

---

[32] Philip M. Hamer, "John Stuart's Indian Policy During the Early Months of the American Revolution," *The Mississippi Valley Historical Review*, Vol. 17, No. 3 (December, 1930), 353.

[33] Ibid.

[34] Sosin, "The Use of Indians in the War of the American Revolution: A Re-Assessment of Responsibility," *Canadian Historical Review*, 117.

[35] J. Russell Snapp, *John Stuart and the Struggle for Empire on the Southern Frontier*, (Baton Rouge, LA: Louisiana State University Press, 1996), 159.

[36] Ibid.

Irreconcilable Grievances

While sick in bed, Stuart received news of a rebel plan to seize his person. He immediately withdrew from Charleston, South Carolina to seek shelter in nearby Savannah, Georgia. His flight so polarized public opinion that he found he could no longer defend his character. This is because two members of the South Carolina Provincial Congress had circulated false accounts that he had been responsible for the murders of thirty-four families on the frontier, and that, in 1760, Stuart had been responsible for the massacre at Fort Loundon, where a group of Indians captured the garrison and massacred its inhabitants.[37] Stuart attempted to plea his innocence to Georgia leaders by presenting his correspondence with his Indian agents. The plan backfired. Although Stuart had showed that the Indians were not being used in any form of military capacity against the colonists, his evidence that the "Indians were very well disposed, and Mr. Cameron particularly had acquainted" him "that he could lead the Cherokees if necessary," was much cause for concern.[38] Stuart was frustrated. He did not believe that any part of his conduct should "induce a Belief that I could Wantonly Use my Influence with the Indians to make them fall upon an Innocent people."[39] His words to William Henry Drayton more clearly convey his frustration, stating, "I know now who it was that propagated such an injurious & False Report, but illiberal as the Word *Villain* may appear to be, the Malicious Author of such a calumny certain Merit's the Appellation."[40]

Stuart's attempt to absolve himself of any wrongdoing led to

---

[37] Hamer, "John Stuart's Indian Policy During the Early Months of the American Revolution," *The Mississippi Valley Historical Review*, Vol. 17, No. 3, 354. See also, Force, *American Archives,* Fourth Series, Vol. 2, 1681-82.

[38] Snapp, *John Stuart and the Struggle for Empire on the Southern Frontier*, 161.

[39] Hamer, "John Stuart's Indian Policy During the Early Months of the American Revolution," *The Mississippi Valley Historical Review*, Vol. 17, No. 3, 356.

[40] Ibid, 357.

his formal impeachment, even though he was not present to defend himself in the proceedings. To make matters worse, agents of Stuart arrived with the standard shipment of gunpowder intended to appease the Indians. Fears heightened, forcing Stuart to flee once again, thus confirming the colonists' suspicions of the Superintendents' designs to arm the "savages" against them.[41]

Following Stuart's initial flight from South Carolina, steps were taken to confiscate all the supplies and ammunition intended to be distributed to the Indians. British provision of supplies to the indigenous tribes was nothing new, having been common practice prior to the Revolution, and having served as a means to maintain peace and security on the Western frontiers. Given the heightened fears, especially after the news of the battles of Lexington and Concord spread, the rebels began to suspect these supplies were being used to persuade the tribes to attack those colonists who rebelled. This theory was strictly cultivated in the minds of the fear-stricken colonists, though, and had no evidentiary basis to prove this was Stuart's intent.

Although the rebels confiscated the supplies and ammunition intended for the Indians, they in turn, redistributed a large portion of it to the tribes. This was done to counter any influence Stuart might have with them.[42] According to Governor Wright, the rebels were sure to convey "the Indians be Acquainted that it is not from the King or from the Government or from the Traders but from the People of the Province."[43] Capturing British provisions and ammunition was nothing new. Rebel parties throughout the entire thirteen colonies took part in such measures, but it was rare for the captured supplies to be used to promote an Indian alliance.

The confiscation of supplies was not the only attempt to prevent Stuart's alleged plan "of turning the power of those

---

[41] Snapp, *John Stuart and the Struggle for Empire on the Southern Frontier*, 162-63.

[42] Edward McCrady, *The History of South Carolina in the Revolution 1775-1780*, Vol. 3, (New York: NY, Paladin Pres, 1969), 18.

[43] Snapp, *John Stuart and the Struggle for Empire on the Southern Frontier*, 162-63.

Savages against" the colonies.⁴⁴ The South Carolina Provincial Congress decided it was also in their best interests to confiscate Stuart's property and to hold his family hostage. The former "will be held as a Guarantee for the quiet & good conduct of the Savages," while the latter was "a barrier against the massacre & butchery of hundreds of Innocent families in Georgia & South Carolina."⁴⁵

Even after being falsely accused, having his property confiscated and his family held hostage, Stuart remained adamantly opposed to the inclusion of the indigenous tribes as military auxiliaries. In August, Stuart conveyed to his agent, Alexander Cameron, to refrain from involving the Indians in any difficulties between the colonies and Great Britain. Cameron replied, "I pray to God" the Indians are not involved in this conflict, "for should the Indians be prompted to take up the Hatchet...the Issue of it would be terrible, as they could not be restrained from Committing the most inhuman barbarities on Women and Children &ca."⁴⁶

On October 3, Stuart was opposed to including the Creek Indians because they were at war with the Choctaws. This would leave the Creeks in a weakened defenseless state if the Choctaws ever attacked them. Stuart was not willing to "expose their women and children to the attacks of their enemies."⁴⁷ He wrote to Gage, "I conceive that an indiscriminate attack by Indians would be contrary to your Excellency's idea, and might do much harm."⁴⁸ Although Stuart disagreed with Gage's attempt to bring

---

⁴⁴ Chesnutt, *The Papers of Henry Laurens*, Vol. 10, Henry Laurens to James Laurens, July 2, 1775, 202.

⁴⁵ Ibid, Henry Laurens to John Laurens, June 23, 1775, 189. Ibid, Vol. 11, Henry Laurens to the Georgia Council of Safety, February 7, 1776, 92.

⁴⁶ Hamer, "John Stuart's Indian Policy During the Early Months of the American Revolution," *The Mississippi Valley Historical Review*, Vol. 17, No. 3, 359.

⁴⁷ Force, *American Archives*, Fourth Series, Vol. 4, 317.

⁴⁸ On September 12, 1775, Gage had requested Stuart to communicate

Dunmore and Connolly's plan to life, he was willing to "dispose them to join in executing any concerted plan, and to act with and assist their well-disposed neighbors."[49] He was against any "indiscriminate Attack" upon the people, but willing to act "to assist his Majesty's Troops and Friends in distressing the Rebells and bringing them to a sense of their Duty."[50]

Whilst he did not initially agree with the use of Indians as auxiliaries in the conflict, Stuart would eventually conform to the idea that employing them was, in the end, in the best interests of the tribes and the British. On May 18, 1776, he addressed the indigenous tribes of the southern frontier, offering whoever is willing to join "his Majesty's forces…shall find protection, and their families and estates [will] be secure from all danger whatever."[51] He also informed the tribes of his plan to "land an army in West Florida, and march them through the Creek nation to the Chickasaws, where five hundred warriors from each nation are to join them."[52] Although Florida's Governor, Patrick Tonyn, supported Stuart's change of heart, he also felt Stuart's delay had cost them dearly. Since the rebels had been successful in stripping the countryside of supplies, causing their acquisition to be "at the risk of life and fortune," Tonyn believed the delay prevented procuring the assistance of the Southern tribes with such supplies. Therefore, Tonyn felt that if only "General Gage's letter of the 12

---

with the Southern Indians, and whenever opporutne, "to make them take Arms against His Majesty's Enemies," and to distress the rebels with all their power "for no terms is now to be kept with them; they have brought down all the Savages they could against us here, who with their Rifle men are continually firing on our Advanced Sentries…no time should be lost to distress a set of people so wantonly rebellious." Sosin, "The Use of Indians in the War of the American Revolution: A Re-Assessment of Responsibility," *Canadian Historical Review*, 113.

[49] Force, *American Archives*, Fourth Series, Vol. 4, 317.

[50] Hamer, "John Stuart's Indian Policy During the Early Months of the American Revolution," *The Mississippi Valley Historical Review*, Vol. 17, No. 3, 361.

[51] Force, *American Archives*, Fourth Series, Vol. 6, 497.

[52] Ibid.

Sepr. been obeyed," it would have been easy to procure supplies to gain favor among the tribes.[53]

With both the British and rebels jockeying for influence over each of the tribes, it was only a matter of time before the indigenous tribes became involved in the conflict. Most of them would side with the British due to the latter's attempts to protect the frontiers against encroachments by colonists and foreign governments.[54] On August 6, 1775, Philip Schuyler wrote to George Washington that the different Indian tribes "are most our enemies."[55] Schuyler's statement was inaccurate at the time he wrote it, but it is almost as if it was foreshadowing the events to come. Many Indians felt "the Revolution was but the culmination of the tension between the two races that had been mounting during the previous decade."[56] Siding with the British was their opportunity to make up for past wrongs committed. There were numerous points under consideration that favored standing by the British. Each tribe had to weigh 1) the future protection of their lands, 2) who would be able to provide them with the essential supplies they desperately needed, and 3) which side would best support their interests.

For over a decade, the Indians had been thwarting white encroachments on their land. The Proclamation of 1763 had been enacted to prevent this. Regardless, colonists ignored the Parliamentary order, seeking to obtain landed interests by any

---

[53] Edward M. Coleman, "Letter From Governor Patrick Tonyn of East Florida to Lord George Germain, Secretary of State for the Colonies, 1776," *Mississippi Valley Historical Review*, Vol. 33, No. 2 (Sep., 1946), 291. Thomas Gage, Lord Dunmore, Guy Johnson, Guy Carleton, John Connolly, and John Stuart were not the only British officials that eventually turned to the indigenous tribes for military assistance. John Johnson made multiple attempts to procure loyalists and Indians to fight against the rebels. Governor Patrick Tonyn and David Taitt also made their own contributions, with the former showing his strong convictions by July 1776.

[54] Graymont, *The Iroquois in the American Revolution*, 88.

[55] Force, *American Archives*, Fourth Series, Vol. 3, 51.

[56] Sosin, *The Revolutionary Frontier*, 87.

means possible. While the rebels were calling the conflict a "war for liberty," most Indians knew, especially with British officials reminding them, that at issue was also a struggle over Indian landed rights.[57] Patriot Edward Bancroft was acutely aware of this point. To "unalterably" secure Indian alliances, Bancroft knew Congress must grant the Indians "full and Absolute" control over their lands.

The ability of the British to supply the indigenous tribes with essential commodities such as furs, blankets, ammunition, arms, and liquor also figured significantly in swaying many tribes' opinions. With increasing white encroachments on their lands, coupled with the depletion of game, many tribes adopted European weapon technology, dress and economic life.[58] Initially, Congress and the Provincial Assemblies made valiant efforts to procure supplies for the different tribes in order to gain favor with them. On January 27, 1776, Congress even authorized the spending of 40,000 pounds sterling to "preserve the friendship and confidence" of the Indians, "and to prevent their suffering for want of the necessaries in life."[59] That notwithstanding, Congress would be unable and unwilling to keep up with the consistent demand. By March 1776, the Congressional Indian Superintendents were in over their head, understaffed, and lacking supplies. Many of the tribes had dealt frequently with the British Superintendents, relentlessly conveying their needs and demands, or as Philip Schuyler stated it to Congress, they come only "begging errands."[60] The Continental officers and Congressional Superintendents were ill prepared for what seemed an endless demand for supplies and services.

The Indians certainly were sincere in their promises of neutrality and friendship to the rebels, but they expected that the

---

[57] Calloway, *The American Revolution in Indian Country*, 23.

[58] O'Donnell, "The South on the Eve of the Revolution: The Native Americans," *The Revolutionary War in the South: Power, Conflict, and Leadership*, 67. Graymont, *The Iroquois in the American Revolution*, 88.

[59] Force, *American Archives*, Fourth Series, Vol. 4, 1656.

[60] Force, *American Archives*, Fourth Series, Vol. 5, 415.

Congressional Indian Department would act similarly, as had the British in the past. They asked for smiths to fix their weapons, clothes to keep warm, and provisions to feed themselves in time of hardship. The interim rebel governments were barely capable of maintaining peace, order, and safety among its own people. As it was, they had not adequately considered the cost of replacing Great Britain economic contribution to the Indians.[61]

When Schuyler was preparing for a meeting with the Northern tribes, he did not possess any supplies to present as a sign of good faith. He wrote to Congress how the Indians "always expect presents on such occasions, but we have nothing to give them."[62] George Galphin held similar sentiments, stating, it "is the greatest Necessity for supplying the Indians at this time to keep them peaceable."[63] Supplying the Indians was not easy for the British either. Governor Patrick Tonyn was concerned with the security of the supply channel which was needed to recruit the Southern tribes. A stoppage of "arms and ammunition," Tonyn feared, shows the "intention of the Government not to employ the Indians." Tonyn had seen the rebels try "every device they could imagine" to recruit the southern Indians, but "their commissaries have labored in vain." He conveyed to Germain that the "Indians have been ready to join the British troops."[64] All that was needed

---

[61] Graymont, *The Iroquois in the American Revolution*, 89-90.

[62] Ibid.

[63] Chesnutt, *The Papers of Henry Laurens*, Vol. 11, George Galphin to Henry Laurens, February 7, 1776, 94. Ibid, Henry Laurens to North Carolina Provincial Congress, February 14, 1776, 103. William Goforth wrote he "Cant help thinking the Supplieng the Indians this Summer is a Matter that deserves Serious Consideration. On the one hand if they are Served with Amunition they may Use it against us. On the Other if they have it not, they have been so long out of the Use of Bows and Arrows that they must Starve which doubtless they will try in time to prevent in time..." Richard B. Morris, *John Jay: The Making of a Revolutionary, Unpublished Papers 1745-1780*, (New York, NY: Harper & Row, 1975), William Goforth to John Jay, April 8, 1776, 250.

[64] Coleman, "Letter From Governor Patrick Tonyn of East Florida to Lord George Germain, Secretary of State for the Colonies, 1776,"

to procure their assistance was the proper supplies and a secure channel.

Of prime importance to the Indians was whether the rebels or British served their best interests. Through the diplomatic successes of Sir William Johnson, the British were in a key position to gain the loyalties of the indigenous tribes. While many of the colonial leaders and border settlers viewed the Indian as an inconvenience to their expansion in the Western frontier, men like William Johnson concerned themselves with the tribes' welfare, taking the time to learn their honor and customs.[65] In the end, the majority of the tribes of the Six Nations sided against the rebels because they ultimately felt the British would be victorious.[66] It was in their best interests to take the side of the projected victor. This would not only allow some to gain vengeance for atrocities committed against them by border settlers, but it would preserve their land interests, thereby preventing future land encroachments.

Tribes such as the Stockbridge and Oneidas, instead, sided with the rebels, reasoning that they stood more to gain. The Stockbridge Indians had lost a significant amount of their landed property during the two years leading up to the American Revolution. Their close proximity to New England settlements caused the tribe to fall victim to colonists' desires to purchase their lands and drive them in debt. The debts owed to the colonists caused the Stockbridge Indians to become heavily reliant on the former, giving the tribe good reason to join the rebel cause.

The Oneida Indians similarily became reliant upon the rebel governments. During the early months of the conflict, the Oneidas and other New England Indians moved in close proximity to the colonists "until the present troubles shall be ended." Joseph Johnson wrote that many of these Indians were "so poor and destitute that they are utterly unable to pursue their journey

---

Mississippi Valley Historical Review, 291.

[65] Graymont, *The Iroquois in the American Revolution*, 89.

[66] O'Donnell, "The South on the Eve on the Revolution: The Native Americans," *The Revolutionary War in the South: Power, Conflict, and Leadership*, 66.

without the charitable aid and relief" of the colonists.[67] It was the potential danger the conflict would pose on the frontier and the "disagreeable situation of affairs" that induced these tribes to move close to the colonists. The majority, being poor and needy, were forced to rely on the contributions and charity of the local rebel governments for livelihood. Initially reluctant to not "intermeddle in this dispute," because the quarrel that seemed to be so "unnatural," the Indians eventually chose to side with the rebels.[68] They were not only grateful for the assistance the rebels provided, but the union proved to work their favor. Besides, the alliance was in the best interests of the rebel governments too. The tribes' close proximity to their settlements served as a deterrent, preventing the New England Indians from siding with the British regardless of the tribes' motives. Moreover, these tribes might induce others to side with them, acting as diplomats, bringing back intelligence on the rest of the Six Nations.[69]

Outside of employing the Stockbridge Indians, the rebels, including Congress, were not immune to employing the other indigenous tribes as military auxiliaries. In June 1775, Congress initially authorized military officers to persuade Indians to join the service on the condition the British employed them first. It was resolved that if any of the Indians were induced "to commit actual hostilities against these colonies, or enter into an offensive Alliance with the British troops," then they should "enter into the same, to oppose such British troops and their Indian Allies."[70] Congress would change their stance to facilitate any form of reconciliation, adopting to exclude Indians from serving in any of

---

[67] Force, *American Archives*, Fourth Series, Vol. 2, 1047.
[68] Ibid, 1116-17.
[69] Alan Taylor, *The Divided Ground: Indians, Settlers, and the Northern Borderland of the American Revolution*, (New York, NY: Alfred A. Knopf, 2006), 84-85. The Oneidas primarily had their own interests in mind. They hoped to supplant the Mohawks, whom they resented, as the most influential member of the Iroquois Nation.
[70] Abbot & Twohig, *The Papers of George Washington*, Revolutionary Series, Vol. 1, 46 n.2.

the "United Colonies." This decision was made even though many strongly believed the British were employing Indians as auxiliaries.

The new policy for military commanders was to maintain neutrality among the indigenous tribes and keep from making any mistakes that might compel them to join with the British. As early as September 1775, Washington cautioned Benedict Arnold not to "insult any of the Inhabitants of Canada," which included the indigenous tribes. Washington knew it was better to make allies with the Canadians and Indians than to induce their allegiance to General Carleton.[71] He felt the inhabitants had been either misinformed of the current conflict, were forced to join with Carleton, or both. Consequently, Washington ordered Arnold to convince "them that we Come at the Request of many of their Principal People, not as Robbers or to make War upon them but as the Friends & Supporters of their Liberties as well as ours."[72] General John Sullivan echoed similar sentiments in his orders, which stated, "Your men are to be frequently cautioned against offering any insult or abuse to the Indians, as one act of rudeness in a soldier might involve America in a dangerous war with a savage enemy."[73] In May 1776 Washington conveyed another problem posed by the sensitive situation with the indigenous tribes. Washington wanted to arrest British officials, including Guy Johnson, but knew that in doing so he would only propagate Indian resentment against the cause. This frustration was conveyed to Philip Schuyler when the General wrote, "Our situation respecting the Indians is delicate and embarrassing."[74]

By June 1776, with the possibility of reconciliation dwindling, Congress would overturn their exclusion on Indian auxiliaries and

---

[71] Ibid, George Washington to Benedict Arnold, September 14, 1775, 456.

[72] Ibid, Instructions to Benedict Arnold, September 14, 1775, 458.

[73] Force, *American Archives*, Fourth Series, Vol. 6, 493.

[74] Ibid, 544. Abbot & Twohig, *The Papers of George Washington*, Revolutionary Series, Vol. 4, George Washington to Philip Schuyler, May 22, 1776, 373.

authorize Washington to employ 2,000 Canadian Indians.[75] Washington supported the inclusion of the Indians and was actually influential in the passing of the resolution. In April 1776, he had received a letter from Schuyler, enclosing intelligence from Colonel Moses Hazzen about the disposition of the Indians.[76] Hazzen believed that "Numbers" of Indians "will come form the interior Country and fall on our Frontiers early in the Spring."[77] This information convinced Washington that it would be "impossible to keep them in a state of Neutrality."[78] He advised Congress to consider "whether it would not be best immediately to engage them on our side, and to use our utmost endeavors to prevent their minds being poison'd by Ministerial Emissaries."[79] Congress sent a Committee of Conference to General Washington to consider the matter and other recommendations. The Committee met from May 25 through the 29, advising Congress to recruit the 2,000 man Indian force.

While Washington interpreted that this force was only to be recruited and employed within Canada, there was much confusion regarding the resolution among the New England governments. Connecticut's interpretation was that Congress authorized them to raise a force among the Stockbridge and Mohegan Indians. Washington queried whether or not Congress meant their June 3 resolution to incorporate such a force. Congress replied, authorizing the General to employ the Indians "in any place where he shall judge they will be most useful."[80] Regardless of the clarification, Washington still preferred the measure to apply to "those who are not Livers Among us, & that Were hostilely

---

[75] Ibid, 1695.
[76] Abbot & Twohig, *The Papers of George Washington*, Revolutionary Series, Vol. 4, Philip Schuyler to George Washington, 55-56.
[77] Ibid, 88 n.3.
[78] Ibid, George Washington to John Hancock, April 19, 1775, 87.
[79] Ibid.
[80] Ibid, George Washington to John Hancock, June 18, 1776, 462-63. Abbot and Twohig, *The Papers of George Washington,* Revolutionary Series, Vol. 5, John Hancock to George Washington, June 18, 1776, 33.

inclined or of doubtful Friendship."[81] His reservations were confirmed when, on June 24, Congress rejected the creation of a force of Stockbridge and Mohegan Indians.[82]

By the spring of 1776, General Washington had become an advocate for the employment of Indians. More importantly, he knew the importance of maintaining good relations with the indigenous tribes. In a letter dated June 20, 1776, Washington asked Schuyler to pay "particular attention" to them and use his "most active exertions for accomplishing and carrying" their alliance into execution." Washington even hoped the new Indian recruits will "make prisoners of all the Kings troops they possibly can."[83] This latter recommendation was actually a resolution passed by the Continental Congress. They had authorized Washington to offer "a reward of one hundred dollars for every commissioned officer, and of thirty dollars for every private soldier of the King's troops that they shall take prisoners in the Indian country, or on the frontiers of these colonies."[84]

Besides Connecticut's desire to make an army out of the Stockbridge and Mohegan Indians, other colonies were making efforts to make allies of the indigenous tribes. On May 20, 1776, the Virginia Convention resolved, "That such Indian Warriors of the neighboring tribes as are willing to be engaged in the service of this country, provided the number so to be engaged doth not exceed two hundred, to be marched down to the assistance of the Regular forces of the Eastern quarter."[85] Even before Congress had authorized Schuyler and Washington to recruit the indigenous tribes, General John Sullivan had formed a brigade of Indians, numbering around two hundred and sixty warriors. Schuyler informed Washington of this unit, with the latter responding, "I am

---

[81] Abbot & Twohig, *The Papers of George Washington*, Revolutionary Series, Vol. 5, George Washington to Philip Schuyler, June 24, 1776, 89.
[82] Ibid, 103 n.2.
[83] Force, *American Archives*, Fourth Series, Vol. 6, 992.
[84] Abbot & Twohig, *The Papers of George Washington*, Revolutionary Series, Vol. 4, 473 n.7.
[85] Force, *American Archives*, Fourth Series, Vol. 6, 1532.

exceedingly Glad that so large a Number of Indians was present at the Review of General Sullivan's Brigade."[86]

In truth, the grievance that the British were responsible for employing the "savages" against the colonies is an assertion that inaccurately portrays the events leading up to the Declaration of Independence. Although both sides attempted to include the Indians in the conflict, there were also individuals on both sides who opposed inclusion. John Adams viewed "employing such savages" as uncivil and inhumane "against any enemy whatever." Adams only accepted their assistance because he knew "little of them," leaving their management to "gentlemen who know a great deal." He also did not object, "provided we cannot keep them neutral."[87]

John Adams and other prominent leaders would ultimately change their minds after the adoption of the Declaration of Independence. Patriots like Henry Laurens felt the British were inventing "horrible Scenes of foreign & domestic Butcheries (not War)." Laurens wrote to William Manning, "While Men of War & Troops are to attack us in [the] front," the Indians will attack from the rear, and the "Tories & Negro Slaves" will "rise in our Bowels."[88] Laurens was not the only colonist to fear this type of British reprisal, because the inclusion of the "savage" Indian was addressed in many of the speeches and documents supporting American autonomy.[89]

Of utmost importance to the inclusion of the Indians was the necessary fear that the other side would employ them. This fear also aided in escalating the conflict from a restitution of grievances to a war for independence. For the Americans, the

---

[86] Abbot & Twohig, *The Papers of George Washington,* Revolutionary Series, Vol. 4, George Washington to Philip Schuyler, May 15, 1776, 309.
[87] Force, *American Archives*, Fourth Series, Vol. 5, 1091.
[88] Chesnutt, *The Papers of Henry Laurens*, Vol. 11, Henry Laurens to William Manning, February 27, 1776, 122.
[89] Force, *American Archives*, Fourth Series, Vol. 5, 1027, 1034. Ibid, Vol. 4, 1018, 699.

British employment of the Indians served as strong evidence that the Crown intended to subject them to a state of servitude. It was an argument passionately conveyed by patriot Oliver Wolcott when he stated the British "had not only cast us out of its Protection but for so long a Time has been carrying on the Most cruel War against us" that was "not only absurd but impious."[90]

The British held a similar and legitimate argument against the colonists. The rebel attempts to persuade the indigenous tribes caused the British to reconsider the manner in which they should address the conflict. The North American British officials had seen first hand what many rebels meant by a restitution of grievances, namely loyalist oppression, establishing radical governments, and conducting ungentlemanly warfare. Hence, it seemed a logical conclusion that the rebels were essentially seeking to employ the indigenous tribes. This reasoning certainly drove Thomas Gage, Lord Dartmouth, Guy Johnson, and John Stuart to making their decisions to recruit the indigenous tribes. In responding to *The Declaration for the Causes and Necessity for Taking up Arms*, James Macpherson felt the rebel inclusion of Indians gave Britain the moral right to do the same. In *The Rights of Great Britain Asserted Against the Claims of America*, Macpherson wrote, "have they not fed every artifice to instigate the Savages to make war on their Sovereign and Mother Country?" Such acts "preceded the just exertions of this kingdom to punish their rebellion."[91]

Just like the inclusion of the Indian-aided Americans in seeking independence, rebel employment of the Indians also helped British officials conclude this was what the colonists initially intended. Gage and other British officials had repeatedly conveyed such sentiments, but Congressional interference with Indian relations drove the point home. Control over the western Indians had long

---

[90] Jerrilyn Greene Marston, *King and Congress: The Transfer of Political Legitimacy 1774-1776*, (Princeton, NJ: Princeton University Press, 1987), 57.
[91] James Macpherson, *The Rights of Great Britain Asserted Against the Claims of America; Being an Answer to the Declaration of the General Congress*, 73.

been recognized as a privilege of the Crown. When Congress appointed commissioners and negotiated treaties, they were exercising an authority reserved only for a sovereign. The right to negotiate treaties was an ancient right, affirming the legitimacy of one's title to govern. Congress recognized that negotiating treaties with foreign governments, such as France and Spain, was inappropriate since such action would denote sovereignty; but they were willing to negotiate treaties with the western tribes although the same principle controlled. Thus, while many delegates were attempting to avoid any conduct that would prevent reconciliation, the creation of an Indian Department accomplished what they were trying to prevent—the perception that they were seeking independence all along.[92]

---

[92] Ibid, 225-27.

Part Five:

Foreign Alliances

Chapter Ten

The Hessian Contribution

I have great reason to think we shall have a severe trial this summer with Britons, Hessians, Hanoverians, Indians, negroe, and every other butcher the gracious King of Britain can hire against us.
Josiah Bartlett to John Langdon, May 19, 1776[1]

The participation of German Hessians in the American Revolution is widely known, owing to their infamous defeat at the Battle of Trenton by George Washington in December 1776. The event has been celebrated in American history as the crucial victory in securing independence. However, the Hessians' participation in the revolutionary conflict was much more influential for what took place before that battle in Trenton. The Declaration specifically accused King George to be guilty of "transporting large Armies of foreign Mercenaries to compleat the works of death, desolation, and tyranny, already begun with circumstances of Cruelty & Perfidy scarcely paralleled in the most barbarous ages, and totally unworthy the Head of a civilized nation."

The Declaration of Independence was the only document to address the grievance in so many words. Though many of the assemblies made declarations about the issue, many others did not forge a formal grievance or suggest cause for seeking autonomy. The Virginia Convention stated Parliament's employment of foreign troops was to aid purely in their "destructive purposes."[2] The Connecticut Assembly simply stated the King has "engaged

---

[1] Smith, *Letters of the Delegates to Congress 1774-1789*, Vol. 4, 39.
[2] Force, *American Archives,* Fourth Series, Vol. 6, 1524.

[in] foreign mercenaries against us."³ The New Hampshire Assembly, Pennsylvania Assembly, Charles County (MA) Assembly, First Battalion of Chester County (PA), and both Wrentham and Scituate (MA) Assemblies similarly listed the sending of foreign mercenaries as a reason for their push towards autonomy.[4]

It is important to note that the grievance was always listed with brevity. This is because it was clear to the Americans that the use of the Hessian soldiers was a gross injustice deserving no explanation. On the surface, the impropriety of sending Hessian soldiers to fight an English civil war seems obvious, especially when one reads the correspondence of the founding fathers. The rebels' disdain for the British government's sending "mercenaries" to handle an internal dispute is well documented, yet the issue was far more complicated.

Both the rebel and parliamentary Whigs' labeling of the Hessian soldiers as "mercenaries" were, in fact, inaccurate. "Mercenaries" were foreigners who voluntarily enrolled themselves as soldiers for a certain time, with certain provisions, for a certain sum of money.[5] Since they did not voluntarily enroll for service, the Hessians did not meet the requirements in this definition. Instead, Hessians qualified as military auxiliaries. In 1758, Emer de Vattel described auxiliaries as when a "sovereign" sends "another sovereign…help in the form of troops or vessels of war." These troops "serve the prince to whom they are sent, in accordance with the orders of their sovereign," and if "they are sent to him without any conditions or restrictions they will be at his service equally for the offensive or defensive war."[6]

Throughout the eighteenth century, all the British ministries had resorted to employing auxiliaries in wartime, especially

---

[3] Ibid, 868.
[4] Ibid, 1030, 755, 1018, 785, 699-700.
[5] Rodney Atwood, *The Hessians: Mercenaries from Hessen-Kassel in the American Revolution*, (Cambridge, MA: Cambridge University Press, 1980), 23.
[6] Ibid, 22.

The Hessian Contribution

Hessians. By 1731, they had became such an integral part in the defense of the British Empire that Baron Walpole described them as "the Triarri of Great Britain, her last Resort in all Cases, both in Peace and War; both at Home and Abroad; howsoever ally'd, or whosesoever distress'd!"[7] In 1745 and 1756, the use of Hessian auxiliaries was so coveted that they were even brought to defend Great Britain from the possible invasion of France and Scotland.[8] Although the use of auxiliaries within Europe was common practice throughout the eighteenth century, and was a continuation of the Middle Ages feudal system, this form of military recruitment was not acceptable within the American colonies.

While the need for a professional fighting force was slowly superseding England's ideology against standing armies, the American colonies remained steadfast to the principle that the military was to consist only of its citizenry. A deep-seated hatred of standing armies—the hiring of foreign troops in the conflict—fuelled feelings of disgust in the hearts of the rebels. For even prior to the outbreak of the revolution, the maintaining and leasing of standing armies by German Princes was viewed with contempt. The connection between the colonists' grievance of standing armies and the British sending of Hessian soldiers is evidenced by the structure of declarations of independence. In the declarations of those colonies, localities and regiments, the employment of mercenaries as a grievance was principally listed immediately following the grievance of either the carrying on of a civil war or the maintenance of standing armies.

Historian Rodney Atwood, who has given the most objective analysis of the Hessian forces that fought in America, contends that when "the British government resolved to use force against the American colonists, it was almost inevitable that they should turn to foreign troops." First, the Americans were aware of Parliament's consistent practice of employing foreign auxiliaries. Second, it was common knowledge that recruiting volunteers to

---

[7] Ibid, 15, *cited as* Horatio, first Baron Walpole, *The Case of the Hessian Forces in the Pay of Great Britain*, (London, 1731), 39.
[8] Ibid, 17.

serve in America would prove difficult, given the politics of the conflict. Lastly, when Parliament successfully recruited enough troops to send to America, training them would take at least a year. Such a period of time was too long for Parliament and the King to act effectively. The move was even supported by British commanders Thomas Gage[9] and Major General Henry Clinton. Both recommended the hiring of foreigners to handle the dispute. If Clinton were to have had a choice, he would have chosen the Russians. He feared that the Hessians would desert, but "with my friends the Russians…They have a language but their own; they cannot desert."[10]

Although the British Tory leadership felt the idea of employing foreign troops to quell the American rebellion was common sense, it must be remembered that no such troops had ever been used to subdue the Mother country's own citizenry. It might have been standard practice for a nation to hire foreign auxiliaries prior to the age of nationalism, but the Whig leadership in Parliament was sure to point out history would not view such an action on its own people favorably.

In a protest against the King's speech supporting foreign assistance, nineteen minority members of the House of Lords stated that they were against the practice, "Because we conceive the calling in of foreign forces to decide domestick quarrels to be a measure both disgraceful and dangerous."[11] During the debate of the treaties with the German princes regarding the use of their auxiliaries, Alderman Bull closed the debate, stating, "Let not the historian be obliged to say that the Russian and German slave was

---

[9] Carter, *The Correspondence of General Thomas Gage with the Secretaries of State, and with the War Office and the Treasury 1763-1775*, Vol. 2, Thomas Gage to Lord Barrington, June 12, 1775, 684.
[10] Atwood, *The Hessians: Mercenaries from Hessen-Kassel in the American Revolution*, 23-24, *cited* in Sir Henry Clinton, *The American Rebellion: Sir Henry Clinton's Narrative of his Campaigns, 1775-1782, with an Appendix of Original Documents*, William B. Willcox, ed., (New Haven, 1954), xvi n. 4.
[11] Force, *American Archives*, Fourth Series, Vol. 6, 15.

hired to subdue the sons of Englishmen and freedom."[12] Bull's point was simple: although it was true that every power in Europe counted on the German lords to fill out the ranks of their armies, this was done to combat the enemy, which always consisted of another nation, not their own people. The rebel Americans certainly viewed themselves as the latter. What's more, they were the defenders of English liberties, not an enemy of the state.

In the fall and winter of 1775, the Parliamentary debate over the use of foreign troops gained more and more controversy. The notion was initiated by King George III in his speech on October 26, 1775. In that speech the King stated, "I have also the satisfaction to inform you that I have received the most friendly offers of assistance; and if I shall make any treaties in consequence thereof, they shall be laid before" Parliament.[13] Although the King implied that troops were only to be employed at the garrisons of Gibraltar and Port-Mahon, the Whigs took the opportunity to address their concerns.

The Marquis of Rockingham believed such action was an "alarming and dangerous expedient." Shelburne was against the employment of such troops because "if Hanover assists us, we must defend her when invaded."[14] John Wilkes thought the employment of "Hanoverians and Hessians...in our domestick quarrels" not only to be dangerous, but illegal and disgraceful to the nation.[15] Despite all the uproar raised by the Opposition, the Whig arguments on the subject found little support. The Tory majority proved too much. The King's notion was supported by people like Lord Bathurst, who recommended to his fellow representatives, "we shall cheerfully concur in whatever may be necessary to enable his Majesty to profit of the friendly dispositions of foreign powers."[16]

---

[12] Edward J. Lowell, *The Hessians and Other German Auxiliaries of Great Britain in the Revolutionary War*, (New York, NY: 1884), 30.
[13] Force, *American Archives*, Fourth Series, Vol. 6, 2.
[14] Ibid, 13.
[15] Ibid, 23.
[16] Ibid, 4.

In the House of Lords, the Duke of Manchester was not so much concerned with the use of foreign troops in Gibraltar, Port-Mahon, or the American colonies, as he was with their possible deployment within England. On November 1, 1775 he issued a petition in the House of Lords, stating, "The bringing into any part of the dominion of the Crown of Great Britain the Electoral troops of His Majesty, or any other foreign troops, without the previous consent of Parliament, is dangerous and unconstitutional."[17] During the debate of the motion, the Earl of Effingham made sure to point out his "disapproval of the measure of bringing foreign troops into any part of" England or "employing them at all in the present contest with America."[18] Although there was some concern over the use of foreign troops in America, the debate rested primarily on the constitutionality of the King employing foreign mercenaries. In the end, however, the petition by the Duke of Manchester was not even permitted to be put to a vote.

In the House of Commons, James Lowther would propose a similar measure two days later. Lowther moved that "the introducing the Hanoverian Troops into any part of the Dominions belonging to the Crown of Great Britain, without the consent of Parliament first had and obtained, is contrary to law." Unlike the Duke of Manchester, however, Lowther was very much concerned with the use of foreign troops against the rebels. He queried, "Why are we to have recourse to foreign mercenaries, instead of our own troops? Why place a dependence upon those who cannot feel the same call for defending the liberty of this country, as the natives of it?"[19] Lowther expressed the concern of many of his Whig supporters: the use of foreigners to handle a country's own disputes was not only unethical but also not as effective, since foreigners were not instilled with the pride of being a free Englishman.

In February 1776, the Whig party would get one more chance to convince their Tory brethren against the use of foreign troops

---

[17] Ibid, 89.
[18] Ibid, 93.
[19] Ibid, 107.

within the American colonies. By the large disparity in the final vote, it can be seen that their efforts were ineffective. Regarding the debate, historian Edward Lowell wrote "there can be little doubt that if the greater number of votes in Parliament was...on the Tory side, the weight of intellect was as decidedly with the Whigs."[20] Lowell's assertion—that all the intelligence regarding the issue was within Whig circles—is loosely supported by the fact that their speeches were far more numerous than those of the Tories. He does later give insight to this disparity by pointing out that the Tories might not have needed to do an equal share of debating. Lowell argues that since the Tories were the majority and that they were certain they would have the vote necessary to approve their stance, why waste valuable Parliamentary time over an issue they already had full support for?[21]

Although Lowell makes a good argument, the Whigs lost the debate because they were not debating the issue properly. Rodney Atwood makes a valid point regarding how some "liberal" historians of the nineteenth century made much of the Opposition speeches in these debates. Throughout the seventeenth century, the issues regarding the employment of Hessian soldiers rested to a greater extent in whether their use was necessary and how much the British taxpayer would have to sacrifice to make the initiative happen.[22] To win their argument, the Whigs would have to answer 'no' to the following questions that Lord North posed. North queried, "Whether the troops proposed to be hired were wanted? Whether the terms on which they were procured, were advantageous? And Whether the force was such as might be deemed fully adequate to effect the operations for which it was intended?"[23] If one expedient could be singled out as to why the Whigs did not gain a larger share of the vote, it would be their

---

[20] Lowell, *The Hessians and Other German Auxiliaries of Great Britain in the Revolutionary War*, 27.
[21] Ibid, 35.
[22] Atwood, *The Hessians: Mercenaries from Hessen-Kassel in the American Revolution*, 28.
[23] Force, *American Archives*, Fourth Series, Vol. 6, 277.

failure to effectively address these questions in the debate.

It is safe to say the Whigs agreed with Governor Johnstone's statement that the "hiring of foreigners to butcher fellow-subjects was...impolitic and cruel," but they were unable to address the issues in the treaties with enough persuasiveness to sway the Tory vote. Nonetheless, the Whigs were able to bring out two valid points regarding the use of Hessian auxiliaries against the Americans. First, there was the fear that the hiring of the Germans would destroy all hopes of reconciliation and thus push the colonists towards autonomy. David Hartley addressed Parliament on this point, stating, "This year, again, your pretext is a pretended commission to offer peace, at the same time tying up the hands of the Commissioners from making any offer but of unconditional submission, with an army of foreign mercenaries." Hartley amplified his aversion to the treaties, forcing the point that "if there could remain any measure exceeding every preceding one in disgrace and barbarity, it is this of introducing foreign troops."[24]

That the colonists could be pushed towards autonomy by the hiring of Hessian soldiers gave reason for a legitimate fear. The colonists were certainly suspicious of Britain's intentions when the sending of the Hessians was finally confirmed. In effect, the failure of the peace commissioners can partly be attributed to Parliament's decision to approve the Hessian treaties. After all, the sending of peace commissioners while deploying foreign troops contradicted each other. From the rebel perspective, how could Great Britain be offering peace and sending a foreign military force at the same time? To the British the answer was simple: peace meant that the colonies would either succumb to their demands or be militarily forced into submission. Washington, who had always held doubts regarding Parliament's intentions in the sending of a peace commission, would write, "I am satisfied that no Commissioners ever were design'd, except Hessians & other Foreigners." He felt Parliament was only stating they were sending commissioners as a means to "deceive, & throw

---

[24] Ibid, 281.

us off our guard-the first it has too effectually accomplished, as many Member of Congress...are still feeding themselves upon the dainty food of reconciliation."[25]

Although Washington and other rebel leaders were mistaken in their assertion that Parliament had no intent of sending peace commissioners, there was good reason, in fact, to reach such a conclusion. Obviously, the sending of Hessian soldiers figured in the assertion, but the continual distribution of intelligence reports that were proven to be false gave rebel leaders even greater cause for mistrust. Rumors about the peace commissioners varied greatly and were dismissed by the rebels as little more than half-truths.

Artemas Ward had received intelligence on May 3, 1776 that twenty-seven commissioners were being sent. Writing to Washington, he believed, if the commissioners were unsuccessful in their efforts that the British would "then burn and destroy all in their power."[26] The *Pennsylvania Gazette* reported thirty-six commissioners were to be appointed, their mission being to treat with each colony separately, not with Congress.[27] In actuality, all the rumors were nothing more than speculation, since King George did not officially appoint but two commissioners until May 3, the same date Ward was certain twenty-seven were in route.[28]

The second valid argument raised by the Parliament Whig opposition concerned the fear of Hessian desertion. Only two of the three treaties with the Hessian princes addressed the issue. The treaty with the Duke of Brunswick read, "in order to prevent desertion in their march, his Britannick Majesty will cause the most precise orders to be given in his Electoral Dominions," and

---

[25] Abbot & Twohig, *The Papers of George Washington*, Revolutionary Series, Vol. 4, George Washington to John Augustine Washington, May 31, 1775, 412.
[26] Ibid, Artemas Ward to George Washington, May 3, 1776, 196-97.
[27] Abbot & Twohig, *The Papers of George Washington*, Revolutionary Series, Vol. 3, Ibid, George Washington to Joseph Reed, February 26-March 9, 1776, 375.
[28] Force, *American Archives*, Fourth Series, Vol. 5, 1176.

that "all necessary measure be taken to stop every deserter from this body of troops."²⁹ The treaty with Hesse Cassel was worded much differently, reading, "All the Hessian desertions shall be faithfully given up, wherever they shall be discovered in the places dependent on his Britannick Majesty; and, above all, as far as it is possible, no person whatever of that nation shall be permitted to establish himself in America without the consent of his Sovereign."³⁰

Even with these provisions in place, James Luttrell expressed his concern of sending Germans to places such as Pennsylvania, "one of the largest and most flourishing Colonies" where "above one-half peopled by Germans." He also feared other flourishing German areas, including the German Flats, which rested off the Mohawk River near New Jersey and New York, and settlements off the Connecticut River, would be too tempting for the Hessians to prevent their desertion. Luttrell and other Whigs believed localities with an overwhelming German presence would be too enticing, since their fellow countrymen had cultivated the land and enjoyed the benefits of living under the freedoms of British subjects. "They will desert and accept lands, which, when they have done, we have hired troops to fight against ourselves," stated Luttrell, further adding "like those who became settlers before them, they see an uncultivated wild grow fruitful and beautiful under their hands, they will readily join in protecting that property and the just rights of America against the oppressive impositions of an enterprising Ministry." The Duke of Richmond concurred. When he moved that a petition be presented to King George against the use of foreign troops, the Duke argued they could not trust foreign troops in this instance because "when they are at so great a distance from their own country and suffering under the distresses of war wherein they have no interest or concern, and with so many temptations to exchange vassalage for freedom, will be more likely to mutiny or desert, than to unite faithfully, and co-

---

²⁹ Force, *American Archives*, Fourth Series, Vol. 6, 272.
³⁰ Ibid, 275.

operate with your Majesty's natural-born subjects."[31]

Much like the incitement of slave insurrections or the inclusion of the Indians in the war, the evidence does not suggest the British employment of foreign auxiliaries came as much of a surprise. Even before the employment of foreign troops was known, Patriot James Duane of New York remarked that the "ministry can expect no Success without the aid of foreign troops."[32] In October 1775, the same time King George III was delivering the speech about employing foreign assistance, the New York Committee of Safety had already heard rumors of foreign auxiliaries having been sent to the colonies. The early reports estimated the auxiliaries would consist of 20,000 Russians, which were to reinforce Boston.[33] By October 3 the intelligence had changed. It was now "confidently" believed 10,000 Hanoverians were to arrive "at any moment."[34] In Philadelphia, the intelligence was just as vague. Reports varied between 4,000 to 45,000 foreign troops depending on whom you asked. In short, the intelligence on the Hessians' date of expected arrival and troop numbers varied daily, with their assured arrival as the only constant.[35]

---

[31] Ibid, 283.
[32] Smith, *Letters of the Delegates to Congress 1774-1789*, Vol. 3, James Duane to Robert Livingston, January 5, 1776, 33.
[33] United States, *Naval Documents of the American Revolution*, Vol. 2, Henry Tucker to St. George Tucker, September 18, 1775, 144-45.
[34] Ibid, Minutes of the New York Committee of Safety, October 3, 1775, 284.
[35] Ibid, Testimony of William Thompson before the New York Provincial Congress, October 10, 1775, 391; Ibid, Journal of the New York Provincial Congress, October 12, 1775, 424; Smith, *Letters of the Delegates to Congress 1774-1789*, Vol. 3, 29, 33, 101, 254, 496, 564, 625-26, 632. James Warren reported to John Adams that 20,000 Hessians were on their way to America. Taylor, *Papers of John Adams*, Vol. 4, James Warren to John Adams, April 30, 1776, 155. Virginia newspapers did not begin reporting on the numbers of Hessians and Hanoverians arriving until May 1776. These papers reported the Hessian numbers between 16,000-20,000 troops. *Virginia Gazette* (Dixon & Hunter), May 4, 1776; *Virginia Gazette* (Dixon & Hunter), May 25,

Irreconcilable Grievances

Upon receiving a steady flow of intelligence assuring the possibility of Hessian troops arriving, the rebels hastened to develop schemes to prompt them to desert. Benjamin Franklin wrote "the German Auxiliaries are certainly coming," but it was "our Business to prevent their Returning."[36] On May 14, 1776, Washington would recommend such a plan to Hancock and the Continental Congress. The general wrote:

> I have not received further intelligence of the German troops since my letter of the 7th instant, covering Mr. Cushing's dispatches; but lest the account of their coming should some companies of our Germans to send among them when they arrive, for exciting spirit of disaffection and desertion? If a few sensible trusty fellows could get with them, I should think they would have great weight and influence with the common soldiery, who certainly have no enmity towards us, having received no injury nor cause of quarrel from us.[37]

Washington had, in fact, already known about the British employment of Hessian soldiers as early as mid-March. Lord Stirling had written to him that Britain had "engaged 4000 Hanoverians and 6000 Hessians...and were in Treaty for 10,000, Russians."[38] Although the General had received this intelligence, he did not make any mention of the use of the Hessians until nearly two months later, when the employment had been reconfirmed by Thomas Cushing. Only then did he forward his

---

1776; *Virginia Gazette* (Dixon & Hunter), June 8, 1776.
[36] Willcox, *The Papers of Benjamin Franklin*, Vol. 22, Benjamin Franklin to John Carroll and Samuel Chase, May 27, 1776, 440. Arthur Lee would later write to Franklin, "It is conceived too that if proper offers are made to the Germans, they will desert in great numbers." United States, *Naval Documents of the American Revolution*, Vol. 4, Arthur Lee to Lt. Governor Cadwallader Colden, April 7, 1776, 1021.
[37] Force, *American Archives*, Fourth Series, Vol. 6, 424.
[38] Abbot & Twohig, *The Papers of George Washington*, Revolutionary Series, Vol. 3, Lord Stirling to George Washington, March 11, 1776, 452.

recommendation of obtaining Hessian desertions to Congress.[39]

Noteworthy is the fact that Washington was not the first to consider the creation of an all-German unit. Nearly a year before, a German hussar veteran had appeared before Congress in full garb, offering his services and that of 50 to 60 others. John Adams described the man, stating he wore:

> A forlorn Cap upon his Head, with a Streamer waiving from it half down to his Waistband, with a Deaths Head painted in Front a beautiful Hussar Cloak ornamented with Lace and Fringe and Cord of Gold, a scarlet Waist coat under it, with shining yellow metal Buttons-a Light Gun strung over his shoulder-and a Turkish Sabre, much Superior to an high Land broad sword, very large and excellently fortified by his side-Holsters and Pistols upon his Horse. In short the most warlike and formidable Figure I ever saw.[40]

Adams supported the hussar's proposition and felt it "a fine Example for their [New England] Imitation, stating, "But what is of more Moment, it would engage the Affections of the Germans, of whom there are many in N.York, Pennsylvania, Maryland and the other Colonies, more intensely in the Cause of America."[41] Even so, the proposition did not receive any attention and seems to have dissolved—and for good reason. In June 1775, Congress and Provincial Assemblies clearly had more pressing issues to deal with than figuring out how to recruit colonists of German ancestry

---

[39] The same day Washington was confirming the sending of Hessian auxiliaries, Thomas Cushing had also relayed such news to John Hancock. United States, *Naval Documents of the American Revolution*, Vol. 4, Thomas Cushing to John Hancock, May 3, 1776, 1390. Artemas Ward confirmed the report on May 9, 1776. United States, *Naval Documents of the American Revolution*, Vol. 5, Artemas Ward to George Washington, May 9, 1776, 6.

[40] Taylor, *The Papers of John Adams*, Vol. 4, John Adams to James Warren, July 6, 1775, 63-4.

[41] Ibid, John Adams to William Tudor, July 6, 1775, 59-60

to their lines. In truth, Congress did not need any more troops because the army at Cambridge was becoming too crowded. By August, Washington had estimated the army ballooned up to 24,450 men and, therefore, told Congress that "a reduction of them seems to be necessary."[42] However, Congress had more pressing issues to face. They had to find sufficient amounts of supplies, arms, gunpowder, and most importantly, try to resolve an end to the conflict. It did not make sense to recruit more troops that couldn't be adequately supplied. Therefore, Adams' hussar company proposition would have to wait until a year later.

It was only once it was confirmed that Hessian auxiliaries were being sent that Congress began to take action resembling the design of Adams' plan.[43] From their proceedings it does not seem that Congress was all that shocked that England was actually going to employ foreign auxiliaries. If anything, Congress felt confident about their hopes to turn the newly arrived Germans into Americans. The first step took place on May 21 when it was resolved to publish copies of the Parliament-Hessian treaties and "prepare an Address to the foreign mercenaries who are coming to invade America."[44] The address was prepared by George Wythe and was supposed to be distributed among the Hessian forces. Although it was never published, it places in context Congress' plan to recruit the Hessians to the American cause. Wythe reminded the Hessians that "all your countrymen who dwell among us were received as friends and treated as brethren, participating in equality with ourselves of all our rights, franchises

---

[42] Abbot & Twohig, *The Papers of George Washington,* Revolutionary Series, Vol. 1, George Washington to John Hancock, August 5, 1775, 222-30.

[43] In May 1776, George Merchant had brought copies of the treaties with Brunswick, Hesse-Cassel, and Hesse-Hanau from England. Congress ordered these treaties published. Lyman H. Butterfield, "Psychological Warfare in 1776: The Jefferson-Franklin Plan to Cause Hessian Desertion," *Proceedings of the American Philosophical Society*, Vol. 94, (Philadelphia, PA: American Philosophical Society, 1950), 234.

[44] Force, *American Archives*, Fourth Series, Vol. 6, 1685; United States, *Journals of the Continental Congress*, Vol. 4, 369.

The Hessian Contribution

and privileges." He hoped that the Hessians had only decided to join the conflict to exchange their German homeland "for happier regions...for a land of plenty and abhorrent of despotism." Exactly why Wythe's address was never reported to Congress is unclear, but it might have been ignored because his plan did not equate to meaningful action. Congress had made numerous petitions to the King and Parliament, all of which had little effect, if any.[45] Perhaps some thought that Wythe's address would also have no effect.

Although Congress did not follow through with their proposed address, they did act on Washington's proposal to create an all German Battalion.[46] The General had left it "for the consideration of Congress" as to whether it would be "advisable & good policy" to adopt the plan. Washington felt a unit totally comprised of Germans would not only provide much needed men for his dwindling forces but, more importantly, may excite "a spirit of disaffection and desertion" among the Hessians.[47] The belief was that this unit would be able to communicate with their Hessian brethren and persuade them to join the American Cause.[48]

After consulting with the delegates from the predominant

---

[45] Smith, *Letters of the Delegates to Congress*, Vol. 4, George Wythe's Draft Address to the Foreign Mercenaries, May 1776, 110-112.
[46] The plan was first accepted by a committee on May 16, 1776. United States, *Journals of the Continental Congress*, Vol. 4, 362. It was not until May 25, 1776 that Congress resolved to raise one battalion of Germans. Ibid, 392.
[47] Abbot & Twohig, *The Papers of George Washington*, Revolutionary Series, Vol. 4, George Washington to John Hancock, May 11, 1776, 279.
[48] Ibid. On June 29, 1776 John Hancock forwarded the good news to George Washington. Congress had resolved to adopt a German Battalion "to be employed in such a Manner, as will be most likely, to defeat the Designs of our Enemies, and to promote the Cause of American Liberty." Abbot & Twohig, *The Papers of George Washington*, Revolutionary Series, Vol. 3, John Hancock to George Washington, June 29, 1775, 149. Washington confirmed the idea of the German Battalion was to solely "counteract the designs of our Enemies." Ibid, George Washington to John Hancock, July 8, 1776, 239.

German populated colonies of Maryland, Pennsylvania, New Jersey, and New York, on June 29, 1776, Congress resolved it to be "expedient to order a German Battalion to be raised, as soon as possible, in the Colonies of Pennsylvania and Maryland." They were to "be employed in such manner as will be most likely to defeat the designs of our enemies, and to promote the cause of American liberty."[49] Congress was so supportive of the plan and so eager for success that a sum of 5,000 dollars was dispersed to both Maryland and Pennsylvania.[50]

Aside from creating their own German units, Congress also initiated a more forthright campaign to recruit the Hessian auxiliaries to their cause. A committee comprised of James Wilson, Thomas Jefferson, and Richard Stockton was enlisted to "devise a plan for encouraging the Hessians...to quit that iniquitous service."[51] The committee induced Congress to adopt a plan offering land to the Hessians. The resolve stated:

> [T]hat these States will receive all such foreigners who shall leave the Armies of his Britannick Majesty in America, and shall choose to become members of any of these States; that they shall be protected in the free exercise of their respective religions, and be invested with the rights, privileges and immunities of natives, as established by the laws of these States; and moreover, that this Congress will provide, for every such person, fifty acres of inappropriated lands in some of these States, to be held by him and his heirs in absolute property.[52]

---

[49] Force, *American Archives*, Fourth Series, Vol. 6, 1132, 1725; United States, *Journals of the Continental Congress*, Vol. 5, 454.
[50] Force, *American Archives*, Fourth Series, Vol. 6, 1294; United States, *Journals of the Continental Congress*, Vol. 5, 487-88.
[51] United States, *Journals of the Continental Congress*, Vol. 5, 640.
[52] United States, *Journals of the Continental Congress*, Vol. 5, 654. On August 27, 1776 it was resolved that all foreign officers whom leave the British armies will be given a land bounty in proportion to their rank and the number of other officers and/or soldiers they induce with them. Ibid, 706-7.

The Hessian Contribution

The idea to swap land for Hessian allegiance was either formulated by Thomas Jefferson, James Wilson, or Samuel Holden Parsons. Exchanging land for military service was an idea that had been circulating among Congress and the Provincial assemblies for some time. The idea had been proposed many times as a means to induce enlistments but, up to this point, had always been defeated. This was because it was felt that a bounty would not recruit the right individuals in the cause of liberty.[53] Just who was the first to hypothesize the idea is unknown, but if Jefferson did, he probably came up with the idea when he received intelligence of German desertions. He had been informed that "Great numbers of the Germans desert daily," but they were too afraid of "ambushes" to desert in greater numbers.[54]

Perhaps it was this intelligence that sparked Jefferson to propose a land bounty to encourage further desertion, or the idea could have been influenced by Wilson. Wilson was also learning of Hessian desertions at the time. In New Jersey, copies of Congress's resolutions had been distributed to the Hessians, offering rewards to those who would desert from service. According to Wilson, these overtures gained the attention of a Hessian Colonel. Wilson queried to Hancock, "Perhaps it is not yet too late to offer additional Rewards to officers in Proportion to their Rank and Pay"?[55]

Samuel Holden Parsons was the first to make mention of the

---

[53] Charles, *Washington's Decision: The Story of George Washington's Decision to Reaccept Black Enlistments in the Continental Army, December 31, 1775*, 115. Following Congressional legislation offering Hessian officers and soldiers to receive land bounties in exchange for leaving the British Service, Congress also adopted a bounty enlistment. After several days of debate, it was resolved that each soldier who enlisted for the duration of the war would receive 100 acres of land and twenty dollar bounty. Jonathan Gregory Rossie, *The Politics of Command in the American Revolution*, (Syracuse, NY: Syracuse University Press, 1975),137.
[54] Smith, *The Letters of the Delegates to Congress 1774-1789*, Vol. 5, Thomas Jefferson to John Page, August 20, 1776, 32.
[55] Ibid, James Wilson to John Hancock, August 22, 1776, 50.

idea. In a letter to John Adams, Parsons put forward the notion while commenting on how the Hessian prisoners should be treated. Since the Hessians were nothing more than "hir[e]d Assassins to mur[d]er Us for Money," he thought "none of their Prisoners should be exchanged if the Fortune of War cast them into our Hands." Although he thought the Hessians should not be given the same gentlemanly military overtures as British troops, he was in favor of encouraging the Germans to "Settle in the Country" by granting them land. Parsons thought such a plan would "infuse a Spirit of Jealousy" among the Hessians, causing them to convert their loyalties to the American cause.[56]

Adams may have forwarded Parsons' plan to Congress, but there no evidence to support that such an action took place.. Whether Jefferson, Wilson, or Parsons initiated the proposal for a bounty for Hessian desertions is unclear. What is certain is that by the end of August Congress decided to adopt the plan when Jefferson drafted his *Report of a Plan to Invite Foreign Officers in the British Service to Desert*. In the document, Jefferson proposed exactly what Wilson had queried to Hancock, that is, that Congress should give lands to officers and non-commissioned officers based in proportion to their rank or pay.[57]

Apart from the need to put in place a plan to recruit the Hessians to their cause, Congress still needed a way to relay this information to the Hessian units. Washington had proposed that members of the American-German battalion would relay information to them. Meanwhile, Wilson preferred distributing copies of the resolutions to the Hessians through secret channels. Franklin had an even more clever method. Franklin had translated some of the resolutions of Congress into German that were to be distributed to the Hessians soldiers in New Jersey. To hide the content of the papers, he would place "Tobacco Marks on the Back" of them and recommended "a little Tobacco" to be "put up in each as the Tobacconists use to do." All that was needed was to

---

[56] Taylor, *Papers of John Adams*, Vol. 4, Samuel Holden Parsons to John Adams, July 7, 1776, 366-67.
[57] Boyd, *The Papers of Thomas Jefferson*, Vol. 1, 509.

place these false tobacco pouches in a canoe that would appear to be washed up on the shore. When the Hessians found the canoe, they would divide the tobacco as plunder "before the Officers could know the Contents of the Papers and prevent it."[58]

It is unknown whether Franklin's plan was ever incorporated, since no copies exist, but Washington and Congress had already put forth a more direct attempt.[59] Prior to Congress authorizing land bounties for Hessian desertions, John Hancock had already begun sending Congressional resolves to Washington, translated in German and ready to be disseminated among the Hessians.[60] General Washington wholeheartedly supported the idea. He knew the task would be difficult and asked Congress to furnish more copies since there will probably be "many miscarriages" until their distribution was perfected.[61]

By the end of August 1776, Washington felt that the plan was working. He was confident that many of the German-translated papers had fallen into the Hessians' hands.[62] He had also received positive news on the subject from Brigadier General Hugh Mercer. Mercer reported that he had had recent conversations with several Hessian officers. These officers gave Mercer "no doubt" that they would join the American cause if Congress gave the "Proper encouragement & opportunity."[63] Given the plan's chance of success, Washington could only ponder whether "It might have

---

[58] Willcox, *The Papers of Benjamin Franklin*, Vol. 22, Benjamin Franklin to Thomas McKean, August 24, 1776, 578-79. Franklin also told Horatio Gates of this plan. Ibid, Benjamin Franklin to Horatio Gates, August 28, 1776, 583.

[59] Butterfield, "Psychological Warfare in 1776: The Jefferson-Franklin Plan to Cause Hessian Desertion," *Proceedings of the American Philosophical Society*, Vol. 94, 238.

[60] Abbot & Twohig, *The Papers of George Washington*, Revolutionary Series, Vol. 6, John Hancock to George Washington, August 16, 1776, 37.

[61] Ibid, George Washington to John Hancock, August 19, 1776, 74.

[62] Ibid, George Washington, to John Hancock, August, 27, 1776, 130.

[63] Ibid, Brigadier General Hugh Mercer to George Washington, August 19, 1776, 79 note 2.

been better had the offer been sooner made."[64]

Although Washington was elated over the success of promoting Hessian desertions, he also became disturbed with a certain practice in November of 1776. Positive news continued to come in regarding Hessian desertions, but the Board of War had informed the general that "Many Prisoners have been desirous to enlist and some have been accepted in our Service."[65] It was a practice that Washington thought "cannot be justified" and was not a "good point of policy."[66]

Washington had been working to exchange his British and Hessian prisoners with General Howe for some time. In eighteenth century warfare it was common practice to exchange prisoners under a gentleman's promise if the prisoners would retire from further participation in the conflict. Washington had written to Congress to prepare such an agreement but, to his dismay, he learned that the prisoners were being enlisted in the American cause. Furthermore, the General had already planned to address Howe on this exact issue. The British Army had been performing the same practice with American prisoners of war, and Washington was planning to put an end to it. He recommended the practice stop when he wrote to the Board of War:

> I would just Observe, that in my Opinion it is nether consistent with the Rules of War, nor politic; nor can I think, that because our Enemies have committed unjustifiable Action by inticing, and in some Instances, intimidating our

---

[64] Ibid, George Washington to John Hancock, August 29, 1776, 155.

[65] Abbot & Twohig, *The Papers of George Washington*, Revolutionary Series, Vol. 7, Richard Peters to George Washington, November 19, 1776, 188; Ibid, Nathanael Greene to George Washington, November 5, 1776, 87-88. The Board of War was responding to George Washington's request to collect all the British and Hessian prisoners for an prisoner exchange with General Howe. Ibid, George Washington to the Board of War, November 15, 1776, 161.

[66] Ibid, George Washington to John Hancock, November 27, 1776, 223.

Men into their Service, we ought to follow their Example.[67]

In any case, Washington could not undo what had already been done. Those prisoners who had already enlisted were allowed to remain in the service. Returning these prisoners would be too dangerous to their welfare once word leaked out of their disaffection.[68] Regarding the future practice of enlisting prisoners, Washington left the matter up to Congress whether "to order them to be returned or not as they shall judge fit."[69] This did not stop the General from giving his opinion, though. He reminded Congress and the Board of War, "the Inlistment of prisoners was not a politic Step." "[I]n time of danger," Washington argued that if such prisoners were to fall "into the Hands of their former Masters," they would receive "no Mercy" and would likely communicate rebel intelligence to the enemy.

Furthermore, Washington did not understand why Congress would want to enlist the enemy. It did not make sense to him. How could anyone respect the character of men who so easily exchanged their loyalties from one side to the other? Would not such men "desert when an Action is expected, hoping by carrying Intelligence" to protect their own interests?[70]

In all probability, Washington's argument convinced Congress because, in May 1778, it was recommended to the states to discontinue the enlistment of deserters or prisoners into the militia.[71] The resolve turned out to be impossible to enforce. The

---

[67] Ibid, George Washington to the Board of War, November 30, 1776, 231.
[68] The Board of War and Washington agreed on this point. See Ibid, Richard Peters to George Washington, November 19, 1776, 188; Ibid, George Washington to John Hancock, November 27, 1776, 223.
[69] Ibid, George Washington to John Hancock, November 27, 1776, 223.
[70] Ibid, George Washington to the Board of War, November 30, 1776, 232.
[71] Lowell, *The Hessians and the Other Auxiliaries of Great Britain in the Revolutionary War*, 288-89.

colonies were always having difficulties filling their militia ranks and meeting Congressional enlistment quotas. Recruiting officers would often take whatever men they could get, including mulattoes, slaves, and free blacks. Thus, with the exception of Washington, the practice of employing deserters and prisoners would continue. The preference against enlisting deserters did not affect the policy of encouraging Hessian desertions. Following the infamous Battle of Trenton, where Washington captured 918 Hessians, Congress took immediate action to change the prisoners' minds about the conflict. They instructed Washington not to exchange the prisoners. The situation afforded Congress too "favorable [an] opportunity of making them acquainted with the situation & Circumstances of many of their Country Men." To effectuate this, they ordered Washington to separate the officers from the soldiers.[72] Washington forwarded Congress' orders to the Pennsylvania Council of Safety, who had taken custody of the prisoners. He also recommended:

> I wish the [officers] well treated, and that the [soldiers] may have such principles instilled into them during their Confinement, that when they return, they may open the Eyes of their Countrymen...[73]

The overall impact of the rebels' plans to entice Hessian

---

[72] Abbot & Twohig, *The Papers of George Washington*, Revolutionary Series, Vol. 7, Executive Committee of the Continental Congress to George Washington, December 28, 1776, 466-67.
[73] Ibid, George Washington to Pennsylvania Council of Safety, December 29, 1776, 482. Washington wrote similar sentiments to Congress. He wrote, "If proper pains are taken to convince them, how preferable the Situation of their Countrymen, the Inhabitants of those Counties, is to theirs, I think they may be sent back in the Spring so fraught with a love of Liberty, and property too, that they may create a disgust to the Service among the remainder of the foreign Troops and widen that Breach which is already opened between them and the British. Ibid, George Washington to the Executive Committee of the Continental Congress, January 1, 1777, 500.

The Hessian Contribution

desertions has never been determined, but evidence suggests the strategy did not have the desired effect.[74] It is not to say that any Hessians held back from deserting. As it turned out, the desertions were fewer in number and frequency that the rebels had anticipated. This is because—just as the Americans were utilizing psychological warfare as a means to entice Hessian desertions—the British had employed similar measures. When the first Hessian units arrived, they were sent to Canada and were often sheltered from any outside contact. They were told of the mistreatment and cruelties the Americans performed on their prisoners. One rebel surgeon recorded in his diary:

> A Number of Hessians...have fallen into our hands. The German officers and soldiers, by a finesse of the British, to increase their ferocity, had been led to believe that Americans are savages and barbarians, and if taken, their men would have their bodies stuck full of pieces of dry wood, and in that manner burnt to death.[75]

In truth, the purpose of Congressional efforts to cause Hessian desertions was just that, but it is interesting to note that the efforts also reflected the Founding Fathers' early attitude on immigration. If one considers the colonists' support of expanding their boundaries west, and the overabundance of land to farm, the vast majority of citizens welcomed the notion of healthy numbers of

---

[74] According to Rodney Atwood, less than six percent of the Hessen-Kassel Hessians had deserted by 1783. Atwood, *The Hessians: Mercenaries from Hessen-Kassel in the American Revolution*, 204. What is for certain is America had a positive influence on the Hessian auxiliaries. Following the conclusion of peace, out of the nearly 30,000 Hessians that came to the colonies, 12,500 decided to remain. Lowell, *The Hessians and the Other Auxiliaries of Great Britain in the Revolutionary War*, 291.

[75] Atwood, *The Hessians: Mercenaries from Hessen-Kassel in the American Revolution*, 189, cited as James Thacher, *A Military Journal during the American Revolutionary War from 1775 to 1783*, (2nd edn, Boston, 1827), 67.

European immigrants arriving. It meant that more people increased economic output, brought an influx of specie, and increased the consumer market. Congress' address to the Hessian auxiliaries was certainly in no way economic in bent but, nevertheless, it represented eighteenth century American sentiment on the topic. The address stated:

> Whereas it has been the wise policy of these States to extend the protection of their laws to all those who should settle among them, of whatever nation or religion they might be, and to admit them to the participation of the benefits of this practice, as well as its salutary effects, have rendered it worthy of being continued in future times.[76]

Historians have been quick to cite the employment of Hessian auxiliaries as an important influence on America independence. As early as January 1776, when their employment was nothing more than mere rumor, Edward Shippen in Philadelphia reported, "Conversions [to the patriot party] have been more rapid than ever." Meanwhile, John Dickinson had been heard to comment that such an act would lead to no alternative but slavery or independence.[77]

While it seems obvious that the employment of foreign troops would help precipitate American independence, the pro-separation patriots also welcomed the idea. Not only would Hessian employment help the patriot cause gain further support, but some even believed the move would prove to be militarily advantageous. One Philadelphia patriot felt confident that the Hessians would join the American cause upon arriving, "because we know that the Germans...will find it much more preferable for

---

[76] United States, *Journals of the Continental Congress*, Vol. 5, 653-54.
[77] Butterfield, "Psychological Warfare in 1776: The Jefferson-Franklin Plan to Cause Hessian Desertion," *Proceedings of the American Philosophical Society*, Vol. 94, 233, cited in as, John C. Miller, *Origins of the American Revolution*, (Boston, MA: Little, Brown, 1943), Letter to Jasper Yeates, 477.

their present comfortable subsistence, as well as a prospect of future happy settlement."[78]

Other patriots welcomed the challenge. Robert Morris was not afraid of the "dogs of war" that were "fairly let loose upon us." He knew the Hessians had been sent over to "Slaughter us" but doubted their success. Morris expected America's "climates will most probably handle them pretty severely before they get seasoned." He felt the American "Troops are pretty well prepared for their Reception," but with the "Fortunes of war being ever uncertain, God only knows what may be the Event."[79] Patriot Caleb Clap was even more confident. He, like many, anxiously awaited their arrival, hoping "to give them a warm Reception (God Willing)."[80]

The employment of Hessian auxiliaries undoubtedly convinced many colonists of the need for separation. Yet it remains unknown as to just how large of an impact it had. Even prior to confirmation of their inclusion, Congress, provincial assemblies, and local assemblies had taken steps towards declaring their independence. Moreover, Congress had been working on establishing foreign alliances themselves. With overtures to France and Spain beginning in the fall of 1775, their hands were not exactly clean, either. If anything, the employment of Hessian auxiliaries may have meant nothing more than another item to pile on the fire of mounting grievances.

Vermont certainly did not view it that way. They immortalized

---

[78] Ibid, cited in as Margaret W. Willard, *Letters on the American Revolution*, (Boston, MA: Houghton Mifflin, 1925), 307. The Americans were not alone in this sentiment. French Ambassador to London, Count De Guines, felt the British maneuver a farce. He too thought the Hessians, "who are slaves at home, will become recruits for the Americans." United States, *Naval Documents of the American Revolution*, Vol. 3, Count de Guines to Count de Vergennes, January 12, 1776, 505.
[79] United States, *Naval Documents of the American Revolution*, Vol. 5, Robert Morris to Silas Deane, June 5, 1776, 384.
[80] Ibid, Diary of Ensign Caleb Clap, July 8, 1776, 973.

the event in their 1777 Constitution, accusing the King of performing "a most cruel and unjust war against them; employing therein, not only the troops of Great Britain, but foreign mercenaries, savages and slaves." John Adams also saw the event as pivotal in that it prevented any form of reconciliation with England. In writing to Isaac Smith, Adams stated:

> [I]f you consider what is doing at New York, New Jersey, Pensilvania, and even in Maryland, which are all gradually forming themselves into order to follow the Colonies to the Northward and Southward, together with the Treaties with Hesse, Burnswick and Waldeck...I believe you will be convinced that there is little Probability of our ever again coming under the Yoke of British Regulations of Trade.[81]

Washington agreed. It did not make sense that Parliament would send foreign troops to the colonies and also hope to convince the colonists to negotiate a peace. Washington queried to his cousin Lund, "[H]ow is it to be accounted for that after running the Nation to some Millions of Sterl[in]g to hire and Transport Foreigners" that "they are willing to give the terms proposed by Congress"?[82] Therefore, though the wheels of independence were moving even before confirming the British employment of Hessian auxiliaries, the act guaranteed that those wheels would continue to move ever forward. Congress now had no intention of working out reconciliation. Indeed, they were hastening to enlist foreign aid of their own—with an alliance that would change the course of the American Revolution and insure the creation of the United States.

---

[81] Ibid, John Adams to Isaac Smith, June 1, 1776, 338.
[82] Abbot & Twohig, *The Papers of George Washington*, Revolutionary Series, Vol. 6, George Washington to Lund Washington, August 19, 1776, 83.

Chapter Eleven

The Need for Foreign Assistance

I expect soon to hear that the Continental Congress have published the Confederacy of the Colonies–compleated the Republic of America–and formed a commercial Alliance with France and Spain. Such tidings will be musick to my ears, as I apprehend nothing short of such a plan will secure our Liberties.
Joseph Ward to John Adams, October 23, 1775

On February 6, 1778, the smoldering embers of the American cause were rekindled when the French Court entered into a formal commercial treaty with the Continental Congress. The commercial alliance eventually flourished into a military one and proved to have a decisive impact on the outcome of the war. The French military's contribution in securing the objective of American Independence is well-known and documented, but what is often overlooked is that France also played a crucial part in the formation and issuance of the Declaration of Independence.

Almost a year to the day that the Declaration of Independence was adopted, Congress had informed King George III of England and the world that "foreign Assistance is undoubtedly attainable" in the Declaration of the Causes and Necessity for Taking Up Arms.[1] Still, Congress certainly had not received any diplomatic overtures. Delegates were simply hoping such words would persuade Parliament to adhere to their demands and quickly work out a reconciliation.

It is ironic that neither author, Thomas Jefferson nor John Dickinson, had so boldly worded their individual drafts of the Declaration of the Causes and Necessity for Taking Up Arms. Jefferson wrote that the colonies may be induced "to avail

---

[1] Boyd, *The Papers of Thomas Jefferson*, Vol. 1, 217.

ourselves of any aid which their enemies might proffer," while Dickinson wrote "our assurance of foreign Assistance is certain."[2] In reality, both statements were accurate since no foreign overtures had been received and would have only given Parliament the impression its colonies would consider foreign assistance. For whatever reason, Congress did not think either statement was persuasive enough, choosing to adopt one that insinuated offers already lay on the table.

Regardless of their intent, the Congressional threat proved to be ineffectual in persuading Parliament to back down, and moreover, failed to convince the outspoken Patriot James Madison. Madison would write to William Bradford that he was "little induced from the confident assertion of the Congress that foreign Assistance…was undoubtedly attainable."[3]

As the civil war progressed into the fall of 1775, the situation had become desperate. When Congress threatened Britain with imaginary foreign alliances, it was confident the conflict was near an end with the recent success of the Battle of Bunker Hill. However, the colonies were sorely ill-prepared and under-equipped to adequately man and supply the conflict for a long duration. The need to restore American commerce became an immediate priority.

Congress and many provincial assemblies were already making efforts to procure supplies from the West Indies and foreign ports, but no matter how much saltpeter, gunpowder, and arms they acquired, it was never enough to meet the ongoing demand. It became clear to American commanders that steps would have to be taken to procure an alliance with France or Spain to secure American efforts of resistance.

Prior to the issuance of the Declaration of the Causes and Necessity for Taking Up Arms, any alliance with France, including a commercial treaty, was far from the minds of the revolutionary leaders. If an alliance was to be formed, one

---

[2] Ibid, 202-03, 211.
[3] Hutchinson & Rachal, *The Papers of James Madison*, Vol. 1, James Madison to William Bradford, July 28, 1775, 160.

The Need for Foreign Assistance

commentator wrote to John Adams that Holland was the "natural Ally" of choice.[4] This is because Americans still harbored mistrust for France for their role in the French & Indian War. Many even feared that if reconciliation could not be quickly achieved, France or Spain would take advantage and claim the colonies for themselves. In April 1775 Dickinson conveyed this exact fear to Arthur Lee, writing:

> While we revere and love our Mother Country, her sword is opening our veins. The same delusions will still prevail, till France and Spain, if not other Powers, long jealous of Britain's force and fame, will fall upon her, embarrassed with an exhausting civil war, and crush, or at least depress her; then turn their arms on these Provinces, which must submit to wear their chains, or wade through seas of blood to a dearbought and at best a frequently convulsed and precarious independence.[5]

A larger and more widespread fear was not that France and Spain would take advantage of Britain's quagmire, but that the three nations would all join forces and partition off North America. As early as January 1775, four months prior to Lexington and Concord, Henry Laurens, the South Carolina Patriot, was the first to hypothesize such a scheme. Laurens was not so afraid of the rumored 17,000 British soldiers that would be arriving at Boston in the coming months. Instead he was concerned that there was more to fear from "the Fleets & Armies of Great Britain perhaps joined by those of France & Spain in a common league." It was from this alliance from which the colonies should "apprehend real danger." Laurens reckoned that if the British were determined to subdue the colonies, and "no other means promised Success," the colonies could be "Sold, bartered,

---

[4] Taylor, *The Papers of John Adams,* Vol. 3, Unknown to John Adams, June 9, 1775, 19.
[5] Force, *American Archives*, Fourth Series, Vol. 2, John Dickinson to Arthur Lee, April 29, 1775, 443.

or left exposed to the Ravages of foreign powers."[6]

While Laurens' views might have seemed like lunacy in January, after nearly a year of armed conflict, the fear began to invade the minds of other founding fathers. There is no evidence to suggest the powers of Europe were actually conspiring to partition America, but word of the scheme somehow spread throughout the colonies. Historian James H. Hutson believes the speculations began springing up in February 1776, with the publishing of the Tory pamphlet, "The True Interest of America Impartially Stated, in Certain Strictures on a Pamphlet Common Sense."[7] The pamphlet was Charles Inglis' response to Thomas Paine's well-received *Common Sense*. Paine had partially justified declaring American independence as a means to gain foreign assistance from France and Spain—an issue Inglis felt obligated to address.

Inglis argued against Paine's assertion that Europe's foreign powers would support American independence. Instead, he believed France would join the British cause as a means to prevent her own colonies from following the example. Certainly, the rulers of Europe were concerned with the repercussions of a successful American revolt. Would not America's success result in similar political uprisings in their respective colonial possessions? Inglis argued if America were to go so far as to declare its independency, Britain would "parcel out this continent to the different European Powers," with Canada restored to France, Florida to Spain, and "additions to each." Inglis reminded his readers to let no man think such a move "chimerical or improbable," because "if every other method failed, she would try some expedient as this." Lastly, Inglis raised many rebel eyebrows when he wrote France and Spain have "actually made an offer of their assistance to Great Britain," which "comes from such

---

[6] Chesnutt, *The Papers of Henry Laurens*, Vol. 10, Henry Laurens to John Laurens, January 22, 1775, 40.
[7] James H. Hutson, "The Partition Treaty and the Declaration of Independence," *The Journal of American History*, Vol. 58, No. 4 (March 1972), 877-896, 877.

The Need for Foreign Assistance

authority as would remove all doubt about the matter, even from our zealous Republicans..."[8]

Copies of the pamphlet were burned throughout the colonies, but many rebels were left to ponder whether there was any truth to his statement. What was Inglis' authority, and was it credible? Historians can only speculate where he got his intelligence, but evidence suggests Inglis' knowledge of a memoir by a double agent, Pierre Roubaud, is what influenced him.

Roubaud had been working behind British political scenes in order to convince the British ministry of the need for French soldiers to quell the rebellion. He argued French assistance was necessary because it would not only inspire the Canadians and Indians to fight for the crown, but such a political maneuver would also secure what remained for France's New World Empire. Roubaud was doing nothing more, though, than blowing hot air. The French were in no way willing to consider such a plan, but the offer was tempting to some British officials. In the end, although the ministry was "really imbrued with the idea," at the time the offer was proposed, the majority felt the rebellion was in its last throes and dismissed it.[9]

Although not adopted, the plan was boisterously broadcast by British officials in an effort to denounce those politicians who argued Parliament's current policies would invoke a coalition

---

[8] Charles Inglis, *The True Interest of American Impartially Stated in Certain Strictures on a Pamphlet Common Sense*, (Philadelphia, 1776), 51-2.

[9] Hutson, "The Partition Treaty and the Declaration of Independence," *JAH*, 881. There is also evidence to suggest that Parliament feared any alliance with the French would only lead to a larger dispute over American land claims. On November 2, 1775, in the House of Commons, Captain Luttrell stated, "Then, sir, when America is conquered, and the flower of your army cut off, your new allies will be prepared to dispute the conquest with you. Is there a man, sir, in this House, that doubts but ever Roman Catholick or either army, or in that country, of any name, description, or situation will not be ready again to assert the right of France to the Colonies of America." Force, *American Archives*, Fourth Series, Vol. 6, 82-3.

between America and France. Moreover, it was the dissemination of these political rants, combined with Inglis' pamphlet, which invoked a fear of partition among many of the rebels.

The proximity of France's West Indies to the colonies did not settle fears either. It served as both a blessing and a curse. It was a blessing because the colonies were able to carry on trade with French merchants for essential goods, but a curse because it offered a strategic military base from which the French could operate, if they chose to side with Britain.[10] George Washington was all too aware of the curse of the West Indies and its potential source of harm. Washington saw the arrival of French troops in that region, coupled with King George III's speech assuring foreign assistance, as being extremely dangerous to the American cause.[11] On February 6, 1776, Charles Lee expressed similar fears when he wrote to Robert Morris his opinions on the subject:

> When I consider the present situation here and at home nothing give me so much uneasiness as the uncertainty we are in with regard to the intentions of the French in the W. Indies...it is amazing that so wise a body as the Congress should sleep over so alarming a circumstance but perhaps they have not...perhaps they have proper instruments of Observation...if the French have a powerful Fleet as well as a large army, we may suppose they intend to attack our Islands, but if they have simply Battalions, we must conclude that there is a conclusion betwixt the two Courts.[12]

The knowledge of the arrival of French troops in the West Indies was not limited to military leaders such as Washington and Lee. In fact, many colonial newspapers and journals were filled

---

[10] According to Willcox, in the summer of 1775, Versailles decided to reinforce the West Indies in fear that the war might spread. Willcox, *The Papers of Benjamin Franklin*, Vol. 22, 357 n.1.

[11] Abbot & Twohig, *The Papers of George Washington,* Revolutionary Series, Vol. 3, George Washington to Joseph Reed, January 4, 1776, 25.

[12] Hutson, "The Partition Treaty and the Declaration of Independence," *JAH*, 885. Cited as Charles Lee to Robert Morris, *Collections of the New York Historical Society for the Year 1871: The Lee Papers*, Vol. 1, 281.

The Need for Foreign Assistance

with information about French troop movements. Of course these publications inflated the troop numbers or were largely inaccurate, but the French had made minor reinforcements of their West Indian garrisons. These fortifications caused much concern for the colonists for what might soon come, especially since rumors of Russian and German auxiliaries were already running rampant.[13]

While there was certainly a cause for concern regarding a Franco-Spanish-British alliance in the early months of 1776, Congress was not utterly shocked that such an alliance might indeed occur. On November 29, 1775, Congress had begun its own attempts to gain foreign allies when it was resolved to form the Committee of Secret Correspondence. The members of the Committee were given the arduous task of opening diplomatic channels "with our friends in Great Britain, Ireland, and other parts of the world."[14]

The Committee wasted no time assuming their duties and immediately began working with Arthur Lee to learn the "disposition of foreign Powers" towards the colonies, warning that "impenetrable secrecy" was necessary in the matter.[15] With Lee being in London, the query letter did not arrive until February 1776. Lee responded that he believed France would favor the exportation of arms and ammunition, but he felt the colonies should not try to obtain military assistance. The colonies should only rely on "her own arm" and "Heaven" for their protection.[16]

Under the penname "Candidus," Samuel Adams secretly disagreed and felt men who held Lee's opinion to be "stupid beyond conception" for delaying any foreign alliance. He posed the question: if they can withstand the tyranny of Britain without allies, why not "better withstand" with an ally? Adams did not fear partition from foreign powers because he knew they had no

---

[13] Ibid, 888.
[14] Force, *American Archives*, Fourth Series, Vol. 3, 1936.
[15] Jared Sparks, *The Diplomatic Correspondence of the American Revolution*, Vol. 1, (Washington, DC: John C. Rives, 1857), 379. Willcox, *The Papers of Benjamin Franklin*, Vol. 22, 297.
[16] Force, *American Archives*, Fourth Series, Vol. 4, Arthur Lee to Benjamin Franklin, February 13, 1776, 1125-26.

legal claim upon the colonies' lands. Their assistance would be purely conditioned on a "share of our commerce as will be convenient to both parties."[17] Although Adams' argument would later become common opinion, the majority agreed with Lee. In the minds of the rebel leadership, there existed an ample body of men in the colonies to assemble a formidable army. Why trust a foreign power's army who might turn their forces upon the rebellion or ask for property of their own?

Patriot Joseph Palmer was concerned any alliance with France or Spain, "offensive or defensive," should be avoided because it would only result in future foreign wars.[18] For the time being, John Adams concurred with his friend Palmer. In a letter to Joseph Warren, Adams did not want to exchange British tyranny for that of the French. Instead, he felt it best to "depend on our own" military forces because both the French and English only intend to "part the Continent between them."[19] Warren jokingly replied he did not want French or English tyranny either, but if he must choose, he preferred the French.[20]

While there was much to debate regarding the potential consequences regarding foreign military assistance, few disagreed with the need for foreign commerce, especially military stores. Adam Stephen thought Congress should apply for foreign assistance in this manner. He wanted "No men from France," and instead agreed to "take what goods and manufactures we wanted from them" as long as they "furnish a Navy Sufficient to protect our Exports, & Convoy them to the best Markets in Europe."[21] Stephens knew the Continental Associations' ban on trade with England was having a negative impact on many merchants. That ban, coupled with the British Navy's attempts to prevent any trade

---

[17] Force, *American Archives*, Fourth Series, Vol. 5, 87-88.
[18] Taylor, *The Papers of John Adams*, Vol. 4, Joseph Palmer to John Adams, February 19, 1776, 37.
[19] Ibid, John Adams to Joseph Warren, April 16, 1776, 122-23.
[20] Ibid, Joseph Warren to John Adams, May 8, 1776, 178.
[21] United States, *Naval Documents of the American Revolution*, Vol. 3, Adam Stephen to Richard Henry Lee
, February 4, 1776, 1127.

The Need for Foreign Assistance

with foreign nations, was having an economically brutal impact. The colonies were in no way prepared to manufacture their raw materials into finished goods. This was especially evident when provincial assemblies began scrambling to procure or produce military supplies. Virginian John Page commented to Thomas Jefferson on the subject, stating the dire need for "Salt, Salt-petre, Sulphur, Gun-powder, Arms, Wollens and Linens." Since several colonies could not produce these items quickly enough, Page hoped "no Time should be lost" in forming a commercial treaty with France to procure them.[22] *The Virginia Gazette* published an editorial from one unknown individual who proclaimed "we must be fools...not to open our ports" to France and Spain as a means to "procure everything necessary for the support of the war."[23]

The rebel leadership faced a major problem in achieving this commercial alliance though. King Louis XVI had promised King George III he would not interfere in the dispute. Louis was both moral and loyal with respect to his commitments. He could have easily taken advantage of the situation but assured King George that he wished a speedy and bloodless end to the conflict. The French King's perspective was simple. The hostilities represented an outright example of disobedience to royal authority, threatening civil disorder not only in England but perhaps throughout Europe.[24] While many historians have ridiculed Louis for not acting against England sooner, it is unclear how such a move would have affected the fragile conflict. Would many of the rebels disarm to come to the aid of England whom they loved so dearly and with whom they were trying to reconcile? Would the loyalists have been consumed with a sense of urgency and rallied to defeat the rebel insurgents?

Whatever the outcome would have been if Louis had interfered, his promise to remain neutral certainly did not prevent zealous

---

[22] Boyd, *The Papers of Thomas Jefferson*, John Page to Thomas Jefferson, April 26, 1776, 288.
[23] Force, *American Archives,* Fourth Series, Vol. 4, 779.
[24] Brian N. Norton & Donald C. Spinelli, *Beaumarchais and the American Revolution*, (New York, NY: Lexington Books, 2003), 31.

Irreconcilable Grievances

French merchants from taking advantage of the situation. Throughout the West Indies, French merchants, and in some cases even government officials, secretly provided military stores for Britain's rebellious subjects. The British government was all too aware of the illegal trafficking and demanded an immediate stoppage. In one instance, the British Ambassador to France, Lord Rochford, informed the French of the rebels' procurement of 30 tons of powder from the West Indies, which was even approved by the French governor himself.[25] In Rochford's eyes the act clearly conveyed "very different ideas" from Louis XVI's affirmation of neutrality. In response, the French government, knowing such reports were probably true, did their best to maintain their rejection of such events. For example, in response to Rochford's intelligence, Horace St. Paul responded by stating that such events were "impossible, a "mistake," and to give "no sort of Credit" to such reports because no trade could occur without the approval of French government in Paris.[26]

The truth was exactly the opposite. Such colonial trade could easily occur without the French government's knowledge, and in some instances this trade even occurred within France itself. Moreover, although Louis XVI had given his allegiance to Britain, his ministers and head officials were working behind his back to keep all diplomatic avenues and possibilities open. Just like the rebel leadership had differing opinions on the repercussions of a Franco-American alliance, so did members of Louis XVI's cabinet.

Count de Guines, the French ambassador to England, was of the opinion that France should form a military alliance with England before the war ended in order to secure any benefits an immediate treaty might offer. Count de Vergennes did not want to act so rashly. Instead, he kept his options open, and in the meantime he showed his full-fledged support for the British. He instructed Guines to ensure the British Ministry that they are not

---

[25] United States, *Naval Documents of the American Revolution*, Vol. 2, Lord Rochford to Horace St. Paul, September, 15, 1775, 718.
[26] Ibid, Horace St. Paul to Lord Rochford, September 20, 1775, 724.

"trying to take advantage of their difficulties and force them into a compromise." He reminded Guines that Louis XVI had no "intention to place the Ministry in jeopardy since it already occupies a most unstable position," and France would "make every effort in order to support it rather than strive to overthrow it." Although Vergennes wanted to maintain the alliance, he was also a realist. He knew "the more the British increase their forces" in America, the more France "must guard against any harmful use they might be tempted to make of them." Vergennes felt that "Anything is to be feared on the part of a nation which behaves more often out of despair than on a matter of principle."[27]

Guines surely wanted to take advantage of the situation and use it as a bargaining chip against Britain, but he followed Vergennes' instructions. In the meantime, Vergennes did his best to stay in the good graces of the British Ministry by instructing colonial commissioners to prevent the trading of "any sort of war material."[28] Vergennes was not against allowing American vessels to enter French ports; he just wanted to ensure measures were adopted to prevent any trade that may damage their current agreement with England. The problem Vergennes faced was how he could prevent Americans from trading arms and ammunition and appease British officials without such a policy "turn[ing] to the detriment" of their trade?[29]

Accomplishing the mission proved to be difficult. In December, Lord Stormont issued another complaint to Vergennes. The few American ships that were being allowed to put into French ports were outrightly seeking arms and ammunition. Stormont wanted to know what Vergennes planned to do about it. Vergennes did what a good diplomat would have done: he assured

---

[27] Ibid, Count de Vergennes to Count de Guines, August 13, 1775, 672-73.
[28] Ibid, Count de Vergennes to Gabriel de Sartine, September 30, 1775, 745. See also Gabriel de Sartine to Count de Vergennes, October 16, 1775, 762 and Gabriel de Sartine to Marine Agent at Lorient, October 16, 1775, 763.
[29] United States, *Naval Documents of the American Revolution*, Vol. 3, Count de Vergennes to Gabriel de Sartine, November 10, 1775, 360.

his ally of their "sincere and constant friendship" by renewing his orders in preventing the exportation of arms.[30]

Vergennes words of friendship to Stormont were worth nothing more than just that. In September 1775, Vergennes had already sent Alexandre Achard de Bonvouloir to America as a secret agent. Bonvouloir had established contacts with many of the rebels' secret committees and Vergennes planned on exploiting the advantage. Through Bonvouloir, Vergennes forwarded the message that French ports were open to American ships and assured them that France had no interest in regaining their losses in Canada after the Seven Years War.[31]

Once Bonvouloir arrived in Philadelphia, he immediately began working to gain the good graces of men such as Franklin and Jefferson. Bonvouloir was cautious not to outrightly commit France to America's cause but assured them France "wished them well" and might aid them, on what terms he did not know. The matter was "too delicate" to give certain advice "for or against it."[32] Although Bonvouloir's visit was only an attempt by Vergennes to get a better understanding of the events in America, it had a significant impact on the politics of Congress and France.

Bonvouloir's contact with Congress let delegates know that France was considering aiding their cause. To what degree was uncertain, but it set in motion events that would lead to the Declaration of Independence. For the French, Bonvouloir's report gave them a trusted eyewitness account of the conflict. Many felt England was handling the situation poorly, and Bonvouloir's letter was the evidence they needed to prove the time to act against England was at hand. Lastly, it affirmed Vergennes' cautious stance on aiding the Americans. Bonvouloir's report stated that Congress hoped to gain the assistance of the French Navy but

---

[30] Ibid, Count de Vergennes to Lord Stormont, December 8, 1775, 414.
[31] Morton & Spinelli, *Beaumarchais and the American Revolution*, 23. Samuel Flagg Bemis, *The Diplomacy of the American Revolution*, (Bloomington, IN: Indiana Univ. Press, 1957), 23.
[32] United States, *Naval Documents of the American Revolution*, Vol. 3, Archard de Bonvouloir to Count de Guines, December 28, 1775, 279-285.

The Need for Foreign Assistance

were reluctant do to so since "many people lean towards the King still." Bonvouloir put it best when he wrote, as of now, there was just too much "uneasiness" to have a "foreign nation mingling in their affairs." Congress needed more time to "win" the people over "and make them feel the need for aid" before they could form any alliance.[33]

Congress also received assurances from two French merchants from Saint Domingue (Haiti), Pierre Penet and Emmanuel de Pliarne. The men were carrying gunpowder to Rhode Island and, upon arriving, posing as agents of the French government, offered to supply the colonies with arms. Penet and Pliarne were, in fact, in no way agents for France. Given the rebel leadership in Rhode Island had no way of knowing this, the Frenchmen were allowed to meet with Washington.[34] Upon meeting them, even Washington thought the men were "very eligible" and recommended them to Congress.[35] Washington, in fact, wrote to Rhode Island Governor Nicholas Cooke that he was "exceedingly obliged" to Cooke for hearing Penet and Pliarne's proposal. Washington knew he was unauthorized to enter into these types of contracts but promised Cooke that he would immediately reimburse Rhode Island "at the Continental expense & Whatever charge you may be at on their Account."[36]

In January, Penet and Pliarne were finally able to meet with Congress and received approval for their plan..[37] All and all, by

---

[33] Ibid, 280. For more on Bonvouloir see Morton & Spinelli, *Beaumarchais and the American Revolution*, 34.
[34] United States, *Naval Documents of the American Revolution*, Vol. 3, Nicholas Brown to John Brown, December 11, 1775, 55-56. Willcox, *The Papers of Benjamin Franklin*, Vol. 22, 311.
[35] United States, *Naval Documents of the American Revolution*, Vol. 3, George Washington to John Hancock, December 14, 1775, 94.
[36] Ibid, George Washington to Nicholas Cooke, December 14, 1775, 95.
[37] Ibid, Penet & Pliarne to Nicholas Brown, February 8, 1776, 1176. Pliarne was very thankful to George Washington for his allowing him and Penet to meet with Congress. He assured Washington "that nothing shall be wanting on our parts to Establish between America & France, a branch of Trade, sufficient to supply all the wants, of the New Empire."

the beginning of 1776 Congress felt they were in position to gain foreign assistance if they chose to do so. Not only had Bonvouloir's words given the delegates this confidence, but so too, had he convincingly won the assurances of Thomas Paine and other writers as to why foreign nations would aid the cause. It was common knowledge that opening the colonies' ports to all nations, especially France and Spain, would be beneficial to all involved. The foreign nations would gain the unfinished goods they needed. Instead of being forced to pay whatever the British charged, the colonies would be paid the market price for their goods and be dually able to acquire manufactured goods at competitive prices. In Williamsburg, Virginia, a writer, identified as "An American," argued this exact point but also supported such a move because it would "humble the pride of our enemies;" instead of being "sufferers for want of their trade, we can do ten times better without it." In short, opening the colonies' ports to all nations would force Great Britain to "court our favor" and "form a commercial league with us."[38]

All this positive information arriving from France was supporting what some radicals from Massachusetts had been saying all along. As far back as October 1775, Joseph Ward had hoped for a commercial alliance with France and Spain. "Such tidings will be musick to my ears," he wrote to John Adams, because Ward believed "nothing short of such a plan will secure our Liberties."[39] At the same time, William Tudor was in favor of acquiring the French Navy to "protect our Coasts" after he had learned of the burning of Falmouth.[40]

By February, all these hopes were dashed with the publication of Inglis' pamphlet refuting *Common Sense* and affirming France and Spain had already formed alliances with England. Surely

---

Abbot & Twohig, *The Papers of George Washington*, Revolutionary Series, Vol. 3, Emmanuel de Pliarne to George Washington, January 11, 1776, 69-70.
[38] Force, *American Archives*, Fourth Series, Vol. 4, 779.
[39] Taylor, *The Papers of John Adams*, Vol. 3, Joseph Ward to John Adams, October 23, 1775, 237.
[40] Ibid, William Tudor to John Adams, October 25, 1775, 251.

The Need for Foreign Assistance

many were skeptical about anything but a commercial alliance with either country, but some of the revolutionary leadership, especially the Committee of Secret Correspondence, had relied on Bonvoilour's previous assurances. The Committee immediately stepped up its efforts to see where France truly stood on the subject by sending Silas Deane.

Deane was to act as an intermediary between the Committee and France and to find the "quantity of arms and ammunition necessary for its defense." Moreover, realizing that France would not openly interfere with the conflict as long as the colonies belonged to England, the Committee queried how France would respond if Congress decided to "come to a total separation." Deane was asked to:

[K]now the disposition of France on certain points...such as whether, if the Colonies should be forced to form themselves into an independent state France would probably acknowledge them as such, receive their Ambassadors, enter into any treaty or alliance with them for commerce or defence, or both? If so, on what principal conditions?[41]

Even the zealous John Adams, who had lobbied for a Franco-American alliance in 1775, grew uncertain of France's disposition by March 1776. In his diary he reflected on whether it was in France's best interest to stand neutral or join with Congress. While Adams knew it was in France's interest to "dismember" the British Empire, he also hypothesized that if reconciliation were accomplished, France would, in all probability, lose the West Indies within six months.[42] Thus, France had much to lose if it made a diplomatic miscalculation in the conflict.

---

[41] Force, *American Archives*, Fourth Series, Vol. 5, Committee of Secret Correspondence to Silas Deane, March 3, 1776, 48-49. Sparks, *The Diplomatic Correspondence of the American Revolution*, Vol. 1, 5-8. Ronald Hoffman & Peter Albert, *Diplomacy and Revolution: The Franco-American Alliance of 1778*, (Charlottesville, VA: University of Virginia, 1981), 3. James Breck Perkins, *France in the American Revolution*, (New York, NY: Burt Franklin, 1970), 62-63.
[42] Butterfield, *Diary and Autobiography of John Adams*, Vol. 2, 235.

Coincidentally, as revolutionaries tried hypothesizing France's disposition to their cause, affirmation of the inclusion of Hessian auxiliaries had arrived—a move some felt would immediately propel France to side with the Americans. John Hancock and other members of Congress had already received intelligence suggesting that if Great Britain employed foreign troops, France would not be "Idle Spectators."[43] As the intelligence was uncertain, however, the pressure to establish some form of a foreign alliance was mounting, and independence was the answer to many of the rebels. Just months earlier, Thomas Paine had argued this exact point in *Common Sense*. Until now, Paine's words had fallen on deaf ears. He had argued that no foreign nation would come to their aid, either as a mediator or ally, as long the colonists were subjects of Great Britain. He believed Congress must assure the foreign courts of their "peaceful disposition" by publishing a "manifesto" that set forth their "miseries" and broke all ties with the "cruel" British court.[44]

When *Common Sense* was initially published in January 1776, Paine's argument for American independence struck most readers in the colonies as simply too radical. Certainly most of the colonists still felt some form of reconciliation could be worked out. It was firmly believed that there had to be another way to gain the assistance of foreign nations without compromising their connection to England, but by March 1776 this hope was dashed. Congress now could only eagerly await word from Silas Deane about the French Court's disposition and hope it was favorable to the American cause. In the meantime, the founding fathers could only speculate about the best approach.

Nathanael Greene was certainly convinced by Paine's argument for foreign assistance, because he himself had posed a similar

---

[43] United States, *Naval Documents of the American Revolution*, Vol. 4, Lord Stirling to John Hancock, March 10, 1776, 284. Ibid, Diary of Richard Smith, March 15, 1776, 350. Abbot & Twohig, *The Papers of George Washington*, Revolutionary Series, Vol. 3, Lord Stirling to George Washington, March, 11, 1776, 452.
[44] Thomas Paine, *Rights of Man, Common Sense, and Other Political Writings*, (New York, NY: Oxford University Press, 1995), 45-6.

argument five days before *Common Sense* was even released. Months earlier, Greene had advocated a declaration of independence as a means to force Britain into peace, but by January he was singing a much different tune. Greene was now in favor of a declaration of independence to "call upon the World and Great God who Governs it to Witness the Necessity, propriety and Rectitude" of the colonies. By doing this, Greene felt Congress could open trade with France and Spain, therefore aiding the cause.[45]

After reading *Common Sense*, patriot Joseph Palmer thought along similar lines. He posed the following questions to John Adams, "If the United [Colonies] shou'd declare independence, and offer their Trade...to Somebody else; would not our Enemies find themselves immediately involved in a War with that Sombody? And would not that involvement break the storm, in some degree, for the present? And can anybody accept such Trade without such an involvement?"[46] Palmer's circular thinking on the subject was another reiteration of Paine's argument. He was simply foreshadowing that the declaring of American independence would aid not only the war effort, but the economy as well.[47]

In January 1776, Greene and Palmer were definitely in the minority when they pledged support for Thomas Paine's call for independence to obtain foreign assistance. Surprisingly, it took until early March before Samuel Adams was on board for the plan. Under the penname Candidus, he was initially in favor of opening trade, but after learning of Parliament's recruitment of Hessian auxiliaries Samuel changed his perspective. He had always known France was keeping a close watch. Samuel had "no Doubt that she [France] would with Chearfulness openly lend her Aid to promote it," but he now supported the argument for the colonies to

---

[45] Showman, *The Papers of Nathanael Greene*, Vol. 1, Greene to Samuel Ward, January 4, 1776, 177.

[46] Taylor, *The Papers of John Adams*, Vol. 3, Joseph Palmer to John Adams, January 23, 1776, 412-13.

[47] Taylor, *The Papers of John Adams*, Vol. 4, Joseph Palmer to John Adams, February 19-20, 1776, 37-8.

affirmatively gain such aid America would have to "declare herself free and independent."[48]

By May, more and more influential patriots began to agree, but the question of what kind of alliance to be entered into remained unanswered. Palmer, like most patriots, preferred only a commercial agreement. "[L]et us not enter into any Treaty offensive or defensive," he wrote John Adams, because otherwise the colonies may be pulled into a European war. Palmer's scheme was to remain militarily neutral and form only a commercial alliance with France and Spain so they "will soon attack G B, but they will not do it 'till the breach between her and the colonies is incurable." In the meantime, Palmer believed America would "grow in Military Strength and Knowledge," and "obtain a Sufficient Stock of Powder and other military stores" to prevent Great Britain from "ever possessing" the colonies again.[49]

The belief that the French would aid the American cause, if independence was declared, even appeared in colonial publications. On April 6, 1776, *The Virginia Gazette* read:

> The French appear exceedingly friendly to the American cause, which they would have promoted by a much larger supply of arms and ammunition than they hitherto imported, had they not been doubtful of the America submission to the claims of Parliament...The common toast among the French, from General down to the merchants, is the independence of America; until which it is declared, they say our war with England can only be looked on as a domestic broil, unworthy of public countenance of those powers who would cheerfully enter into friendship and alliance with them, could it be done with propriety.[50]

The report was pure speculation since no affirmative word from

---

[48] Cushing, *The Writings of Samuel Adams*, Vol. 3, Samuel Adams to Samuel Cooper, April 3, 1776, 275.
[49] Taylor, *The Papers of John Adams*, Vol. 4, Joseph Palmer to John Adams, February 19-20, 1776, 37-8.
[50] United States, *Naval Documents of the American Revolution*, Vol. 4, Dixon and Hunter's *Virginia Gazette*, April 6, 1776, 570-71.

the French Court had arrived, but that did not prevent the rumor from spreading, making many feel independence had to be declared soon. Charles Lee was not certain whether the rumors were true, but like most patriot supporters it did not prevent him from holding an opinion on the subject. Lee believed that, given all the considerations, he was convinced the French would "immediately and essentially assist" the cause "if independence is declared." He conveyed these sentiments to fellow Virginian Patrick Henry, informing the latter it was their "duty to adopt the measure as by procrastination our ruin is inevitable."[51]

Richard Henry Lee wrote a similar plea to Henry, asking him to move heaven and earth to see the Virginian delegation in Congress propose a declaration of independence to secure America "from the despotic aims of the British Court by Treaties of alliance with foreign States." He reminded Henry that "whilst we are hesitating about forming alliances," Parliament was certainly not. Lee believed Great Britain would soon conclude "she cannot conquer us alone," and when she did the colonies' ruin will be sealed by the "signing of a Treaty of partition with two or three ambitious powers."[52]

Patrick Henry agreed, describing gaining the French Alliance as "everything." He, too, believed the British were offering partition to France, which "may induce her to aid [in] our destruction."[53] Moreover, Henry did not disappoint his fellow patriots' cries. On May 15, when the Virginia Convention passed the famous resolution ordering its delegates to propose a declaration of independence, Henry was the principle mover. He wrote to Richard Henry Lee it better to "anticipate...the efforts of the enemy by instantly sending Ambassadors to France" rather

---

[51] *The Lee Family Papers*, (Charlottesville, VA: University of Virginia, 1966), Charles Lee to Patrick Henry, May 8, 1776. See also, Force, *American Archives,* Fifth Series, Vol. 1, 95-6.
[52] Ballagh, *The Letters of Richard Henry Lee*, Vol. 1, Richard Henry Lee to Patrick Henry, April 20, 1776, 176-78.
[53] Taylor, *The Papers of John Adams*, Vol. 4, Patrick Henry to John Adams, May 20, 1776, 201.

than let France be "allured by the partition."⁵⁴ John Adams could not agree more, writing to Henry that the "importance of an immediate application to the French court" was "clear."⁵⁵

Thanks to Henry's motion, by June 7th the wheels of American independence began moving faster than ever before. It was on this day that Richard Henry Lee conveyed the Virginia Convention's belief that a declaration of independence was necessary, because "it is expedient forthwith to make the most effectual measures for forming Alliances." Thus, as many contemporary Americans primarily view the vote for a declaration of independence as a break from Europe, it was actually more of a formal attempt to create foreign alliances.⁵⁶

It is easy to be drawn in by Jefferson's eloquent wording in the preamble. The famous words "We hold these truths to be self-evident, that all men are created equal" spur inspiration that few other lines in history can accomplish. These words do not comprise the entire meaning behind the Declaration of Independence though. The Declaration was primarily a legal document and is to be taken in its entirety, not in piecemeal sections. It was a document that explained to the American colonists, King George III, Parliament, and the world why the colonies had to "dissolve the political bands" that connected them with England. Beyond the Declaration's preamble and list of grievances, Congress announced to the world its new governmental powers. Outside of their power to dissolve their "Allegiance" and "connection" to Great Britain, Congress could now "levy War, conclude Peace, contract Alliances, establish Commerce, and do all the other Acts and Things which Independent States may of right do."

What Congress was trying to accomplish by concluding the

---

[54] William Wirt Henry, *Patrick Henry: Life, Correspondence, and Speeches*, Vol. 1, Patrick Henry to Richard Henry Lee, May 20, 1776, 410-11.
[55] Taylor, *The Papers of John Adams*, Vol. 4, John Adams to Patrick Henry, June 3, 1776, 234-35.
[56] William C. Stinchcombe, *The American Revolution and the French Alliance*, (Syracuse, NY: Syracuse University Press, 1969), 7.

The Need for Foreign Assistance

Declaration with this announcement, was that it had the legal authority to form foreign alliances. The founding fathers were hoping Paine was right when he argued such a resolution would entice France and Spain to aid them. Certainly no time was wasted making sure France knew of America's newly declared independence. The Committee of Secret Correspondence immediately sent a copy of the Declaration to Silas Deane, following its approval. Dean was instructed to "communicate the piece to the Court of France and send copies of it to the other Courts of Europe." Furthermore, to gain the support of the French people, it was advised to have it "translated in French so it could be published throughout France."[57]

The timing of the issuance of the Declaration of Independence and the colonies' need for foreign assistance was, by any means, no accident. Certainly the Declaration was adopted for many reasons, depending on which delegate you asked, but the two issues were undoubtedly politically intertwined. Just days before Patrick Henry proposed the Declaration, the Committee of Secret Correspondence was still hypothesizing the disposition of the French Court. They even sent William Bingham to West Indies to not only know "the designs of the French assembling so large a Fleet with great Numbers of Troops," but to also find if they "mean to act for or against America."[58]

Furthermore, just one day following the Congressional decision to appoint a committee to draft the Declaration, a committee was created to "prepare a plan of treaties to be proposed to foreign powers." In short, American independence and foreign assistance went hand in hand. John Adams and others had come to believe that independence was necessary if a treaty was to be formed, and a treaty was necessary if independence was to be maintained.[59] Adams went to work right away in drafting what would be known

---

[57] Willcox, *The Papers of Benjamin Franklin*, Vol. 22, The Committee of Secret Correspondence to Silas Deane, July 8, 1776, 503.
[58] Ibid, The Committee of Secret Correspondence to William Bingham, June 3, 1776, 443-47.
[59] Taylor, *Papers of John Adams*, Vol. 4, Plan of Treaties, 260-61.

Irreconcilable Grievances

as the Plan of Treaties. The treaty echoed what Adams and the majority of the delegates preferred in any alliance—purely commercial without any political or military ties.

While Congress might have affirmed the Declaration to "contract Alliances," most preferred not to have the French militarily involved. What if the French preferred to be militarily involved to ensure the success of their diplomatic investment? How would Congress deal with such an overture? James Warren probably conveyed the vicarious situation best, writing to John Adams, "I don't want a French Army here," but if he had to have one, Warren would "want to have one Employed against Britain."[60]

Adams also thought it better to have the French Army pitted against the British rather than the colonies, but that did not mean he was about to offer such an option in his Plan of Treaties. He ensured the document was primarily a commercial agreement. Offering any nation the right to trade with the newly formed United States was thought to be sufficient for any foreign aid given to the Americans, even if such an agreement led that nation to be at war with Great Britain. The basis of the treaty would form the foreign policy of the nation for decades to come—perfect neutrality in either European or foreign wars.[61]

The calculated maneuver by Congress to declare independence as a means to gain foreign assistance was risky. They had no assurance of knowing their calculated maneuver would be successful. Even in late June, Adams correspondence shows there were still pessimists that believed the Declaration would only put them "in the Power of foreign States." They felt France would only take advantage of the situation, "demanding terms of Us, and That Spain will sit idle" and "rejoice to see Britain and America wasting each other." Even in the face of all these doubts, the Declaration still would go through because of steadfast men like Adams. He felt such fears and arguments have "no Weight with me," because the "Advantages" from the Declaration were "very

---

[60] Ibid, James Warren to John Adams, May 8, 1776, 178.
[61] Ibid, Plan of Treaties, 261.

The Need for Foreign Assistance

numerous, and very great."[62]

Fortunately for the founding fathers, Adams was right. In the winter of 1775, men like Pierre Augustin Caron, who was later named "de Beaumarchais," and Lauraguais were working non-stop to convince the French Court to aid the American cause. These men are rarely mentioned in American history texts, but their contribution to the success of American Independence has proven to be immeasurable. It was through their efforts that King Louis XVI would change his position on the conflict.

Just about the time the Declaration of Independence was being signed by the delegates in Philadelphia, the Committee of Secret Correspondence had been assured of Louis XVI's resolve. Monsieur Dumas wrote to the Committee:

As to you first demand [a military alliance], the King is a true Knight: his word is sacred; he have given it to the English to live in peace with them; he will hold it. While France is not at war with the English, he will not ally himself against them with the Colonies...[63]

Certainly such news was not well received, but Congress could only wait and hope certain events would turn in their favor so Louis XVI's would change his resolve. Those events involved the political maneuvering of Beaumarchais, the Comte de Lauraguais, and the Count de Vergennes. As early as November, Vergennes knew if Congress declared America independent it would increase the possibility of foreign entanglements greatly, but it was Beaumarchais who began formally addressing Louis XVI on the subject.[64]

It began January 1776 when he proposed to Louis XVI a plan to secretly aid the Americans. The plan called for the King to place one million livres into a fake trading company called

---

[62] Ibid, John Adams to John Winthrop, June 23, 1776, 331.
[63] Force, *American Archives*, Fourth Series, Vol. 6, Monsieur Dumas to the Committee of Secret Correspondence, May 14-21, 1776, 443-44.
[64] United States, *Naval Documents of the American Revolution*, Vol. 3, Count de Vergennes to Count de Guines, November 19, 1775, 377.

Roderigue Hortalez & Co. It was a simple, yet ingenius, idea to prolong the American conflict as a means to weaken the British Empire and give France time to bolster its Navy. First, Roderigue Hortalez & Company would take half the money to purchase tobacco from the Americans, which would provide the latter with immediate funds to maintain the war effort. Second, the company would use the remaining half to procure the necessary powder and saltpeter the Americans.

To save expenses in procuring powder and saltpeter, Beaumarchais preferred purchasing the powder secretly from the Louis XVI's own stores, thus saving costs and allowing him to resell the articles to the Americans at a much greater profit. Beaumarchais hypothesized this would increase the half-million livre investment to nearly 2.5 million livres, providing a 2 million livre profit. It was this profit that would allow Roderigue Hortalez & Company to perpetually stay in the business of aiding the Americans without further financing from the Court.[65]

Louis XVI and his ministers did not initially take to the plan, deciding, rather, to remain steadfast in their decision to maintain their neutrality. The decision did not shake Beaumarchais' resolve though. He was adamant about supplying the American cause, not only for the political benefit of France, but for his own personal wealth and gain. On February 27, Bonvouloir's report, detailing the success of the American forces, arrived at the French Court. Just two days later, Beaumarchais reasserted his plan. The letter dramatically stated:

> The notorious dispute between America and England, which will soon divide the world and change the European system, requires each power to examine carefully how it can be affected by this separation and if the consequences will be beneficial or prejudicial. The most concerned power of all is certainly France whose sugar islands have been, since the last war, the object of constant regret and hope on the part of the English; desires and regrets which will unfailingly bring us war unless, because of an inconceivable weakness, we agree

---

[65] Ibid, Caron de Beaumarchais to Louis XVI, January 22, 1776, 525-30.

The Need for Foreign Assistance

to sacrifice our wealthy possessions in the gulf of chimera of a shameful peace, more destructive than this war which we fear.[66]

Beaumarchais' argument was simple: the sooner the conflict in America ended, the worse off France would be. Beaumarchais left the King to ponder whether England would redirect its military forces to the West Indies following any American pacification or peace. France could limit this, however. By aiding the American cause, the conflict would drag on, allowing France to expand its Navy, thus providing further protection to the valuable West Indies. Finally, France's aid would remain purely secret through the American colonies' agent Arthur Lee.

Louis XVI surely questioned Beaumarchais' motive and intelligence regarding the conflict, but the King had also received a letter from Comte de Lauraguais supporting Beaumarchais' arguments.[67] Furthermore, Vergennes prepared a persuasive letter to the King and the French Cabinet, entitled "Considerations on the Affair of the English Colonies in America." The letter left the issue of French intervention to the council but openly advocated for secretly aiding the Americans. Vergennes was clearly in favor of continuing "to feed with dexterity the security of the English Ministry as to the intentions of France and Spain." Although interfering in England's colonial affairs might "not accord with the King's dignity," why should not France put itself "in a position which may either restrain the English, render their attacks uncertain, or ensure the means of punishing them"?[68]

---

[66] United States, *Naval Documents of the American Revolution*, Vol. 4, Caron de Beaumarchais to Louis XVI, February 23, 1776. Document was received on February 29, 1776, see Morton & Spinelli, *Beaumarchais and the American Revolution*, 34.
[67] United States, *Naval Documents of the American Revolution*, Vol. 4, Count de Lauraguais to Count de Vergennes, February 24, 1776, 930-31; Morton & Spinelli, *Beaumarchais and the American Revolution*, 35.
[68] United States, *Naval Documents of the American Revolution*, Vol. 4, "Considerations of the Affair of the English Colonies in America," March 12, 1776, 966-70.

Irreconcilable Grievances

On May 2, Louis XVI made the crucial decision. He agreed to provide the Americans with one million livres for arms through Beaumarchais' Roderigue Hortalez & Company, and to expand the French Navy.[69] The steps taken by France were just the beginning of what would become an indispensable relationship in ensuring the success of the American Revolution. In July 1776, few in Congress saw such a commercial relationship with France flourishing into an all-out military alliance. Neither France nor Congress wanted to commit to such an agreement, but within the year following the Declaration of Independence certain events were set in motion. These events would force England to declare war against France, and induce France to send military aid to America.

* * * * * * * * *

Many factors undoubtedly played an influential role in Congress adopting the Declaration of Independence. Historians have formulated different arguments as to what ultimately led to its inception, but it was certainly not the pageant of freedom many have portrayed. The political influences of the first year of the Revolutionary War were not much different than the political influences of today. Just as social events dictate domestic and foreign policy in twenty-first century America, the same held true in eighteenth century.

Another parallel between the events portrayed in the latter grievances of the Declaration and today's events is there can be very little "black and white" or "right and wrong" interpretation. The founding fathers and the colonists' hands were often just as guilty or guiltier of the atrocities they accused Parliament of committing. The Patriots' hands were certainly not clean, and no

---

[69] Morton & Spinelli, *Beaumarchais and the American Revolution*, 40; Willcox, *The Papers of Benjamin Franklin*, Vol. 22, 454. United States, *Naval Documents of the American Revolution*, Vol. 4, Count de Vergennes to Louis XVI, May 2, 1776, 1084.

other example echoes this more than the treatment of loyalists before, during, and after the war.

It remains unquestionable that the founding fathers were influenced by the natural rights of man and the ideological principles of leading philosophers. The colonists were a constitutional people. They were raised and governed by certain constitutional principles which were echoed in their colonial charters and petitions to Parliament. The most notable principle was the same as set forth in the Glorious Revolution of 1688: that the relationship between the people and their government was a social contract. The Declaration of Independence resonates this principle in the opening paragraph:

> When in the Course of human events it becomes necessary for one people to dissolve the political bands which have connected them with another and to assume among the powers of the earth, the separate and equal station to which the Laws of Nature and of Nature's God entitle them, a decent respect to the opinions of mankind requires that they should declare the causes which impel them to the separation.

While the political issues between the colonies and Parliament assuredly played a major role in escalating hostilities, they were not the driving force behind the adoption of the Declaration of Independence. The Declaration possessed an all-inclusive list of grievances, not all playing an important role in convincing the people to separate from the mother country. It was primarily England's alleged inciting of slave insurrections, bombarding of coastal towns, inclusion of Indian and Hessian auxiliaries, and the need for foreign assistance that led to the Declaration's adoption. Each event or series of events affected the colonists differently, depending on multiple sociological factors. Thus, no particular event in the colonies determined whether an individual believed that independence was the solution.

Index

Acland, Major John Dyke, 34, 36
Abigail Adams, 149, 150, 151
Adams, John, 1, 4, 7, 59, 74, 147, 149
    Appoints Washington, 81
    Boston Massacre trial and, 73-74
    Burning of Charlestown and, 151
    Continental Navy and, 181-182
    David Hume and, 55 n.6
    Declaration of Independence Committee and, 5
    Foreign assistance and, 6, 301, 306, 312-313, 318, 320-321
    Hessians and, 298
    Hessian desertions and, 290
    Indian employment and, 268
    King George III's speech and, 40
    Militia and, 76
    Motion for independence, 4
    Olive Branch Petition and, 29
    Peace Commissioners and, 47
    Plan of Treaties and, 319-320
    Prohibitory Act and, 40
    Proposes Hussar regiment and, 285-286
    Reconciliation and, 5-6
    Selection of Continental Army officers and, 80
    Slave insurrections and, 119
    Standing armies and, 75-76
    Thoughts on Government and, 75
Adams, Samuel, 53, 74
    Appoints Washington, 81
    Foreign assistance and, 305-306, 315
    King George III's speech and, 26
    List of Infringements and Violations of Rights, 73
    Militia and, 76-78
Alexander, Robert, 48
Allen, Ethan Colonel, 226, 236, 241-242
American Revolution,
    Social influences, 18-19
Anderson, Oliver, 44
Andrew Doria, 185
Arnold, Benedict, 228, 237, 241-242, 265
Articles of Confederation, 46, 82
Atwood, Rodney, 275, 279
Avery, Robert, 148
Bailey, Jacob, 165
Bailyn, Bernard, 57
Bancroft, Edward, 247, 261
Bancroft, George, 17
Barkley, Andrew Captain, 142, 175
    Cuts off supplies to Portsmouth, 177-178
    Fort William & Mary and, 174
    Guard boat fired on, 176-177
    Portsmouth and, 174
    Warns Portsmouth to cease and desist, 176
Barrington, Lord, 30, 114-115, 234-235
Barry, John, 184
Beaumarhais, Pierre Augustin Caron, 321-324
Betts, Azor, 189
Bill of Rights,
    American, 64

327

Bill of Rights *continued*,
    British, 56, 59, 72
Bingham, William, 319
Blackstone, William, 51, 68
Bonvouloir, Achard de, 310-312
Boston Assembly, 56
Boston Chronicle, 188
Boston Gazette, 235
Boston Massacre, 1, 73-74
Boston Port Act, 1, 39, 73
Boston Tea Party, 1
Bradford, William 118, 300
Broughton, Nicholas Captain, 183
Bulloch, Archibald, 106
Bunker Hill, Battle of, 27-28, 43, 115, 150, 152, 173, 300
Burgh, James, 74
Burke, Edmund, 35, 39, 49, 53, 125, 215
Burrows, Edwin, 18
Butler, Benjamin, 189-190
Cabot, 185
Cambridge, Massachusetts, 1, 79, 91
Camden, Lord, 32
Cameron, Alexander, 256, 258
Campbell, Archibald, 196
Campbell, William, 122-123
Canada, 143
Canceaux, HMS, 156-162
Caractacus, 79
Carleton, Guy, 8 n.18
    Indians and, 235, 237, 239-240, 242-243, 247-248, 265
    Slaves and, 125
Carter, Landon, 107-108, 129, 194
Carter, Robert, 107
Cary, Archibald, 128
Cassel, Hesse, 282
Charles I, 65, 67
Charles II, 62, 67
Chase, Samuel, 28, 29, 74, 184
Cherne, Leo, 1
Clap, Caleb, 297
Clinton, Henry, 129, 276

Coercive Acts, 2, 137
Collet, John, 116-117
Committee of Secret Correspondence, 305, 313, 319, 321
Common Sense, 2, 302, 312, 314-315
Connecticut, 6, 116, 189
    British Navy and, 136
    Employment of Indians and, 266-268
    Hessians and, 273-274
Connolly, John, 215-216
    Indian auxiliaries and, 249-254, 259
    Lord Dunmore's War and, 219-220, 249
Constitution,
    American, 64, 82
    British, 2, 29, 53-54, 63, 71, 109
    John Adams reference to, 4
    Virginia, 58
    Whig interpretation of, 53-59
Continental Army, 43, 76, 79
    Appointment of officers, 80-81
    Black soldiers serving in, 91
    Committee of Conference and, 166
    Enlistments and, 286
    Falmouth may cause dissolution of, 166-167
    Poorly equipped, 138, 227
    Portsmouth and, 181
Continental Association, 90, 306
Continental Congress, 37, 65
    Allegedly defamed, 190
    Appointment of Continental Army officers, 80
    Black soldiers approved, 91
    British Navy and, 135
    Communication with Washington and, 142
    Creates Committee of Secret Correspondence, 305

Continental Congress *continued*,
  Dunmore's Proclamation and, 101, 110-111
  Fear of partition, 301
  Foreign Assistance and, 9-10, 297, 299-300, 306-307, 310-314, 318-320
  German unit and, 285-288
  Independence and, 3, 5, 166
  Indian affairs and, 243-244, 261-262, 264-267, 270
  Informs King George foreign assistance is available, 299
  King George III's speech and, 25-26
  Militia Bill and, 76-80
  Naval operations and, 183-184
  Offers land bounty to Hessian deserters, 288-291
  Opens trade to all nations, 166
  Peace Commissioners and, 48
  Portsmouth and, 178, 181
  Reconciliation and, 12, 28-30, 41-52
  Response to Lord North's Conciliatory Proposal, 8-9
  Rhode Island plan and, 184
  Second, 92
  Standing Armies and, 11-12
  Supplying Continental Army and, 286, 300
  Treaty with France, 299
  Uses burning of coastal towns to recruit Indians, 171 n.123
  Virginia Convention and, 98
Continental Navy,
  American autonomy and, 182
  Creation attributed to burning of coastal towns, 181, 209
  Establishment of, 171, 181-186
Cooke, Nicholas, 165, 167, 311
Coventry, Earl of, 32-33
Cowley, William, 253
Cromwell, Oliver, 57, 80

Cushing, Samuel, 91
Cushing, Thomas, 25, 284
Dartmouth, Lord, 30, 36, 42, 90, 96, 100, 116, 122, 127, 190, 207, 219, 234-236, 244, 252-255, 269
  British Navy and, 136
  Orders gunpowder seized, 93, 137
  William Johnson's death and, 218
Davies, William, 103
Deane, Silas, 74, 313, 319
Declaration of the Causes and Necessity for Taking Up Arms, 7-8, 9-10, 65
  Foreign assistance and, 299-300
  Indians and, 87
  Response to, 269
  Slavery and, 87
Declaration of Independence, 16, 25, 48, 131, 132, 250, 268, 317, 324-325
  Causes of, 15
  Coastal bombardments and, 190-191, 210
  Congress assembles committee for, 5
  Dunmore's Proclamation and, 129-132
  French alliance and, 299, 310, 318-321, 324
  Grievances in, 5, 7, 12-15
  Grievances compared to other petitions, 19-21
  Hessians and, 273, 282
  Indians and, 213
  Influenced by Virginia Declaration of Rights, 2
  Legal document and, 318
  Modeled after 1689 Declaration of Rights, 58, 59, 64
  Opening paragraph, 325

329

Declaration of Independence
  continued,
  Slave insurrections and, 85
  Standing armies and, 64
  Suspending and dispensing
    with law, 64
Declaration of Indulgence, 62
Declaration of Rights,
  Of 1689, 2, 56, 57, 59, 60, 61,
    66, 67
  Virginia, 2, 75, 130, 186
Declaration of Rights and
  Grievances, 65
Declaratory Act, 11
Deer Island, 149-150
Defiance, 185
De Guines, Count de, 96
Delaware, 75, 189
Denbigh, Earl of, 37
Dickinson, John, 74, 87, 296, 299-
  301
Dispensing power, 62-65
Drayton, William Henry,
  Argues King George III
    vacated throne, 58
  British Navy and, 136
  Compares American
    Revolution to Glorious
    Revolution, 55 n.6, 59-61
  John Stuart and, 256
  Prohibitory Act and, 40
  Standing armies and, 72
  Suspending and dispensing
    power and, 63
Drummond, Lord, 40, 43-44
Duane, James, 3, 283
Dudley, Viscount, 32
Dundas, Henry, 35
Dunmore, Lord John Murray, 113,
  115, 119, 123, 137
  Armory and, 93-94
  Burning of Norfolk and, 193,
    197-201
  Chesapeake and, 185
  Great Bridge and, 197, 199
  Gunpowder incident and, 93-
    94, 95-97, 248
  Indians and, 96, 239, 249-254,
    259
  Kemp's Landing and, 98, 100,
    119, 195, 196
  Land grants and, 90
  Lord Dunmore's War and,
    219-220
  Mentioned in draft of
    Declaration of Independence,
    20-21
  Navy and, 182, 190
  Norfolk printing press and, 98,
    185-187, 190, 194
  Plot to kidnap Martha, 191-
    192
  Proclamation to free slaves,
    15, 85-86, 91-92, 96, 98-105,
    107-112, 124-125, 127-132,
    190, 196, 199, 248-249, 253
  Reconciliation with Virginia
    Assembly and, 96-97
  Requests loyalists be given
    protection, 200
  Requests supplies, 199
  Runaway slaves and, 190
  Strength doubled, 100
  Threatens to arrest Virginia
    Assembly, 92
  Withdraws from Norfolk, 198
Easton, John, 242
Eden, Robert, 94-95, 99, 127, 137
Eliot, Andrew, 71
Elliot, Thomas Colonel, 193
Falcon, 160
Falmouth, 170, 175, 179, 180, 191,
  193, 203
  Bombardment begins, 164
  Burning of, 136, 154-171, 173,
    192
  Burning establishes
    Continental Navy, 171
  Burning used to recruit
    Indians, 171 n.123

Falmouth *continued*,
 Captain Coulson and, 156, 157
 Committee of Inspection and, 156
 Committee of Safety and, 159
 Delivered arms to Mowat, 162-163
 First run in with British Navy, 155-156
 Graves removal and, 204
 Inhabitants compare situation to Gloucester, 160
 Marines land to burn, 164-165
 Mowat issues ultimatum to, 161-162
 News of Lexington & Concord reaches town, 156
 Sons of Liberty dispatched to, 163
 Thompson's soldiers leave, 158
 Town committee meets with Mowat, 162-163
Ferguson, Adam, 35
Fields, William, 65
Fletcher, Andrew, 69
Flinn, Thomas, 147
Fort Johnson, 117
Fort Loundon, 256
Fort Pitt, 251
Fort Ticonderoga, 235, 239, 241
Fort William and Mary, 8-9, 173-176, 180
Fowler, William, 182, 183
France, 68
 Alliance with colonies, 310-314, 321-324
 Impact on American independence, 316-320
 Neutrality andm, 307-309
 Partition and, 301-305
 Trade with colonies and, 310
 West Indies and, 304-305
Franklin, Benjamin, 74, 103, 310

Committee of Conference and, 167
Declaration of Independence Committee and, 5
Falmouth's burning and, 165
Hessians and, 284, 290-291
Indian recruitment and, 240
French & Indian War, 35, 54, 216, 301, 310
Frey, Sylvia, 118, 127
Gadsden, Christopher, 181-182
Gage, Thomas, 127, 137, 145, 185
 Bunker Hill and, 152-153
 Burning of Charlestown and, 151-153
 Colonial port towns and, 143
 Communication with England and, 142
 Dunmore and, 95-96
 Fears American Independence, 30-31
 Fort William & Mary and, 8-9
 Hessian employment and, 276
 Indian affairs and, 217, 221-222, 230, 233-239, 244, 252, 254, 258, 260, 269
 Lexington & Concord and, 8, 96, 152, 174
 Loyalists and, 114-115
 Receives word Governor Wentworth has fled, 177
 Responds to Graves' request to burn coastal towns, 154-155
 Slave insurrections and, 113-114
 Strategy of in Boston, 138
 Supplying troops and, 137
 William Johnson's death and, 218
Galphin, George, 262
Gardener, Savage, 144
Gates, Horatio, 80
Gazetter, 188
George III, King, 17, 18, 51, 61, 127, 182, 281, 307, 318

331

King George III *continued*,
　Accused of exciting Indians, 213
　Address to colonies, 21
　Blamed for slave insurrections, 87
　Claims colonies to be in open rebellion, 26
　Charged with maintaining slavery, 130
　Charges against, 3
　Compared to James II, 57
　Frustrated with Graves, 208
　Hessians and, 273, 276
　Naval strategy and, 137
　Opinion on Graves, 204
　Plan to subdue colonies, 31
　Proclamation of, 151
　Restricts arms and munitions to colonies, 222
　Speech to Parliament and effect of, 25-28, 41, 43, 126, 182, 276-277, 283, 304
　Standing armies and, 72
　Suspending and dispensing power and, 63-64
　Vacating throne and, 58-59
Georgia, 3, 119, 131, 239
　Fear of Indian attacks and, 256-57
　Tybee Island, 106
Germain, George, 203, 262
Gerry, Elbridge, 7
Gibson, John, 253
Glorious Revolution of 1689, 15, 18, 21, 325
　Compared to American struggle, 55-64, 109
　Social contract and, 56-57
　Standing armies and, 66-68, 71, 76
Glover, John, 183
Goold, William, 153 n.65, 154 n.66, 155 n.69
Grafton, Duke of, 33, 34, 49, 208

Grape Island, 149
Graves, Samuel, Vice-Admiral, 30, 127, 208-210
　American vessels harass, 183
　Appointed command of North America, 138
　Asks Howe if he wants Charlestown burned, 152-153
　Communication with England and, 142
　Complaints of, 205-206
　Implementing British strategy and, 137-139
　Infuriated by rebels, 145, 149
　Knows rebellion not limited to Massachusetts, 142-143
　Labeled poor administrator, 138 n.11,
　Lexington & Concord and, 139-140, 152
　Orders Mowat to attack Gloucester, 154 n.67, 159
　Orders received, 138, 140-141
　Orders sent, 145, 159, 177
　Portsmouth and, 174, 178
　Rebellion and, 209
　Receives orders to attack Falmouth, 155
　Recommends Charlestown, MA burned, 152
　Recommends ruthless warfare, 138, 139, 141
　Removal of, 142, 203-208
　Requests Gage's permission to attack coastal towns, 154
　Responds to attack on Moore, 149
　Supplying British and, 175
　Viewed as tyrant, 141-142
　Warns Charlestown inhabitants, 153 n.65
Grievances, 12
　Latter, 19-20
　List of in Declaration of Independence, 2, 5, 7, 19-20

Grievances *continued*,
    List of in Declaration of Causes, 7
    List of in Lord North's Conciliatory Proposal, 7-8, 11
    List of in Olive Branch Petition, 10
    In Virginia Declaration of Rights, 2
    Unlisted grievance in Declaration of Independence, 20-21
Great Britain,
    American allegiance to, 5
Greene, Jacob, 27
Greene, Nathanael, 27
    Falmouth's burning and, 165-166
    Foreign assistance and, 314-315
Greven, Phillip, 17
Guines, Count de, 127, 203, 204, 308-309
Hallowell, Benjamin, 204
Hancock, John, 1, 28, 51, 74, 314
    Dunmore and, 192
    Hessians and, 290-291
    Reconciliation and, 42
Hannah, 183
Hardy, Dave, 65
Harrington, James, 67, 68, 74
Harrison, Benjamin, 167
Hartley, David, 55, 280
Hawke, David, 129
Hay, George, 40
Hazzen, Moses Colonel, 266
Henry I, 65
Henry II, 65
Henry, Patrick, 4, 110, 195, 317-319
Hessians, 214, 235, 314-315, 325
    American independence and, 273-274, 296-298
    As auxiliaries, 274-275
    Colonies anticipate arrival of, 283-284
    Debated in Parliament, 275-280
    Desertion enticed and, 290-296
    Effects of inclusion, 16
    Employment of, 19, 21
    Land bounty offered to deserters, 288-290
    Parliament fears desertion and, 281
    Treaties and, 281-282
Hinchcliffe, John, 33
Hinds, Peter, 121
Holland, 68, 301
Holt, John, 185, 187-188, 190
Hopkins, Samuel, 90-91
Howe, Richard, 49
Howe, Robert Colonel, 49, 152, 192-194, 201-202
Howe, William Major General, 49, 152-153, 203, 292
Hume, David, 55 n.6, 74
Hutcheson, Francis, 70
Hutchinson, Thomas, 53, 64
Hutson, James H., 302
Hyde, Elijah, 152
Indentured Servants, 90
Independence,
    Bombardment of coastal towns and, 151
    British Navy and, 135
    Brunswick, Massachusetts and, 56
    Buckingham County, Virginia and, 56
    Congress and, 5
    Declaration of, *See* Declaration of Independence
    Falmouth and, 166
    Founding Fathers and, 2
    France's impact on, 299, 316-320
    Glorious Revolution and, 53

Independence *continued*,
- Hessians and, 273-274, 296-298
- History and, 16-19
- Indians and, 213-214
- People's support and, 1, 7, 15
- Richard Henry Lee's resolve for, 4-5
- State Conventions and, 5
- Taxation, 53
- Timing of, 5
- Vote for, 2-3, 5

Indians,
- British compared to, 116, 151
- British-Colonies disputes and, 220-221
- British promote neutrality and, 229
- British sentries killed and, 235
- Canesadaugans, 226
- Catawba, 255
- Caughnawaga, 224, 242
- Cherokee, 216, 255-257
- Chickasaws, 259
- Choctaw, 258
- Choosing sides and, 238-244, 260-261, 263-264
- Creek, 106, 258
- Employment of generally, 21, 113-114, 214-215, 268-270
- Employment of by British, 215, 228, 234-240, 247, 251-254
- Employment of by rebels, 223-230, 236, 257-258, 263-270
- Falmouth's destruction used to recruit, 171 n.123
- French assistance and, 303
- General fear of attack by colonists, 222-223
- Hohnogwus, 226
- Mahicans, 229
- Mickmac, 171 n.123
- Moheconnuck, 225
- Mohawks, 223, 229-231
- Mohegan, 266
- Montauks, 229
- Narragansetts, 229
- Neutrality and, 248
- Niantics, 229
- Northern colonies fear of attack and, 222-223, 248
- Oneida, 227, 229, 231, 263
- Ottawas, 219
- Pennsylvania and, 215-216
- Pequots, 229
- St. Francis, 226, 248
- St. Johns, 171 n.123
- Shawnee, 215-216, 220, 249-251
- Six Nations, 218, 226, 229-232, 238-239, 248, 253-254, 263-264
- Southern colonies fear of attack and, 222, 248-259
- Stockbridge, 225-227, 235, 238, 263-264, 266
- Swagaches, 226
- Threat of, 87
- Tuscarora, 227
- Wabash, 216
- *See also*, Guy Johnson, William Johnson, John Stuart, John Connolly, Lord Dunmore, Thomas Gage, Samuel Kirkland, Continental Congress

Inglis, Charles, 302-303, 312
Izard, Ralph, 128
James II, 57, 60, 62-63, 66, 67, 68, 72
Jefferson, Thomas, 1, 5, 25, 59, 65, 74, 77, 100, 105, 135, 185, 307
- Attacks slave trade, 130-131
- David Hume and, 55 n.6
- Declaration of Independence Committee and, 5
- Draft of Declaration of Independence, 132

Jefferson, Thomas *continued*,
  Dunmore's Proclamation and, 77, 101, 130
  Foreign assistance and, 299-300, 310
  Hessian desertions and, 288-290
  Models Declaration of Independence on Declaration of Rights, 58, 64
  Norfolk and, 191
  Standing armies and, 64
Jeremiah, Thomas, 122
Johnson, Guy, 218, 221-222, 227, 229-234, 236-237, 248, 253-254, 265, 269
Johnson, Joseph, 220-221, 263-264
Johnson, William, 215-221, 230, 232, 263
Jones, Ichabod, 145-146
Kaplan, Sidney, 132
Kent, Benjamin, 40
Kettel, John, 235
Kirkland, Samuel, 230, 243-244
Lane, John, 242
Lauraguais, Comte de, 321, 323
Laurens, Henry, 40
  Dunmore's Proclamation and, 105, 128
  Independence and, 7
  Indian employment and, 268
  Partition and, 301-302
  Reconciliation with Great Britain and, 7
Laurens, John,
  Prohibitory Act and, 40
Le Cras, Edward, 209
Lee, Arthur, 121, 301, 305-306
Lee, Charles, 80
  Falmouth and, 165, 166
  Fear of French West Indies and, 304
  French assistance and, 317
  Reconciliation and, 45

Lee, Richard Henry, 2, 26, 105, 128, 186, 194, 317-318
Legge, William, 92
Lewis, Andrew Colonel, 220
Lexington and Concord, 5, 7, 28, 95, 117, 151, 156, 207, 215, 222-223, 255, 257, 301
  Battle of, 1, 60, 115, 139-140, 174
Lind, John, 64
Linzee, John Captain, 160
Little, Paul, 161
Liverpool, 199-200
Livingston, Roger R., 5
Locke, John, 1
Lombard, Calvin, 157
London Charter, 65
London Gazetteer, 45
Lord Dunmore's War, 219-220, 248-249
Lord North's Conciliatory Proposal, 7, 11, 75
Louis XVI, 203, 307-309, 321-324
Lovejoy, David, 168-169
Lowell, Edward, 279
Lowther, James, 278
Loyalists, 54, 98, 114-115, 131
  Falmouth and, 157, 157-158 n.77
  Intimidated, 159
  Norfolk and, 185-186, 194, 199-200
  Presses and, 144, 187-188
  Suppressed, 189-190, 255
Luttrell, James, 282
Luttrell, Temple, 38-39, 49
Lynch, Thomas, 25, 42-43, 167
Lyons, James, 146
Lyttleton, William Henry, 33, 124
Machaivelli, 74
Mackenzie, Frederick, 238
Macpherson, James, 269
Madison, James,
  Dunmore's Proclamation and, 99

335

Madison, James *continued*,
  Foreign assistance and, 300
  Slave insurrections and, 118-119
Magdalen, HMS, 93
Magna Charta, 65
Maier, Pauline, 5, 58, 59, 193
Maine,
  Machias, 145-149
Manning, William, 268
Margaretta, HMS, 145-149
Martin, Josiah, 94, 103, 117, 127, 137
  Gunpowder and, 94
  Slave insurrections and, 115-116
Maryland, 75, 99, 184
  Annapolis, 95
  Baltimore, 191, 202
  British Navy and, 136
  Charles County, 136, 274
  Gunpowder and, 94-95
  Delegates leave Congress, 3
  Dunmore's Proclamation and, 128-129
  Frederick County, 51
  German unit and, 288-289
  Hagerstown, 253
  Independence and, 132
Mason, George, 2, 74, 75
  Declaration of Rights and, 130, 186
  Dunmore's Proclamation and, 99
Massachusetts, 4, 6, 31, 33, 50, 56, 63, 75, 136, 209, 312
  Boston, 137, 138, 143, 152, 156, 167, 182, 230, 233, 238-239, 252
  Brunswick, 156
  Burning of Charlestown, 136, 150-154, 180, 191, 193
  Burning of Falmouth, 136, 154-171, *See also* Falmouth
  Cambridge, 1, 79, 91, 227
  Charlestown Neck, 138, 152, 235
  Gloucester, 154 n.67, 160
  Malden, 150
  Nantasket, 150
  Provincial Congress recruits Indians, 223-225, 227
  Roxbury, 152
  Scituate, 72, 274
  Wrentham, 274
Mein, John, 188
Mercer, Hugh General, 291-292
Mercury, HMS, 98
Meyhew, Jonathan, 74
Mifflin, Thomas, 74
Militia,
  American system of, 70, 76
  Virginia Declaration of Rights and, 75
Militia Bill, 76-80
Molesworth, Robert, 69, 74
Montagu, John Admiral, 138
Moore, James Captain, 145
  Attacked by rebels, 146-147
  Killed in attack, 148-149
  Ordered to surrender, 148
  Repels rebels, 147-148
  Threatens to fire on Machias, 147
Morris, Robert, 40, 297, 304
Mowat, Henry, 145, 180
  Allegedly misrepresents Falmouth situation, 154 n.66
  Captured by Thompson, 156-157
  Decides not to burn Falmouth, 158
  Deviates from Graves' orders, 155
  Engages rebel schooner, 159
  Falmouth does not think he will burn, 158-159, 158 n. 79, 160
  History's inaccurate interpretation of, 155 n.69

Mowat, Henry *continued*,
   Indians and, 240, 245, 247-248
   Loyalists support, 157-158 n.77
   Only tells Graves what he wants to hear, 155 n.67
   Ordered to attack Gloucester first, 154 n.67
   Orders Arms delivered from Falmouth, 162-163
   Orders from Graves, 159
   Receives orders to chastise coast, 138, 141, 141 n.23
   Sends ultimatum to Falmouth, 161-162
   Starts bombardment of Falmouth, 164
   Under martial law by Thompson, 157
   Warns Falmouth he will fire, 157-158
Moylan, Stephen, 183
Moyle, Robert, 69
Mutiny Act, 71
Nationalism, British, 53-54
Navy, British, 15, 31, 181
   Accused of burning coastal towns, 19, 21
   American independence and, 135
   Bombardment of coastal town, 149-156
   Change of command, 206
   Compared to Corsairs of Barbary, 151
   Guerilla tactics and, 139
   Munitions trade stopped, 135-137
   Prevents trade with colonies, 306-307
   Strategy of, 136
   Strict guidelines of, 139
   Supplying British troops and, 137, 149-150
   Viewed as oppressors, 208

   See also James Wallace, Andrew Barkley, Samuel Graves, Henry Mowat, Massachusetts, Rhode Island, James Moore, Portsmouth, Norfolk, Falmouth, Norfolk
Navy, Continental, *See* Continental Navy
Nelson, Thomas, 187
New Hampshire, 8, 15, 75, 179, 274
   Hillsborough County, 180
   Portsmouth, *See Portsmouth*
New Jersey, 48-49, 282, 288-289
New York, 3, 63, 171, 239, 282-283, 288
   British Navy and, 136
   Committee of Safety and, 189
   Confiscate Guy Johnson's property, 232-233
   Congress recruits Indians, 227, 229-232, 242, 248
   Long Island, 149-150
New York Journal, 170
Newport Mercury, 144, 168
Nicholas, Robert Carter, 130
Norfolk, Virginia, 98, 100, 103, 251
   British accused of burning, 191, 192
   Burning of, 136
   Burning rejoiced by rebels, 191
   Considered to be Tory infested, 185-186, 194, 199, 201
   Dunmore fires on, 200-201
   Howe wants to destroy, 201
   Inhabitants fear rebels will burn town, 195-197
   Printing press and, 185 n.45
   Rebel account of burning, 192-194
   Rebels capture, 198

Norfolk, Virginia *continued*,
    Report by commissioners on burning, 193
    Virginia Committee of Safety denies will be burned, 197
    Word of burning spreads, 202-203
Norman Conquest, 65
North, Lord, 11, 26, 42, 49, 124-125, 204, 214-215, 279
North Carolina, 52, 75
    British Navy and, 135
    Brunswick, 117
    Gunpowder and, 94
    Independence and, 132
    New Bern, 115
    Provincial Congress and, 46-47
    Slave insurrections and, 115-117
    Wilmington, 116
Nova Scotia, 174
Olive Branch Petition, 6, 8 n.18, 10, 28-30, 51
    Debated in Parliament, 33-36, 38, 214
Olwell, Robert, 120
Otis, James, 74
Otter, 185, 187-188, 198
Page, John, 100, 103, 201-202, 307
Paine, Thomas, 2, 18, 192, 302, 312, 314-315
Palmer, Joseph, 306, 315-316
Parliament, British, 65-66, 300
    Examination of John Penn, 36-38
    Graves and, 207
    Hessian employment and, 275-283
    Indian employment and, 214-215
    Investigates naval bombardments, 203
    Olive Branch Petition and, 33-36, 214

    Partition plan and, 303-304
    Peace Commissioners and, 49-50
    Quartering troops and, 71
    Reconciliation with colonies and, 6-7, 31-36
    Right to taxation, 37-38
    Slave insurrections and, 117-118, 124-127
    Suspending and Dispensing power and, 62-64
Parsons, Samuel, 289-290
Partition,
    Colonies fear of, 301-305
Pasteur, William, 95
Peace Commissioners, 45-47, 49, 280-281
Pendleton, Edmund, 105, 131, 186, 197
Penet, Pierre, 311
Penn, John, 36-38, 216, 220
Pennsylvania, 59, 75, 78, 274, 282, 294
    German unit and, 288-289
    Indians and, 215-217
    Lord Dunmore's War and, 219-220
    Philadelphia, 92, 296, 310, 321
    Pittsburg, 219
Pennsylvania Evening Post, 144
Pennsylvania Gazette, 45, 281
Petition of Right 1628, 66
Pliarne, Emmanuel de, 311
Popish Plot, 67
Portsmouth, New Hampshire,
    Attack British, 177-178
    Committee of Safety and, 178-179
    Defends itself against British, 175
    Plead with Barkley, 176
    Receives aid from Washington, 179
    Relationship with Crown, 173
    Treasury seized, 178

Pote, Jeremiah Captain, 157
Prescott, William Captain, 153
Preston, 207
Printing Presses, 187
Privateers,
    Congress recruits, 171 n.122
Prohibitory Act, 25, 39, 44, 48,
    124, 214
    Colonies react to, 40-42, 45
Proclamation of 1763, 89, 216-217,
    218, 260
Providence Gazette, 144
Quarles, Benjamin, 99-100
Quartering Act, 1, 70
Quebec, 12, 43
Quincy, Josiah, 73-74
Randolph, Peyton, 93, 103
Reconciliation, 2, 6-7
    Arguing from a position of
    strength, 7
    British attempts at, 21
    Congress and, 12
    Hessians and, 16
    Lord North's Conciliatory
    Proposal and, 11
Reed, Joseph, 27, 79, 192
    Prohibitory Act and, 40
    Reconciliation and, 46
Restoration, English, 66
Rhode Island, 165
    Bristol, 168-171, 173, 179,
    180, 191, 193
    Connanicott, 143
    Newport, 167-171
    Proposes Navy to Congress,
    184
    Providence, 167
Richmond, Duke of, 37, 282
Rivington, James, 188
Robinson, Thomas, 189
Rochford, Lord, 205, 308
Rockingham, Marquis of, 32, 277
Roderigue Hortalez & Co., 322-324
Romes, George, 170
Rose, HMS, 143-144, 167

Roubaud, Pierre, 303
Rutledge, Edward, 128, 184, 185
St. Paul, Horace, 308
Sandwich, Earl of, 34, 37, 204, 205
Savelle, Max, 54
Scarborough, 174, 177, 178
Schuyler, Philip, 233, 243, 248,
    253, 260, 262, 265, 267
Scituate, Massachusetts, 72
Scorpion, HMS, 122
Seven Years War, 70, 72
Sewell, Jonathan, 206
Shay, Daniel, 82
Shelburne, Earl of, 33, 38, 214, 277
Shippen, Edward, 296
Shuldham, Molyneux Admiral,
    206-207
Sidney, Algernon, 68-69, 74
Slavery,
    American fear of being
    subjected to, 9, 28
    British accused of using
    against colonies, 20-21
    King George III charged with
    maintaining, 130
Slaves,
    Employed in conflict, 98-99,
    101, 125-126
    Employ Indians to get rid of
    rebellious, 106
    Importation of, 88-91
    Literacy and, 118
    Manumissions and, 107
    Masters offer their protection,
    105-107
    Revolts and, 90, 85
    Sent to West Indies, 88, 105,
    110, 123
    Tybee Island and, 106
    See Also Josiah Martin, John
    Stuart, Lord Dunmore, John
    Collet, Thomas Gage
Snowden, Leonard, 189
South Carolina, 15, 60, 88, 120,
    124, 131, 239, 301

South Carolina *continued*,
  Assembly and, 108, 113
  British Navy and, 136
  Charleston, 59, 113, 121, 123, 136
  Cheraws District, 51
  Fears Indian attack, 113-114, 256-258
  Slave insurrections and, 119, 120-121
South Carolina Gazette, 88, 121, 123
Spain, 300-302, 312, 315, 319, 323
Squire, Matthew Captain, 187-188, 190, 200
Stamp Act, 1, 71
Standing Armies, 11, 64-82
  Machiavellian principle and, 68
  Quartering of troops and, 64-67, 73
Stephen, Adam, 306
Stevens, Phillip, 204, 209
Stirling, Lord, 284
Stockton, Richard, 288
Stono Rebellion, 90
Stuart, John, 115, 217, 222, 269
  Falsely accused of inciting Indian attacks and, 255-259
  Indian plot and, 113, 259-260
  Keeps Indians neutral, 254-255
Sullivan, James, 26
Sullivan, John, 8, 166
  Assaults Fort William & Mary, 173-174, 180
  Defending Portsmouth and, 179-181
  Indians affairs and, 265, 267-268
  Uses British Bombardment to inspire Portsmouth, 180-181
Temple, Robert, 46
Thaxter, John, 147, 149
Third Amendment, 64

Thompson, Samuel Colonel, 156-157
Thoughts on Government, 75
Toland, John, 69
Tonyn, Patrick, 259-260, 262
Tories, 16
Townshend, Viscount, 32
Treaty of Paris of 1763, 15
Trenchard, John, 67, 74
Trenton, Battle of, 273, 294
Trumbull, John, 54, 116, 240
Tucker, Daniel, 161, 165
Tudor, William, 312
Tupper, Benjamin Captain, 149-150
Tyng, William, 164
Vattel, Emer de, 274
Vergennes, Count de,
  American alliance and, 309-310, 321-324
  British alliance and, 308-309
  Norfolk's burning and, 203
Vermont, 75, 297-298
Veterans, American Revolution, 1
Virginia, 2, 115, 120, 128, 129, 215, 307
  Alexandria, 252
  Augusta County, 90
  Buckingham County, 56, 59, 72
  Charlotte County, 59, 132
  Dunmore's Proclamation and, 15, 102-112
  Fear of Indian attack and, 254-255
  Fredericksburg, 96
  Great Bridge, 98, 197, 199
  Gunpowder and, 93-94, 95-97
  Hampton, 196
  Independence and, 132
  List of Grievances and, 52
  Lord Dunmore's War and, 219-220
  Kemps Landing, 98, 100, 119, 195, 196

Virginia *continued*,
  Motion for independence, 4
  Norfolk, *See* Norfolk
  Princess Anne County, 90
  Printing Press and Norfolk and, 186
  Williamsburg, 187, 193, 202, 312
Virginia Assembly/Convention,
  British Navy and, 135-136
  Declaration of Rights and, 130
  Disavows Norfolk will be burned, 197
  Dunmore's Proclamation and, 103, 105, 109-112
  Given proposal to destroy Norfolk, 201
  Hessians and, 273
  Indian affairs and, 267
  Manumissions and, 106
  Proposes American independence, 317-318
  Raises a body of troops, 93
  Receive plans for Indian attack, 253
  Receives word of Norfolk's burning, 192-193
  Reconciliation with Dunmore, 96-97
  Refuses supplies to Dunmore, 199-200
  Slave importation and, 88
  Slave insurrections and, 87-88
  Tories and, 199
Virginia Gazette, 98, 103-104, 185, 187, 191, 198, 307, 316
Wallace, James Captain, 182, 184
  Attacked by Newport inhabitants, 170
  Bristol, RI and, 168-171
  Engaged with rebel sloop, 143-144
  Newport, RI and, 167-171
  Operations in Narragansett Bay, 143-145
  Requisitions supplies, 167-168
Wallace, Michael, 18
Walpole, Baron, 275
Ward, Artemas, 81, 281
Ward, Joseph, 29, 47-48, 166, 312
Ward, Samuel, 165
Warren, James, 6, 40, 77, 320
  Continental Navy and, 182
  Falmouth's burning and, 166
  King George III's speech and, 26
  Olive Branch Petition and, 29
  Reconciliation and, 45
Warren, Joseph, 306
Warren, Mercy Otis, 45-46, 151
Washington, George, 1, 25, 48, 74, 186
  Battle of Trenton and, 273
  Believes British will attack coast, 179
  Black soldiers and, 91-92, 125
  Communication with Congress and, 142
  Council of War and, 179, 180
  Creation of Navy and, 183
  Dunmore's Proclamation and, 91-92, 105
  Dunmore's Seizure of printing press and, 185
  Fears Dunmore will attack Alexandria, 191
  Fears Falmouth will cause dissolution of army, 167
  Fears for Martha Washington's safety, 191-192
  Foreign assistance and, 311
  French West Indies and, 304
  Hessians and, 284, 290-294, 298
  Indian affairs and, 233, 253-254, 260, 265-267
  King George III's speech and, 27-28
  Military school of thought, 80-81

341

    Militia and, 76, 79
    Orders Portsmouth Tories seized, 181
    Own slaves flee to British, 107
    Prisoner exchange and, 292-293
    Prohibitory Act and, 40
    Peace Commissioners and, 45-46, 50-51, 281
    Recommends all German unit, 284, 287, 290
    Reconciliation and, 42-44
    Requests Sullivan's Return, 180
    Selection as Commander in Chief, 80-81
    Uses Falmouth to inspire army, 167 n.110
Washington, Martha, 191-192
Wedderburn, Alexander, 35
Wentworth, John, 175-179
West Indies, 35, 88, 105, 110, 123, 300, 304-305, 308, 313, 319, 323
Wheelock, Eleazer, 242
Wilkes, John, 36, 277
William and Mary of Orange, 57, 66, 68
Wilson, James, 74, 288-290
Wood, James Captain, 250
Woodford, William Colonel, 193, 195-200
Woolsey, George, 191, 240
Wythe, George, 286-287

About the Author

Patrick Charles is the author of *Washington's Decision: The Story of George Washington's Decision to Reaccept Black Enlistments, December 31, 1775*. Mr. Charles graduated from the George Washington University with Departmental Honors in History, and also in International Affairs—Conflict and Security, and European Affairs. He is a former Marine Sergeant with Marine Security Guard Battalion, and has also worked for the Department of State. He currently resides in Cleveland, Ohio, where he is finishing his Juris Doctorate at Cleveland-Marshall School of Law.

www.ingramcontent.com/pod-product-compliance
Lightning Source LLC
Chambersburg PA
CBHW070229230426
43664CB00014B/2247